Trading in Knowledge

Development Perspectives on TRIPS, Trade and Sustainability

Edited by

Christophe Bellmann, Graham Dutfield and Ricardo Meléndez-Ortiz

ICTSD

International Centre for Trade and Sustainable Development

Earthscan Publications Ltd
London • Sterling, VA

First published in the UK and USA in 2003
by Earthscan Publications Ltd

The views expressed in this publication are those of the authors and do not necessarily reflect the views of ICTSD, DFID or the institutions to which the authors are affiliated

A catalogue record for this book is available from the British Library

ISBN: 1-84407-044-1 paperback
1-84407-043-3 hardback

Typesetting by MapSet Ltd, Gateshead, UK
Printed and bound in the UK by Creative Print and Design (Wales), Ebbw Vale
Cover design by Yvonne Booth

For a full list of publications please contact:

Earthscan Publications Ltd
120 Pentonville Road, London, N1 9JN, UK
Tel: +44 (0)20 7278 0433
Fax: +44 (0)20 7278 1142
Email: earthinfo@earthscan.co.uk
Web: **www.earthscan.co.uk**

22883 Quicksilver Drive, Sterling, VA 20166–2012, USA

Earthscan is an editorially independent subsidiary of Kogan Page Ltd and publishes in association with WWF-UK and the International Institute for Environment and Development

A catalogue record for this book is available from the British Library

Library of Congress Cataloging-in-Publication Data

Trading in knowledge : development perspectives on TRIPS, trade, and sustainability / edited by Christophe Bellmann, Graham Dutfield, and Ricardo Meléndez-Ortiz.
p. cm.
Includes bibliographical references and index.
ISBN 1-84407-044-1 (pbk.) -- ISBN 1-84407-043-3 (hbk.)
1. Intellectual property (International law) 2. Sustainable development. I. Bellmann, Christophe, 1971- II. Dutfield, Graham. III. Meléndez-Ortiz, Ricardo.

K1401.T73 2003
341.7'58–dc21

2003011359

This book is printed on elemental chlorine-free paper

Contents

TRIPS and Public Health

IPRs and the Protection of Traditional Knowledge

PART THREE – IMPLEMENTING THE TRIPS AGREEMENT

Regional Initiatives

National Legislative Reforms

List of Tables and Boxes

Tables

Boxes

List of Contributors

Adronico Oduogo Adede (Kenya) is Chief Executive Officer of L'Etwal International in Nairobi.

Frederick Abbott (US) is Edward Ball Eminent Scholar Chair in International Law, Florida State University College of Law.

Grethel Aguilar (Costa Rica) works for the IUCN – Regional Office for Mesoamerica in Costa Rica.

K Balasubramaniam (Sri Lanka) is Advisor and Coordinator for Health Action International Asia-Pacific, based in Colombo, Sri Lanka.

John Barton (US) is George E Osborne Professor of Law at Stanford University, and formerly chaired the UK Commission on Intellectual Property Rights.

Christophe Bellmann (Switzerland) is Programmes Director at the International Centre for Trade and Sustainable Development in Geneva.

Jorge Cabrera Medaglia (Costa Rica) is Professor at the Universidad de Costa Rica and a consultant to the National Biodiversity Institute (INBio) in Costa Rica.

Boniface Guwa Chidyausiku (Zimbabwe) is Ambassador of the Permanent Mission of Zimbabwe to the World Trade Organization (WTO) in Geneva.

Carlos Correa (Argentina) is Director of the Centro de Estudios Interdisciplinarios de Derecho Industrial y Economico (CEIDIE), Universidad de Buenos Aires. He was a member of the UK Commission on Intellectual Property Rights.

Biswajit Dhar (India) was a Senior Fellow at Research and Information System for the Non-Aligned and Other Developing Countries in Delhi. He is currently Professor and Head at the Centre for WTO Studies, Indian Institute of Foreign Trade in New Delhi.

Graham Dutfield (UK) is Herchel Smith Research Fellow at Queen Mary Intellectual Property Research Institute, Queen Mary College, University of London, and also Senior Research Associate at the International Centre for Trade and Sustainable Development (ICTSD).

Johnson A Ekpere (Nigeria) is Professor at the University of Ibadan in Nigeria, and was formerly Executive Secretary and a consultant to the Scientific, Technical and Research Commission of the Organization of African Unity.

Rosine Jourdain (France) is Head of Mission for Médecins Sans Frontières in Burkina Faso.

Atul Kaushik (India) is Deputy Secretary of the Cabinet Secretariat of the Government of India.

Demba Kebe (Mali) is Scientific Coordinator at the Institute for Rural Economy in Mali.

Jakkrit Kuanpoth (Thailand) is a Barrister-at-Law of the Thai Bar Association, Associate Professor of Law at Sukhothai Thammathirat Open University, and Director of the Research and Rule of Law Bureau, Office of the National Human Rights Commission in Thailand.

Robert J L Lettington (UK) is an advisor to the Director-General of the International Centre of Insect Physiology and Ecology and a frequent consultant to the Secretariat of the Food and Agriculture Organization (FAO) Commission on Genetic Resources for Food and Agriculture on policy and regulatory issues.

Francis Mangeni (Uganda) is Counsellor at the African Union Office in Geneva.

Ricardo Meléndez-Ortiz (Colombia) is the Executive Director of the International Centre for Trade and Sustainable Development (ICTSD).

Oumar Niangado (Mali) is Delegate for the Syngenta Foundation for Sustainable Agriculture in Bamako, Mali.

Ruth Okediji (Nigeria) is William L Prosser Professor of Law, University of Minnesota College of Law.

James Otieno-Odek (Kenya) is a Senior Lecturer at the University of Nairobi.

Manuel Ruiz (Peru) is Director of the International Affairs and Biodiversity Programme at the Sociedad Peruana de Derecho Ambiental (SPDA) in Lima.

Suman Sahai (India) is Convenor of the Gene Campaign in India.

Silvia Salazar (Costa Rica) is Legal Adviser on Intellectual Property at the University of Costa Rica.

Ana María Hernández Salgar (Colombia) is Researcher for the Policy and Legislation Programme of the Alexander von Humboldt Institute for Research on Biological Resources in Colombia.

Ghate Utkarsh (India) is a consultant based at the Foundation for Revitalisation of Local Health Traditions (FRLHT) in Bangalore, India.

Begoña Venero (Peru) is an Associate Administrative Judge of the Intellectual Property Tribunal of the National Institute for the Defence of Competition and Protection of Intellectual Property in Peru.

David Vivas Eugui (Venezuela) is Programme Manager on Intellectual Property, Technology and Services at the International Centre for Trade and Sustainable Development (ICTSD).

Weerawit Weeraworawit (Thailand) is Minister (Commercial Affairs) at the Ministry of Commerce in Thailand. He is also an Associate Judge of Thailand's Central Intellectual Property and International Trade Court.

Rosemary A Wolson (South Africa) is Intellectual Property Manager at the University of Cape Town.

Narendra Zaveri (India) is an advocate for and consultant to the India Drug Manufacturers Association (IDMA).

Jeanne Zoundjihekpon (Benin) is Programme Manager in Francophone Africa for Genetic Resources Action International (GRAIN), based in Cotonou, Benin.

Foreword

Over recent decades, there has been an unprecedented increase in the scope and level of protection of intellectual property rights (IPRs). Protectable subject matter is being widened, new rights are being created, and standards relating to IPRs are being harmonized throughout the world. As industrialized countries increasingly rely on new technologies including information and communication technologies and biotechnologies – which require considerable research and development but can be fairly easily copied or replicated – IPR protection of exported products and technologies becomes a key concern. At the global level, this trend has resulted in a significant shift in the balance of interests between private innovators and society at large, which has provoked serious tensions around key public policy concerns such as public health, food security, education or biodiversity management. As the policy options and flexibilities available to developing countries to use IPRs in support of their broader development strategies are being rapidly narrowed down, many experts have questioned the 'one-size-fits-all' approach to intellectual property (IP) protection and advocated a substantial rebalancing of the global IP regime.

The challenges that developing countries face when designing and implementing IP policy at the national and international levels are huge. First, although empirical evidence on the role of IP protection in promoting innovation and sustainable development in these countries remains limited and inconclusive, what evidence exists suggests that appropriate levels of protection will vary widely. For example, developing countries that are relatively advanced in economic and technological terms have greater opportunities to benefit from IPRs than least developed countries, for which the implementation of international IP rules represents a net short-term financial loss that, it may be plausibly argued, is unlikely to be offset by economic and social gains for a very long time.

Second, IPR regulations affect a broad range of stakeholders concerned with multiple agendas such as the protection of traditional knowledge, the right of farmers to save and exchange seeds, patentability criteria for living organisms, access to medicines and technology transfer. This cross-cutting nature of IPRs makes it difficult for governments to understand the complex web of interests and concerns surrounding IP policy, which are only partially – and sometimes inconsistently – addressed by a variety of international instruments such as the Agreement on Trade-related Aspects of Intellectual Property Rights (TRIPS), the Convention on Biological Diversity (CBD), the Food and Agriculture Organization (FAO) International Treaty on Plant Genetic Resources and the International Union for the Protection of New Varieties of Plants (UPOV).

Finally, developing countries must negotiate at different levels simultaneously. While much of the debate still focuses on TRIPS and the CBD, new multilateral treaties are being negotiated and adopted. These include the World Intellectual Property Organization (WIPO) Copyright Treaty, the Patent Law Treaty and the WIPO's draft Substantive Patent Law Treaty. At the bilateral level, the EU and the US particularly are encouraging developing countries to adopt higher standards (TRIPS-plus), with narrowed-down exceptions. Most of them lack technical and institutional capacities to follow these closely interlinked negotiations, understand how they affect their national interests, and define consistent strategies and positions at the multilateral, regional, bilateral and national levels.

In sum, integrating IP policy in sustainable development strategy requires a multi-disciplinary and multi-level approach. An approach that takes into account differences in economic development. An approach that reflects the diversity of interests and the richness of the debate in the developing world. While intellectual property rights have been the focus of a considerable amount of research and analysis, there has been a significant scarcity of authors from the South and particularly from a non-Anglo-Saxon perspective.

This volume intends to attenuate this shortcoming by offering a unique selection of think pieces, analysis and proposals by developing country authors from a wide range of perspectives taking in civil society, farmers and grassroots organizations, researchers and government officials. It also provides an opportunity for key African, Asian and Latin American authors to convey their leading-edge thinking to stakeholders both in the South and in the North.

The chapters presented herein were commissioned for a series of Regional Multi-stakeholder Dialogues on IPRs and sustainable development designed to respond to the urgent need to strengthen developing countries' capacities to advance their public policy objectives through the implementation or review of TRIPS.[1] The dialogues aimed to provide an opportunity for the Geneva-based developing country negotiators to listen to, and draw on, specific national and regional experiences; enhance the understanding of national policy-makers and the representatives of civil society of the TRIPS processes; and identify strategic approaches to effectively participate in ongoing negotiations on TRIPS.

As in previous similar undertakings of the International Centre for Trade and Sustainable Development (ICTSD), these dialogues were jointly designed and implemented with local partners[2] in five developing country regions who helped ICTSD identify key actors and relevant topics to be addressed in each specific region. Participants originated from a wide range of perspectives and backgrounds, such as negotiators – more than 20, including chairmen of the TRIPS Council – ministries of trade, health, agriculture and environment, IP offices, grassroots movements, farmers' associations and indigenous groups, NGO activists, moderate engagers, experts and scholars. Geographically, 42 countries have been covered, in South and Central America, Africa and Asia.[3] These events created unique spaces and opportunities for non-trade actors to engage and interact in open and sometimes lively discussion. In particular, they have brought to the table stakeholders who would otherwise find it highly difficult or impossible to relate to trade decision-makers. In several instances, these dialogues have acted as a catalyst for continued interaction at the national level.

Ex-post evaluation of the effectiveness of these events has encouraged ICTSD to launch a second phase of dialogues and pursue similar types of sustained capacity building efforts by enabling and facilitating dialogue as a sine qua non condition for better policies. In this context, the publication and wide dissemination of this collection, complemented by four chapters commissioned by ICTSD and the UN Conference on Trade and Development (UNCTAD), does not only intend to contribute to existing literature. It also responds to the pressing need to create a critical mass of well-informed stakeholders, who are able to define their own public policy agenda in the field of IPRs and sustainable development and advance it efficiently at the regional and multilateral levels. In reading through this collection, it becomes evident that both the analytical research papers and the more advocacy-oriented pieces contained here are essential inputs in advancing today's international negotiations on IPRs and in ensuring better policy-making processes.

Christophe Bellmann
Programmes Director – ICTSD

Ricardo Meléndez-Ortiz
Executive Director – ICTSD

NOTES

1 The five regional dialogues were held respectively in Cusco, Peru (February 2001), Nyeri, Kenya (July 2001), Tikal, Guatemala (September 2001), Rajendrapur, Bangladesh (April 2002) and Dakar, Senegal (July to August 2002).

2 ICTSD partners included: in Geneva, the Quaker United Nations Office (QUNO); in Latin America, the United Nations Economic Commission for Latin America and the Caribbean (ECLAC), the Sociedad Peruana de Derecho Ambiental (SPDA – Peru), and ANDES (Peru); in Eastern and Southern Africa, the African Centre for Technology Studies (ACTS – Kenya); in Central America, the World Conservation Union, Regional Office for Mesoamerica (IUCN – Costa Rica), the Central American Commission for Environment and Development (CCAD), and the Guatemalan Association for the Conservation of Nature, Cänan K'aax (Guatemala); in Asia, the Centre for Policy Dialogue (CPD – Bangladesh), and the Bangladesh Environmental Lawyers Association (BELA – Bangladesh); in West and Central Africa, ENDA Tiers Monde (Senegal), Solagral (France), and Oxfam West Africa Programme.

3 Argentina, Bangladesh, Benin, Bolivia, Brazil, Burkina Faso, Cameroon, Chile, Colombia, Costa Rica, Ecuador, El Salvador, Ethiopia, Gabon, Guatemala, Guinea, Honduras, India, Indonesia, Ivory Coast, Kenya, Mali, Mauritania, Mexico, Namibia, Nicaragua, Niger, Nigeria, Pakistan, Panama, Peru, Philippines, Senegal, South Africa, Sri Lanka, Tanzania, Thailand, Togo, Uganda, Venezuela, Zambia, and Zimbabwe.

Acknowledgements

For the completion of this first series of dialogues and the publication of this volume, we are particularly grateful to: Graham Dutfield for his tireless dedication in reviewing, editing and polishing most of the texts contained herewith; Marie Chamay for the patience and efficiency she demonstrated in coordinating the overall production of this volume; and our partners in the regions, Manuel Ruiz and Jorge Caillaux at Sociedad Peruana de Derecho Ambiental (SPDA – Peru), Alejandro Argumedo at ANDES (Peru), Marianne Schaper at the UN Economic Commission for Latin America and the Caribbean (ECLAC), John Mugabe, then executive director of ACTS, and Susan Murunga at the African Centre for Technology Studies (ACTS – Kenya), Grethel Aguilar at the World Conservation Union, Regional Office for Mesoamerica (IUCN – Costa Rica), Mario René Mancilla at the Guatemalan Association for the Conservation of Nature, Cänan K'aax (Guatemala), Debapriya Bhattacharya and his excellent team, Fatema Yousuf and Mustafizur Rahman at the Centre for Policy Dialogue (CPD – Bangladesh), Syeda Rizwana Hasan at the Bangladesh Environmental Lawyers Association (BELA – Bangladesh), Taoufik Ben Abdallah, Cheikh Tidiane Dieye and Awa Dione at ENDA Tiers-Monde (Senegal), Anne Chetaille at Solagral (France), and Sally Baden at Oxfam West Africa Programme (Senegal), for their enthusiasm, and invaluable support in the substantive and logistic organization of the dialogues.

We are also very grateful to Dr Toufiq Ali at the Permanent Mission of Bangladesh in Geneva, Falou Samb, then second counsellor at the Permanent Mission of Senegal, and Robert Lettington at the International Centre of Insect Physiology and Ecology in Kenya, for their propitious advice and constant assistance. Also to H E Amb Amina Chawahir Mohamed of Kenya, H E Amb Eduardo Perez Motta of Mexico, Susan Bragdon at the International Plant Genetic Resources Institute (IPGRI), Carlos Correa of Argentina, David Hathaway of Brazil, Antonio Jacanamijoy at Coordinadora de las Organizaciones Indígenas de la Cuenca Amazonica (COICA), Leo Palma of the Philippines and Monica Rosell at Communidad Andina (CAN) for their active and insightful participation. And not least to Brewster Grace and Geoff Tansey at the Quaker UN Office in Geneva (QUNO) for their inputs and collaboration in initiating the regional dialogues series.

Many thanks also go to those at ICTSD who contributed to the success of the dialogues, including El Hadji Diouf and, particularly, Heike Baumüller for her generous help in preparing the Tikal event in the midst of taking care of many other responsibilities. And, of course, many thanks to all the authors for their readiness to collaborate and the amount of work they have put into their contributions, as well as to all participants – many of whom dedicated a considerable amount of travel time to be with us – for fascinating and incredibly enriching discussions.

Finally, ICTSD is grateful to the sponsors of the five dialogues, the Swedish International Development Cooperation (SIDA) and, particularly, Carl Gustav Thornström for his constant support and assistance; and the UK Department for International Development (DFID). This publication has been made possible in part by funding from the UK Department for International Development (DFID).

Christophe Bellmann and
Ricardo Meléndez-Ortiz,
Geneva, March 2003

List of Acronyms and Abbreviations

AB	Appellate Body (of TRIPS)
ABS	access (to genetic resources) and benefit sharing
ACC	Anti-Counterfeit Code
ACTS	African Centre for Technology Studies
ALIDES	Central American Alliance for Sustainable Development
ARIPO	African Regional Industrial Property Organization
AU	African Union
BELA	Bangladesh Environmental Lawyers Association
CBD	Convention on Biological Diversity
CBD-COP	Convention on Biological Diversity – Conference of the Parties
CBR	Community Biodiversity Register
CCAD	Central American Commission on Environment and Development
CEAD	Centre for Environment and Agriculture Development (India)
CGIAR	Consultative Group on International Agricultural Research
CGRFA	Commission on Genetic Resources for Food and Agriculture (of the FAO; formerly CPGR)
CIPR	Commission on Intellectual Property Rights
CIPRO	Companies and Intellectual Property Registration Office (South Africa)
CISEC	Centro de Investigaciones y Servicios Comunitarios (Colombia)
CITES	Convention on International Trade in Endangered Species of Wild Fauna and Flora
CoFaB	Convention of Farmers and Breeders
CONCAUSA	Joint Declaration of Cooperation between the United States and Countries of the Alliance
COP	Conference of the Parties (of the CBD)
CPGR	Commission on Plant Genetic Resources (of the FAO, now CGRFA)
CSIR	Council for Scientific and Industrial Research (India)
CTE	Committee on Trade and Environment (of the WTO)
DEAT	Department of Environmental Affairs and Tourism (South Africa)
DoA	Department of Agriculture (South Africa)
DST	Department of Science and Technology (South Africa)
DTI	Department of Trade and Industry (South Africa)
EEC	European Economic Community (now the EU)
EPC	European Patent Convention

EPO	European Patent Office
EU	European Union
FAO	Food and Agriculture Organization (of the United Nations)
FRLHT	Foundation for Revitalization of Local Health Traditions (India)
GATT	General Agreement on Tariffs and Trade
GMP	good manufacturing practice
GSP	Generalized System of Preferences
IDMA	Indian Drug Manufacturers Association
ICTSD	International Centre for Trade and Sustainable Development
IGC	Intergovernmental Committee (on Intellectual Property and Genetic Resources, Traditional Knowledge and Folklore)
IISc	Indian Institute of Sciences
IK	indigenous knowledge
IKS	indigenous knowledge systems
ILO	International Labour Organization
IMF	International Monetary Fund
INDECOPI	National Institute for the Defence of Competition and Protection of Intellectual Property (Peru)
IP	intellectual property
IPR	intellectual property right
ISM	Indian Systems of Medicine
ITC	International Trade Commission (US)
IU	International Undertaking (on Plant Genetic Resources)
IUPGR	International Undertaking on Plant Genetic Resouces
KARI	Kenya Agricultural Research Institute
LDC	least developed country
MEA	multilateral environmental agreement
MFN	most favoured nation
MIHR	Centre for the Management of Intellectual Property in Health R&D
MLS	Multilateral System
MTA	material transfer agreement
MTN	Multilateral Trade Negotiation
NAFTA	North American Free Trade Agreement
NBSAP	National Biodiversity Strategy and Action Plan (India)
NGO	non-governmental organization
NISCOM	National Institute of Science Communication (India)
NVNI	non-violation nullification or impairment
OAMPI	African and Malagasy Industrial Property Office
OAPI	Organisation Africaine de la Propriété Intellectuelle
OAU	Organization of African Unity (now African Union)
OECD	Organization for Economic Co-operation and Development
PBR	plant breeders' right; People's Biodiversity Register (India)
PCT	Patent Cooperation Treaty
PIC	prior informed consent
PLT	Patent Law Treaty
PVP	plant variety protection

R&D	research and development
RIS	Research and Information System for the Non-Aligned and Other Developing Countries
SCP	Standing Committee on the Law of Patents (of WIPO)
SIECA	Central American Economic Integration System
SMEs	small and medium enterprises
SPLT	Substantive Patent Law Treaty
TBGRI	Tropical Botanic Garden and Research Institute (India)
TK	traditional knowledge
TKDL	Traditional Knowledge Digital Library
TNC	Trade Negotiations Committee (of the MTN)
TPD	Transvaal Provincial Division (of the High Court of South Africa)
TRIPS	Agreement on Trade-related Aspects of Intellectual Property Rights
UNCTAD	United Nations Conference on Trade and Development
UNEP	United Nations Environment Programme
UNESCO	United Nations Education Scientific and Cultural Organization
UPOV	Union Internationale pour la Protection des Obtentions Végétales (International Union for the Protection of New Varieties of Plants)
USPTO	United States Patent and Trademark Office
USTR	United States Trade Representative
WCT	WIPO Copyright Treaty
WHO	World Health Organization
WIPO	World Intellectual Property Organization
WPPT	WIPO Performances and Phonograms Treaty
WTO	World Trade Organization
WWF	World Wide Fund for Nature

1

Introduction

Graham Dutfield

INTELLECTUAL PROPERTY, TRADE AND SUSTAINABLE DEVELOPMENT: MOUNTING CONTROVERSY

Intellectual property rights (IPRs) have never been more economically and politically important than they are in today's so called 'knowledge-based society'. Neither have they ever been so controversial. IPRs are frequently mentioned in discussions and debates on such diverse topics as trade, investment, technology transfer, industrial policy, public health, food security, education, human rights and the widening gap between the income levels of the developed countries and the developing countries.

IPRs are legal and institutional devices to protect creations of the mind, such as inventions, works of art and literature, and designs. They also include marks on products to indicate their difference from similar ones sold by competitors. Internationally accepted IPRs presently consist of the following: patents, copyrights and related rights, industrial designs, trade marks, trade secrets, plant breeders' rights, geographical indications, and rights to layout designs of integrated circuits. Of these, patents, copyrights and trade marks are arguably the most economically significant.

To proponents, IPRs contribute to the enrichment of society through: (i) the widest possible availability of new and useful goods, services and technical information that derive from innovative activity and (ii) the highest possible level of economic activity based on the production, circulation and further development of such goods, services and information. These objectives are supposed to be achieved because owners can seek to exploit their legal rights by turning them into commercial advantages. The possibility of attaining such advantages, it is believed, encourages innovation and creativity. But after a certain period of time, these legal rights are extinguished and the now unprotected inventions and works can be freely used by others. In short, IPRs are designed to balance conflicting aims and interests in order to most effectively achieve certain public policy goals. However, striking such a balance is very difficult for policy-makers. There are three reasons for this. First, IPR policy-making relies on scarce expertise, which is especially lacking in developing countries. Second, there is a lack of reliable economic data upon which to estimate the long-term effects of a given level of IPR protection. Third, the economic stakes involved are very high, in consequence of which, balancing the interests of creators, users of intellectual property and the public through the design of IPR systems is not just a matter of economic calculation, but is an inherently political exercise. This situation favours the rich and powerful and not the poor and powerless.

At the international level, the most important legal document on IPRs is probably the 1994 Agreement on Trade-related Aspects of Intellectual Property Rights (TRIPS), one of the main outcomes of the Uruguay Round of the General Agreement on Tariffs and Trade (GATT), which is administered by the Geneva-based World Trade Organization (WTO). TRIPS establishes enforceable global minimum (and high) standards of protection and enforcement for virtually all of the most important IPRs in a single agreement.

TRIPS attracted controversy from the start. This is due not only to concerns about the development impacts of the agreement but also because of the way it was negotiated. As the chapters by Adede and Kuanpoth in this volume demonstrate, TRIPS resulted from a highly successful attempt by the US, Europe and Japan, supported by business associations representing transnational corporations, to place IPRs on the agenda of the Uruguay Round of GATT, and then to force through an agreement covering a wide range of IPR standards going far beyond the original aim of preventing counterfeiting of trade marked goods and piracy of copyrighted works. Indeed, one of the main purposes of the dialogues at which most of these chapters were presented was to help developing countries to enhance their capacity to negotiate by identifying where their interests are at stake and developing strategies to advance them domestically, regionally and internationally with other like-minded governments.

The concerns about IPRs are not just to do with designing IPR systems that further national developmental objectives. IPRs are considered by many people to be actually harmful. Specifically, critics have argued that IPRs – or at least the way they are currently contoured – have such deleterious effects as: raising the prices of essential drugs to levels that are too high for the poor to afford; limiting the availability of educational materials for developing country school and university students; legitimizing the piracy of traditional knowledge; and undermining the self-reliance of resource-poor farmers. Understandably, debates on these issues are polarized and emotional. However, policy-makers need to be able to separate out the truth from the propaganda so that they can design IPR laws and policies that best meet the needs of the people they represent and negotiate effectively in future agreements.

Unfortunately, it is impossible to calculate with any certainty the long-term impacts of TRIPS on developing countries and their populations. It is possible that, ultimately, every country will benefit. But this is pure speculation. We can be certain, though, that developing and least developed countries will incur short-term costs in the form of administration, enforcement and rent transfers, and that these will outweigh the benefits. The cost–benefit balance will vary widely from one country to another, but in many cases the costs will be extremely burdensome. According to the World Bank's *Global Economic Prospects and the Developing Countries 2002* study:

> *If TRIPS were fully implemented, rent transfers to major technology-creating countries – particularly the United States, Germany, and France – in the form of pharmaceutical patents, computer chip designs, and other intellectual property, would amount to more than $20 billion* (World Bank, 2001).

Stated baldly, this means that TRIPS represents at least a $20 billion transfer of wealth from the technology importing nations – many of which are developing countries – to the technology exporters – few, if any, of which are developing countries – that may or may not be outweighed by future gains.

Developing countries are justifiably concerned that TRIPS furthers the interests of the advanced industrialized countries much more than their own. A good example of the built-in biases that critics see in the TRIPS Agreement is that while protection must be extended to high-technology fields such as semiconductors, biotechnology, pharmaceuticals and software, traditional knowledge and folklore are entirely excluded. While there may be legitimate reasons for such 'discrimination' in modern IPR law, it is important to note that many developing countries feel they have a potential competitive advantage in the area of commercially applicable traditional knowledge.

In 2002, the UK Commission on Intellectual Property Rights (CIPR), established by the UK Department for International Development (DFID) and chaired by John Barton, an eminent law professor at Stanford University and a contributor to this book, published a very timely report called *Integrating Intellectual Property Rights and Development Policy* (CIPR, 2002). The commission was mandated to look at how IPRs might work better for poor people and developing countries by providing balanced, evidence-based policy recommendations. The document contains some quite far-reaching recommendations directed at the global IPR system including the institutions within it and national IPR policy-making, and covering the following six areas: intellectual property and development; health; agriculture and genetic resources; traditional knowledge, access and benefit sharing (ABS) and geographical indications; copyright, software and the internet; and patent reform.

Overall, the commission expressed serious doubts about whether the international IPR regime in its present form, and current processes to further strengthen IPR protection, are in the interests of the poor. It also noted that the TRIPS Agreement imposes onerous costs on most developing countries. In raising these doubts and concerns, the commission did not break new ground. But what is truly significant is their source. This is a high-level commission established by a developed country government which also appointed the six members. These members are all widely respected authorities on intellectual property, from developed and developing countries, with expertise covering science, law, ethics and economics, and working in industry, government, academia and the legal profession. As such, the commission could hardly be accused of bias against the intellectual property system. Moreover, their findings drew upon not only their own varied backgrounds but also on fact-finding missions to developing countries on three continents, consultations with stakeholders, eight expert workshops, a series of study papers commissioned by international authorities on different aspects of intellectual property protection, and an international conference.

The report made many telling points. Overall, it made an overwhelming case that a one-size-fits-all approach to IPR protection simply does not work, especially when the required levels of protection are as high as they are today and are likely to become even higher in the near future. At certain stages of development, weak levels of IPR protection are more likely to stimulate economic development and poverty alleviation than strong levels. The commission presented well-documented historical evidence to support this view. Present-day empirical data is, as the commission reveals, somewhat lacking. But what there is points to the same conclusion. A clear inference of the commission's findings in this regard is that the TRIPS Agreement can be regarded as an experiment being conducted on the poor to see whether the lessons of history are applicable to the present-day situation or not.

The commissioners presented strong evidence for their critical stance with respect to the international intellectual property regime, but at the same time avoided the error of treating developing countries as a homogeneous group of countries. Rather they argued that due to their different scientific and technological capacities and social and economic structures, an optimal IPR system is bound to vary widely from one country to another. For example, developing countries that have relatively advanced scientific and technological capacities like India and China may well benefit from high levels of IPR protection in some areas, whereas the least developed countries, such as Bangladesh or Senegal, almost certainly will not. In this context, it is important to point out, as the Barton and Correa chapters clarify, that IPRs can be a tool for development if designed appropriately.

THE INTERNATIONAL IPR FRAMEWORK: A DYNAMIC SYSTEM

As if TRIPS was not enough for developing countries to contend with, there is a great deal more to the international law of intellectual property than this single agreement. The architecture of the global intellectual property regulatory system includes an increasing and, to some, bewildering diversity of multilateral agreements, regional conventions and instruments, and bilateral arrangements.

A wide range of multilateral IPR treaties are administered by the World Intellectual Property Organization (WIPO), a specialized UN agency that is also located in Geneva. Prominent examples include the Paris Convention for the Protection of Industrial Property and the Berne Convention for the Protection of Literary and Artistic Works. Most multilateral IPR agreements are administered by this agency, but there are some important non-WIPO treaties such as the International Convention for the Protection of New Varieties of

Plants, which is administered by the Union Internationale pour la Protection des Obtentions Végétales (UPOV), and, of course, TRIPS. Not all such treaties deal primarily with intellectual property. Two important non-IPR agreements, that are covered in this book, containing important provisions dealing with, or having implications for, intellectual property, are the Convention on Biological Diversity and the International Treaty on Plant Genetic Resources of the Food and Agriculture Organization (FAO) of the UN.

There is a large and growing number of regional agreements and instruments. These include the European Patent Convention, the EU Directive on the Legal Protection of Biotechnological Inventions, the Bangui Agreement Establishing an African Intellectual Property Organization (OAPI), the Harare Protocol on Patents and Industrial Designs within the Framework of the African Regional Industrial Property Organization, and the Andean Community Common Regime on Industrial Property. Some of these, such as Chapter 17 of the North American Free Trade Agreement (NAFTA), are components of trade agreements rather than stand-alone IPR treaties.

In recent years, there has been a proliferation of bilateral agreements on trade and investment. These tend to require parties to introduce stronger IPR protection than TRIPS requires (so-called 'TRIPS-plus' provisions), which is why they are popular with the US and the EU. A recent example is the 2000 Free Trade Agreement between the US and Jordan, but there are many others.

The quantity of international agreements has continued to increase since TRIPS came into force. New treaties adopted since then include the two 1996 'internet treaties', which are the WIPO Copyright Treaty and the WIPO Performers and Phonograms Treaty, and the 2000 Patent Law Treaty. Negotiations are currently underway to draft a Substantive Patent Law Treaty, which would advance the process of harmonizing patent law to a much higher level, leading perhaps one day to a world patent system. These developments and their implications are analysed by Okediji in Chapter 8. It is perhaps sufficient to mention here that at a time when many developing countries are still unclear how best they should implement their TRIPS obligations, such rapid evolution in the international IPR regime and the trend towards harmonization causes them great concern.

KEY AREAS OF DISCUSSION

While the whole of the TRIPS Agreement has implications for sustainable development, the part that developing countries have expressed most concern about is the section on patents. According to Article 27.1, 'patents shall be available for any inventions, whether products or processes, in all fields of technology, provided that they are new, involve an inventive step and are capable of industrial application'. Moreover, 'patents shall be available and patent rights enjoyable without discrimination as to the place of invention, the field of technology and whether products are imported or locally produced'. Evidently, this constrains developing countries from providing the kinds of subject-matter exclusions that many European countries had in their patent laws until quite recently, such as on pharmaceuticals and food products. For example, France only allowed pharmaceuticals to be patented from 1960, Ireland from 1964, Germany from 1968, Japan from 1976, Switzerland from 1977, Italy and Sweden both from 1978 and Spain from as late as 1992. To many countries, as we will see, the health implications of this are disturbing given the potential effects of patent monopolies on the prices of much-needed drugs.

If anything, Article 27.3(b), which deals with exceptions to patentability in the area of biotechnology and plant breeding, has attracted even more attention than Article 27.1. (See Chapter 9 by Chidyausiku which explains the particular concerns of African countries.) According to this subparagraph, WTO members may exclude from patentability:

> *plants and animals other than micro-organisms, and essentially biological processes for the production of plants or animals other than non-biological and microbiological processes. However, Members shall provide for the protection of plant varieties either by patents or by an effective sui generis system or by any combination thereof.*

This means that with respect to products, plants and animals may be excluded from patentability. As regards processes, essentially biological processes for the production of plants or animals may also be excluded. But patents must be available for micro-organisms as products and for non-biological and microbiological processes for producing plants or animals. Patent protection need not be available for plant varieties but an effective IPR system is still obligatory. This may be an UPOV-type plant variety right system, an alternative system yet to be devised, or some combination of systems.

Undoubtedly, this part of TRIPS is extremely important for developing countries. What is less clear is how they can take advantage of its provisions to further their sustainable development objectives. It is thus hardly surprising that they are still unsure about where their national interests lie with respect to the paragraph's provisions, and have barely implemented any part of it, except by default in the sense of continuing to not allow plants and animals to be patented.

Nowadays, developing country concerns about TRIPS are focused mainly on the following areas, all of which are also key themes of this book:

- TRIPS and public health
- TRIPS, biodiversity and genetic resources
- Plant varieties and the sui generis option
- Patenting life
- Traditional knowledge and folklore

TRIPS and public health

In the last few years, increasing attention has been centred on the relationship between patents and the availability and price of essential drugs. In particular, a number of governments and health and development non-governmental organizations (NGOs) have condemned pharmaceutical companies for taking advantage of their patent monopolies in two ways: first, by charging high prices for treatments for diseases that heavily affect poor people that are unable to afford them; and second, by putting pressure on developing country governments to prevent the local manufacture or importation of cheaper copied versions of the drugs produced in countries where either they cannot be patented or where the patents are not respected.

Many of these issues have been brought to the fore by the current HIV/AIDS pandemic. This is now one of the world's most serious public health crises. Africa is the most severely affected continent with millions of infected people there destined to die in the next few years unless they can be treated with anti-retroviral drugs. Yet in many developing countries, only a tiny proportion of HIV/AIDS sufferers receives these treatments.

High prices for AIDS drugs are not the only factor limiting patients' access to them. Poor people often live far away from clinics and hospitals. Also, many countries are short of medical practitioners trained to prescribe anti-AIDS drugs to patients in the appropriate combinations and dosages. Nonetheless, high prices obviously have a profound impact on the ability of poor people to acquire them. And, at least in principle, patent monopolies can place the companies holding them in a strong position to set prices at high levels.

In the face of the health crises affecting many developing countries, discussions have been taking place on finding ways to make better use of the flexibilities inherent in TRIPS by virtue of its ambiguous language and, alternatively, to relax the international patent rules that restrict the manufacture and sale of generic versions of patented drugs. Chapters 13, 14 and 15 in this volume by Balasubramaniam, Jourdain and Zaveri assess the scale of the policy challenges for developing countries and identify possible solutions.

TRIPS, genetic resources and biodiversity

One of the major challenges for developing countries is to ensure policy coherence so that implementation of TRIPS is consistent with two international agreements that deal specifically with genetic resources and biological diversity, namely the Convention on Biological Diversity and the International Treaty on Plant Genetic Resources for Food and Agriculture, which is yet to enter into force.

The Convention on Biological Diversity

'Biological diversity' and its contracted form 'biodiversity' are neologisms which date back to the early 1980s when several prominent biologists were calling attention to the dangers of an anthropogenic global mass extinction event. Biodiversity is not intended to be purely a scientific term. Indeed, it was coined specifically to pursue a conservationist agenda. Given that 'biological diversity' should so quickly become the title of an international treaty, the Convention on Biological Diversity (CBD), the strategy was a clear success.

The CBD, which entered into force in 1993, has as its three objectives 'the conservation of biological diversity, the sustainable use of its components and the fair and equitable sharing of the benefits arising out of the utilization of genetic resources'. Intellectual property rights and particularly patents are considered to be most relevant to the third of these objectives, that of fair and equitable benefit sharing.

Agreeing a text acceptable to governments of the biodiversity-poor industrialized world and of the biodiversity-rich developing countries turned into an unexpectedly long, difficult and contentious process. Some developing countries complained that it was unfair for influential conservation organizations and developed country governments to expect them to protect their forests and forgo the economic benefits from selling timber or converting them to other uses. These countries argued vociferously that a quid pro quo for biodiversity preservation was fair and necessary. Realizing the potential economic value of their biodiversity wealth and needing to improve their scientific, technological and financial capacities to exploit it, their position was that they had the right to set conditions on those seeking *their* resources, including the fair and equitable sharing of benefits such as the transfer of technology and financial resources. Needless to say, perhaps, developed countries and transnational corporations wanted as few restrictions and conditions as possible on access to biological resources.

The relationship between intellectual property rights and the CBD tends to be treated as most relevant to the regulation of access to genetic resources, and the development of measures to ensure fair and equitable benefit sharing with commercial users, states and holders of traditional knowledge. The most important parts of the convention here are Articles 15 and 8(j). Article 15 recognizes the sovereign rights of states over their natural resources and their authority to determine access to genetic resources, and that access, where granted, shall be on mutually agreed terms and subject to the prior informed consent of the provider party. Article 8(j) requires parties to 'respect, preserve and maintain knowledge, innovations and practices of indigenous and local communities embodying traditional lifestyles relevant for the conservation and sustainable use of biological diversity and promote their wider application with the approval and involvement of the holders of such knowledge, innovations and practices and encourage the equitable sharing of the benefits arising from the utilization of such knowledge, innovations and practices'.

Intellectual property is only explicitly referred to in the context of technology transfer, which is supposed to be one of the main kinds of benefit for provider countries to receive. Article 16 on access to and transfer of technology requires parties to the convention to undertake to provide and/or facilitate access to and transfer of technologies to other parties under fair and most favourable terms. The only technology referred to is biotechnology, but the article is concerned with any technologies 'that are relevant to the conservation and sustainable use of biological diversity or make use of genetic resources and do not cause significant damage to the environment'. Recognizing that technologies are sometimes subject to patents and other IPRs, access to such technologies must be 'on terms which recognize and are consistent with the adequate and effective protection of intellectual property rights'.

Paragraph 16.5 requires the parties to cooperate to ensure that patents and other IPRs 'are supportive of and do not run counter to' the CBD's objectives. This reflects the profound disagreement during the negotiations – which remains unresolved – between those who believed that IPRs conflict with the CBD's objectives and others that saw no contradiction. Such disagreement has not gone away. Chapter 7 by Dhar provides an excellent and very helpful analysis of the relationship between the CBD and TRIPS.

The International Treaty on Plant Genetic Resources for Food and Agriculture

During the 1980s the FAO became the principal battleground of what became known as 'the seed wars' (Kloppenburg and Kleinman, 1987). The main bone of contention was that the developed countries were allegedly abusing the free exchange principle. The main criticisms were, first, that most of the world's major crop genetic resource collections were held in the developed world even though most of the samples had come from the developing world. Second, while folk varieties were treated as being the common heritage of humankind, plant breeders in the developed countries were securing IPR protection for their own varieties.

At the 1981 FAO biennial conference, a resolution called for the drafting of a legal convention. In 1983, the over-ambitious demand for a convention was replaced by a call for a non-binding 'undertaking', and for the creation of a new FAO Commission on Plant Genetic Resources (CPGR) where governments could meet for discussion and monitor what became known as the International Undertaking on Plant Genetic Resources (IUPGR). The objectives of the IUPGR were 'to ensure the safe conservation and promote the unrestricted availability and sustainable utilization of plant genetic resources for present and future generations, by providing a flexible framework for sharing the benefits and burdens'.

The 'farmers' rights' concept was included in the IUPGR from 1989 – in response to the developed countries' insistence on excluding IPR-protected plant varieties from application of the common heritage principle. CPGR Resolution 5/89 defined farmers' rights as 'rights arising from the past, present and future contributions of farmers in conserving, improving and making available plant genetic resources particularly those in the centres of origin/diversity. Those rights are vested in the international community, as trustees for present and future generations of farmers, and supporting the continuation of their contributions as well as the attainment of overall purposes of the International Undertaking [on Plant Genetic Resources].'

In 1993, CPGR Resolution 93/1 called for the IUPGR to be revised in harmony with the CBD. To this end, the commission, now called the Commission on Genetic Resources for Food and Agriculture (CGRFA), held a series of negotiations to revise the International Undertaking. These lengthy negotiations were finally concluded in November 2001, when a revised agreement was not only agreed upon, but was turned into a legally binding agreement known as the International Treaty on Plant Genetic Resources for Food and Agriculture. Recognizing both the sovereign rights and the interdependence of countries over their plant genetic resources, the International Treaty established a multilateral system to facilitate access and benefit sharing (ABS). ABS is to be regulated principally by means of a standard material transfer agreement (MTA), a kind of contract, which will apply also to transfers to third parties and to all subsequent transfers. The negotiations leading to the adoption of the International Treaty are presented and analysed in this volume in Chapter 6 by Lettington.

Plant varieties, the sui generis option and food security

The International Convention for the Protection of New Varieties of Plants (the UPOV Convention) was adopted in Paris in 1961 and entered into force in 1968. It was revised in 1972, 1978 and 1991. The 1978 Act entered into force in 1981, and the 1991 Act in 1998. The convention established the International Union for the Protection of New Varieties of Plants, which is based in Geneva and has a close association with WIPO to the extent that the latter organization's director-general is also secretary-general of UPOV.

The UPOV Convention is the only sui generis system recognized in international law for plant varieties, and is being promoted by the developed countries and the organization itself as the most convenient and effective way for the developing countries to fulfil their obligations under TRIPS to provide IPR protection for plant varieties as an alternative to patents.

The UPOV Convention's provisions are extremely detailed and specific. To be eligible for protection, plant varieties must be novel, distinct, stable, and uniform (in UPOV 1991) or homogeneous (in UPOV 1978). To be novel, the variety must not have been offered for sale or marketed, with the agreement of the breeder or his successor in title, in the source country, or for longer than a limited number of years in any other country. To be distinct, the variety must be distinguishable by one or more characteristics from any other variety whose existence is a matter of common knowledge. To be considered as stable, the variety must remain true to its description after repeated reproduction or propagation. Unlike patents there is no written disclosure requirement. Instead, applicants are required to submit the plant material for which protection is sought to the responsible governmental authority for testing to ensure that the above eligibility requirements have been met. This material may then be used by a government institution to demonstrate stability and homogeneity conclusively through propagation trials.

UPOV 1978 defines the scope of protection as the breeder's right to authorize the following acts: 'the production for purposes of commercial marketing; the offering for sale; and the marketing of the reproductive or vegetative propagating material, as such, of the variety'. The 1991 version extends the scope of breeders' rights in two ways. First, it increases the number of acts for which the prior authorization of the breeder is required. These include 'production or reproduction; conditioning for the purpose of propagation; offering for sale; selling or other marketing; exporting; importing; stocking for the above purposes'. Second, such acts are not just in respect of the reproductive or vegetative propagating material, but also encompass harvested material obtained through the use of propagating material, and so-called 'essentially derived' varieties.

However, the right of breeders both to use protected varieties as an initial source of variation for the creation of new varieties and to market these varieties without authorization from the original breeder (the 'breeders' exemption') is upheld in both versions. One difference is that UPOV 1991 extends rights to varieties which are essentially derived from the protected variety.

There is no reference in the 1978 version to the right of farmers to re-sow seed harvested from protected varieties for their own use (often referred to as 'farmers' privilege'). Thus, countries that are members of the 1978 convention are free to uphold farmers' privilege or eliminate it. Most of them uphold it, either explicitly or by default.

The 1991 version is more specific about this. Whereas the scope of the breeder's right includes production or reproduction and conditioning for the purpose of propagation, governments can use their discretion in deciding whether to uphold the farmers' privilege. According to Article 15, the breeder's right in relation to a variety may be restricted 'in order to permit farmers to use for propagating purposes, on their own holdings, the product of the harvest which they have obtained by planting ... the protected variety'. There is therefore a strong possibility that some governments will further restrict or eliminate farmers' privilege, but this remains to be seen. At present the strength of the farmers' privilege varies quite widely.

UPOV 1991 extends protection from at least 15 years to a minimum of 20 years. This later version is silent on the matter of double (that is, both patent and plant breeders' rights) protection whereas the earlier version stated that members 'may recognise the right of the breeder provided for in this Convention by the grant either of a special title of protection or of a patent'. Removing the bar on double protection was intended to ensure that the US remained compliant with UPOV.

The overwhelming majority of the more than 50 UPOV members are in Europe, North America, Latin America, the Far East and Australasia. This seems to reflect the fact that in many developing countries, especially in Africa, private sector involvement in plant breeding and seed supply is quite limited. Moreover, in many of these countries small-scale farming communities are responsible for much of the plant breeding and seed distribution, as they have been for centuries. Consequently, until recently there would have been few domestic beneficiaries of a plant breeders' rights system, especially if state involvement in breeding was also quite limited.

Critics of the UPOV system, which includes some developing country governments, point out that the convention was initially developed to meet the conditions in the advanced industrialized countries and is therefore inappropriate for their countries. Moreover, concerns have been raised that the plant breeders' right and patents on plants may have the effect of undermining the food security of communities in developing countries. They may do this in three ways. First, by encouraging the cultivation of a narrow range of genetically uniform crops including non-food cash crops, with the possible consequences that people's diets will become nutritionally poorer and crops will be more vulnerable to outbreaks of devastating diseases. Second, by limiting the freedom of farmers to acquire seeds they wish to plant without payment to breeders, and thereby impoverishing them further. And third, by restricting the free circulation of plant genetic resources, which is generally considered essential for the development of new plant varieties.

Patenting life

The 'patenting life' controversy was triggered in the US by the 1980 Supreme Court decision in Diamond v Chakrabarty that living things may constitute patentable inventions, and in Europe in the late 1980s by the European Commission's drafting of a directive on the protection of biotechnological inventions (which was finally adopted in 1998). Chapter 11 by Salazar provides a useful overview of the extension of patent protection to this new field of activity.

Political opposition and critiques have highlighted aspects of extending patent law into this area that they find problematic. These include: first, the moral significance of treating as property such 'inventions' as plants, animals, micro-organisms and (in some jurisdictions) functional or structural components of life forms including gene sequences, proteins and cell cultures; second, the way that these patents appear to overturn some of the basic ground rules of patent law, such as that substances existing in nature are discoveries and cannot therefore be patented; third, the possibility that basic research may be discouraged when overly broad patent claims are allowed, which may also overlap with claims in other patents, and biotechnology research tools such as gene sequences are privatized through the patent system; fourth, that allowing patents on life forms supports the practice of 'biopiracy', which is the misappropriation of genetic resources and/or of traditional knowledge relating to these resources; and fifth, that patents on plants and plant breeders' rights infringe the basic right of farmers to freely dispose of harvested seed as they see fit including to sell it.

Traditional knowledge and folklore

Traditional knowledge plays an important role in the global economy. Traditional peoples and communities are responsible for the discovery, development, and preservation of a tremendous range of medicinal plants, health-giving herbal formulations, and agricultural and forest products that are traded internationally and generate considerable economic value.

The fact that traditional knowledge is being so widely disseminated and commercially exploited with such a small proportion of the benefits flowing back to provider peoples and communities raises the question of ownership and IPRs. Can IPRs such as copyright, patents and trade secrets be used for the protection of traditional knowledge? At the international level, the idea of applying copyright law to protect intangible cultural expressions including those of traditional peoples and communities dates back to the 1960s. The term commonly applied to such manifestations of culture was not traditional knowledge but folklore, or 'expressions of folklore'.

Over the years many traditional peoples and communities have condemned the unauthorized reproduction of their fixed and unfixed cultural expressions such as artistic works, handicrafts, designs, dances, and musical and dramatic performances. Not only do outsiders frequently neglect to ask permission to do so, but also fail to acknowledge the source of the creativity, and even pass off productions and works as authentic expressions or products when they are not.

Yet they find it difficult to prevent such practices. Similarly, the IPR system is frequently implicated in the misappropriation of traditional knowledge associated with biodiversity, a practice often referred to as 'biopiracy'.

It is conceivable that IPRs such as copyright, patents and trade secrets could be used to protect traditional knowledge and folklore. However, these are far from ideal and use of them for such a purpose may be impractical, at least without some reforms. It is because no adequate solutions have been found that the development of legal measures to protect traditional knowledge and/or folklore has become an integral part of the work of several inter-governmental organizations. These include the WTO, WIPO, the CBD, the UN Conference on Trade and Development (UNCTAD), and the World Health Organization (WHO).

INTERGOVERNMENTAL NEGOTIATIONS

The World Trade Organization

In future times, historians of trade law may point to 1999 as a year that marked a shift in the balance of power at the WTO. While the Quad countries (the US, EU member states, Japan and Canada) were still disproportionately powerful, developing countries became more proactive and assertive. Developing countries have begun not only to complain in an organized fashion about TRIPS, but also to make proposals in a coordinated way. Thus, not only have developing countries actively opposed the raising of IPR standards, but they have even proposed that TRIPS be revised in order to circumscribe certain rights, to maintain or even expand the exceptions, and to create new IPR frameworks.

According to UNCTAD Secretary-General Rubens Ricupero, who had been strongly advocating a positive developing country approach to trade negotiations, more than half of the 250 proposals submitted to the WTO General Council during the preparations for the 1999 Seattle Ministerial Conference came from developing countries (Ricupero, 2001). Of these 250 proposals, 15 were on TRIPS and 8 came from developing countries (UNCTAD, 2000). And while many factors contributed to the collapse of the Seattle Conference, criticisms by many developing countries that they were being excluded from key negotiations probably contributed to its failure to launch a new trade round or even to agree on a declaration at all.

In October 1999, 12 developing countries from Asia, Africa and Latin America submitted two joint papers to the General Council detailing the implementation issues to which they were seeking solutions.[1] The two papers put forward several TRIPS-related proposals. One of these argued that TRIPS is incompatible with the CBD and sought a clear understanding that patents inconsistent with Article 15 of the CBD, which vests the authority to determine access to genetic resources in national governments, should not be granted. Several other proposals were directed to Article 27.3(b) and the review of its substantive provisions. Thus, the 12 countries requested that the list of exceptions to patentability in Article 27.3(b) of the TRIPS Agreement should include the WHO's list of essential drugs,[2] and also that the subparagraph should be amended in light of the provisions of the CBD and the FAO International Undertaking taking fully into account the conservation and sustainable use of biological diversity, the protection of the rights and knowledge of indigenous and local communities, and the promotion of farmers' rights. The review should also: (i) clarify artificial distinctions between biological and microbiological organisms and processes; (ii) ensure the continuation of the traditional farming practices including the right to save, exchange and sell seeds, and sell their harvest; and (iii) prevent anti-competitive practices which will threaten the food sovereignty of people in developing countries.

It is noteworthy, first, that most of the proposals were directed to the patents section of TRIPS, and especially the provision relating to biological and genetic resources. Second, they reflected a serious effort to harmonize positions held by the same governments at the CBD Conference of the Parties (CBD-COP) and the FAO-CGRFA. Third, they incorporated positions that a certain number of influential Northern and Southern civil society organizations had been articulating for several years.

Traditional knowledge has become an especially important concern for many developing countries, as Chapters 16, 18 and 19 by Weeraworowit, Aguilar and Hernández Salgar, among others, make very evident. On 6 August 1999, two important documents were submitted to the General Council. One of these, from the Permanent Mission of Venezuela,[3] proposed that the next review of TRIPS, inter alia, should 'establish on a mandatory basis within the TRIPS Agreement a system for the protection of intellectual property, with an ethical and economic content, applicable to the traditional knowledge of local and indigenous communities, together with recognition of the need to define the rights of collective holders'.

The African Group of countries[4] proposed that, in the sentence on plant variety protection in Article 27.3(b), 'a footnote should be inserted stating that any sui generis law for plant variety protection can provide for [inter alia]: (i) the protection of the innovations of indigenous farming communities in developing countries, consistent with the Convention on Biological Diversity and the International Undertaking on Plant Genetic Resources'. This communication, which attracted considerable civil society organization support worldwide, also warned that, 'by mandating or enabling the patenting of seeds, plants and genetic and biological materials, Article 27.3(b) is likely to lead to appropriation of the knowledge and resources of indigenous and local communities'.

While Article 27.3(b) and traditional knowledge continue to be important areas of concern for many developing countries, at the century's end the need to resolve the access to medicines problem understandably became the most contentious TRIPS-related issue. This is of course mainly due to the current HIV/AIDS pandemic, which is the most serious public health crisis for many developing countries, especially in Africa. Millions of people throughout the world have already died and millions more infected people will do so in the next few years unless they can be treated with anti-retroviral drugs. Yet, as mentioned above, a tiny proportion of HIV/AIDS sufferers receives these extremely expensive treatments.

In April 2001, the Council for TRIPS accepted a request by a grouping of African countries known as 'the African Group' to hold a Special Discussion on Intellectual Property and Access to Medicines. This was held the following June. Prior to the discussion, the African Group and 16 other developing countries prepared a paper which affirmed that 'nothing in the TRIPS Agreement should prevent Members from taking measures to protect public health'.[5] This was submitted at the discussion along with another African Group paper proposing that WTO members issue a special declaration at the forthcoming Doha Ministerial Conference including the same language. This proposal was endorsed at the Discussion by Tanzania on behalf of the least-developed WTO members.[6] The US, the EU and Switzerland found such unity difficult to resist and accepted that a declaration was inevitable. Consequently, their aim was not to prevent it but to ensure that the strong rights provided by TRIPS would not be weakened.

In the event, the Doha conference adopted the Declaration on the TRIPS Agreement and Public Health, incorporating very similar language to that proposed by the developing countries (in fact, it states that 'the TRIPS Agreement does not and should not prevent Members from taking measures to protect public health'). The declaration consists of seven paragraphs. Paragraph 5 clarifies the freedoms that all WTO members have with respect to compulsory licensing, their determination of what constitutes a national emergency or other circumstances of extreme urgency, and the exhaustion of rights. Thus, the declaration reaffirms the right to use to the full the provisions in TRIPS allowing each member 'to grant compulsory licences and the freedom to determine the grounds upon which such licences are granted'. The declaration explicitly mentions that public health crises 'relating to HIV/AIDS, tuberculosis, malaria and other epidemics, can represent a national emergency or other circumstances of extreme urgency'. Moreover, WTO members are free to establish their own regime for exhaustion of IPRs. This is important because it means that, if national laws indicate that patent rights over drugs are exhausted by their first legitimate sale, countries can then import drugs legally purchased in countries where they are sold at a lower price.

The process of developing and negotiating the declaration has been a valuable experience for developing countries in Africa and elsewhere. The process was a unique collaborative effort, involving trade negotiators, NGOs working in the areas of health and development, and academics, that reflects an enhanced capacity to negotiate on important but technically complex issues in a united, effective and informed manner. The determination of the developing countries to have a meaningful declaration was such that last minute attempts to dilute the text were headed off, ensuring that the outcome was a balanced document that was nonetheless fully compliant with TRIPS.

The World Intellectual Property Organization

In September 1999, WIPO's Standing Committee on the Law of Patents (SCP) held its third session, which was to be devoted mainly to discussing a draft Patent Law Treaty (PLT). The PLT was intended to harmonize certain patent procedures while steering clear of matters relating to substantive patent law.

The Colombian delegation at the session submitted a brief document entitled 'Protection of biological and genetic resources'[7] that turned out to be quite controversial. The delegation proposed that the PLT include an article based on the two proposals that the document comprised. The first was that 'all industrial property protection shall guarantee the protection of the country's biological and genetic heritage. Consequently, the grant of patents or registrations that relate to elements of that heritage shall be subject to their having been acquired legally.' The second was that 'every document shall specify the registration number of the contract affording access to genetic resources and a copy thereof where the goods or services for which protection is sought have been manufactured or developed from genetic resources, or products thereof, of which one of the member countries is the country of origin'.

This idea of linking patent filing with access and benefit sharing regulations gained the support of several other developing countries. Predictably it did not go down well with some of the other delegations, including the US, the European Community, Japan and Korea, all of which argued that the proposed article related to substantive patent law and therefore had no place in the Patent Law Treaty.

As a compromise, the SCP invited WIPO's International Bureau to do two things. The first was to include the issue of protection of biological and genetic resources on the agenda of that November's meeting of the Working Group on Biotechnological Inventions. The second was to arrange another meeting specifically on that issue. This Meeting on Intellectual Property and Genetic Resources took place in April 2000 and reached a consensus that 'WIPO should facilitate the continuation of consultations among Member States in coordination with the other concerned international organizations, through the conduct of appropriate legal and technical studies, and through the setting up of an appropriate forum within WIPO for future work'.[8]

Two months later, at the Diplomatic Conference for the Adoption of the Patent Law Treaty, WIPO's director-general Kamil Idris read out an agreed statement announcing that 'Member State discussions concerning genetic resources will continue at WIPO. The format of such discussions will be left to the Director General's discretion, in consultation with WIPO Member States'.[9]

For the 25th Session of WIPO's General Assembly, the secretariat prepared a document which invited member states to consider the establishment of an Intergovernmental Committee on Intellectual Property and Genetic Resources, Traditional Knowledge and Folklore (IGC). The WIPO Secretariat suggested that the IGC constitute a forum for members to discuss three themes that it had identified during the consultations. These were 'intellectual property issues that arise in the context of (i) access to genetic resources and benefit sharing; (ii) protection of traditional knowledge, whether or not associated with those resources; and (iii) the protection of expressions of folklore'.[10] This suggestion was enthusiastically supported by a large number of developing countries and was approved without formal opposition.

The first session of the IGC convened in April 2001, and the second took place the following December. Substantive discussion at the two meetings focused mainly on two subjects: operational principles for contractual agreements concerning access to genetic resources and benefit sharing, and traditional knowledge as prior art. There was a clear division between those countries that favour the creation of new legal norms (mainly from Latin America and the African Group) and those opposed to them, including the US and Canada. The latter group of countries, along with industry representatives, considered that solutions should be sought within existing legal frameworks and, while willing to contemplate additional obligations, would prefer these to be non-binding.

The committee also agreed that WIPO should continue its work to establish model IPR clauses for contractual agreements regulating access and benefit sharing, possibly including the development of a database of such clauses to help guide negotiations. Approval was also given to continuation of WIPO's work on the IPR aspects of documenting public domain traditional knowledge, the aim of which is to ensure that patent examiners are able to prevent cases where patents whose claims extend to traditional knowledge are improperly awarded. (See Chapters 17, 20 and 27 by Sahai, Utkarsh and Kaushik, which discuss some traditional knowledge documentation initiatives in India.) Towards the end of the meeting, several developing countries proposed, without objections from other participating countries, that WIPO should produce a document providing elements for model sui generis protection for traditional knowledge.

The Conference of the Parties to the Convention on Biological Diversity

To review implementation of the CBD, the Conference of the Parties (COP) (composed of all contracting parties) meets periodically (usually biannually). IPRs are most frequently discussed in deliberations on such topics as access to genetic resources, benefit sharing, and the knowledge innovations and practices of indigenous and local communities, and not so much transfer of technology. The COP has become a forum in which TRIPS and IPRs are debated, critiqued (and defended) in a fairly open way. There are two reasons for this. First, the national delegations consist largely of civil servants from environment ministries. They tend to be concerned mostly about conservation, sustainable development and food security, and often have little contact with their trade ministry counterparts. Second, there are close links between many of the national delegations and well-organized networks of highly articulate and politically astute activists representing international civil society organizations that attend virtually all inter-governmental meetings relating to the CBD. The openness of the CBD forums (not just the COP, but also the Experts' Panel on Access and Benefit-Sharing, and the Ad hoc Open-ended Inter-sessional Working Group on Article 8(j) and Related Provisions) has made the building of such links easier.

It is difficult to envisage the COP, even without the US, ever adopting a protocol to the CBD that would require parties to reform their patent or plant breeders' right systems to give effect to certain CBD provisions such as those dealing with benefit sharing. Even if it did, many developed countries would simply refuse to ratify it. On the other hand, several developing countries have already introduced measures regulating IPRs to support the CBD's objectives. These include Costa Rica (see Chapters 18 and 26 by Aguilar and Cabrera Medaglia) and the Andean Community countries (see Chapter 25 by Ruiz).

At the Sixth Meeting of the Conference of the Parties, which took place in The Hague in May 2002, the Bonn Guidelines on Access to Genetic Resources and Fair and Equitable Sharing of the Benefits Arising out of their Utilization were officially adopted. The guidelines, which are intended to be used when developing and drafting legislative, administrative or policy measures on ABS and contracts, have a number of interesting provisions relating to IPRs. Parties with genetic resource users under their jurisdiction are suggested to consider adopting 'measures to encourage the disclosure of the country of origin of the genetic resources and of the origin of traditional knowledge, innovations and practices of indigenous and local communities in applications for intellectual property rights'. This possibility is elaborated on and analysed in this volume in Chapter 21 by Vivas Eugui.

VIEWS FROM DEVELOPING COUNTRIES

This book shows that the views coming from developing countries are diverse. It should also be evident that the developing world does not and cannot speak with one voice on every issue affecting them, including those covered in this book. What unites these voices, though, is a common determination that developing countries should be active players in international negotiations and that they can and should work together where doing so enables them to be more effective in advancing their interests.

This book also gives ample testimony to the fact that developing countries are not just waiting for favourable international-level settlements before embarking on the design and implementation of domestic and regional laws and policies that seek to harmonize their obligations under TRIPS, particularly relating to Article 27.3(b) and other agreements like the CBD. Peru recently broke new ground by passing legislation to protect the collective knowledge of indigenous peoples relating to biodiversity (see Chapter 30 by Venero). Costa Rica has passed a law which seeks to implement the CBD while limiting IPRs in ways that are considered to conflict with the Convention's objectives (see Chapter 18 by Aguilar). Indian, Kenyan and South African legislators have also been highly active, as demonstrated in Chapters 27, 28 and 29 by Kaushik, Wolson and Otieno-Odek. Countries have also collaborated to develop regional agreements and model laws, such as the countries of Central America (see Chapter 26 by Cabrera Medaglia), the Andean Community (Bolivia, Colombia, Ecuador, Peru and Venezuela) (see Chapter 25 by Ruiz), and the African countries through the African Union (formerly the Organization of African Unity). The latter organization has drafted a model law which, as Chapters 24 and 23 by Ekpere and Mangeni should make clear, is likely to be very influential throughout that continent and possibly beyond it as well.

NOTES

1 These papers were: (1) World Trade Organization – General Council (1999) 'Preparations for the 1999 Ministerial Conference. Implementation issues to be addressed before/at Seattle. Communication from Cuba, Dominican Republic, Egypt, El Salvador, Honduras, India, Indonesia, Malaysia, Nigeria, Pakistan, Sri Lanka and Uganda' [WT/GC/W/354]; and World Trade Organization – General Council (1999) 'Preparations for the 1999 Ministerial Conference. Implementation issues to be addressed in the first year of negotiations. Communication from Cuba, Dominican Republic, Egypt, El Salvador, Honduras, India, Indonesia, Malaysia, Nigeria, Pakistan, Sri Lanka and Uganda' [WT/GC/W/355].

2 This is not a particularly ambitious demand, since 95 per cent of drugs on the WHO essential list are already off-patent. In fact, it is partly the relative cheapness of the drugs listed (due in large part to their patent-free status) that makes them 'essential' and thus worthy of inclusion.

3 World Trade Organization – General Council (1999) 'Preparations for the 1999 Ministerial Conference. Proposals regarding the TRIPS Agreement (Paragraph 9(a)(ii) of the Geneva Ministerial Declaration). Communication from Venezuela' [WT/GC/W/282].

4 World Trade Organization – General Council (1999) 'Preparations for the 1999 Ministerial Conference. The TRIPS Agreement. Communication from Kenya on behalf of the African Group' [WT/GC/W/302].

5 World Trade Organization – TRIPS Council (2001) 'TRIPS and public health. Submission by the African Group, Barbados, Bolivia, Brazil, Dominican Republic, Ecuador, Honduras, India, Indonesia, Jamaica, Pakistan, Paraguay, Philippines, Peru, Sri Lanka, Thailand and Venezuela' [IP/C/W/296].

6 World Trade Organization – TRIPS Council (2001) 'Special discussion on intellectual property and access to medicines' [IP/C/M/31].

7 World Intellectual Property Organization – Standing Committee on the Law of Patents (1999) 'Protection of biological and genetic resources. Proposal by the Delegation of Colombia' [SCP/3/10].

8 World Intellectual Property Organization (2000) 'Matters concerning intellectual property and genetic resources, traditional knowledge and folklore. Document prepared by the Secretariat' [WO/GA/26/6].

9 Ibid.

10 Ibid.

REFERENCES

Commission on Intellectual Property Rights (2002) *Integrating Intellectual Property Rights and Development Policy. Report of the Commission on Intellectual Property Rights*, London: Department for International Development.

Kloppenburg Jr, J, and D L Kleinman (1987) 'Seed wars: common heritage, private property, and political strategy', *Socialist Review* 95.

Ricupero, R (2001) 'Rebuilding confidence in the multilateral trading system: closing the "legitimacy gap"', in G P Sampson (ed), *The Role of the World Trade Organization in Global Governance*, Tokyo: United Nations University.

United Nations Conference on Trade and Development (2000) 'Elements of a positive agenda', in UNCTAD, *Positive Trade Agenda for Developing Countries: Issues for Future Trade Negotiations*, Geneva: UNCTAD.

The World Bank (2001) *Global Economic Prospects and the Developing Countries 2002: Making Trade Work for the World's Poor*, Washington DC: The World Bank.

PART ONE

THE INTERNATIONAL ARCHITECTURE

TRIPS and Development

TRIPS and the International System on Genetic Resources

The WIPO Agenda

Chapter 2

Origins and History of the TRIPS Negotiations

Adronico O Adede

This chapter is designed to give readers a sense of the political and trade interests, including legal and scientific considerations, that influenced the inclusion of intellectual property protection issues on the agenda of the Uruguay Round of multilateral trade negotiations resulting in the establishment of the World Trade Organization (WTO) and the adoption of a series of international legal instruments. Chief among them is the Agreement on Trade-related Aspects of Intellectual Property Rights (TRIPS), whose Article 27.3(b) is given special attention in this chapter.

Specifically, the chapter seeks to answer the following questions:

- Why, how and when did intellectual property rights (IPRs) become an issue for discussion predominantly under the multilateral trade negotiations and in the context of the WTO, thus overshadowing the treatment of the subject under the World Intellectual Property Organization (WIPO)?
- What were the considerations that influenced African and other developing countries to participate in the Uruguay Round negotiations which resulted in the TRIPS Agreement?
- What is the scope of the 'review of the provisions' of Article 27.3(b) as distinguished from the 'review' under other articles of TRIPS?
- What role did the industry, non-governmental organizations (NGOs) and civil society play in the negotiation of TRIPS?

THE INCORPORATION OF INTELLECTUAL PROPERTY RIGHTS IN MULTILATERAL TRADE NEGOTIATIONS

The Uruguay Round of multilateral trade negotiations, which was launched at Punta del Este, Uruguay, in 1986, took place against the background of claims by US industries in such sectors as computer software and microelectronics, entertainment, chemicals, pharmaceuticals, and biotechnology that they were suffering heavy losses from the absence of adequate protection of their IPRs in foreign markets. In 1987, a survey by the US International Trade Commission (ITC) confirmed, on the basis of public hearings held and questionnaires administered, that US firms were losing some US$50 billion a year from lack of overseas intellectual property protection. The conclusion was that something had to be done, and the idea of taking up the issue of IPRs within the General Agreement on Tariffs and Trade (GATT) framework began to receive support from the US.

However, there was a general feeling among developing countries that the concern with IPR protection was being expressed by the US government on behalf of its industries, and that all such efforts towards the establishment of an effective international IPR regime were aimed at furthering the interests of Western businesses and not those of the developing countries. This feeling was not without foundation, because the private sector, in which the pharmaceutical industry played a major role, had led the effort to treat IPRs as a trade-related matter. Thus, Edmund T Pratt, chairman of Pfizer, initiated the process in 1984 by saying: 'We must also work to get more broadly based economic organizations, such as the OECD [Organization for Economic Co-operation and Development] and the GATT, to develop intellectual property rules, because intellectual property protection is essential for the continued development of international trade and investment (Cottier, 1991).'

Accordingly, the developing countries resisted the idea of making the question of IPR protection a subject for discussion under the multilateral trade negotiations with such a strong industry influence and specific agenda. They considered intellectual property to be an issue that belonged exclusively within the competence of WIPO and pointed to their own initiatives in the 1970s to revise the Paris Convention on the Protection of Industrial Property. The developing countries were thus worried about the link that may be established between the TRIPS Agreement under the GATT forum and the existing intellectual property rights conventions such as the 1886 Berne Convention for the Protection of Literary and Artistic Works, the 1961 Rome Convention for the Protection of Performers, Producers and Broadcasting Organizations, and the 1989 Treaty on Intellectual Property in Respect of Integrated Circuits. Linking intellectual property to the negotiation under the GATT framework was equally not enthusiastically endorsed by the European Community in the beginning, at least not until 1990 as shown below.

The US was, on the other hand, not happy with the progress made towards intellectual property rights protection within WIPO. It pointed out the failure of conferences between 1980 and 1984 to revise the Paris Convention on the Protection of Industrial Property, and therefore preferred the GATT forum for negotiating an effective regime for the protection of IPRs. They pointed out that the GATT forum provided for effective enforcement of agreements and for dispute settlement mechanisms which were practically lacking in the WIPO-administered conventions. Thus, the US continued with their efforts to introduce, in the GATT forum, an item dealing with IPRs to address the problem of counterfeit products and, later, of copyright piracy, which had been increasing in developing countries in the 1980s.

Counterfeiting and copyright piracy increased in the 1980s because of the desire of developing countries to catch up in the industrialization process and to have access to printed educational material which they needed in that context. The situation was accelerated by the following factors: the advent of copy-prone electronic-based technologies and products; the growing competitiveness of newly industrialized developing countries in the manufacturing sector; the increasing globalization of the market-place; and the growing perception of intellectual property by the enterprises of the developed countries as a strategic asset. Thus, there was tension between the quest for tighter protection of IPRs for the promotion of creativity being pursued by the industrialized owners of the property, and the policy of maximization of social welfare arising from an impeded diffusion of that creativity being pursued by the developing countries through more relaxed protection of IPRs.

The US, joined by what were then the EEC countries, attempted to champion an Anti-Counterfeit Code (ACC), which they produced during the Tokyo Round of negotiations,[1] in response to the above situation. But the counterfeit code was not adopted by the Tokyo Round. However, the US did not give up. When the GATT Ministerial Conference convened in Punta del Este, Uruguay, from 15 to 20 September 1986, to discuss the mandate of the next round of negotiations, the US mounted a campaign to include IPRs, beyond the question of counterfeiting and piracy, among the issues for discussion under the Uruguay Round of multilateral trade negotiations. The result was that, borrowing from the language used in another item on the proposed mandate – Trade-related Economic Measures – the trade ministers at Punta del Este, coined the expression 'Trade-related Aspects of Intellectual Property Rights (TRIPS)' and included it on the agenda of the Uruguay Round.

The inclusion of TRIPS issues on the agenda of the Uruguay Round did not, however, mean that the developing countries had abandoned altogether their reluctance to have intellectual property rights issues discussed under the GATT forum. It appears from the subsequent developments that the inclusion of TRIPS on the agenda was a last-minute political compromise whose legal foundation was yet to be clarified. As observed elsewhere, the TRIPS item 'featured almost as a footnote on a crowded agenda [of the Uruguay Round] and it was uncertain whether that contentious item would survive the end of the round'(Bronckers, 1994), as may be gleaned from this brief discussion of the economic and political backdrop to the inclusion of the item on the agenda.

According to the Ministerial Declaration of 20 September 1986, the mandate of the Uruguay Round of trade negotiations, included the following issues for discussion: tariffs, non-tariff measures, tropical products, natural resource-based products, textiles and clothing, agriculture, subsidies and countervailing measures, safeguards, GATT articles, Multilateral Trade Negotiation (MTN) agreements and arrangements, dispute settlement, trade-related investment measures, and trade-related aspects of intellectual property rights including trade in counterfeit goods. The negotiating objectives were stated as follows:

> *In order to reduce the distortions and impediments to international trade, and taking into account the need to promote effective and adequate protection of intellectual property rights, and to ensure that measures and procedures to enforce intellectual property rights do not themselves become barriers to legitimate trade, the negotiations shall aim to clarify GATT provisions and elaborate as appropriate new rules and disciplines.*
>
> *Negotiations shall aim to develop a multilateral framework of principles, rules and disciplines dealing with international trade in counterfeit goods, taking into account work already undertaken in the GATT.*
>
> *These negotiations shall be without prejudice to other complementary initiatives that may be taken in the World Intellectual Property Organization and elsewhere to deal with these matters.*

One of the arguments for conducting the discussions on the question of effective protection of intellectual property rights within the GATT forum (the Uruguay Round), and not in WIPO, as further explained in the next section, was advanced as follows. Under the GATT forum, the developing countries have the opportunity to use bargaining power and secure trade-offs in negotiating favourable terms on issues such as textiles and clothing, agriculture, tropical products and safeguards, as part of the package that included IPRs. The consideration of such trade issues clearly went beyond the limited discussion of whether or not to establish high standards for the protection of IPRs, as would be the case in negotiations within the framework of the WIPO.

By expanding the scope of issues for discussion, ranging from the TRIPS Agreement to those aimed at producing a series of agreements on the other specific areas mentioned above, the Uruguay Round was billed as presenting a unique opportunity for developing countries to achieve tangible gains at the negotiations. This argument on possible useful trade-offs in the results of the negotiations, encouraged the developing countries to assess more closely the positive and negative elements associated with their continued rejection of the inclusion of IPR issues in the Uruguay Round. The pressure was mounting on them. With the support of the other industrialized states, the US kept on pushing for the discussion of IPRs on the agenda of the Uruguay Round along with the new subjects such as trade in services and related investment measures. In fact, the US had already began to use its domestic law (Super/Special 301) unilaterally to undertake trade retaliation against states whose practices with respect to IPRs it considered to be 'unfair', and made the enactment of effective legislation by developing countries for the protection of IPRs a mark of good conduct to be rewarded.

Further consideration of the possible package deal helped some developing countries to warm to the idea of the inclusion of TRIPS on the Uruguay Round agenda. But they still largely gave a rather restrictive interpretation of the Punta del Este Mandate by: (i) finding it hard to depart from their original view that WIPO should remain the organization with competence over substantive standard setting for IPRs; (ii) continuing to limit the negotiations under the mandate to counterfeit and strictly trade-related issues; and (iii) stressing the importance they attached to transfer of technology and developmental policies as a quid pro quo for intellectual property protection.

Intensive lobbying and discussions on the actual commencement of negotiations on TRIPS continued between 1986 until 1989. During the ministerial meeting held in Montreal in December 1988 to carry out the Mid-Term Review of the Uruguay Round the ministers reached an agreement on 11 of the 15 subjects under negotiation according to the mandate. However, the ministers failed to agree on the commencement of negotiations on four areas: agriculture, textiles and clothing, safeguards, and the trade-related aspects of intellectual property rights, including trade-related aspects in counterfeit goods. They then decided that the Trade Negotiations Committee (TNC) should meet in Geneva during the first week of April 1989 to continue discussions and agree upon the remaining areas and review the entire package. The pressure was to be applied upon the so-called 'big' developing countries to abandon their resistance.

On reaching agreement on the remaining issues at the April 1989 meeting, the following further clarifications were made concerning TRIPS (Trade Negotiations Committee, 1989):

> *Ministers agree that negotiations on this subject shall continue in the Uruguay Round and shall encompass the following issues:*
>
> *(a) The applicability of the basic principles of the GATT and of relevant international intellectual property agreements or conventions;*
> *(b) The provision of adequate standards and principles concerning the availability, scope and use of trade-related intellectual property rights;*
> *(c) The provision of effective and appropriate means for the enforcement of trade-related intellectual property rights, taking into account differences in national legal systems;*
> *(d) The provision of effective and expeditious procedures for the multilateral prevention and settlement of disputes between governments, including the applicability of GATT procedures; and*
> *(e) Transitional arrangements aiming at the fullest participation in the results of the negotiations.*
>
> *Ministers agree that in the negotiations consideration will be given to concerns raised by participants related to the underlying public policy objectives of their national systems for the protection of intellectual property, including development and technological objectives.*
>
> *In respect of (d) above, Ministers emphasize the importance of reducing tensions in this area by reaching strengthened commitments to resolve disputes on trade-related intellectual property issues through multilateral procedures.*

> *The negotiations shall also comprise the development of a multilateral framework of principles, rules and disciplines dealing with international trade in counterfeit goods.*
>
> *The negotiations should be conducive to a mutually supportive relationship between GATT and WIPO as well as other relevant international organizations.*

There was, therefore, a delay of three years between the decision to include TRIPS in the Uruguay Round in 1986 and the actual agreement to take it up for discussion in 1989, by the Negotiating Group 11 of the TNC of the MTN.

The discussion on the TRIPS Agreement began with a number of legal texts prepared, first in March 1990 by the members of the EEC. The submission of a complete text of a TRIPS agreement by the EC, which thereby abandoned its earlier doubt about bringing the negotiation on TRIPS under the GATT framework, triggered an important phase of the negotiations. This was followed by a series of similar drafts of complete texts of TRIPS agreements, submitted in May 1990 by the US, Switzerland, and Japan, all of which 'borrowed substantially from the Community's text' (Reinbothe and Howard, 1991). These proposals represented one approach to the negotiation on TRIPS, envisaging a single TRIPS agreement encompassing all the areas of negotiations and dealing with all categories of intellectual property on which proposals were made. Under this approach, the TRIPS Agreement would be implemented as an integral part of the general agreement that was intended to produce the World Trade Organization.

It was also not until May 1990 that a group of 12 developing countries (Argentina, Brazil, Chile, China, Colombia, Cuba, Egypt, India, Nigeria, Peru, Tanzania, and Uruguay), later joined by Pakistan and Zimbabwe, agreed to participate in the actual negotiations on the TRIPS Agreement by producing their own detailed proposal, which consisted of two parts.

The first dealt mainly with the norms and principles to be applied to trade in counterfeit and pirated goods. It provided for the establishment of certain procedures and remedies to discourage such trade, while trying to ensure an unimpeded flow of trade in legitimate goods. The second part covered standards and principles concerning availability, scope and use of IPRs, setting out the objectives and principles underlying an agreement on such standards and specifying the basic standards relating to different categories of IPRs.

By presenting the proposed text of a TRIPS agreement into two parts, the developing countries wanted, in the first instance, to signal their determination to emphasize the part dealing with trade in counterfeit goods while minimizing the part relating to substantive standards on IPRs. Secondly, with regard to the latter part, the developing countries wanted to highlight the importance of the public policy objectives underlying national IPR systems, the necessity of recognizing those objectives at the international level and the need to specify some basic principles which could subsequently elucidate the application of any standards established in the TRIPS Agreement. Thirdly, they insisted on the need to respect and safeguard national legal systems and traditions on IPRs, in view of the diverse needs and levels of development of states participating in the IPR negotiations.

The proposals thus represented another approach to the negotiations on TRIPS under which the resulting agreements would be implemented in the relevant international organizations, account being taken of the multi-disciplinary and overall aspects of the issues involved.

As a basis for negotiations towards a TRIPS agreement, the chairman of the Negotiating Group 11, using the four proposals mentioned above, produced a composite text in which he grouped related points and arranged alternative proposals on the same issues and conveniently identified them, emphasizing that the composite text itself did not seek to prejudice the question as to how the instrument would be implemented and thus left that question wide open. Successive revisions of the composite text occurred as a result of further negotiations leading to the revision of the text which was placed before the Ministerial Meeting in Brussels on 3–7 December 1990. The Brussels meeting produced tangible results and intensive negotiations resumed during the last quarter of 1991, leading to the tabling of the Draft Final Act in December 1991. In fact, this Final Act was close to the complete agreement on TRIPS. Thus, the subsequent discussions did not yield many substantive provisions different from it, apart from the addition of a provision on semiconductor technology in Article 31(c) and the introduction of paragraphs 2 and 3 of Article 64 on the settlement of disputes, which were added to the final version of the agreement adopted at Marrakech in 1994.

It is beyond the scope of this paper to discuss the unique negotiating systems under the GATT framework, which resulted in the adoption of a number of instruments by the Uruguay Round, including the TRIPS Agreement. A negotiating system emerged within the GATT framework under which the issues are first placed before a smaller group to be thrashed out and then before a larger group of the members. Moreover, the issues, as we have already seen in the agenda of the Uruguay Round, may not strictly speaking be those presented only in the context of North–South differences. There are also those which require a North–North accommodation and even South–South compromises. Thus the WTO uses the so-called 'green room' negotiating system. Under the system, a group of 'five plus five' is convened to undertake negotiation on an issue. The result is then presented to a larger group of 'ten plus ten' as an agreed package, representing a consensus which needs no further substantive discussion. The 'ten plus ten' then presents the agreed proposal to, say, a group of 30, which also receives it as a consensus text. After that the proposal is put before the Ministerial Committee for formal endorsement. This negotiating system has been criticized by the developing countries, claiming that it tends to place on the negotiating table, proposals and agreements which have been largely negotiated by the major players such as the US, the EU and Japan, for the endorsement by the rest of the membership of the WTO, who are thus excluded from the actual negotiation on the issues. The 'green room' negotiating system has thus been contrasted with another selective negotiating system, namely, the 'Vienna setting',[2] that has been reportedly used more acceptably by the Conference of the Parties (COP) to the Convention on Biological Diversity (CBD).

Given the negotiating system followed by the Uruguay Round, which even developing country sovereign states complained about, it is easily apparent that the non-governmental organizations and civil society had next to no opportunities for influencing the negotiations of the TRIPS Agreement during the conference processes between 1990 and 1994. They may, however, have had opportunities for organizing informal workshops and seminars to discuss TRIPS-related issues, but these were completely outside the official GATT negotiating procedures. The interests of developed country industries, on the other hand, were actively pursued by their respective governments, as evidenced by the active role played by the US in bringing IPRs to the negotiating table at the launch of the Uruguay Round. The fact that NGOs and civil society were excluded from the negotiations resulting in the creation of the WTO and the agreements it administers, including TRIPS, may explain why they subsequently became so uncompromising towards the WTO, as shown when they helped to paralyse the 1999 Seattle Ministerial Conference, where it was expected that a Millennium Round would be launched.

THE FACTORS WHICH INFLUENCED AFRICA'S PARTICIPATION IN THE NEGOTIATIONS

It is useful to recall briefly here that the developing countries, as observed in our discussion on the backdrop to the inclusion of IPRs on the agenda, generally considered the management and control of patent-related activities as a key element in development policy. They tended to see patents as an obstacle to technology transfer, which they need for development and for enhancing their capacity to undertake research leading to patentable inventions of their own. In contrast, the developed countries regard the existence of an effective patent protection system as the necessary prerequisite for investment in research and development and an essential incentive for technology transfer. These opposing views on patent protection should be kept in mind as we outline the factors influencing African and the other developing countries as they negotiated what became the TRIPS Agreement.

The first factor was the expectation of gains in other trade areas. The underlying rationale for the traditional GATT practice of holding rounds of trade negotiations is that this allows for trade-offs between different areas of negotiation, thus making it possible for the negotiators to reach compromises and achieve progress towards a desired goal. If each area of negotiation were taken in isolation, the chances for a successful agreement on each of the issues would have proved difficult. This factor made the negotiations on TRIPS, which included other issues jointly taken up for discussion, more manageable and, therefore, different from the negotiations that take place at WIPO, which generally deal exclusively with IPRs. As latecomers to the industrialization process, the developing countries demonstrated their unwillingness to strengthen IPR protection on account of their weak technological capacities. This situation precluded their budding enterprises from being able to take full advantage of incentives provided by stronger IPRs. Thus, the benefits gained from such protection (including the incremental contribution to technological progress worldwide) would be outweighed by the disadvantages of being unable to acquire and adapt foreign technology without cooperation with its creator, or to import new products and processes from alternative sources. The developing countries thus saw TRIPS negotiation as a threat. On the other hand, the developed countries, in their rush to establish stronger protection of IPRs against imitation and piracy, which was resulting in loss of royalties and competitive edge in foreign markets, saw IPR negotiations under the GATT framework as the answer.

However, once the package included trade disciplines in other areas, such as agriculture, textiles and clothing, tropical products, and safeguards, that allowed for improved market access in developed country markets, the success of the Uruguay Round appeared more attractive to both sets of countries. They realized that it would not be possible to have a successful outcome to the Uruguay Round without a viable TRIPS agreement being part of the package. In other words, both the developing and the developed countries saw the need to protect the integrity of the Uruguay Round of negotiations to produce its desired results. This factor became evident to all the negotiators as early as 1989 during the Mid-Term Review of the Uruguay Round.

Another factor that influenced the developing countries to go along with the negotiation of TRIPS was the recognition of the benefits of a multilateral resolution of the differences in the intellectual property area. A multilateral framework came to be perceived by the developing countries as a lesser evil than bilateral settlements. Moreover, it became clear also that only a multilateral negotiating framework designed to provide a credible dispute settlement mechanism would have reasonable prospects for ensuring that trade conflicts relating to intellectual property would be handled objectively and effectively, and also for discouraging the unilateral use of trade sanctions by the developed states to extract IPR-related concessions. For political and economic reasons the developing countries changed their stance. As Cottier explains:

> *Firstly, it is evident that the United States' threats to use 'Super 301' procedures and retaliate against what the US administration unilaterally considers to be insufficient protection and unfair trade have greatly enhanced the attractiveness of an overall multilateral framework. Many consider it more beneficial to defend their interests in a multilateral system with well-defined standards rather than being exposed to unilateral determination. Moreover, a failure of negotiations could also lead to similar policies on the part of the European Economic Community and Japan. Secondly, it should not be underestimated that increased standards of protection in intellectual property also reinforce retaliatory powers of LDCs [less developed countries] in trade disputes where their own export interests are affected. But beyond trade and politics, the process also began to shift legal and economic attitudes towards the functions of IPRs for the benefit of long-term social and economic development* (Cottier, 1991).

The third factor influencing African participation was that, for purely national reasons, and consistent with the changing attitudes, a higher degree of IPR protection was increasingly seen as an important part of the general move in many developing countries towards more open, market-based economic policies and towards increasing interest in attracting foreign investment. Moreover, the economic development that had already taken place in some of the more advanced developing countries had led to the emergence of powerful lobbies favouring intellectual property protection, in tandem with the lobbying of the so-called Cairns Group of countries (developed and developing), which are major exporters of agricultural products. For these reasons, the negotiations cannot be depicted as purely North versus South conflicts.

It should also be noted that TRIPS was billed as an agreement to further not just the interests of IPR owners and of countries that are net exporters of intellectual property, but also those of users and of net importing countries. It was therefore important to agree on the conditions under which, for example, the developing countries would be prepared to accept an obligation to protect inventions in virtually all areas of technology, including pharmaceuticals, for a period of 20 years. The conditions therefore included defined limitations and exceptions to the rights defined in the agreement. Accordingly, discussions focused on questions of the flexible and proper application of such concepts and areas as compulsory licensing, parallel importing, exhaustion of rights, transitional arrangements and the control of anti-competitive practices in pursuit of a balanced protection of interests. All these were aimed at the establishment of market-based economic policies in the developing countries, which went beyond the trade-offs in the identified areas, and sought to attract foreign investment in general.

It is also important to observe that the proposed TRIPS regime meant that many developing countries would have to make very substantial changes to their intellectual property laws and practices, involving not only changes in legislation but also the building up and reinforcement of intellectual property offices and enforcement authorities. For this, the developing countries would rely on technical assistance made available to them through bilateral sources and, significantly, from appropriate multilateral sources such as WIPO, the UN Education Scientific and Cultural Organization (UNESCO) and the UN Conference on Trade and Development (UNCTAD), all of which made significant contributions to the technical discussions on TRIPS.

THE EXCLUSIONS FROM PATENTABILITY AND THE SCOPE OF THE REVIEW OF ARTICLE 27.3(B)

The patents section of TRIPS was the most politically and economically controversial in the entire TRIPS negotiation. Article 27.3(b), which deals with exceptions to patentability in the context of products and processes relating to living things, has proved particularly contentious.

According to TRIPS, the provisions of Article 27.3(b) were to be reviewed four years after the date of entry into force of the WTO Agreement, which was 1999. Despite this, since that year, there has been considerable disagreement over the review's scope. To start up the process, in December 1998 the WTO secretariat circulated a questionnaire to member states for them to be complete.

Since only a few responses were received (33 from member states as well as from the Food and Agriculture Organization (FAO), the International Union for the Protection of Varieties of Plants (UPOV), and the secretariat of the CBD) by October 1999 when the first review session was held, the council invited members who had not yet done so to provide their responses. This resulted in another document by the WTO secretariat incorporating this new information.

Some of the developed countries such as the US took the position that the review process on the implementation of Article 27.3(b) had thus taken place and that there would be nothing to gain by further discussion on the subject. African and other developing countries, on the other hand, took the position that the scope of the review envisaged under the article required substantive discussion on the content of the provision of the paragraph. It was the position of the developing countries that such a discussion had not yet taken place and that it had to be pursued. The developing countries' position was the correct one, and it is in this connection that we offer below the views of the African governments, raising a number of substantive issues which may lead to amendment of the article.

The African Group made its views known collectively through a document presented on their behalf by the government of Mauritius at a meeting of the council in March 2000. Subsequently, six issues were raised by the African governments in their proposal presented to the TRIPS Council at its June 2001 meeting.

The first issue concerned the link between the provisions of Article 27.3(b) and development. The African states asserted that they had yet to realize the promise of benefits from globalization, from joining the multilateral trading system, the biotechnology revolution and from the mutuality of benefits under TRIPS.

The second concerned the terminology. Specifically, the African states argued that the distinction made in the article between plants, animals, essentially biological processes for the production of plants or animals, which may be excluded from patenting, and micro-organisms, non-biological and microbiological processes, which are patentable, is artificial and violates the basic principles of intellectual property law.

The third concerned the sui generis protection of plant varieties. The African states observed that although the 'sui generis system' is not defined, they are required to put the said system into place. The current model, which is that of UPOV, has certain defects which make it less attractive to the developing countries.

The fourth related to the ethics of patenting life forms. The African states maintained their position that patenting life forms (human, animal or plant life) raises serious ethical, religious and cultural questions and should therefore be rejected, as should the commodification and marketing of life.

The fifth was the relationship between TRIPS and the conservation and sustainable use of genetic resources. The African states emphasized that the continent's rich biological diversity benefits the whole world and therefore needs to be conserved and used sustainably. Consequently they maintained that their development partners should support the condition of access to genetic resources, based on the sharing of benefits on mutually agreed terms, prior informed consent, as envisaged under the CBD. There is general support for this sound position by a number of experts commenting specifically on the relationship between TRIPS and the CBD.

The sixth was the relationship between TRIPS and traditional knowledge and farmers' rights. The African states affirmed that local farming communities have their own systems of knowledge that are applied to conservation and sustainable use of biological diversity, and which ensure their food security and sustenance. Accordingly, they argue that such knowledge systems should be recognized both at regional and international level. They also point out that TRIPS is based on the Western concept of individual ownership of rights and therefore does not recognize the communal property rights over traditional knowledge.

CONCLUSION

It would appear from the foregoing that the motive of the developed countries has been to expand their commercial control of the world's biodiversity within the industrial sector, relying on instruments such as TRIPS. The developing countries prefer WIPO or the CBD as the forums for the development and implementation of legal instruments dealing with the issues of IPRs and biodiversity as these are embodied in TRIPS. It is clear that they were reluctant from the start to place IPRs on the agenda of the Uruguay Round. But they agreed on the basis that it would enable them to gain concessions in other areas of particular interest to them, such as agriculture, textiles and clothing, tropical products, and safeguards. Alas, subsequent trade negotiations have revealed that developing countries have still not realized the benefits promised in these areas under the Uruguay Round. Specifically, increased access to rich country markets for developing country exports has not occurred. Also, no gains have been realized from the supposed phasing out of textile quotas. In addition, abuse or misuse of the anti-dumping measures against products from developing countries has not abated. And finally, the implementation of the WTO Agreement on Agriculture has not reduced the heavy protection of domestic agriculture producers in the rich countries.

It is not surprising, therefore, to find that five years after the entry into force of the TRIPS Agreement, its usefulness and acceptability to the developing countries is still debated. There are clear hints that unless the views of developing countries are taken into account seriously, they will call for substantial amendments to certain articles of TRIPS.

The point was made at the outset of this chapter that the government of the US undertook a study in 1987 and produced empirical evidence confirming that a number of their firms were losing billions of dollars due to lack of proper protection of their IPRs abroad, particularly in the developing countries. The conclusive empirical evidence led to the government's decision to seek better protection for IPRs by focusing on their trade-related aspects and to bring up the issue for discussion at the Uruguay Round. On the basis of this observation, the question of the need for similar empirical evidence for supporting African claims, has now become a constant theme. Thus, Ambassador Chidyausiku of Zimbabwe has called upon fellow African negotiators to provide empirical evidence to support the criticisms they have made of specific aspects of TRIPS in their existing proposals, or which they may raise as the negotiations continue.

NOTES

1 See Agreement on Measures to Discourage the Importation of Counterfeit Goods. GATT Doc L/4817, 31 July (1979).

2 Known as such because of the city in which it was first used in the process of negotiations towards the Biosafety Protocol, it gives seats at the table to two representatives from each of the five major groups and they speak for their respective groups at the informal negotiations conclusively unless a member of a group sees the need to intervene.

REFERENCES

Bronckers, M (1994) 'The impact of TRIPS: intellectual property protection in developing countries', *Common Market Law Review* 31.

Cottier, T (1991) 'The prospects for intellectual property in GATT', *Common Market Law Review* 28.

Reinbothe, J and Howard, A (1991) 'The state of play in the negotiations on TRIPS (GATT/Uruguay Round)', *European Intellectual Property Review* 5.

Trade Negotiations Committee (1989) 'Mid-Term Meeting', GATT Doc No MTN.TNC/11, 21 April, p21

Chapter 3

The Future of IPRs in the Multilateral Trading System

Frederick Abbott

Issues for the Mexico Ministerial Conference

The first question to address is which issues developing countries should pay special attention to for the forthcoming Mexico Ministerial Conference (10–14 September 2002). Seven are identified in this chapter.

Public health

The Council for TRIPS was instructed by Paragraph 6 of the Doha Declaration on the TRIPS Agreement and Public Health to report to the General Council before the end of 2003 regarding an expeditious solution to the problem of members facing difficulty in using compulsory licensing because of insufficient or no manufacturing capacity for products in the pharmaceutical sector. At this time, there is uncertainty regarding (i) whether and when agreement on a proposal will be reached in the TRIPS Council, and (ii) what the modality of such a proposal would be. Many developing country members consider that prospects for a favourable result are enhanced by seeking an 'early harvest' agreement (preceding Cancun). The EC, however, suggested that any recommendation to the General Council be put into a 'single undertaking' basket to be adopted by ministers. Assuming that the Paragraph 6 matter is not resolved before then, this is a matter to which developing countries should pay particular attention for the forthcoming Ministerial Conference.

I agree that it is preferable to aim for an early harvest agreement. If this matter is left for Mexico, developed country members will offer the solution as a major 'concession' to developing country members for which reciprocal concessions will be demanded. This might have a significant impact on developing country interests both within and outside the TRIPS context.

Non-violation causes of action

Developing countries have a substantial and immediate interest in resolving the question whether and under what conditions non-violation nullification or impairment (NVNI) causes of action may be initiated under the TRIPS Agreement. Although developing country members might initiate NVNI actions, as a general proposition it seems more likely that developed country member intellectual property (IP) interest holder groups will seek to expand the scope of TRIPS actions through this mechanism. If the de facto moratorium on NVNI actions is lifted, it may be very difficult to re-engage on limiting such actions. For this reason, it is important that the issue be addressed now, rather than as a longer-term agenda item. (Matters such as the Convention on Biological Diversity (CBD) relationship, for example, do not have the same short fuse.)

Transfer of technology

Developing country members may press for concrete proposals on technology transfer from the developed countries. This would necessarily include commitment on funding. So far, assistance under the TRIPS Agreement has largely consisted of technical programmes to implement IP laws. Developing country members might agree on one or two very specific proposals, rather than continuing to address this subject matter in the abstract.

Convention on Biological Diversity and Article 27.3(b)

The relationship between the CBD and the TRIPS Agreement assumed a concrete character during negotiations at the Food and Agriculture Organization (FAO) on the International Treaty on Plant Genetic Resources for Food and Agriculture. The question was whether an obligation to pay a royalty imposed on inventors of patented agricultural products deriving from materials taken out of the Multilateral System would violate the Article 27.1 of the TRIPS Agreement rule against discrimination as to field of technology. Without addressing the merits of that question, those who suggest that there is no conflict or potential conflict between the TRIPS Agreement and CBD might be referred to that incident.

The proposal that patent applicants be required to disclose the source of material from which genetic research (or related traditional medicine-based research) is conducted seems reasonable, and the arguments offered so far in opposition are weak.

Issues have been raised by certain developing countries regarding Article 27.3(b) and the patenting of life forms, including genetic material. This is argued to constitute 'discovery' in contrast to 'invention'. It has been suggested that Article 27.3(b) might be amended to exclude such life forms from patenting. As an alternative, it might at least be made clear that such materials do not constitute 'micro-organisms' and therefore are excludable.

In the light of the EC's adoption of the Biotechnology Directive to cover this subject matter for internal market purposes (resolving debate over the meaning of Article 53(b) of the European Patent Convention – EPC), and US jurisprudence so far on the subject, it will be very difficult to obtain an amendment to affirmatively exclude such subject matter (in its 'non-natural' state). Even obtaining agreement on optional excludability might be very difficult given the centrality of this matter to the pharmaceutical industry. This might be a case in which developing countries with an interest should state a position on the record, and let the matter be put before a panel at some stage.

Developed country members arguing that the 1991 version of the International Union for the Protection of New Varieties of Plants (UPOV) Convention is the only effective sui generis system of plant variety protection seem to have a very weak case. At the moment there is considerable flexibility provided by Article 27.3(b) regarding this subject matter. The most appropriate tactic may be to resist further elaboration on this, leaving the matter to member discretion.

Geographical indications of origin

This is a very difficult area for the developing countries because of the difficulties inherent in predicting whether there will be 'net' advantage to them if greater general levels of geographical indications protection are afforded. The basic problem is that the EC asserts extensive rights in geographical indications that developing countries might be required to recognize if more extensive protections are provided. This might affect developing country producers (being required to rename their products) and consumers (paying higher prices). This must be weighed against the analogous rights that developing countries will claim. Certainly there are some important areas where developing countries consider their interests are being neglected (eg rice, tea, textiles). However, in some of these areas, there may be competing claims among developing countries that will need to be resolved before profitable advantage of strengthened geographical indications protection can be taken.

Before the geographical indications subject matter is given a priority, I would recommend waiting for further identification of specific developing country economic benefits.

Traditional knowledge and folklore

It may be useful to pursue rules against the 'misuse' of traditional knowledge such as through foreign patent claiming based on publicly available information, prior to attempting to define 'positive' ownership rights in traditional knowledge, which involves a far more complex set of issues.

From a TRIPS-economic standpoint, it seems doubtful that rights in traditional expression will have a 'material' impact on development. While the protection of such expression is important on cultural grounds, and will have an impact in certain micro-economic settings, it may be preferable to pursue such protection at the World Intellectual Property Organization (WIPO) or another UN affiliate, where cross-concessions are less likely to be demanded.

Pandora's box

The question inevitably arises whether opening the TRIPS Agreement to any amendment is opening a 'Pandora's box' in that the developed countries have demands of their own that will be used to counterbalance any gains that developing countries may seek to achieve. There is certainly a risk that if the TRIPS Agreement is reopened, bilateral pressures will be applied toward achieving higher levels of protection. Two areas this is *less likely* to affect are (i) medicines, where the public interest is sufficiently high that a single purpose change might work; and (ii) non-violation causes of action that do not involve a reopening as such.

LESSONS DRAWN FROM TRIPS COUNCIL NEGOTIATIONS AND WTO–TRIPS JURISPRUDENCE

Lessons from success

The most successful negotiations in the TRIPS Council up until now from the standpoint of the developing countries involve access to medicines, and there are some important lessons that may be derived from that. There were several distinctive elements to the negotiations leading up to the Doha Declaration on the TRIPS Agreement and Public Health.

The developing countries shared not only a common interest, but also a compelling public interest. The strong element of common interest facilitated the establishment of a common negotiating position.

The developing countries *led* the pre-Doha negotiations. The Ambassador of Zimbabwe chaired the TRIPS Council, and focused the attention of the council on access to medicines. The developing countries formulated a number of cohesive policy papers that were circulated to the TRIPS Council. The developing countries submitted the first fully articulated draft of a declaration to the council. There was a sense of commitment among the developing countries not to 'break ranks' when the final negotiations took place in Doha. These elements combined to place the developed countries in a defensive posture.

Public pressures were generated by two major external forces. Major NGOs (such as Médecins Sans Frontières and Oxfam) geared up highly visible public relations campaigns in support of the developing countries' position. This placed considerable pressure on trade negotiators in terms of home constituencies. The events of 11 September 2001, led to a negotiating vulnerability on the part of the US, which came into the Doha negotiations with a compelling national interest not to repeat the Seattle fiasco. There was significant pressure to successfully conclude a Doha deal, with the terms of the deal having assumed a secondary role.

On the 'risks' side, it should be recalled that a number of the developing country Geneva TRIPS Council delegates were in more subordinate diplomatic positions when the end game negotiations took place in Doha. More senior diplomats from the home capitals were not always as conversant with the issues as the TRIPS Council delegates, and were placed under a new set of pressures from developed country diplomats. A lesson to be derived from this 'risk factor' is that close attention should be paid to briefing senior diplomats prior to the ministerial conferences. It may be more difficult to control for the risk factor of developed country diplomatic pressures that may come from outside the TRIPS arena (relating, for example, to IMF or World Bank funding).

Replicating the conditions of success

Distinctive elements of the Doha Declaration success may be subject to replication in certain contexts, but not in others. Four factors should be borne in mind. First, developing countries do not always share common interests in TRIPS matters. Second, most issues are not as publicly compelling as access to medicines issues. Third, NGOs may not build public support on technical IP issues. This will vary depending on context. Fourth, trade negotiating vulnerability cannot be anticipated as a recurring feature of negotiations.

This may suggest that developing countries would benefit by attempting to make calculations in advance concerning the extent to which elements more likely to lead to success will be present. Developing countries may find that their interests are better served by prioritizing negotiations in areas where they are able to identify strong common interests, public resonance and NGO participation. While developed country vulnerability in the sense of the Doha negotiations cannot be anticipated, a substitute for that kind of vulnerability may be a careful analysis of the concessions that developed countries are expected to pursue from the developing countries.

TRIPS jurisprudence

The evolved jurisprudence on TRIPS has not yielded many surprises. In the India – Mailbox case the Appellate Body (AB) emphasized the importance of the express language of the TRIPS text, in contrast to 'legitimate expectations'. This has generally been interpreted as favourable to developing country interests because it dampens the prospects that developed country interest groups will be able to secure TRIPS-plus interpretations of the agreement. Nonetheless, the AB did not give India free rein to self-interpret and apply the agreement, signalling that national legislation would be reviewed for compliance with the express text.

The most important TRIPS decision is the panel report in Canada – Generic Pharmaceuticals. This decision has elements both favourable and unfavourable to likely developing country interests. On the less favourable side, the panel articulated a fairly narrow interpretation of the literal language of Article 30. On the positive side, the panel identified 'discrimination' as the key term of Article 27.1, and defined it in a way that should allow substantial flexibility in adopting bona fide differential treatment.

The panel report in US – Homestyle Exemption reiterated a narrow approach on express language for exceptions. This case involved a fairly aggressive claim to exemption by the US, one that the US IP/copyright industries in fact opposed.

The AB's decision in Canada – Patent Term reinforced the line of decision in India – Mailbox concerning the centrality of express language.

The most unusual case is US – Havana Club. The EC came in with a very poor legal position, arguing against a widely accepted view of the proper interpretation of the Paris Convention. Understandably, the EC's claims were rejected by the panel and AB. There were, however, two elements of importance to developing countries, one positive, one perhaps negative.

On the positive side, the AB affirmed that the US had the right to make determinations regarding the ownership of IP interests (in this case trademarks) based on public policy considerations. That is, because Cuba had failed to compensate the original trade mark holders (its own nationals), the US could choose to delegitimize Cuba's claim of successor ownership.

On the negative side, the AB found national treatment and most favoured nation (MFN) inconsistencies against the US based on a highly improbable set of hypothetical circumstances that might result in discrimination under the literal language of the US statutory and regulatory scheme. If the AB pursues such a rigorous interpretation of the national treatment and MFN rules in other contexts, there may be very little flexibility for differential treatment in favour of more localized developing country interests.

Dispute settlement decisions under the TRIPS Agreement must of course be read in light of decisions in other WTO areas. The most important from the developing country context may be (a) the Shrimp-Turtles decision and (b) the EC – Asbestos decision. In both these decisions the AB signalled some interest in considering the normative or policy context of its ruling, including in the Shrimp-Turtles decision the relevance of non-WTO agreements. The latter is relevant to the relationship between the TRIPS Agreement and CBD.

One point that may be extracted from the totality of AB decisions in the TRIPS and other socially relevant contexts is that the AB is not isolated from its political/public context. In a case involving a compelling public interest, such as access to medicines, the AB may be sympathetic to policy claims. However, attempting to predict the responses of a quasi-judicial body in ambiguous cases may be a 'fool's errand'. In respect to the AB, for example, the outcome might well be influenced by which three panellists are selected to decide the case. The lesson may be that, given a choice, it is preferable that agreement be obtained by diplomatic means, rather than leaving matters to the discretion of the judiciary.

STRATEGIZING TO DEAL EFFECTIVELY WITH THE TRIPS REVIEW PROCESS

This may be the most important issue for purposes of medium to long-term planning regarding the TRIPS Agreement. It involves the question of process in contrast to matters of substance.

Each developing country may have analysed and determined its national interest in a particular TRIPS subject matter prior to engaging in the multilateral context. This would appear to be desirable from the standpoint of multilateral negotiations since this would reduce the possibility that the Geneva negotiator will eventually be undercut by his or her home constituency. However, developing countries may have different capacities in respect to effectively analysing TRIPS issues, and in this context the availability of external analytical assistance will be important from the outset. The development of internal-domestic capacity to analyse TRIPS issues from a local standpoint is a matter addressed by others in this programme.

Over the past 50 years, there have been a number of efforts to achieve solidarity or common positions among developing countries in international forums. At the broad multilateral level there was (and are) the Group of 77, and the movement for a New International Economic Order. At the regional level, the Andean Pact in the early 1970s developed a rather sophisticated common plan to address technology and IP issues (ie Decisions 84 and 85). Yet these efforts were largely unsuccessful in shifting the balance of negotiating leverage away from developed countries. In fact, developing country common efforts to reform the Paris Convention in the late 1970s and early 1980s are routinely cited as the triggering event for movement of intellectual property negotiations to the GATT.

This history is recalled for two reasons: (i) it is useful to be reminded that we are not the first to consider whether the developing countries might be more successful in achieving common objectives with coordinated strategies; and (ii) that solutions based on 'better or more sophisticated policy analysis' of developing country interests may yet run into a wall of 'countervailing power' on the developed country side. This suggests that any strategy for effectively negotiating in the TRIPS Council should include components relating both to effectively determining what the optimal positions are *and* how negotiations might be conducted such that enough diplomatic pressure is brought to bear to achieve desired outcomes.

Formulating positions

The formulation of common negotiating positions is an inherently problematic exercise. Developing countries do not share uniform characteristics in terms of (i) level of overall economic development, (ii) technology infrastructure, (iii) trained research and development personnel, and so forth. Nor do developing countries necessarily confront the same problems. The US, EC, Japan and Switzerland differ with each other on TRIPS negotiating objectives, and developing countries at least arguably face even more disparate characteristics than these highly developed countries.

This suggests that an attempt might initially be made to identify developing countries that share characteristics from the standpoint of IP, and perhaps consider policy options, initially at least, within subgroups of countries.

It would seem highly desirable that a relatively stable policy analysis group be established on a subgroup or issue level. A problem confronting developing countries in Geneva is the rotating nature of diplomatic positions. At the point when a diplomat has spent a number of years on a particular subject matter and become adept at it, he or she may be transferred to a different negotiating arena. For the EU and US, which have a number of delegates dealing with the same sets of issues, and with large policy groups in the home capital, rotation is less of a problem.

Another problem is that developing countries are in economic competition with each other, and each may perceive that its advantage would lie in accepting incentives from developed countries (including making itself more attractive to investors in relation to other developing countries), rather than working on a common position. This was very likely the context that doomed the Andean Pact's otherwise well-developed technology strategy – that is, developed country investors had other places to invest, so were more or less free to reject the Andean Pact's strict conditions.

The foregoing suggests that effectively strategizing for TRIPS Council review and negotiations may involve: (i) building toward a developing country common position through stages that first identify the interests of subgroups, then attempting to reconcile potentially competing interests; (ii) creating a stable policy analysis group with a longer-term memory; and (iii) overcoming the desire to maximize individual gains at the potential expense of a common objective.

Addressing the wall of countervailing power

Developing countries face an enormous disadvantage in any trade negotiations with the developed countries. First, the developing countries are not able to offer comparable concessions (or the threat of withdrawing existing concessions). Second, the developing countries are highly dependent on the developed countries as the source of capital, whether it is provided through the IMF or World Bank, or through investment bankers and securities exchanges. In the TRIPS arena, developing countries are heavy net importers of technology, and dependent on continued developed country supply of technology.

TRIPS negotiations do not take place in isolation from other trade and finance negotiations. In this sense, no matter how reasonable from a public welfare policy standpoint a developing country negotiating demand is, the demand may not be accepted unless (i) the developed countries do not perceive their interests as adversely affected, or (ii) the developing countries amass a sufficient amount of leverage to overcome resistance.

The 'easiest' way to achieve negotiating objectives would be to identify positions that are aligned with developed country interests. This is plausible in some cases. For example, the developing countries may find that they have common cause with the EC on the issue of non-violation nullification or impairment, and (perhaps) on geographical indications. A second but more costly way to achieve objectives is by offering reciprocal concessions. In some cases, for example, competition negotiations, the developing countries may decide that they would not be adversely affected. This may facilitate pursuing common cause (for example, with the EC on the competition issue). A third way is through public relations offensives, perhaps in common cause with NGOs.

Whether the developing countries could plausibly threaten a general market access boycott in a way comparable to a US Section 301 threat of market access restriction is debatable, but at least worth considering at some level. The central problem is one of establishing a disincentive for breaking ranks, and overcoming the problem faced by the Andean Pact in the availability of multiple potential sites for investment and exports. One alternative to a general developing–

developed country market access restriction strategy would be to offer favourable treatment to one developed country or region over another based on favourable treatment in TRIPS negotiations. Developing and implementing a strategy of this nature would be highly complex.

DEMANDS FOR HIGHER STANDARDS IN LIGHT OF THE INSUFFICIENT OR COMPLETE LACK OF DATA AND EVIDENCE TO SUPPORT THOSE DEMANDS

The problem of indeterminacy in the economic analysis of TRIPS-related issues arising, inter alia, from the lack of adequate objective data is likely to persist for the foreseeable future. However, while the tools of economic analysis may not provide concrete answers to questions facing TRIPS negotiators, these tools are useful in identifying factors that may play a role in determining whether the introduction of new and higher standards of IP protection will benefit or harm consumers and producers in developing countries.

The problem of indeterminacy might be addressed by framing the matter as a 'burden of proof' issue. That is, by demanding empirical proof of a positive effect of the introduction of higher levels of IP in the particular contexts faced by developing countries (at different stages of development, and so forth).

I would not place too much emphasis, however, on this. Developed country policy researchers are adept at manipulating information, including data and statistics, to suit their objectives.

From the outset of negotiations in 1986, TRIPS demands have not been based on serious claims that developing countries will benefit from introducing higher standards of protection. They have, instead, been a matter of 'protecting First World IP assets'. Recall that in recent medicines negotiations, the US argued that the price of medicines is but one of several factors preventing developing countries from addressing public health needs, and this was used as the basis for denying the relevance of patent protection. If the trade representative of the leading industrial power can argue that the price of goods is irrelevant to consumer welfare, this suggests that improvements in economic argumentation may not be the answer to claims for higher levels of protection.

Each developing country must decide for itself whether and in what contexts the introduction of IP protection will be beneficial for national welfare. Resistance to demands for higher levels of protection might be based on concepts of good governance and political responsibility towards citizens.

Chapter 4

The Political Economy of the TRIPS Agreement: lessons from Asian countries

Jakkrit Kuanpoth

The main objective of this chapter is to provide an overview of the politico-economic implications surrounding the TRIPS Agreement with particular reference to the experience of Thailand and with a focus on patents. It starts by tracing the history of the international patent system. It then covers the adoption of patent systems by Asian countries. The third part of the chapter describes the negotiating history of the TRIPS Agreement and the key role of the US. The final sections offer an Asian perspective on these developments.

HISTORICAL DEVELOPMENT OF THE INTERNATIONAL PATENT SYSTEM

The historical development of intellectual property law, particularly the patent system, is a long one. The first patent statute was enacted by the Venetian State in 1474. In England, the Crown issued a monopoly right in the form of 'letters patent' for the first time in 1331 to foreigners who wished to practice their craft in the country. The patent system was introduced to encourage the transfer of new technologies and the establishment of new industries. The monopoly right was provided on condition that the holder should work his imported invention in the country for a specific time and that the patentee should teach the invention to others. Subsequently, the monopoly right was abused by the Crown, becoming a source of patronage and revenue rather than an encouragement to invent. The 1623 Statute of Monopolies was enacted in order to curb such practices. The statute declared all monopolies void but with the exception that 'any declaration before mentioned shall not extend to any letters patent and grants of privilege, for the term of fourteen years, or under, hereafter to be made, of the sole working or making of any manner of new manufactures within this realm, to the true and first inventor and inventors of such manufactures, which others at the time of making such letters patents and grants shall not use'.

The Statute of Monopolies is regarded as a landmark in the development of the modern patent system. The basic objectives of the statute were to encourage industrial activity, employment and economic growth, rather than to reward the 'true and first inventor' for his effort. In the early days of the English patent system, the patent holder was obliged to introduce new trades and to teach the details of his invention to indigenous tradesmen. In the early 18th century, the condition for disclosure changed from the working of the invention to describing it by a written specification. This disclosure was what society gained in exchange for granting the patent to the inventor.

In the US and France, the first patent laws were enacted in 1790 and 1791 respectively. Apart from the recognition of the inventor's right, the first US Patent Act was intended to promote inventive activities for the progress of science and useful arts in accordance with the constitution, which declares that 'the Congress shall have power … to promote the progress of science and useful arts, by securing for limited times to authors and inventors the exclusive right to their respective writings and discoveries'.

The 1791 French patent law was passed to respond to 'the backwardness of French industry, the threats posed to the French economy by the penetration of English products, and the desire of the French government to ameliorate the situation of the French industrial worker' (UNCTAD, 1975). The first French patent law was enacted on the basis that an inventor has 'a property right in his invention', and the right of the inventor over his invention was regarded as 'one of the fundamental rights of man'.

After the Statute of Monopolies was adopted in England, the systematic use of monopoly privileges for inventors gradually spread to other countries and by the end of the 19th century several of the present developed countries established their own national patent laws to encourage and reward the invention of new technology.

Although national patent laws became widespread in Europe and North America, legal protection under the patent system was limited to national boundaries. Moreover, the detailed provisions of national patent laws varied considerably in many respects. There was no international treaty establishing common standards of patent protection, and the protection of foreign inventions therefore depended on reciprocity principles under bilateral agreements between nations. This led to uncertainty and insufficiency in protecting foreign intellectual property rights (IPRs).

As industry and commerce among nations increased and became closer, the need was felt for countries to establish international rules setting minimum standards for national patent laws in order to facilitate the acquisition and maintenance of patent protection in different countries.

This need was a consequence of two developments. The first was the increasing importance of international trade and investment to the economies of the major industrialized countries. The limitation of patent protection within national boundaries was 'an obstacle to the expansion of international economic relations' (Anderfelt, 1971). The second was the unsatisfactory situation caused by differences between the patent laws of different countries and the attendant disadvantage at which foreign inventors were placed. For instance, the laws of some countries contained provisions that discriminated against foreigners. Foreign patent applicants were unable to obtain the same rights and obligations provided in the patent law as the nationals of those countries. The lack of uniformity between national patent laws and the discrimination against foreigners caused problems for economic enterprises operating in several countries.

In 1883, the first international agreement in this area was adopted. The Paris Convention for the Protection of Industrial Property was adopted in 1883 and came into force the following year. Since then, the Paris Convention has been revised six times, most recently in 1967. The Paris Convention is a multilateral arrangement that continues to serve as a systematic framework for the international protection of industrial property. It is indeed the precursor of the modern international protection system for industrial property protection.

THE DEVELOPMENT OF PATENT LAW IN ASIA

In Asia, the legal systems of many countries were heavily influenced by colonization. With the exception of Japan and Thailand, most Asian countries were colonized by Western countries and this led to the import of legal culture from the West during the colonial era. The Philippines, for example, established laws to protect IPRs under Spanish rule and overhauled its intellectual property systems after its colonization by the US. Indonesia introduced intellectual property laws while a colony of the Netherlands. In Singapore and Malaysia, intellectual property laws were largely modelled on the British system, and common law still has a major influence on the legal systems of both countries. China and Taiwan set up their intellectual property systems from scratch and have recently tried to improve them to comply with TRIPS.

Unlike other Asian countries, Japan and Thailand never endured colonial rule, and their intellectual property laws were not imposed by colonial powers. Both countries designed their patent systems to accelerate industrial production and trade expansion. Japan, among Asian countries, has the longest tradition of patent protection. The introduction of the patent system in 1885 was a component of its economic development strategy. Since then, industrial property rights have become a vehicle for industrial policy and the driving force behind Japan's remarkable economic success.

Thailand has experienced a relatively short period of legal development in the field of industrial property compared to Japan and many developed countries. Although establishing a patent system was first considered in 1913, there was no legal protection for inventions until 1979. The first Thai patent law, called the Patent Act BE 2522, came into effect on 12 September 1979. The reason for the enactment of a patent law in 1979 was to enhance industrial and economic development, and facilitate the transfer of technology from overseas.

In the post-colonial period, many countries in Asia decided to replace their existing laws with new patent rules in order to reduce dependence on their former colonial masters. After the TRIPS Agreement, many countries again completely overhauled their intellectual property laws in compliance with the requirements of TRIPS. As this chapter explains, this was triggered by external influences, especially intensive Western and US pressure.

THE NEGOTIATING HISTORY OF THE TRIPS AGREEMENT AND THE ROLE OF THE US

Intellectual property was incorporated into the Uruguay Round of GATT talks because some advanced member nations, in particular the US, held that the protection of IPRs was an essential component of their international trading interests and a vital element in their economic success. As we saw in Chapter 1 of this volume, developed countries became more and more concerned that IPRs owned by their enterprises, such as patents, copyrights and trademarks, were being widely infringed in foreign countries, particularly in the developing world. The growth of counterfeit products both at home and in foreign markets created problems for the developed countries' industries. The main industries affected by IPR violations generally were those dealing in high technology, luxury goods and the entertainment industry.

It was also contended that the lack of adequate protection and enforcement of IPRs in the developing world had led to serious distortions and increasing damage to world trade. This situation led enterprises, whose competitiveness directly depended on IPR protection, to put considerable pressure on their governments. They called for the improvement of international standards and the enhanced protection of IPRs worldwide.

The enforcement of intellectual property laws is basically limited to each national jurisdiction. This territorial limitation renders the domestic laws of states inadequate to protect innovators from unauthorized imitation in a foreign country. The basic inadequacy of these international conventions lies in the lack of national enforcement of intellectual property protection and the absence of dispute settlement mechanisms.

In addition, the substantive standards of protection in the existing agreements are too narrow to deal with some crucial areas of modern technological advances such as biotechnology, computer software, and semiconductor chips. The 1883 Paris Convention for the Protection of Industrial Property, which is administered by the World Intellectual Property Organization (WIPO), for example, contains no specific requirement for its state parties to provide patent protection. The parties are, therefore, free to determine their own level of protection according to the level of national development.

It is worth noting that there was an unsuccessful attempt in the 1973–1979 Tokyo Round of multilateral trade negotiations to adopt a code on trade in counterfeit goods. The proposal was rejected because there was widespread belief among the GATT parties that intellectual property should not come under the jurisdiction of GATT which had until then basically dealt with trade in goods. It was argued that IPR protection was not directly related to international trade, and there was no evidence that counterfeiting had trade implications. Developed countries, led by the US, attempted to counter this response by arguing that technology and intellectual property had now become international in character, and were now directly involved in many aspects of international business transactions, in particular trade in counterfeit products.

Bringing IPRs into GATT would provide a vehicle for the international enforcement of IPRs by increasing the scope for imposing meaningful sanctions, and resolving disputes through the GATT dispute settlement mechanism. Developed countries firmly maintained that strengthening international and national protection of IPRs would help governments to reduce the widespread circulation of copied goods, which seriously distorts legitimate trade. For this reason, intellectual property issues should be brought into the ambit of GATT, so that international efforts could be targeted at the trade-related aspects of IPRs, not on intellectual property per se.

During the TRIPS negotiations, the US maintained principally that effective and adequate protection must be given to inventions in any technological field including some particular products which were often excluded from protection in many of the developing countries' patent laws. These included foods, chemicals, biotechnology, and pharmaceutical products. However, the EC proposal in this respect was less stringent than that of the US, as it excluded the patenting of plants and animal varieties and essentially biological processes for the production of plants or animals.

The particular concern of many developing countries is that these products, particularly pharmaceuticals and crop seeds, are basic requirements for their deprived populations. Stricter IPR protection would increase monopoly power of the right holders, generally foreign firms, and this might lead to overpricing and restricted supply of those essential products in their countries. In addition, because the developing nations view scientific and technological advancement as the vehicle for industrialization and economic development, the improvement of international standards and the strengthened national protection of IPRs, in their view, might increase the cost of modern technologies because of the inherent monopoly feature of the IPRs and the possible abusive practices of the patent holder.

Developing countries maintained that the TRIPS negotiations should come up with proposals to achieve developmental goals, by promoting long-term economic and industrial development and technology transfer in each individual country to a greater extent than providing exclusive privileges as a reward to the creator.

Apart from their national economic sovereignty, another concern of developing countries is directed at their socio-economic development. Developing countries have often suffered from the unstable prices of raw materials, foods and semi-manufactured products, which are their main foreign exchange earners. The acceleration of the development of their economies, therefore, depends on industrial and technological progress, which has been the driving force behind the developed countries' economic success, which entails diversifying their exports. However, it should be accepted that the current economic imbalance between the developed and developing countries is the main obstacle to the latter nations' development in science and technology. Strengthening legal protection of IPRs, regardless of specific needs and social priorities of each country, may sharply reduce the developing countries' industrial and technological competitiveness and will give rise to stronger dependencies on the more powerful economies.

The role of the US Trade Representative (USTR) was very important in the TRIPS negotiations. The USTR is a central organ of the US government, whose responsibility is to implement US trade policy. The USTR, which is appointed by the president on the approval of the senate, is conferred a right to enter into international negotiations with all trading partners. The USTR had requested consultations with some developing countries in Asia and Latin America on IPR issues before and during the Uruguay Round. On the bilateral level, the US demanded a higher degree of IPR protection from its trading partners. This strategy, it was hoped, would improve the possibility of achieving favourable results in the multilateral trade negotiations.

The US employed (and continues to employ) such bilateral strategies as placing tremendous pressure on certain foreign governments to give greater respect to the protection of IPRs by withdrawing, or threatening to withdraw, trade preferences under the Generalized System of Preferences (GSP). Moreover, the US trade legislation, in the form of Special 301 of the Omnibus Trade and Competitiveness Act of 1988, has been used as a coercive economic measure for the fulfilment of demands on IPR protection.

The GSP is a scheme established under the GATT umbrella. It is designed to assist industrial and economic development of developing nations. Generally speaking, the GSP allows advanced industrial countries to accord priority to reducing or eliminating duties and other barriers for certain products from eligible developing countries with a view to ensuring that developing countries expand access to world markets and to markets of granting nations.

The US implemented its own scheme of generalized and non-reciprocal treatment in favour of developing countries. The GSP programme was adopted as part of the 1974 US Trade Act, which was subsequently amended by the Trade and Tariff Act of 1984. The Trade Act confers authority on the president, under the guidelines provided in the act, to designate whether a country will be classified as a 'beneficiary developing country' to receive GSP benefits, what products are eligible, and what conditions should be attached. However, a developing country that fails to reach the US standards on intellectual property protection may be deemed ineligible for US duty-free benefits. The withdrawal of Thailand's GSP status is a good example of US practice.

In January 1989, as recommended by the USTR, President Reagan decided to withdraw the 1989 GSP benefits from Thailand's eight export items on the ground of failure to provide an adequate and effective protection of IPRs. Again, in May 1991, the USTR used the GSP to combat Thai government IPR policies by removing preferential status from 17 export items. It is interesting to note that Thailand's GSP privileges in the US market are quite considerable. For example, US government statistics show that in 1989, 23 per cent of Thailand's total exports to the US gained GSP benefits equivalent to US$1200 million. Therefore, the suspension of GSP status generated significant negative economic impacts.

From the foregoing, it can be argued that although the GSP programme was designed to encourage the economic and industrial development of developing countries by introducing the 'non-reciprocity' standard, its application has produced the opposite effect. Legal features of the GSP and its economic significance are now examined.

First, the GSP does not subject the donor country to any binding obligation, so it may withdraw trading privileges at any time. Developed nations may introduce the scheme if they wish. The preferential benefits are unilateral concessions of the granting country. In withdrawing the concessions, the granting nation, therefore, is not liable to pay any compensation or any retaliatory measure.

Second, since the term 'least developed countries', which can enjoy GSP benefits, is not clearly defined, the donor nation may lay down its own criteria to identify whether a country should be qualified for preferential treatment, and what condition should be attached. For example, the US trade law provides a 'minimum competitive needs limit' principle. The idea of the minimum competitive needs limit is to impose a ceiling on imports from a particular country. This means that an exporting country can be easily excluded from the US preferential scheme when its total exports reach the ceiling stipulated by the law.

Third, according to the graduation concept introduced in the Tokyo Round of GATT negotiations, when developing countries reach a certain level of economic development, trade preferences granted to them will be terminated. This means that after a developing country has reached the stage where it is no longer ranked as a least developed country, it should not be entitled to preferential treatment and it must be subject to the same obligations as other developed nations. However, as for the possibility that developing countries can make reciprocal concessions by abandoning preferences, there are no criteria to evaluate the economic development of the developing countries. The solution to the problem, therefore, seems to be a decision taken by the donor. This could be seen when the US decided to unilaterally withdraw the GSP status from Singaporean exports on the ground of graduation. Although Singapore had yielded to the US demand by enacting its Copyright Act in 1987 its GSP was still revoked.

Fourth, since the structure of GSP is based on the unilateral discretion of the donors, it is obvious that the superior position of the granting country will serve the interests of the more economically powerful countries by allowing them to press another condition on a recipient in exchange for the GSP. This is seen in the US Trade Act which links the GSP not only with intellectual property but also with other issues such as foreign investment, international terrorism and trade in narcotics. Even though the recipient country yields to the US demand by modifying its intellectual property law, it is possible that the US may demand some further condition for retaining GSP status.

Fifth, the GSP seems to be designed to assure the technically, uninterrupted supply of cheap products to advanced nations. This is reflected in the unilaterally discretionary power of granting states to select a recipient country. Why should there be such a preference for eligible countries if there is true equality among trading nations?

The above discussion demonstrates the feebleness of the GSP, which has often been used politically as a bargaining tool rather than to promote economic development. Although developing countries want to gain benefits from trade preferences, in order to accelerate their economic development, this expectation is still doubtful. For this reason, increased national protection of IPRs should be made on the basis of its contribution to national technological and economic development, rather than in exchange for the uncertain benefits of the GSP.

The key mechanism to combat the infringement of US IPRs is established under a special provision of the Omnibus Trade and Competitiveness Act of 1988 called 'Special 301'. The 1988 Act was passed by congress to modify the Trade Act of 1974 in order to strengthen US retaliatory power. Congress believed that the new trade legislation would reduce unfair foreign trade barriers and persuade foreign governments to reform their intellectual property laws for the benefits of US commerce.

According to the procedures under Special 301, the USTR is required to investigate cases on an annual basis against those countries that 'deny adequate and effective protection of intellectual property rights'. Annually, the USTR is required to submit a report called the National Trade Estimate Report to congress on foreign acts, policies, or practices that are significant barriers or distortions to trade, including the estimation of their economic impact on US commerce. Within 30 days after the submission of the National Trade Estimate Report to congress, the USTR must assess the adequacy and effectiveness of foreign nations' IPR laws. In addition, the USTR must identify 'priority foreign countries' that fail to provide adequate and effective protection of IPRs or deny market access to US exports. The identification must be conducted on the initiation of the USTR, but may be exempted if the USTR considers that the identification would be detrimental to US economic interests.

Since the 1988 Trade Act became law, the USTR has created three lists for those foreign countries which fail to meet the US standards on intellectual property protection. These lists are: (i) priority foreign countries; (ii) a priority watch list; and (iii) a watch list. The countries put on the lists may be subject to trade retaliation from the US.

The 1988 Trade Act allows the USTR to identify those countries whose practices are deemed to constitute barriers to US commerce, as well as to conduct an investigation concerning their practices. The USTR also enjoys full authority to take any action it deems appropriate to retaliate against the foreign country concerned. This means that in considering each case, the USTR will act as investigator, prosecutor, judge and executioner all at the same time. There is no doubt that nothing guarantees other countries' rights when they are charged under the US Trade Act. The final solution to a dispute, therefore, seems to depend on the bargaining power of the parties concerned.

It is clear from the foregoing discussion that the US trade law is designed as a powerful tool to enable the US administration to enforce US rights and to scale down foreign trade barriers. However, the imposition of trade leverage is incompatible with WTO's substantial provisions for dispute settlement, which requires a member to request consultations with the other party concerned to resolve the dispute before trade concessions can be suspended.

The use of economic coercion by the US, under whatever guise, amounts to a clear contradiction of WTO principles. In practice, US restrictive trade practices constitute more of a distortion to free trade than the purely domestic policies of many developing countries trying to participate in the international trading system. Undoubtedly, national laws are only operational within a country's territorial jurisdiction, but when such laws violate internationally acceptable conventions and treaties, they debase the sense and spirit of international cooperation. This is a more accurate interpretation of Section 301 in the present circumstances.

PROTECTION OF IPRS IN ASIAN COUNTRIES

It is worth noting that distrust of IPRs is still deep-rooted in many Asian countries. They view them with suspicion and believe that their introduction on the basis of high standards of protection would entail a fairly high risk. In addition, the protection of IPRs seems to clash with the traditional social or religious beliefs of those countries. According to their cultural traditions, most Asian countries consider intellectual works as a communal good and their copying as a means to disseminate learning. In part, due to these cultural differences, Asian countries provided a lower level of IPRs protection. For example, India, Korea and Thailand did not protect pharmaceutical products. In India, process patents for pharmaceuticals only lasted for five years.

The US responded to the problem posed by the apparent loss of revenues due to counterfeit goods by imposing considerable governmental pressure on a number of countries in Asia. Thailand, Indonesia, Malaysia, the Philippines, Singapore, Taiwan, and the Republic of Korea were among those countries viewed by the US as primary sources of IPR piracy. The USTR, due to the lobbying of certain national industries, demanded the tightening of domestic legislation in Asian countries through bilateral consultations. In the early 1990s, the USTR put several Asian countries on its watch list for trade retaliation.

The USTR requested consultations with countries in Asia on IPR issues before and during the Uruguay Round. The use of bilateral trade pressure against such countries helped the US to achieve the aim of IPR protection. For example, many Asian countries introduced legislation to bring their IPR laws into conformity with the norms and standards demanded by the US even before the conclusion of the Uruguay Round. This strategy also led to the establishment of an acceptable framework within the multilateral trade negotiations of an agreement on minimum IPR standards that became the TRIPS Agreement.

Although many Asian countries had identical experiences, the case of Thailand will be discussed in detail as an illustration. From the late 1980s, Thailand's exports had experienced rapid and sustained expansion. The performance of Thai products in international markets was highly successful. Thailand enjoyed the distinction of being the world's fastest growing economy until it faced an economic crisis in 1997.

Thailand's most important trading partner is the US. Previously, its trade balance with the US was regularly in deficit, but from 1985 Thailand succeeded in transforming a visible trade deficit with the US into a surplus. This imbalance raised concerns in the US. In order to achieve a reduction of its foreign trade deficit, the US administration decided to use its trade leverage against Thailand along with other Asian countries. In 1989 and 1991 the US removed GSP privileges from some Thai export products on the grounds of alleged inadequate protection for copyrights and pharmaceutical patents.

Due to Thailand's lack of effective enforcement, it was claimed that in 1988 US copyright owners had lost revenues estimated at US$61 million due to piracy (International Intellectual Property Alliance, 1988). In the case of patents, the failure of Thailand to provide patent protection for pharmaceutical products had, it was claimed, severely affected US drug producers. According to Mossinghoff, patent and trade mark infringements in Thailand added up to huge losses of trade and income, almost US$2000 million, for ten US pharmaceutical companies (Mossinghoff, 1990).

The USTR called for consultations with Thailand on this matter. A meeting between the two countries was held in Amsterdam on 22–24 April 1991, in which the US made three demands. First, Thailand must modify its copyright, trade mark and patent laws, in order to protect some particular products such as pharmaceuticals, computer software and living organisms. Second, the term of patent protection must be longer than that provided in the existing law. This included the extension of the protection period from 15 years to 20 years and backdated protection for drugs already invented but not yet licensed for use in Thailand (this is known as 'pipeline protection'). Finally, the US called for tighter penalties and elimination of provisions designed to prevent abuse of monopoly power arising from patent protection, particularly compulsory licensing.

Thailand, along with India and China, was named by USTR as a priority foreign country under Section 301 of the US Omnibus Trade and Competitiveness Act of 1988, subject to trade retaliation. This forced the Thai government to meet US demands in the hope of avoiding retaliation because it was realized that the US market is an essential part of Thailand's economic success.

As to copyright, Thailand and the US could reach a compromise on the computer software issue by deferring the legal ambiguity of such protection under the Thai Copyright Act to be tested in Thai courts. However, under great pressure from the US, Thailand then decided to amend its copyright law in 1997 by adopting Copyright Act BE 2537. The new law provides protection for computer programs and databases in line with the TRIPS standards. In addition, the Thai government has enforced the Copyright Act more vigorously. A large number of copyright cases were successfully prosecuted, and the average penalties for such illegal practices have substantially increased.

In the cases of trade marks and patents, Thailand decided to adopt two laws, Trademark Act BE 2534 and Patent Act BE 2535. The new Thai Patent

Act extends patent coverage to pharmaceutical products, micro-organisms, biotechnological processes, food, beverages and agricultural machinery. The new law extends the patent term from 15 to 20 years.

It is worth noting that the attempts to amend the patent law were attacked by many domestic interest groups and academics on the grounds that the law yielded too much to US demands, and that the amendments would cause adverse effects on indigenous industries and the well-being of the poor.

The above discussion demonstrates the US determination to tighten its trade policy to combat what it considers to be unfair trade barriers, including a lack of adequate IPR protection, which the country views as a major contributor to its balance of trade deficits. The US Trade Act, including its Special 301 provision, is often used to influence domestic legislation in foreign countries to comply with its demands. Frequently, such countries have no option but to surrender if they want to avoid serious retaliatory measures.

APPRAISAL

The introduction of TRIPS into the Uruguay Round of global trade talks, combined with the use of GSP benefits and Section 301 of the Trade Act, indicates the determination of world economic superpowers to defend their national interests regardless of the international rules and the resulting damage to the economies of other countries.

In an attempt to impose a high level of IPR protection on other countries' statutes, it is clear that the US intends to use its own standards as the international minimum standards for other countries' laws. This approach is unreasonable and inappropriate because it ignores the widely varying socio-economic circumstances of other countries. It should not be forgotten that countries differ in their social values, cultures, philosophies and levels of economic growth and industrial development. The perceptions of countries about the protection and violation of individual property cannot always be identical. Any international framework must, of necessity, take these differences into account.

In accordance with the self-determination principle of international law, every state has a right to choose its political, economic, social and cultural systems. This notion has been recognized by the Paris Convention as it grants participants considerable discretion in determining criteria and degree of industrial property protection in accordance with their stage of development and public policy.

It may be noted that the Uruguay Round agreements are ostensibly premised on the notion that world trade should be liberalized and expanded through negotiations to reduce tariff and non-tariff barriers and to prevent countries from applying protectionist measures to safeguard their own domestic industries (except under certain prescribed conditions). The inclusion of IPRs, which is founded on protectionism, seems to be inconsistent with the spirit of the international trade regime. Liberalization means non-protectionism, while IPRs presuppose protectionism. Undoubtedly, the attempt to include IPRs in the Uruguay Round and the WTO underscored the desire of the advanced economies to reserve the freedom to adopt one or the other contrasting ideas of liberalization and protectionism, whichever suits their interests at any given time.

REFERENCES

Anderfelt, U (1971) *International Patent Legislation and Developing Countries*, The Hague: Martinus Nijhoff.

International Intellectual Property Alliance (1988) *Trade losses due to piracy and other market access barriers affecting the US copyright industries*, Washington DC: IIPA.

Mossinghoff, G J (1990) 'Drug trade seeks leverage on patents', *Chemical Marketing Report* 238.

UNCTAD (1975) *The Role of the Patent System in the Transfer of Technology to Developing Countries*, TD/B/AC.11/19/Rev 19, para 228.

Chapter 5

Integrating IPR Policies in Development Strategies

John Barton

Now is a good time for thinking about the role of intellectual property rights (IPR) strategies in development. The Doha Ministerial Declaration recognizes that the new round of international trade negotiations will be, more fundamentally than any previous negotiation, a negotiation between developed and developing nations, and it reflects a move towards balance on issues such as technology transfer and access to medicines. In September 2002, the UK Commission on Intellectual Property Rights (CIPR) completed a substantial study that carefully explored developing nation concerns (Commission on Intellectual Property Rights, 2002). An important review of the patent system is to be published by the US National Research Council. And institutions such as the Centre for the Management of Intellectual Property in Health R&D (MIHR)[1] are seeking to help find ways within the IPR system to develop new technologies for developing nation needs.

Upcoming International Issues

The CIPR report identifies two IPR issues of great importance to developing countries that are on, or very close to, the current international agenda.

The first of these is the move to harmonize patent law. This negotiation, already underway, is strongly supported by the EU and the US as a way to avoid duplication of the costs of patent searching and granting, because, with harmonized standards, a search (and possibly a decision) in one office can be accepted in another. There is, however, an important implication for the developing world: a harmonized treaty would probably leave significantly less flexibility than does TRIPS. This is a problem if the harmonized structure ends up, as is likely, as a compromise between the US and the European systems, for such a compromise is likely to include a low inventive step standard and a very broad subject matter standard, standards that are not in the interest of developing nations (nor, in the judgement of many, of the developed nations either). The question is what is the right strategy for the developing nations: to attempt to participate and seek a positive standard? To attempt to participate and seek special provisions for developing nations? To refrain from participation?

The second is a negotiation over appropriate arrangements for digital material, especially in relation to the internet. Here, the driving force is the concern of the music and cinema industries that digital material can be readily copied, thus making impossible an adequate return on the investment in content production – but the principles involved will almost certainly affect computer programs and perhaps scientific information as well. These concerns have led to a desire to provide 'technological protection,' such as encryption, for such material, and to seek international treaties and statutes, eg the 1996 World Intellectual Property Organization (WIPO) Copyright Treaty and the 1998 US Digital Millennium Copyright Act, to prohibit circumvention of such technological protection. This may interfere with fair use rights and thus not be in the interests of the developing world. There will certainly be an effort to extend such anti-circumvention legislation and treaties to the entire world, and the developing nations will need to consider how to respond.

But it may be possible for the developing nations to think more boldly – the new technology can permit a fundamentally new approach to the economics of information. The transition is as profound as that from the scribe to the printing press (which led, indirectly, to the creation of copyright law). If information can be reproduced at zero cost a system of incentives based on charging for the making of copies seems unlikely to be successful in the long run. Is there a way for developing nations to take the lead in designing ways to take advantage of this ease of dissemination while also maintaining incentives for development and creation of digital material?

MAKING THE CURRENT IPR SYSTEM WORK AS WELL AS POSSIBLE

A second set of tasks is to find ways to make the current IPR system work as well as possible for developing nations. This is particularly an issue for the patent system, for it is an especially expensive system, but also an issue for other areas. And there is the obvious question of who should pay for the strengthening of developing nation IPR systems. In some cases, the costs may be appropriately borne by the World Bank or national donors. In other cases, where they may not properly be high-priority development areas, the funding should rather come from the international intellectual property community, as through fees by patent applicants or support from WIPO (which comes in large part from Patent Cooperation Treaty – PCT – filing fees).

Developing country IPR law design

The obvious first example is the creation of model laws and grant of technical assistance in drafting national laws. As the CIPR report shows, the laws most adapted to developing nations are not the same as those currently used by developed nations. That report goes quite far in defining appropriate patent systems; it does not give the same level of detail for copyright. In developing the detail needed by developing world legislators and law reformers additional studies may be useful, as may a series of working-level meetings among intellectual property (IP) offices and practitioners from the developing world. The development of workable TRIPS-compatible compulsory licence procedures is particularly important. And it may be desirable to strengthen regional IP systems, in order to save costs and create larger markets that may be more likely to attract research investment.

Other areas of law

In the face of strong political pressure and building on substantial technical assistance that is generally based on a developed world model, most developing nations have adopted the basic IP legislation needed to protect global IP rights holders. They have been much slower, however, in adopting the legislation that might help them in meeting their own specific needs. The obvious examples are the legislation (or regulation) needed to help wisely transfer public sector technology into the private sector – this includes a definition of the relative rights of public sector employees and of public sector employers, as well as a reasonable licensing procedure. After all, in most developing nations, public sector research far outweighs private sector research. For some nations, there may be a need for legal arrangements to manage genetic resources or traditional knowledge. For some, there may be a need to elaborate price control procedures. And for some, the need may be to develop antitrust principles that can complement IP legislation.

Human resources

None of these areas of law is useful without human resources, nor can developing nation concerns be effectively represented in specific transactions or in general national and international policy-making without such resources. This requires people who understand not only the formalities of the law, but also the way to operate effectively in the international arena on behalf of developing nation clients. It is a need almost certainly beyond the ability of the existing short-term study programmes or general-purpose graduate law programmes. Perhaps a one-year programme at a major university, possibly with an externship or clinical component, is essential, but it may be possible to achieve significant benefits with a six-week or summer programme. It is essential to find ways that such programmes can be organized and funded.

Access to developed world IPR systems

Another need identified in the CIPR report is to enable developing country scientists to use the IP system in the developed world. The international legal system provides for reciprocity – the developing country scientist can file for a patent in the developed world (where, because of the large market size, the patent is most likely to be valuable) just as the developed world scientist can file for one in the developing world. But the developing world scientist often doesn't have the funds to have the application prepared, so the reciprocity is often meaningless in practice. Are there mechanisms to solve this problem – pro bono obligations for developed world law firms? International legal assistance systems on the pattern of the Advisory Centre on WTO Law?

BEYOND THE CURRENT IPR AGENDA: TOWARDS REAL TECHNOLOGY POLICY

All the points so far are essentially about making the IPR system as useful as possible. But the crucial issue is not IPR but technology for development. It is clear that IPR systems can play only a slight role in actually encouraging the creation of that technology – and it seems essential to move the debate beyond a reactive one focusing on IPRs to a proactive one focusing on technology (in which IPRs may play some role). This must be done in a way that recognizes the enormous difference between the world that led to the technology-transfer debates of the 1970s and today's world. Those debates involved minimizing the costs of technology imported for import-substitution purposes; today, the need is for technology for use in a global economy.

In the first instance, there is an important intellectual agenda – we know from economics studies that technology was extremely important to the development of the US and probably of other developed nations as well. We know much less, however, about how to shape the technological input to development in developing nations today. What is it that contributes to a take-off, in the sense of the take-off of the East Asian nations over the last generation? Does a new nation have a chance without a new technology, such as the steel and rail technologies that were central in the way the US and German competed with the UK or the move to semiconductors and computers that played such an important role in East Asia? GATT and the WTO have given the world the benefit of substantially free trade – and also therefore deprived developing nations of approaches based on infant industry protection. Similarly, TRIPS has deprived them of approaches based on imitation. Yet, under today's global regime, production economies of scale arise far beyond the national level and markets must be global – so the traditional infant industry or imitation industrialization strategies may no longer be practical anyway. How can the necessary thinking best be encouraged? Through an existing international institution like UNCTAD or the UN Industrial Development Organization? As a cooperative project of national academies of science? Through symposia designed to attract the interest of academic economists?

The appropriate strategies must be thought out nation by nation, and sector by sector, if not firm by firm, for the needs differ from case to case. But it is especially important to think further about the needs of the technologically more advanced developing nations, such as India and Brazil. These nations were not emphasized in the CIPR report, which concentrated on the poorest. For these more advanced nations, unlike the poorest nations, IPR systems may encourage domestic innovations, and for the larger ones, or those in appropriate regional groupings, such systems may even encourage outside innovation focused on the special needs of the particular nations. But these nations face a new group of problems beyond poverty – how to enable their firms to participate in a global business community. In today's world, the leading firms in that community (and these are almost always developed world firms) hold strong IP positions that may be used to defend their existing oligopolies against new entrants. It is hard, for example, to see how a new firm, from anywhere in the world, could become a semiconductor or an agro-biotechnology major. Certainly, firms within these nations can start as licensees or strategic allies of global majors, but can they become more independent industrial competitors? The difficulty of entry into markets dominated by multinational oligopolies is thus compounded by the international IP system. What can reasonably be done in response? Are there international antitrust approaches that might be helpful? National antitrust arrangements in the developing world alone may well be inadequate, for a licence created under national IP-antitrust principles does not necessarily permit export of products to major markets with different IP-antitrust principles. Can new international patent-antitrust principles be negotiated in an area as intellectually difficult and strategically important as this? Is the WTO or the Organization for Economic Co-operation and Development (OECD) the right place to begin?

Programmes are emerging to provide global public goods, such as medical and agricultural research, especially oriented toward the developing world. At this point, these are fundamentally public programmes, such as those of the US National Institutes of Health and of the Consultative Group on International Agricultural Research (CGIAR) centres, and there are many efforts integrating the public sector with the private sector, such as the new partnerships for HIV, tuberculosis and malaria. The fundamental problem in these areas is persuading the taxpayers in wealthy nations that the programmes are worth funding. But there are also IPR problems being faced by almost all these institutions, because of the variety of patents held by both universities and the private sector on fundamental research technologies. These research institutions are in turn being assisted by a new generation of intermediaries designed to help with such IPR problems, but it is not yet clear that these intermediaries will be successful. Might there be value in more legislative solutions, such as creating an international analogue of the public use provision of US patent law, which allows use of patents by or for the government without licence, albeit subject to an obligation of reasonable and entire compensation? Perhaps, there might be some other form of automatic licence, at least for research uses? Is such a licence already available under an appropriate interpretation of TRIPS, perhaps of Article 30? Are there ways that the availability of such a licence could be clarified so that it would be politically acceptable and would not undercut private sector incentives? Are there other IP needs of global research that might be met by some form of global negotiation?

Access to medicines

There is an additional important and immediate issue associated with access to medicines that are already available on the market. Article 6 of the Doha Declaration on TRIPS and Public Health called for consideration of ways to enable nations with insufficient manufacturing capabilities to use compulsory licensing, an issue posed by the language of Article 31(f) of TRIPS, which states that any use of a patent without authorization of the right holder must be 'predominantly for the supply of the domestic market of the Member authorizing such use'. Such negotiations are taking place. Unfortunately, as the CIPR report points out, resolution of the technical legal issue will not resolve the real world economic problem. After 2005, there will probably not be a generic industry anywhere in the world making generic substitutes for new products on patent. Hence, production under compulsory licence will require that a firm learn how to produce the particular product, carry out the necessary quality control (which may require bioequivalence testing), and scale up a production facility. This will require significant expense that must ultimately be covered by those using the product (or by the world public sector) – it will not be possible to rely on others to cover this expense as is the case with production by the current developing world generic industry.

The choice of a solid economic alternative is unclear, but there are at least three directions that should be explored. One is to find some way to maintain what amounts to a standby generic industry, in which there is some mechanism to spread the start-up costs of producing a new product. A second is a public sector approach, perhaps based on the pattern of public sector pharmaceutical production in Brazil. And a third is to find ways to obtain strong enough commitments from the pharmaceutical industries that alternative production capabilities are not needed. Each direction has its pros and cons; it would be useful to explore them carefully prior to any form of international negotiation. And the appropriate forum for the exploration and negotiation is not yet clear – it might be well to begin with the World Health Organization or the World Bank.

Technology transfer treaty

For the developing nations a critical component is the creation of a scientific and technological human resource infrastructure. This is the heart of a 'sound and viable technological base', as sought in TRIPS Article 66.2. There are already many bilateral and regional agreements to encourage the cooperative development of new technologies that, in general, provide a framework within which specific public sector collaborations can be negotiated. These include, for example, a 1994 Agreement Relating to Scientific and Technical Cooperation between Australia and the European Community, a 1994 Memorandum of Understanding on Scientific Cooperation between the United States of America and the Russian Federation, and a 1999 Agreement on Scientific and Technical Cooperation between the Caribbean Community and the Kingdom of Spain. Why not expand this network into a global process through an international treaty designed to strengthen commitment to science and technology, to education in it, and to its sharing, particularly with developing nations? Such a treaty might itself state key commitments; it might also, in the pattern of the WTO General Agreement on Trade in Services, provide a framework for negotiating further commitments.

There might be procedural provisions encouraging negotiations and arranging for dispute settlement; possible substantive provisions might include:

- Commitments by all nations to maintain specific levels of funding of education and research. The educational commitments might be cast as performance specifications; those for research may be more reasonably funding specifications. The commitments might differ according to the income level of the nation.
- Commitments by developed nations to assist developing nations in achieving these educational and scientific/technological goals. These are, after all, among the areas in which international assistance is most effective – a treaty commitment may be especially useful, since the economic benefit is often long-term so that short-term political incentives for such support may be weak.
- Commitments to ensure that the benefits of publicly funded research are made available to all and not just to nationals. Although preferences to national recipients are politically understandable, there is neither scientific nor economic logic to restricting the beneficiaries of research to nationals. Removing such restrictions on a basis of reciprocity would be of benefit to all.
- Similar reciprocal commitments against favouritism to national firms in treatment of such issues as ability to participate in research consortia or ability to achieve the benefit of research-oriented tax benefits.
- Commitments against visa restrictions that limit the ability of students to study at universities in another nation, or restrict the ability of scientists or engineers to gain experience at firms in another nation.
- Commitments to ensure international access to scientific conferences.
- Commitments to ensure access to scientific literature and databases. This might, at least in respect to developing nations, include fair use provisions that would help shape the application of intellectual property law.
- Appropriate arrangements for intellectual property associated with international scientific and technological collaboration.
- Appropriate protections for national security and technology proliferation concerns, as with respect to military uses of biotechnology, but such protections should be no broader than essential.
- Regular meetings and review procedures to evaluate the actual degree of scientific and technological cooperation, its mutual benefit, and its benefit for developing nations.

There are many questions that must be explored in designing such an agreement. The focus might be more on science and education or it might be more on technology and entrepreneurial activity. The former would concentrate more on human resources and basic research; the latter would recognize the importance of the private sector in much technology flow, but might raise greater concerns about threats to trade secrets and industrial competitiveness.

Moreover, the focus might be more on encouraging the flow of technology generally or more on specifically benefiting developing nations. After all, scientific and technological progress builds upon the work of predecessors and colleagues, and the exchange of scientific and technological ideas among nations accelerates the progress of science and technology and makes it possible for the benefits of free trade to be expanded. Thus, a global treaty is in the interests of the developed nations themselves (and serves essentially the same goals as cooperative scientific programmes within the EU). With strong enough commitments such a treaty would contribute extensively to the rate of development of science and technology in the world and would therefore benefit all; it would be in some sense an extension of WTO past goods and services and IP to technology itself. A global treaty would particularly benefit developing nations, by providing the prerequisites for real technology transfer to these nations. But it might be better to pursue such a treaty as a new generation development treaty, concentrating on differential treatment and tailoring the provisions to the needs for technology transfer from developed to developing nation.

There are several forums in which such an arrangement might be negotiated, and the choice depends on the focus of the agreement. Among the options are a WTO Code on International Access to Technology (perhaps beginning with the WTO Working Group on the relation between trade and the transfer of technology), an UNCTAD Agreement on Technology Transfer, or a UNESCO Agreement on Strengthening International Scientific and Technological Cooperation.

NOTES

1 MIHR is an organization dedicated to promoting access to health technologies for the poor through improved management of intellectual property in research and development. See http://www.mihr.org.

REFERENCES

Commission on Intellectual Property Rights (2002) *Integrating Intellectual Property Rights and Development Policy*, Report of the Commission on Intellectual Property Rights, London: CIPR

TRIPS AND THE INTERNATIONAL SYSTEM ON GENETIC RESOURCES

Chapter 6

TRIPS and the FAO International Treaty on Plant Genetic Resources

Robert J L Lettington[1]

INTRODUCTION

Agriculture was almost without doubt the world's first example of globalization. The principles of cultivation and domestication spread from no more than eight or ten centres of origin and the world's major crops and livestock from a similar number of centres of origin. This process began some 10,000 to 20,000 years ago and still continues today through the mechanisms of crop and livestock improvement. Private and community initiatives probably constitute the bulk of activity in this field with up to 80 per cent of the population of the developing world engaged in farming and the majority of these farmers employing some form of conservation and improvement techniques regarding their crops and livestock. The products of these initiatives are distributed informally at the local level, and until recently have also travelled globally by similar means, with exchange between scientists and institutions also being informal more often than not. However, in the last 30 to 40 years public research has become the main vehicle for the transmission of agricultural developments around the world. In the last 10 to 20 years the private sector has undergone dramatic concentration and at the same time begun to eclipse the public sector. Unlike the public sector, the private sector is driven by a proximate profit motive.[2] Producing a single product with the widest possible application, and ideally limiting the source of that product to a single company generally captures maximum profits for that single company. However, homogenization in agriculture undermines the diversity that ensures its continued vitality, and indeed viability, while limiting access to the means of production threatens the immediate food security of those without the ability to leverage that access.

FROM THE INTERNATIONAL UNDERTAKING TO AN INTERNATIONAL TREATY

In 1983 the Food and Agriculture Organization (FAO) Commission on Plant Genetic Resources (now the FAO Commission on Genetic Resources for Food and Agriculture, or CGRFA) adopted the non-binding International Undertaking on Plant Genetic Resources (1983 IU). The aim of this agreement was to ensure the conservation, sustainable use and continued free flow of germplasm for the crops of major importance to world food security. The theory was that a diversity of germplasm provides insurance for crops against changes in climate, the impacts of pests and the prevalence of disease, while also providing the scope for future improvements in the desired traits of particular crops. The dramatic concentration of agro-industries, the rise of agro-biotechnology, the entry into force of the Convention on Biological Diversity (CBD) and the TRIPS Agreement have created fundamental changes in the dynamics of the use and, above all, ownership and transfer of biological material. In response to these events the FAO Conference requested the CGRFA to open negotiations for the revision of the IU as a legally binding agreement that would reflect these new realities, recognize the special needs and significance of agriculture and in particular operate in harmony with the CBD. The basic principles underlying the revision were agreed to be the interdependence of the world's regions for the germplasm that guarantees their major crops and the urgent need to achieve and maintain food security for all. At 3.30am on 1 July 2001 the CGRFA, at its Sixth Extraordinary Session concluded some seven years of formal negotiations and adopted an Agreed Text of the International Undertaking on Plant Genetic Resources (IU) to be forwarded to the FAO Conference in November 2001 for adoption and opening for signature.

The Revised International Undertaking on Plant Genetic Resources

In developing a legally binding agreement from the basis of a 20-year-old non-legally binding predecessor there are obviously many detailed changes from the 1983 IU in the agreed text of the IU adopted by the Sixth Extraordinary Session of the CGRFA. However, the key operative changes can be found in relatively limited areas. The following section is not intended to provide a comprehensive overview of the IU but rather simply to cover the key elements of the agreement and some of the major sources of conflict in the negotiations. Moving sequentially, and in no particular order of priority, the first indications of significant change can be found in the preamble.

Farmers' rights

In paragraphs 7 and 8 the preamble of the agreed text refers to farmers' rights, which, in short, can be seen as a sort of 'freedom to operate' for small farmers complemented by an international framework of tangible support. Paragraph 7 simply recognizes the basis and existence of these rights. Paragraph 8 is substantive in that it references the details of such rights, as later iterated in Article 10. This is somewhat controversial as the repetition of the detail in both the preamble and the actual article could be interpreted as giving it greater weight, meaning that the details of farmers' rights are as fundamental to the objectives of the agreed text as the broader concept. This is essentially a North–South issue but also raises questions relating to the multifunctionality[3] of agriculture debate between the Cairns Group and the European Union (EU) and Japan in the World Trade Organization (WTO). The weighting of the details of farmers' rights also has significance in terms of the implementation of these rights at the national level. If the details are as significant as the concept then governments have less leeway in interpreting these details in implementation. This has implications for the final line of paragraph 8, which affirms the need for the 'promotion of Farmers' Rights at national and international levels'. This is a purely North–South question, with the issue being the concern of developing countries over the sincerity of the developed countries in the recognition of farmers' rights. The implication is that developing countries will recognize such rights in a tangible form while developed countries will not, leaving a situation where farmers' rights create no actual benefits for farmers. To prevent such a situation, developing countries pushed strongly for the international recognition of farmers' rights while key developed countries adamantly opposed such recognition on the grounds of feasibility. Paragraph 8 of the preamble thus represents a compromise on the question.

Coverage of the Multilateral System (MLS)

As the IU is a legally binding instrument the question of coverage becomes far more significant than it was under the 1983 IU. This is particularly true in light of the provisions on facilitated access and even more so because of those on benefit sharing. There are three basic categories of plant genetic resources that are included in the MLS. The first includes material held under the management and control of the states party to the IU. This would include national collections and in situ resources found on public property. It is also likely to be understood so as to include in situ plant genetic resources found on private land in states that vest the rights to genetic resources in the state rather than in the landowner. The second category is the ex situ collections of the Consultative Group on International Agriculture Research (CGIAR) and other international institutions that agree to submit their collections to the authority of the governing body of the IU, an arrangement similar to that which is currently in force between FAO and 12 CGIAR centres. The final category is other private collections that shall also be encouraged to submit to the authority of the governing body.

A critical point to note about the coverage of the agreed text is the distinction between the physical and the conceptual control of crops and forages listed in Annex I to the IU. The IU expressly states its intention to respect property rights of all kinds and thus one is clearly not talking about the physical ownership of all examples of a crop or forage becoming public. What one is talking about, are the conceptual elements of the crop or forage being public. A rough analogy might be with buying a car. When you buy a car nobody else has rights to take that individual example of a car away from you but equally you have no right to prevent anybody else from using the same type of car, or to stop the manufacturer from producing more of the same. Thus the fears, expressed by some developed country delegations, that the agreed text would mean that governments would be giving themselves the rights to enter into private property and remove plant genetic resource specimens for public distribution, are unfounded.

Facilitated access

Along with the list of crops and forages, facilitated access constitutes the bedrock of the MLS. The basic idea is that for any listed crop or forage access shall be provided either free or at cost with all available associated information, subject to certain limitations. As with the current 'black box' accessions held by the CGIAR, plant genetic resources under development at the time of a request may be withheld during the period of that development. Equally the requirements for facilitated access will respect any intellectual property rights held over particular material, something that may or may not limit its availability depending upon the circumstance. The final 'negative'[4] limitation is that access to in situ plant genetic resources will be subject to any relevant national laws and/or standards that the governing body of the IU may establish. Where this final limitation leaves plant genetic resources in farmers' fields[5] is not entirely clear as such material could be considered in situ or ex situ depending upon your perspective. There are also several 'positive' limitations. First and foremost is the restriction that 'intellectual property or other rights that limit facilitated access' may not be claimed on plant genetic resources accessed from the MLS. The exact nature of this limitation is one of the key outstanding issues in the agreed text of the IU and is discussed in greater detail below. A further significant positive limitation is that any material accessed from the MLS and conserved by the recipient must continue to be available under the system. This must be read in the context of the material under development provisions, as there may be unfair competition implications.

The idea of facilitated access has created some difficulties in understanding, particularly in relation to the question of non-parties. Principally the question is whether one can have access that is not facilitated, ie can you access material covered by the MLS on bilateral terms and without accepting the wider obligations of the IU? Developing countries in general are understandably hostile to this idea on the basis that it may provide a means for non-parties to 'buy their way out of the system'. They can simply use their greater resources and negotiating power to negotiate bilaterally for whatever they want and thereby avoid contributing to the maintenance of the system.

Benefit sharing

The main benefit to be gained from participation in the MLS is one that is explicitly mentioned in the IU but that is rarely given much credence by negotiators, perhaps due to the difficulty of explaining its immediate value in political terms. This is the continued free flow of germplasm at the global level, the main objective of the IU. The first, global, benefit is that the free exchange of germplasm promotes the vitality of crops throughout the world, thus guaranteeing their future. In the shorter term, exchange is critical to both developed and developing countries for slightly different reasons.

In developed countries the increasing homogenization of crops within an industrial agricultural framework creates an immense vulnerability to unforeseen events. Such events may be climatic or involve pests and diseases. The genetic uniformity of industrial crops means that they have limited, if any, ability to develop resistance to these events and are thus dependent on external sources of germplasm to provide the necessary resistance. The example of the devastation that wheat rust caused to US crops in the mid-1970s is a classic example of this vulnerability. Equally the collapse of the rice harvest in Indonesia in the 1960s was a similar example of the vulnerability of industrial crops, albeit that this took place in a developing country.

In most developing countries, and particularly those in Africa, the homogenization of crops through industrial agriculture is not yet a major problem. However, the market effects of the International Union for the Protection of New Varieties of Plants (UPOV) system of plant breeders' rights, the possibility of patents on plants and above all the strategies of multinational agrochemical corporations may be encouraging many African states in this direction. This can be witnessed by the activities of UPOV among the country members of the Organisation Africaine de la Propriété Intellectuelle (OAPI), Kenya, South Africa and Zimbabwe, and at its extreme with the case of the application of biotechnology in countries such as Kenya and South Africa. The main problem currently facing African countries is that, while industrial agriculture is not yet dominant, farmers are highly susceptible to unforeseen events anyway due to their limited access to credit, limited sophistication in pest and disease control and frequently the harsh and unpredictable environment. Thus the diversity of their crops is the main insurance policy for African farmers and this depends on the constant exchange of germplasm, something that would not be feasible if the transaction costs of exchange were to be increased.

A further type of benefit present in the agreed text is one that can be found frequently in other international agreements, including TRIPS. These are the provisions on technology transfer, capacity building, exchange of information and similar measures. The inclusion of, and likely future debate over, these provisions provides ready comparisons to some of the recent discussions in the TRIPS Council about the efficacy of such measures in the absence of a clear determination by developed countries to implement them. Any successful outcome of the discussions for the possible review of the implementation of these measures under TRIPS might provide a clear benchmark that could be used to leverage their use under other agreements. There is also, of course, the clear linkage that the success of technology transfer and capacity building measures under agreements such as the IU could be used to argue that the same activities provide the fulfilment of TRIPS requirements, since in TRIPS the requirements are non-technology specific. These interlinkages, combined with the apparent concern of some developed countries regarding attacks on the TRIPS framework, may well constitute an opportunity for real technology transfer in various fields provided that the pressure is maintained under TRIPS.

The key novel element of benefit sharing under the agreed text of the IU is the mandatory contributions derived from the commercialization of products derived from plant genetic resources accessed under the MLS. The exact mechanism to be used to implement this has been one of the major points of controversy throughout the entire history of the negotiations for the revision of the IU. The agreed text triggers payments when a product incorporating plant genetic resources accessed under the MLS is commercialized, thus broadly avoiding problems with possible effects on intellectual property rights that were raised with earlier suggested mechanisms. The payment is mandatory in the event that the commercialized product has limits on its availability for use in further research and breeding, and voluntary in the event that the product is freely available for such purposes. This limitation is principally intended to distinguish plant varieties protected by plant breeders' rights under the UPOV system, which generally allows research and breeding, from other types of protection, particularly patents, that do restrict research and breeding. This kind of distinction clearly raises intellectual property rights issues and some developed countries have argued that it constitutes a discrimination that violates TRIPS provisions. The argument has been dropped mainly because its proponents wanted the exclusion for plant breeders' rights, and, thus once the principal trigger was changed from IPRs in general to commercialization, they found they were arguing against themselves. Despite this it is important in terms of the TRIPS Council and the WTO dispute settlement procedure that agriculture is clearly understood as a collection of technical fields rather than a technical field in and of itself, and that the IU provisions thus do not constitute discrimination between technical fields. A further potential problem with TRIPS has been raised in terms of whether the levying of a charge might affect a patent holder's enjoyment of their rights. First, the IU does not discriminate between IPR holders and others in terms of the application of its benefit sharing provisions. However, it could be argued that while it does not explicitly do so it does in practice. In the event that such an argument was accepted, which it could be due to the distinction between products available for further research and breeding and those that are not, one would turn to Article 28 of TRIPS ('Rights Conferred'). Nowhere does this article make any reference to immunity from any kind of charges or levies associated with the holding of a patent; indeed intellectual property offices routinely make fees a requirement for the processing of a patent application and for the maintenance of a patent once granted. This latter point may well be worth bearing in mind in other contexts as well: patents only grant limited rights and one should be clear as to exactly what those rights are.

Unfortunately the political importance of the commercial benefit sharing provisions has far outweighed any likely tangible benefits, particularly due to their linkage to the question of intellectual property rights. It is extremely unlikely that these provisions will generate substantial funds, the seed industry is simply not that profitable a business in global terms and the likely royalty rate that will be accepted by industry is going to be low, probably substantially less than 1 per cent of sales. The problem seems to be that some delegations and commentators are thinking in terms of the profit margins of the pharmaceutical industry rather than the agricultural sector. The fact that the bulk of the agricultural sector does not make such profits is one of the justifications for the IU; agriculture with its current form and practices could not sustain the transaction costs of a purely bilateral system. Indeed the continued slump in commodity prices and the difficulties of farmers throughout the world illustrate this fact very clearly. Perhaps one might have been better off seeking a proportion of direct and indirect subsidies to products rather than of the profits they generate, since for the OECD countries alone subsidies are estimated to amount to 110 per cent of the combined GDP of Africa!

A final point worthy of note is that the commercial benefit sharing elements of the MLS embodied in the IU reinforce the concept at the heart of Article 15 of the CBD, that it is not just the finished product that is of value when one is dealing with biological material, there is an inherent value in the elements that go to make up that product and in the broader environment that conserves and provides those elements. The novelty lies in the fact that a system has been developed to recognize this without creating unduly burdensome transaction costs that might actually harm the very people the system was developed to benefit.

The CGIAR and other international institutions

The Consultative Group on International Agricultural Research centres and other international institutions have been given special consideration in the IU due to their significance to agricultural research and development, particularly in developing countries. The CGIAR centres have been the main element of this discussion due to the size and significance of their ex situ collections. Discussions largely represented a three-way discussion between the centres themselves, seeking the simplest and most open system possible; developed countries, seeking to ensure the maintenance of an open CGIAR system; and several developing countries concerned that the CGIAR collections might be used as a means for abusing the IU. The resolution of these issues is a system where institutions holding ex situ collections are expected to sign agreements submitting their collections to the authority of the governing body of the IU. Broadly institutions signing such agreements will be expected to manage any material they hold that is covered by the IU, by means of inclusion in Annex I, 'List of Crops Covered under the Multilateral System', in line with the provisions of the IU. Since CGIAR centres were seeking broader coverage for their collections there are also provisions covering non-listed material in their collections, the key sticking point in discussions. The solution is that this material will be covered by a standardized material transfer agreement (MTA) that will broadly conform with the provisions of the IU. There are also provisions covering non-listed material that may be acquired by institutions subsequent to the entry into force of the IU. Such material will be handled on the basis of whatever terms the particular institution is able to reach with the country providing the material, ie in accordance with the CBD and current practice.

OUTSTANDING ISSUES AND POTENTIAL OUTCOMES

The agreed text of the IU adopted on 1 July left several key issues outstanding. All of these issues involve what have come to be intensely political questions and it is thus perhaps appropriate that they have been left to be addressed directly at the ministerial and heads of state level when the FAO Conference holds its biannual session in November 2001. However, they do have the potential to unravel the agreement at the last moment and in at least two instances bear on discussions in the TRIPS Council.

List of crops covered under the multilateral system

While a list of several dozen crops and forages has been agreed upon there is still considerable discussion on the question of including further crops that are considered to be of critical importance. Europe, with some support from others, is providing the driving force in this discussion by its strong statements that the current list is unacceptably short and would lead to its not supporting the IU, thus unravelling the G77–EU alliance that has brought negotiations this far. The sticking point has largely been the politics of the G77. For most of the discussions the G77 agreed to stick to a short list of crops unless the benefit sharing provisions met their expectations. However, as discussion on the benefit sharing provisions came to a close it became clear that several countries within the G77 were determined to take this position further. Some countries clearly seem to be attempting to prevent the inclusion of crops for which they are the centres of origin, playing zero-sum politics and thus trying to take the benefits of the system without contributing to it. Others, in contrast, seem to be trying to pursue a strategy that has lost its usefulness. Clearly the inclusion of crops in the list benefits those who cannot afford access to privatized collections the most. One delegate even went so far as to liken the position supporting a short list of crops to a child threatening to hold his breath until he dies unless you give him what he wants. If it was just this position that mattered the issue might be resolved quickly. However, it has given other countries the ability to maintain their more destructive objections without becoming overly isolated in doing so. Unfortunately in this instance G77 solidarity has been misused to allow some members of the group to use others to further their own particular national interests.

Clearly for the IU to succeed and achieve its stated objectives the list of crops must be expanded. It is expected that informal contacts between governments between July and November 2001 will at least lead to some of the developing countries dropping their objections, thus leaving the others in an untenable position. If this does not happen then the future of the entire agreement could be at stake.

Relationship with other agreements

This is once again a debate between the EU and the Cairns Group. In realistic terms the discussion is not about the status of the IU in relation to all other international agreements but rather just of its relationship to the agreements in the WTO framework, in particular TRIPS and the Agreement on Agriculture. The EU position is that this is something that must be dealt with generally, and thus be discussed in the WTO framework, while others are determined that the WTO agreements must be established as primary, partly because of concerns over intellectual property rights but more importantly because of the ongoing battles over distorting and non-distorting subsidies in agriculture. Given that developing countries, if they have a position at all, object to all subsidies, they are at best on the sidelines of this debate. It is expected that this will be resolved in the same manner as it was in the Cartagena Protocol on Biosafety, ie the issue will be ducked by means of ambiguous language.

Genetic parts and components

The outstanding issue of greatest relevance to discussions in the TRIPS Council is the question of language in the definition of plant genetic resources for food and agriculture and in the main text referring to restrictions on intellectual property rights that makes reference to 'genetic parts and components' of plant genetic resources for food and agriculture. The key question behind this is that of invention vs discovery and thus the main protagonists are the US on one side and developing countries on the other. Developing countries have generally taken a compromise view of this issue in recent times by separating it from that of the question of intellectual property rights and thus the patenting of life forms. Their position now is that the only operative aspect of this language will be that the use of genetic parts and components of plant genetic resources covered by the MLS will trigger benefit sharing in the same way as use of the plant would, thus ensuring that classical plant breeding and biotechnology are treated equally. Indeed, one could argue that the current US position actually violates TRIPS as it constitutes discrimination against classical plant breeding in favour of biotechnology! However, the US is instinctively afraid that this is an attack on its patenting practices and Article 27 of TRIPS. The solution may lie in finding compromise language that assuages US concerns while ensuring the equal treatment of technical fields in benefit sharing and leaving the invention vs discovery debate to another forum. This could perhaps be the TRIPS Council, but since TRIPS does not define 'invention' one may have to look to the World Intellectual Property Organization's (WIPO's) Intergovernmental Committee on Genetic Resources.

AFRICAN COUNTRY PARTICIPATION

African participation throughout the negotiations for the revision of the IU, in terms of physical presence, has been significant and to a large degree consistent. In line with its representation in the CGRFA, Africa made up more than one quarter of the delegations at the Contact Group discussions and consistently sent the same individuals allowing for familiarity with the issues. However, generally the delegates were scientific representatives with only limited capacity in the legal and, most importantly, political aspects of discussions. This was at its most glaringly obvious in the unfamiliarity of African delegations with the trade debates between the US and EU that came to the fore in negotiations in late 2000. Having said this, representation was above average and in almost all cases competent, in comparison to higher profile forums such as the CBD, perhaps actually due to the lower profile of the forum. Delegates generally seemed to have considerable freedom in their positions and strategies, something that at times allowed for constructive compromises that might not otherwise have been possible. The weakness of this was seen in the fact that there were very few clear national positions to be seen as these were the responsibility of individuals and few delegates had the opportunity to prepare thoroughly. Generally the effectiveness of African delegations could be measured by the breadth of experience of individual delegates.

On familiar issues, such as farmers' rights, the African Group had a fairly strong voice, but this weakened considerably when faced with the less familiar territory of complex legal or trade issues. The key defining position was that taken on the list of crops; that a large list would only be agreed to if substantive benefit sharing provisions were realized. While this served a purpose in earlier stages of negotiations as it became increasingly redundant it did seem to have created some differences within the Group. However, in general terms due to the lack of prepared positions the African Group tended to be dominated by a few key personalities and maintained unified positions, in spite of what are often radically different practices at the national level.

CONCLUSION: AMPLIFYING THE AFRICAN VOICE

The art of war

As the Chinese warrior philosopher Sun Tzu noted in his oft quoted treatise 'The Art of War' battles are mostly won before they are fought. A key weakness of African negotiators in the revision of the IU, as with many other international processes, has been inadequate preparation.

Preparation should consist of various elements that could be broken down into the two basic categories of strategy and tactics. Strategy includes the broader elements of the negotiations, particularly one's ultimate goals and interrelationships with other negotiations and processes. Tactics includes the more particular details of how best to arrive at the desired outcome. In the revision of the IU it is clear that the possibility of a cohesive G77 in alliance with the EU, and wherever possible Japan, has been decisive in the progress that has been made in the negotiations since the Eighth Regular Session of the Commission on Genetic Resources for Food and Agriculture in 1998. It is clear that various elements play into the strength of this grouping, particularly the positions of the EU and the Cairns Group on the agriculture negotiations at the WTO. The current stories being played out in the TRIPS Council and WIPO are also a major influence. A key factor in the EU and Cairns Group positions is concern over the implications of the IU in these other forums. It seems likely that an IU that carves out of these forums, rather than impinging upon them, is one that will work as it will provide the requisite enforceability while calming the fears of the Cairns Group that the IU will simply become a loophole in the WTO system. At the same time separating agricultural issues from the heat of debate in the TRIPS Council provides some easing of discussions there while providing tangible benefits for developing countries. An African strategy can play upon these fears to extract compromises that might not otherwise be acceptable and thus create a win–win situation. Questions of tactics play into the issue of strategy as they should be the detailed means of implementing the strategy in the negotiating sessions. The question of the list of crops is one such tactic that needs to be recognized as such. It is useful while it does not threaten one's strategic strengths, in the case of the IU the alliance with the EU.

In the context of the negotiations for the revision of the IU it is clear that there was a need for more thorough planning and consultation prior to negotiations, at both the national and regional level. Ideally the Organization of African Unity (OAU), or now the African Union (AU), would provide a forum for such preparation but as yet it has failed to reach such a detailed level. Both scientific and political considerations were involved in the negotiations and the two would ideally have been merged in preparatory work, with scientists, lawyers and diplomats cooperating in the preparation of strategies and tactics. The options and implications need to be weighed and alternatives developed. Such preparation begins with thorough discussions in capitals but due to the realities of weak individual national voices from Africa must be followed up by regional meetings. The relative success of the African Group position at the Third Interministerial Conference of the WTO in Seattle should be a lesson in terms of its thoroughness, but it should also be learnt that such ad hoc development of regional positions cannot be relied upon for consistency; a more formal approach should be adopted. For such an approach to be ultimately successful it will require two further elements: a maximizing of Africa's assets and clear action and commitment at the national level.

Maximizing assets

Africa possesses the expertise to successfully negotiate in international forums. It has world-class lawyers, economists, scientists and diplomats. Unfortunately these voices are only randomly heard in the development of positions for international negotiation. In high-profile forums experts are obviously somewhat at the mercy of politicians and their input thus sometimes uncertain. However, many negotiations take place without senior politicians and thus delegates have the ability to consult with, and sometimes even bring to negotiating sessions, the expertise that they require. In the current situation of most African governments the responsibility for achieving this falls exclusively on the delegate who will be present as part of their competent representation of their country's interests. Any good manager knows that the ability to effectively consult and delegate is probably their greatest asset and a head of delegation is no different from any other form of manager in this respect.

Actions speak louder than words

A final issue that is generally not within the power of individual delegates or delegations is the question of how their position matches actual practice in the capital. In the case of African countries there is frequently a dislocation between the two. The African Group position at the TRIPS Council and Kenyan government policy is a classic example of this. While at the international level Kenya opposes patents on life forms, at the national level the first speech of Dr Bonaya Godana to the Kenya Agricultural Research Institute (KARI), as newly installed Minister of Agriculture, focused on the need to encourage KARI's research and his intention to provide the additional funding necessary to patent this research. In more general terms delegates at the international level may achieve greater impact in their capitals by means of wider consultation with those in the capital, and not only their colleagues in public service but also other experts and researchers who can be expected to have some influence on national processes. At the same time they should always try to highlight to their superiors in capitals the options that their activities have created, being realistic about the relative values and priorities of such options in national life. Wherever possible this information should also be distributed to other actors who may be able to assist the delegate in lobbying in the capital.

NOTES

1 This paper represents the opinion of the author and in no way represents the views of any of the organizations with whom he works.
2 The term 'proximate' is used on the understanding that the public sector does have an 'ultimate' profit motive in terms of benefits for society as a whole, otherwise it would be a pointless exercise, but that this differs from the profit motive of the private sector, which is more immediate and focused on shareholders.
3 Experience in the negotiations for the revision of the IU has shown that not all countries are aware of the concept of multifunctionality and the controversy it has created in the WTO. The basic idea, chiefly propounded by the EU and broadly supported by Japan, is that agriculture plays a multifunctional role in society rather than being simply an industrial process significant for food production. Depending on particular perspectives this multifunctional role may include cultural and environmental values of agriculture. The Cairns Group objects to the concept of multifunctionality in the belief that it is an excuse for subsidies and protectionism in agriculture. An abortive attempt to broaden the debate was recently made in the context of the Kyoto Protocol by the US Energy Secretary when he declared that energy consumption was also multifunctional in that above average energy consumption was a cultural attribute of US citizens.
4 'Negative' and 'positive' are seen here in terms of the MLS, a 'negative' limitation limits the system, while a 'positive' limitation protects the scope of the system.
5 Although one could of course argue that since traditional farmers are constantly experimenting with and improving their plant genetic resources they are constantly under development and thus permanently unavailable if the farmer so wishes.

Chapter 7

The Convention on Biological Diversity and the TRIPS Agreement: compatibility or conflict?

Biswajit Dhar

Introduction

When it was formally opened for signature at the 1992 Earth Summit, the Convention on Biological Diversity (CBD) was seen as the first decisive step taken by the global community to ensure conservation and sustainable use of the world's biological resources. For the genetic resource-rich developing countries, the CBD was particularly important on two counts. In the first instance, it recognized that the rights over their genetic resources lay with the sovereign states. Secondly, it recognized the need to preserve and maintain the knowledge, innovations and practices of indigenous and local communities from the point of view of conservation and sustainable use of biological diversity. This, according to the CBD, was to be achieved through fair and equitable sharing of benefits arising from the utilization of such knowledge, innovations and practices.

The adoption of the CBD, which provided a framework for the conservation and sustainable use of biodiversity, was followed by the formalization of the TRIPS Agreement where the emphasis was laid on protecting the rights of inventors and other producers of intellectual works. In fact, the regime of intellectual property rights (IPRs) defined by the TRIPS Agreement marks a major departure from the past in that the balance of rights and obligations between the inventors and the society at large has been decisively shifted in favour of the former. This change in the basic tenets of IPRs has come at a time when the world's genetic resources have been exploited like never before as a result of the expansion of the biotechnology industry.

Although TRIPS and the CBD have largely been on parallel tracks thus far, there are at least two compelling reasons why their compatibility needs to be examined. The first is that both TRIPS and the CBD are products of the Multilateral System and therefore any points of inconsistency that may arise in the two agreements would have to be addressed in order that the signatory countries are able to meet the requirements for complying with both. This has in fact been tacitly recognized in the 2001 Doha Ministerial Declaration. Paragraph 19 of the declaration 'instruct[s] the Council for TRIPS, in pursuing its work programme including under the review of Article 27.3(b), the review of the implementation of the TRIPS Agreement under Article 71.1 and the work foreseen pursuant to paragraph 12 of this Declaration, to examine, inter alia, the relationship between the TRIPS Agreement and the Convention on Biological Diversity, the protection of traditional knowledge and folklore, and other relevant new developments raised by Members pursuant to Article 71.1'.

The second reason for looking at TRIPS and the CBD closely arises in the context of the functioning of the WTO Committee on Trade and Environment (CTE). The CTE is mandated to bringing the objectives of the Uruguay Round agreements and those of the multilateral environmental agreements (MEAs), including the CBD, on an even keel. This dimension of the WTO's work programme was moved onto the fast track by the ministerial declaration.

The aim of the present chapter is to analyse the CBD and TRIPS and to bring out the manner in which the issue of IPRs has been approached by the respective multilateral treaties. The chapter has four sections. In the first, we discuss the key provisions of the CBD that impact on the IPR regime. In the second section, we analyse TRIPS. Our discussion is restricted to patents, which are considered to have the most significant implications for biodiversity. In the third section, we indicate the inconsistencies between the two treaties that need to be addressed. Finally, we briefly indicate the way forward towards reconciling the CBD–TRIPS incompatibility.

THE CONVENTION ON BIOLOGICAL DIVERSITY

Any analysis of the CBD needs to begin by looking at the objectives of the Convention stated in Article 1. The objectives of the CBD 'are the conservation of biological diversity, the sustainable use of its components and the fair and equitable sharing of the benefits arising out of the utilization of genetic resources, including by appropriate access to genetic resources and by appropriate transfer of relevant technologies, taking into account all rights over those resources and to technologies…'.

The objectives of the CBD thus delineate two sets of rights in respect of genetic resources. The first set of rights comprises those that can be exercised over the genetic resources per se, while the second set of rights relate to the technologies which have been developed using the genetic material. While the former concerns the countries that are the depositories of the genetic resources, the latter largely concerns the corporate interests that are engaged in developing the ever-growing range of biotechnologies. A significant third dimension of the CBD, cross-cutting both sets of rights mentioned above, deals with the rights of the traditional communities who are the custodians of genetic resources and holders of associated knowledge, and who sustainably exploit the genetic resources.

Two features of the provisions of the CBD that have an impact on the IPRs regime need to be mentioned. The first relates to access to genetic resources and the second is the benefits arising out of the use of genetic resources. Benefits from the use of genetic resources, according to the framework that the CBD has evolved, are seen to accrue both directly and indirectly, the latter taking such forms as access to proprietary technology at affordable terms. In both the dimensions, as should be evident from the discussion below, the interests of the countries holding the genetic resources have been given primacy over the commercial interests that have been exploiting these resources to develop technologies.

According to the framework provided by the CBD, the rights over the genetic resources in any given country have to be established through an iterative process. In the first instance, the CBD provides that the nation states have sovereign rights over their own biological resources. The preambular statement that defines the rights of the states also emphasises that the states have to bear the responsibility for the conservation and sustainable use of their biological resources.

In the exercise of their rights, governments can determine physical access to the genetic material that lies in areas within their jurisdiction by enacting suitable legislation (Article 15.1). These rights to fully determine access to genetic material in its territory provide a government, particularly that of a developing country signatory to the CBD, the opportunity to ensure that it can secure benefits from any commercial exploitation of its genetic material. Towards ensuring that the above mentioned is realized, Article 15.4 states that access to genetic resources, wherever granted, shall take place on terms that are mutually agreed to by the providers and receivers of the genetic material.

Article 15.5 strengthens the provisions of Article 15.1 by providing that access to genetic resources be subject to prior informed consent of the contracting party providing such resources. This, in other words, implies that any use of genetic resources without the consent of the country possessing the resources would be deemed as a violation of the provisions of the CBD.

One of the key features of the CBD is that it recognizes the ever-increasing exploitation of genetic resources consequent upon the advent of biotechnology. Hailed as the technology of the future, biotechnology has been able to bring about a transformation in the use of genetic resources, generating in the process a wide range of products that could fundamentally alter human existence. However, much of these technologies are being developed in the research laboratories of the industrialized world, which are controlled and financed by the transnational corporations. The large-scale privatization of research in biotechnologies has given rise to a situation where access to such technologies has become a major area of contention, a problem that has been acutely felt by the developing countries in particular.

The CBD has addressed this issue of access to biotechnologies concerning countries in the developing world, which have been the main suppliers of genetic material. In the first place, it provides that every contracting party to the

CBD shall make efforts to develop and carry out scientific research based on genetic resources provided by other state parties with the full participation of, and to the extent possible, within the countries supplying the genetic material. Through this provision, contained in Article 15.6, the CBD has tried to ensure that the developing countries are able to participate in the process of technology generation where the technologies utilize their genetic resources. The significance of this provision needs to be understood in the context of the ongoing discussions in several multilateral forums, which have emphasized that improving the technological competence of the developing countries is a sine qua non for ensuring economic development. Although initiatives have been taken in the past to establish collaborative programmes between the developing and the developed countries in the area of science and technology aimed at improving the core competence of the former set of countries, the impact of these initiatives was not felt. This was largely because the private sector in the industrialized world could not be involved in any meaningful manner. Article 15.6 of the CBD can thus be seen as a departure from the past initiatives in that it introduces a binding commitment for countries to undertake collaborative research ventures in the area of biotechnology. It must, however, be pointed out that the provisions of this article leave a possible window of opportunity for those industrialized countries unwilling to collaborate, by adding that they can decide whether or not such collaboration in scientific research is possible. This qualification thus appears as a challenge for the implementation of Article 15.6 of the CBD without seriously diluting its spirit.

The objectives of Article 15.6, referred to above, have been elaborated further in Article 19, which provides for the adoption of mechanisms for handling biotechnology and distributing benefits arising from the use of this frontier technology. At the outset, Article 19 provides for the adoption of legislative, administrative and policy measures by every CBD state party that could ensure 'effective participation in biotechnological research activities by those Contracting Parties, especially developing countries, which provide the genetic resources for such research, and where feasible in such Contracting Parties'. Thus, not only does Article 19 require that the developing countries be enabled to participate in biotechnological research, but it also emphasizes that the research centres should be established in the developing countries. Article 19.2 provides for equitable sharing of benefits arising out of use of biotechnologies between the countries developing the technologies and those that make the genetic resources available for the development of such technologies. This article is singularly important insofar as it provides explicit recognition to the economic value of the genetic resources.

As was mentioned in the foregoing, one of the lacunas in past initiatives to provide developing countries with an enabling mechanism in this area of technology development was the non-participation of the private sector. This important issue is addressed in Article 16. This article holds the key in that several of the issues concerning access to and transfer of technology have been raised in a manner that could change the technological paradigm which has been emerging over the past decade. This paradigm has been strengthened by the provisions of TRIPS, which we shall discuss in the next section.

Article 16.1 deals with access to and transfer of technology. It recognizes that 'both access to and transfer of technology [including biotechnology] among Contracting Parties are essential elements for the attainment of the objectives' of the CBD. Given this, Article 16.1 makes it imperative for every party 'to provide and/or facilitate access for and transfer to other Contracting Parties of technologies that are relevant to the conservation and sustainable use of biological diversity or make use of genetic resources and do not cause significant damage to the environment'.

The problems that developing counties have experienced in obtaining technologies that they require to further their developmental objectives have been addressed in Article 16.2. This article provides that developing countries shall have access to technologies on 'fair and most favourable terms, including on concessional and preferential terms where mutually agreed…'. This article further provides that 'in the case of technology subject to patents and other intellectual property rights, such access and transfer shall be provided on terms which recognize and are consistent with the adequate and effective protection of intellectual property rights'. Article 16.2 thus represents an attempt to balance the interests of the owners of the technologies and the countries desirous of using them.

The terms of technology transfer which, according to Article 16.2, have to be fair and 'most favourable' are extremely significant given that the major impediment to developing countries' access to technology has been the unaffordable terms which the transnational corporations set to license their technologies. The corporations are able to set such terms because of their control over the market for technology. This control is underpinned by the monopoly power provided by patents and other IPRs. As a result, North to South technology transfer is seriously restricted.

The response of the CBD to this piquant problem is provided in Article 16.3. This article makes it mandatory for the CBD parties to 'take legislative, administrative or policy measures, as appropriate, with the aim that Contracting Parties, in particular those that are developing countries, which provide genetic resources are provided access to and transfer of technology which makes use of those resources, on mutually agreed terms, including technology protected by patents and other intellectual property rights…'. Article 16.2 thus clearly indicates that it is incumbent upon each state party to put in place appropriate legislative, administrative or policy measures which can be used to ensure that organizations involved in the technology generation processes, including the private sector, can be called upon to provide technologies based on genetic resources of the developing countries to the countries supplying these genetic resources on affordable terms. The last mentioned objective is sought to be realized by introducing the added proviso that technology transfer shall take place on 'mutually agreed terms'.

The problems in the area of technology transfer arising out of the exercise of market control by the private sector are specifically addressed in Article 16.4. This article provides that 'each Contracting Party [to the CBD] shall take legislative, administrative or policy measures, as appropriate, with the aim that the private sector facilitates access to, joint development and transfer of technology … for the benefit of both governmental institutions and the private sector of developing countries…'.

The provisions of the CBD discussed in the foregoing are aimed at laying down the core principles upon which mechanisms for the transfer of gene-based technologies between the developed and the developing countries can be established. What is particularly significant is that these provisions seek to establish a balance between the rights of the owners of the technology and the potential users of these technologies in the developing countries. This has been one of the more contentious issues in several multilateral forums.

An important dimension of the CBD relates to its recognition of the contribution made by the local communities to the conservation of biodiversity. Article 8(j) of the convention provides that the contracting parties should: '(i) respect, preserve and maintain knowledge, innovations and practices of indigenous and local communities embodying traditional lifestyles relevant for the conservation and sustainable use of biological diversity, (ii) promote their wider application with the approval and involvement of the holders of such knowledge, innovation and practices, and (iii) encourage the equitable sharing of benefits arising from the utilization of such knowledge, innovations and practices'. Based on the provisions of Article 8(j), state parties have to develop instruments for protecting the rights of the traditional communities and to put in place a mechanism that can allow fair and equitable sharing of benefits arising out of the commercial exploitation of either the genetic resources or the associated knowledge.

The broad thrust of the approach of the CBD to the issue of IPRs has thus been to identify the various stakeholders who have been involved in the conservation and sustainable use of biodiversity and to make it mandatory for the governments to develop instruments through which the benefits arising out of any commercial exploitation of genetic resources and the associated knowledge can be shared in a fair and equitable manner. In so doing, the CBD has also taken care of the critical dimension of intergenerational equity, by including all the potential beneficiaries, above all, the local communities.

The perspective that the CBD sets out while defining the framework for access and use of genetic resources, including the terms on which technologies based on genetic resources should be made available, needs to be understood in the context of the debate that several multilateral organizations witnessed from the 1970s, which was centred on the need to evolve a new international economic order. Two elements of this debate were particularly important in light of the above discussion. The first stemmed from the recognition that the existing arrangements for technology transfer from the developed to the developing countries were disadvantageous to the latter. Towards addressing this problem, the UN Conference on Trade and Development (UNCTAD) proposed the adoption of an international Code of Conduct for the Transfer of Technology. The second, not entirely unrelated to the first, was the proposed reform of the global regime of intellectual property protection, in the main, the patent system. In this area, efforts were made by both UNCTAD and the World Intellectual Property Organization (WIPO) to develop a patent system that responded to the development needs of the developing countries.

Fundamentally, therefore, the structure of the CBD can be seen to reflect the unfinished agenda of the 1970s.

THE WTO–TRIPS INTELLECTUAL PROPERTY REGIME

The patent regime that TRIPS seeks to introduce has two distinguishable features. First, the norms and standards of patenting (and other forms of IPR) are applied nearly uniformly in all countries, implying a near harmonization of patent standards. Secondly, the norms and standards set by the agreement would be effectively imposed through the WTO's elaborate dispute settlement mechanism.

At the outset we should dwell on the specific nature of protection that TRIPS requires countries to introduce in the area of patents. We would argue that the patents regime introduced by TRIPS is a response to the narrow objectives of trade rather than to sustainable development.

The Norms and Standards of Patent Protection

The rights of the patentees have been strengthened in two ways. First, the nature and scope of protection has been expanded considerably beyond that available thus far, either in the domestic legislations of any country or in the global regime for patent protection as defined by the Paris Convention for the Protection of Industrial Property. Second, the obligations on the patentees have been diluted. The latter, in particular, pertains to the commonly adopted condition that patents must be worked in the country that grants the rights.

The rights of the patentee have been made more pervasive by extending the coverage of patentable subject matter. Biotechnological inventions have been brought under the ambit of patent protection by including micro-organisms and non-biological and microbiological processes. Barring a few exceptions, which include plants and animals, patents are to be available for all fields of technology. Countries can exclude areas from being patented to protect public order, morality or to prevent serious threat to their environment. Although WTO members can exclude plants from patent protection, they have to provide protection for plant varieties whether by patents or an 'effective sui generis system'.

The patent regime confers the right to the patentee to prevent third parties from the acts of making, using, offering for sale, selling, or importing the product that is covered by the patent. Countries can only provide limited exceptions to the exclusive rights that patents provide, and the legitimate interests of patent holders as well as those of third parties must not be unduly prejudiced. The above mentioned quite clearly shows that while there is clear enunciation of the rights of the patentee, the grounds for providing even limited exceptions are exceedingly specious.

TRIPS imposes two obligations on patentees. The first pertains to the disclosure of the 'invention in a sufficiently clear and complete manner' so as to allow 'a person skilled in the art' to use the invention. This disclosure provision, however, does require the patentee to provide information on the source of any genetic material that may be used in the patented product or process.

The second obligation that has been imposed on the patentee pertains to the working of the patent in the country of grant, that is, using the patent for commercial exploitation. The requirement of 'working' was in the manner of 'benefit sharing' between the patentee and the society at large. In order to ensure that patents were indeed worked in the country of grant, the patent system allowed for the use of the instrument of compulsory licensing. Thus, compulsory licences could be issued to anyone desiring to exploit the patent if the patentee did not comply with the 'working' requirements within a given period of time. It is noteworthy that the Paris Convention for the Protection of Industrial Property allows compulsory licences to be issued in the event of non-working of a patent by a patentee three years after it is granted. The compulsory licensing provisions governing 'working of patents' were thus introduced to bring about a balance between rights and obligations of a patentee.

TRIPS changes the balance between rights and obligations of the patentee by making the condition for working the patent almost non-existent. The first limiting clause introduced in the agreement relates to treating 'importation as working of the patent'. Article 27.1 and 28 of the TRIPS Agreement provide for this possibility. Article 27.1 states, '… patents shall be available and patent rights enjoyable without discrimination as to the place of the invention, the field of technology and whether products are imported or locally produced'. The rights conferred on the patent holder, as was mentioned above, provide that the right to import is to be included as an exclusive right granted to the patentee.

The real significance of these provisions can be seen in the context of technology transfer, particularly from the developed to the developing countries. We had indicated earlier that one of the most important problems that developing countries have been facing while trying to promote their industrial development was getting access to the advanced technologies that corporations in developed countries own. This problem, we have explained, has been addressed by the CBD, but TRIPS, in allowing importation to be treated as 'working', could now act as a constraining factor for developing countries seeking advanced technologies.

The unequal relations between developed and developing countries in the market for technology, that is manifest in the unfavourable licensing arrangements the latter are forced to enter into, will become more pronounced as a result of the dilution of the requirements of working as provided in Article 31 ('Other use without authorization of the right holder'). No grounds are explicitly given under which a compulsory licence, as provided in the Paris Convention, can be issued except in the case of pharmaceuticals where compulsory licences can be issued to ensure access to address public health concerns. This follows the adoption of the Doha Ministerial Declaration on the TRIPS Agreement and Public Health. It may be argued that in all other fields of technology TRIPS does not explicitly provide for the grant of compulsory licences either as a measure against abuse of monopoly rights conferred by a patent or to ensure working of the patent within the patent-granting country. This runs contrary to the Paris Convention where, as mentioned above, apart from the fact that the instrument of compulsory licensing is available to ensure working, non-working of a patent was considered to be an abuse.

The conditions under which the patent can be worked, as per TRIPS, are extremely narrow. Article 31(b), laying down the conditions of 'working', indicates that only under circumstances of extreme urgency or national emergency can a patent be compulsorily 'worked'. Under such circumstances, where a patent is 'worked', the patentee has to be paid 'adequate remuneration ... taking into account the economic value of the authorization (licence)'. This provision shifts the bargaining counter almost completely in favour of the patentee, as the determining authority to decide on the value of the licence he is willing to issue rests with him.

Article 31(g) adds further to the rights of the patent holder by providing grounds for revocation of any licence that is provided for working. This article states that 'authorisation ... shall be liable ... to be terminated if and when the circumstances which led to it cease to exist and are unlikely to recur'. This makes the provision very fragile for use by anybody who wants an authorization to use the patent and set up a commercial venture. No manufacturer will come forward to seek an authorization and take the risk of working the patent when he does not know if the circumstances under which the authorization was made will continue or not. In addition to these clauses referred to above, Article 31(f) allows the patentee to impose restrictive clauses on any authorization to prevent use of his patent for production aimed at the export market. The last-mentioned article in effect gives substance to the now well-documented tendency of the multinational corporations to licence technology to developing countries only for the exploitation of the latter's domestic markets and to prevent export of goods manufactured by imposing restrictive clauses.

These provisions are aimed at strengthening the rights of the patent holder. This has been done with an understanding that IPRs are above all private rights and that the nature of protection afforded by the regime should help only in maximising the returns for the owners of the intellectual property. This new IPR regime is in fundamental conflict with the larger objectives of sustainable development, due consideration of which was given while evolving the framework of the CBD. In the section below, we will highlight some of the major conflicts between the provisions of TRIPS and the CBD.

CONFLICTS BETWEEN THE CBD AND TRIPS

The most striking point of departure between the CBD and TRIPS lies in their objectives. The CBD considers intellectual property protection as a means to achieving conservation and sustainable use of biodiversity, and equitable benefit sharing. TRIPS, on the other hand, considers strengthening of IPRs as an end in itself. This leads to a very significant difference in that while the former establishes a more inclusive regime where the largest number of stakeholders is brought together to realize a common good, the latter essentially emphasizes the need to protect the sole interests of the owners of intellectual property. The position obtaining in the latter is, in fact, contrary to what has been conventionally maintained in respect of IPRs. The system of patents evolved at the end of the 15th century as a means to encourage individual inventors to

Table 7.1 *A comparison of the provisions of the CBD and the TRIPS Agreement*

Provisions of the CBD	*Provisions of the TRIPS Agreement*
1 Conserving biodiversity is the key objective of the treaty	Realization of the objectives of free trade as the prime motive force for the regime of intellectual property protection
2 Nation states have sovereign rights over their genetic material	Intellectual property rights over biotechnological inventions have to be granted without any consideration as regards the source of the genetic material
3 Local communities have to be recognized for their contribution to the conservation and sustainable use of biodiversity	Corporate interests or individuals can alone be assigned IPRs. Limited scope for granting collective rights
4 Any use of genetic material requires prior informed consent of the nation states or the local communities who are identified as custodians of the biodiversity	Patent holder need not disclose the source of genetic material on which a patent may have been granted
5 Use of genetic material must be accompanied by the sharing of benefits between the stakeholders	Patent holder would be sole beneficiary of any rights arising out of IPRs
6 Developing countries supplying genetic material must be involved in biotechnological research	No reference as to the involvement of developing countries in biotechnological research activities. The framework considers only the post-research phase where protection of the products and processes arising out of research activities is the sole objective.
7 Transfer of proprietary technology to developing countries supplying genetic material on terms to be decided by mutual consent	'Economic value of the licence' would be the guidepost for determining terms of technology transfer

exploit their inventions so that the public at large could benefit from their efforts. An element of benefit sharing thus typified the patent system as it evolved over the centuries.

This approach is echoed in the provisions of the CBD. In these provisions, the rights of the intellectual property holders have been tempered with corresponding benefits for the other stakeholders in the system. In fact, rather than establish the primacy of the rights holder, as has been the case with TRIPS, the CBD provides that the benefits should be shared by the largest number. Thus, the ownership of the sovereign states over their genetic resources has been given more importance than the ownership of IPRs. This fundamental difference in the understanding of the place of IPRs in society, as between the two treaties, has given rise to several specific points of departure (see Table 7.1). These points of departure will have considerable bearing as countries start the process of giving effect to the two treaties.

Three specific issues of conflict between the CBD and TRIPS need to be highlighted in this context. These are: (i) in cases where patentable inventions are based on biological material, TRIPS does not clearly provide for either the disclosure of the source of material utilized in the inventions or the obtaining of prior informed consent of the country of origin of the material; (ii) the conventional forms of intellectual property rights included in TRIPS are inadequate to protect traditional knowledge in an effective manner; and (iii) transfer of technology as provided for in the CBD cannot take place in a regime where the rights of intellectual property owners appear insurmountable. The post-Doha work programme on the CBD–TRIPS relationship will have to take into consideration these issues as a starting point to resolve the incongruities between the two treaties.

THE WAY FORWARD

This section briefly discusses the possible approaches towards reconciling the differences between the CBD and TRIPS in the three specific areas mentioned above. It needs to be pointed out that the suggestions are of a preliminary nature and that they have been made to facilitate further discussion.

One of the first steps needed towards reconciling the CBD and the TRIPS Agreement should involve incorporating the element of prior informed consent, as provided for in Article 15.5 of the CBD, into the TRIPS Agreement. This would essentially entail amendment of Article 29 of TRIPS so as to make mandatory mention of the origin of biological material should an invention seeking patent protection use such material. The applicant should also provide evidence that the prior informed consent of the country of origin of the biological material was obtained.

Protection of traditional knowledge and its holders has been raised as a critical concern by most developing countries. This issue has gained prominence ever since the cases of biopiracy and patenting of products and processes based on traditional knowledge have come to light. Although various options have been suggested, a dominant view has been that development of sui generis systems for the protection of traditional knowledge would be the most appropriate mechanism. Rendering the sui generis systems of protection consistent with TRIPS would be the most significant step towards making these systems effective. Among others, this could require another look at Article 27.3(b), which is currently being reviewed.

The third issue that needs to be addressed to ensure compatibility of the CBD and TRIPS relates to transfer of technology. As was mentioned earlier, TRIPS does not encourage the transfer of technology from the developed to the developing countries. In all fields of technology, except in the case of pharmaceuticals, granting of compulsory licences by the authorities in the developing countries could face resistance from the patent holders. Even with pharmaceuticals, where the terms for compulsory licensing were clarified somewhat by the 2001 Doha Ministerial Declaration on the TRIPS Agreement and Public Health, licensing terms could be the impeding factor for developing countries. In other words, TRIPS could render ineffective the provisions of Article 16 of the CBD, which are aimed at providing access to and transfer of technology to the developing countries 'under fair and most favourable terms'. Given this inconsistency between the CBD and TRIPS, Article 31 of the latter agreement needs to be reviewed.

Chapter 8

New Treaty Development and Harmonization of Intellectual Property Law

Ruth L Okediji[1]

INTRODUCTION

The prolonged negotiation of TRIPS might have suggested that international efforts in regulating intellectual property would abate for some time. Instead, however, two significant treaties in the area of copyright were negotiated in 1996, not long after the obligatory implementation of the TRIPS Agreement in developed countries. The World Intellectual Property Organisation (WIPO) Copyright Treaty (WCT) and the WIPO Performances and Phonograms Treaty (WPPT) deal with a new and very much unsettled frontier in copyright law, namely the application of copyright in the digital economy. In addition to these treaties, WIPO has worked on a patent law treaty to facilitate greater harmonization in the area of patents while work on the trade mark issues, specifically geographical indications, remains part of the international intellectual property agenda.

The unparalleled degree of harmonization of intellectual property norms, standards and enforcement mechanisms established by the TRIPS Agreement raises important concerns about the implications of these relatively high, 'minimal' standards of intellectual property protection for development interests. Recently, the debate about the impact of TRIPS on development objectives has focused primarily on issues such as access to essential medicines and the protection of traditional knowledge. However, harmonization also has important implications for other development concerns such as education, technology transfer and diffusion, and foreign direct investment including basic R&D investment activity. In theory, stronger levels of intellectual property protection via the agency of the TRIPS Agreement enforced at similar levels throughout the global community and monitored by the supranational authority of the WTO TRIPS Council is expected, in the long term, to strengthen the domestic economies of developing countries. While this expectation remains contested, there is consensus that harmonization at the levels established in the TRIPS Agreement will, in the short term, engender significant transfers of wealth from developing countries to developed countries.

This contribution presents a brief discussion of some development concerns associated with the evolving trajectory of intellectual property harmonization, including some practical considerations for study and strategy.

DEVELOPING COUNTRIES AND HARMONIZATION OF INTELLECTUAL PROPERTY RULES

Historically, countries joined the harmonization process only when their own levels of development and domestic priorities were consistent with the objectives of the harmonizing treaty. Indeed, the impetus for harmonization typically commences with an attempt to coordinate domestic laws for the mutual benefit of participating countries. Such coordination consists of identifying common principles for a basic framework of international cooperation in the subject area. Once a framework is established, countries progressively identify common objectives and negotiate legal standards in different degrees of specificity. As membership increases and the subject matter becomes more complex due to changes in the market-place (whether related to labour costs or technological developments) there is typically a corresponding increase in the scope of the treaty. Consequently, additional rights are negotiated by members to deal with these new challenges and to give creators opportunities to exploit their works in new media and in new markets. A review of the two primary intellectual property unions established by the Paris Convention for the Protection of Industrial Property and the Berne Convention for the Protection of Literary and Artistic Works is paradigmatic of this evolution. As is well known today, these two treaties established the framework (and informed many of the substantive provisions) of the TRIPS Agreement.

The harmonization process has been the primary, and preferred, mechanism for integrating developing countries into the international intellectual property system. Despite a few exceptions designed to address the interests of developing countries, the evidence is clear that harmonization generally tilts the balance of interests at stake in intellectual property regulation to favour owners of intellectual property and, de facto, developed countries. In general, harmonization exerts an upward force on national laws and policies; this process has consistently (if gradually) resulted in stronger and more expansive rights for owners. Correspondingly, the scope of limitations or exceptions tends to be narrower. The 'one-size-fits-all' approach that is fundamental to harmonization efforts makes it difficult for developing countries to tailor domestic laws to address local problems. Further, harmonization compels developing countries to negotiate new standards and rules of intellectual property without necessarily having had the benefit of experience of or expertise with the rules. It is thus more difficult for these countries to effectively evaluate the costs and benefits of membership in the treaty with respect to specific domestic priorities.

There is an abundance of literature that suggests that higher intellectual property standards attract foreign direct investment and encourage technology transfer. However, for most countries the empirical evidence is far less supportive of these propositions. This should not be understood as a problem of harmonization per se, but simply that intellectual property protection is only one piece of the development puzzle. How significant high levels of protection may be to a country's development is dependent on a balance of multiple factors that must be examined carefully within the particular conditions of each region, the changing dynamics of technology development and models of foreign direct investment.

In addition to the increased difficulty of shaping national intellectual property policy for development objectives, harmonization also has direct effects on local inventors. Higher standards mean that domestic innovators and investors assume higher risks in the creative process than the level of development indicates should be the case. This observation is particularly important when one considers that in developed countries, young industries and new technologies generally enjoy lower intellectual property (IP) standards in order to encourage innovators to engage in optimal levels of creativity.[2] All this might suggest that harmonization, in general, has facilitated greater gains for creators in developed countries at the expense of those in developing countries with no significant corresponding increase in short-term welfare for the developing world. The chart below summarizes some costs and benefits of harmonization.

Table 8.1 *Harmonization chart*

Examples of Some Benefits	*Examples of Some Costs*
Uniform standards which increase market confidence (ie investors willing to introduce new products in the market-place).	Less flexibility to tailor domestic IP policy to needs of local investors and domestic peculiarities.
Facilitates easier development of new global rights.	Less discretion over nature and scope of IP rights. Forced acceleration of development in non-IP areas such as education policy, industrial policy, and public health policy.
Centralized institutions responsible for monitoring, collecting and preserving information. More efficient use of resources by pooling efforts of different domestic offices.	Adverse effect on the development of a domestic IP culture and policy. Employment effects on local practitioners, judges, and other professionals (eg patent agents).
Uniform Fees/Single application with relevance in multiple jurisdictions.	Loss of income from domestic applications. Less likely that domestic innovators can afford the fees no matter how low.

Given that harmonization will continue to dominate the international regulation of intellectual property rights, several questions should be considered and evaluated for development purposes:

- How can harmonization efforts be structured to ensure that development objectives are clearly incorporated into the main text of the agreement?
- What mechanisms exist in international law to allow developing countries to strategically implement the harmonized terms of a treaty?
- How does the digital environment alter the fundamental assumptions that inhere in the classical justifications for intellectual property?
- How can/should developing countries engage in the harmonization process? At what stage in the process should they engage?
- What role does/can regional harmonization play in efforts to implement intellectual property rights in a manner consistent with development objectives?

DISTINGUISHING TYPES OF INTERNATIONAL TREATIES

To think effectively about these issues, it is helpful to distinguish between types of international intellectual property treaties and how these categories affect development priorities and efforts. Two broad classifications exist: substantive and administrative. There has been a tendency in development literature to treat these two types of treaties uniformly. However, each category functions differently with distinct effects on development strategies and priorities.

Substantive treaties

Substantive treaties are evolutionary in nature in the sense that they establish legal platforms that inform future negotiations in the particular subject matter. These treaties determine doctrines, legal standards, definitions of terms and general precepts of intellectual property protection that will bind all member states. They regulate the nature, scope and conditions of substantive protection of various categories of intellectual property. Examples of such treaties include the Berne Convention, the Paris Convention and to a lesser extent, the TRIPS Agreement. The proposed patent law treaty also falls within in this category.

Administrative treaties

Administrative treaties coordinate the practices and activities related to the administration of intellectual property rights. Examples of these include the Madrid Agreement concerning the International Registration of Marks, the Hague Agreement concerning the International Deposit of Industrial Designs and the Patent Cooperation Treaty (PCT). These treaties establish taxonomies for intellectual property to facilitate the organization, registration, identification and processing of information regarding the specific subject matter of the treaty. In general, administrative treaties have the potential to facilitate development goals in a more direct manner than substantive treaties. For example, administrative treaties provide a rich source of information for developing countries; they can constitute avenues to participate in the generation of data, and may be a source to identify owners of intellectual property and structure opportunities for access.

One immediate development concern may be that such classification can be artificial and problematic for certain kinds of creative works, particularly traditional knowledge products which are not easily amenable to rigid categorization. Protection of traditional knowledge includes both the substance of the knowledge, and the practices of using, preserving and transmitting the knowledge to successive generations. Treaties designed for traditional knowledge protection must integrate elements of 'administration' and 'substance.'

Points of action

There are a number of points of action that should be noted as important elements of a framework/agenda for developing countries in the area of intellectual property harmonization. As an initial matter, an important undertaking is to identify how the major treaties under each category interact with development goals of member states generally, and in specific industries targeted for purposes of exploiting comparative advantage. There are over 50 treaties that affect international intellectual property regulation. There is an important need to chart, compare and synthesize these treaties to help developing countries identify development losses associated with multiple memberships in overlapping, conflicting or superfluous agreements. Streamlining these treaties will also allow for more effective planning, allocation and use of scarce resources. Further, this work will help developing countries identify what development gains are available under their current obligations to better avoid bargaining these away under later bilateral and multilateral negotiations.

A notable number of bilateral trade agreements between developed countries (principally the EU and the US) and developing countries providing for 'TRIPS-plus' protection of intellectual property rights have already been negotiated. Other regional free trade agreements with similar 'TRIPS-plus' provisions are currently under negotiation. There is a need to consider how best to obtain the gains of bilateral and regional trading agreements without sacrificing the flexibility currently available under the TRIPS Agreement. In negotiating such agreements, developing countries need to assess the import of TRIPS-plus provisions in the context of technology transfer priorities, access to essential medicines and existing opportunities to exploit the inherent malleability of standards and limitations of the TRIPS Agreement.

Related to the problem of increasing bilateralization/regionalization of TRIPS-plus intellectual property rules through free trade agreements is the need to develop an understanding of the relationship, as a matter of international law, between various treaties that deal with intellectual property regulation. Prominent examples are the relationship between the Convention on Biological Diversity (CBD) and TRIPS, the impact of various human rights treaties on TRIPS interpretation and implementation, and the relationship between post-TRIPS intellectual property treaties such as the WIPO copyright treaties mentioned earlier, and other future treaties. The relationship between these various legal regimes is certainly complex and imbued with tensions and competing principles. Nevertheless, the multifaceted and dynamic nature of the development process will require methodologies to reconcile the obligations imposed by these treaties in a rational, coherent and balanced strategy of implementation. At the very least, this suggests that not every country will or should implement all these agreements in the same way. Monitoring agencies such as the WTO TRIPS Council should recognize this fact and evaluate compliance strategies of developing countries with some consideration of the development goals of particular countries. Indeed, such an approach to evaluating TRIPS compliance is consistent with the objectives set forth in the preamble of the TRIPS Agreement.

With regard to legalizing development objectives and concerns, the structure of international intellectual property treaties must also be considered very strategically. Where, in the treaty, should development objectives be integrated? Scepticism about the operational and legal force of the TRIPS preamble (where most of the development objectives of TRIPS were placed) and the fact that at least several WTO dispute panels which had the opportunity did not refer to the development-oriented objectives of TRIPS, suggest that the placement of such clauses is indeed a matter that should be carefully revised for future negotiations. There is also the recent practice of negotiating 'Agreed Statements' to complement treaties. What is the legal effect of these agreed statements? Is the practice of making exceptions for developing countries still a viable model for a world economy with open markets? Should such welfare enhancing limitations be construed as 'developing country exceptions' or more broadly as consumer exceptions? The recent report of the UK Commission on Intellectual Property Rights (CIPR)[3] indicates that there has been little use by developing countries of exceptions in existing treaties. Indeed, a few developing countries even have stronger intellectual property laws than some developed countries. It is important to understand what social, economic and political/institutional pressures are responsible for this situation and how to reverse this trend.

Another possibility is to consider the efficacy of models of compliance that are not centred around legal rules as such. For example, in other areas of international harmonization such as environmental law, there has been success with the use of 'soft law' agreements. These are agreements that focus on normative principles that guide the behaviour of member states, as opposed to explicitly stated obligations. It will be increasingly important to explore such models in areas such as standard setting, exceptions to proprietary rights, technical cooperation and new subjects of intellectual property treaty negotiations.

Finally, there is an urgent need to consider the effect of information technology on the administration and coordination of treaty obligations. How can the economies of scale made possible by information technology be translated in the intellectual property context to assist in (i) gains for developing countries with regard to access to technology (patents), content (copyright) and products (products such as medicines or other goods) and; (ii) reducing costs of participation in negotiation, drafting and coordination between the various regional and international intellectual property offices?

CONTEXT, CONSIDERATIONS AND PROBLEM SPOTTING

In addition to the need for a more precise identification of existing treaties and corresponding development goals, there remain some important points of focus for future consideration, reform and other action.

Regional harmonization and regional institutions: appraising strategic roles and benefits

Although there are several regional intellectual property institutions in developing regions, evidence of the pro-development role/benefit of these institutions is, at best, mixed. Regional institutions have served primarily as outposts for foreign intellectual property owners seeking regional recognition/protection for their creative works. Some things to consider, particularly in light of the recent CIPR report confirming, again, low levels of creative activity in developing countries, include:

- What are the existing regional offices and what are their roles?
- Can these institutions be restructured in a way that utilizes them as development agents for the region?
- How can these institutions serve the needs of local innovators?
- Can they constitute alternative sources of model laws in different subject matter areas?

The CIPR report presents empirical evidence that is useful for determining how best to utilize existing regional offices and what needs are best served by their existence.

Pre-emptive/advance identification of issues

Developing countries are typically caught unawares or unprepared when issues for new treaty negotiations are submitted. As a strategic matter, it is important for developing countries to think ahead about issues that may be introduced in multilateral negotiations. Other subject matter of possible harmonization already on the horizon includes database protection, traditional knowledge and competition laws. Developing countries must consider the implications of these initiatives for their priorities by advance study of the debates that have taken place in the developed countries, and by ascertaining development interests related to each subject matter.

INVOLVEMENT IN NEGOTIATIONS OF THE NEW TREATIES

The relatively successful experience of developing countries during negotiation of the WIPO digital treaties demonstrates the importance of developing country involvement in the early stages of negotiations. Negotiations over these treaties were aided by the alliance built between developing countries and public interest groups from developed countries. As a result, the WIPO digital treaties were a more balanced reflection of interests between owners and users than might otherwise have been the case.

In negotiating new treaties, attempts to coordinate with other developing countries should be made to identify common grounds of interest and/or concern prior to introduction and negotiation in the broader international forum. Early identification and interjection of issues of concern for development objectives should be an integral part of the discussions, particularly in WIPO-led treaty initiatives or in other inter-governmental forums.

INTEGRATION OF TREATY LANGUAGE IN NATIONAL LAWS

It is increasingly the case that developing countries incorporate, verbatim, treaty language in their domestic laws. This practice may have some adverse consequences for development purposes, particularly since treaty language often reflects a particular understanding of the treaty and this tends to be viewed in a strong protectionist light. It is important to evaluate which countries have done this, and to suggest ways of incorporating treaty norms in domestic laws in ways that are sensitive to development concerns and that avoid importing interpretive limitations directly associated with the negotiating stages of the treaty.

RELATIONSHIP BETWEEN OLD TREATIES AND NEW TREATIES

As mentioned earlier, the legal relationship between TRIPS and the WIPO treaties, or TRIPS and CBD obligations, is complex and unsettled. Often, developing countries do not know how to comply with their obligations in a consistent and complementary fashion. There needs to be a thorough review of the legal relationship between new and old treaties and how this relationship may affect development concerns. Further, evidence of state practice has important ramifications for how a treaty-based obligation may be interpreted. Developing countries need to understand what constitutes 'state practice' and how to establish such practices. 'Regional practice' rather than state practice should also be considered to strengthen a pro-development construction of treaty obligations and to provide a regional baseline for treaty implementation.

THE PROBLEM OF 'PIGGY-BACKING'

Increasingly, treaties are being subsumed or incorporated in new negotiations. For example, membership in the WTO is a de facto membership in the Berne Convention and the Paris Convention; membership in regional organizations like Organisation Africaine de la Propriété Intellectuelle (OAPI) requires membership in the PCT, and so on. The result is that membership in a new treaty often entails joining several other treaties. For developing countries that are already lagging behind in many respects, this means their economies must absorb all at once what developed countries absorbed over many years, sometimes over centuries. Staggered implementation of treaty obligations was a strategy employed by developing and least developed countries with regard to implementation of the TRIPS Agreement. Such an approach is a necessary part of ensuring that the development process and participation in the international intellectual property system are not mutually exclusive.

USE OF INFORMATION TECHNOLOGY

With regard to information technology, a primary issue is to understand how it can be used to enhance the knowledge base in developing countries, particularly in the administration of intellectual property rights. Information technology can be of exceptional value in: (i) upgrading human resource capacity through distance education; (ii) expanding databases of information pertaining to intellectual property in developed countries; (iii) protection and use of information technology in administering local intellectual property offices, particularly enhancing the quality and quantity of interaction between administrators and creators; and (iv) building institutional alliances with public sector organizations involved with intellectual property issues in developed countries.

CONCLUSION

It is important to keep in mind that the momentum to harmonize intellectual property rights is likely to continue well into the foreseeable future. First, there are numerous perceived gains from harmonization. These include efficiency gains from the standardization of rules, such as the relative ease of administering and enforcing the rights from country to country, consistency in interpretation of terms and the development of a common culture oriented towards similar levels of intellectual property protection. Second, harmonization is considerably easier since countries now share a substantive common baseline established by the TRIPS Agreement. Further, it should be noted that one of WIPO's fundamental activities is to initiate new negotiations in areas where it believes member countries will benefit from harmonized rules. Thus, as a regulatory matter, harmonization will continue to play a central role in international intellectual property regulation.

Not every development concern can be addressed for each intellectual property treaty that exists. An integral part of development strategy in the immediate future is to identify global-specific, region-specific and some country-specific development priorities. Strategies should concentrate heavily on areas where these three converge. A working list of such areas of convergence, and relevant sectors implicated, should be used for preparations to negotiate common ground between developing countries. Some consideration should also be given to creating alliances with some developed countries in areas where those countries may share similar concerns. This was a strategy that worked very well during the TRIPS negotiations as well as during the WCT/WPPT negotiations.

Finally, it should be noted that harmonization and development are not mutually exclusive processes. Indeed, harmonization that establishes 'maximum,'[4] as well as minimal, standards can be a useful tool to reconcile the interests of owners and users of intellectual property, and to encourage a development of international rules that recognize the welfare goals intrinsic to intellectual property protection particularly under the common law tradition. The next five years will require constructive and strategic, theoretical and coherent exercises that include dialogue, technical assistance and innovative concepts to facilitate the true integration of development concerns in the fabric of international intellectual property law making.

NOTES

1 This paper is a slightly revised version of a discussion note prepared for the UNCTAD/ICTSD Conference on 'Setting an Agenda for Intellectual Property Negotiations in the Next Five Years,' held at the Bellagio Rockefeller Conference Center, Bellagio, Italy, October 30 – November 2, 2002. Many thanks to the Rockefeller Foundation, UNCTAD/ICTSD and the group of participants.

2 By 'lower' standards, I mean to suggest that the application of core patent principles such as 'novelty' or 'non-obviousness' are applied differentially to inventors working in new sciences. A recent example of this practice is the case of biotechnology patents in the US. It should be noted that within the TRIPS Agreement, developing countries also have some flexibility in applying the required principles within their own domestic system. Developing countries should endeavour to develop guidelines for interpretation and application that take advantage of this flexibility, particularly to encourage local innovation.

3 Commission on Intellectual Property Rights (2002) *Integrating Intellectual Property Rights and Development Policy*, Report of the Commission on Intellectual Property Rights, London: CIPR

4 A treaty that employs maximum standards as a strategy would mean that countries could not implement higher standards than those established by the treaty. In addition to preventing the extraction of higher terms of intellectual property protection through bilateral economic pressure, this approach also more explicitly allows for a range of options for implementing the treaty obligations in the domestic environment.

PART TWO

POLICY AND SYSTEMIC ISSUES

PLANT VARIETY PROTECTION AND PATENTS ON LIFE FORMS

TRIPS AND PUBLIC HEALTH

IPRS AND THE PROTECTION OF TRADITIONAL KNOWLEDGE

PLANT VARIETY PROTECTION AND PATENTS ON LIFE FORMS

Chapter 9

Article 27.3(b) of the TRIPS Agreement: the review process and developments at national and regional levels

Boniface Guwa Chidyausiku

This chapter covers three areas. The first is the current debate over patents on life forms. The second is Article 27.3(b) and the review process in the TRIPS Council. The third area is the African Group position and the contribution of African regional and national policies and initiatives to the first two topics.

THE DEBATE OVER PATENTS ON LIFE FORMS

The issue of patents on living organisms is a current topic of worldwide debate. Several factors have led to the emergence of this debate. First, the advances within the last decade in the field of biological sciences, including the ability to isolate and manipulate genes, have resulted in a rapid development of genetic engineering and the growth and expansion of the biotechnology industry. This development has been accompanied by an increased interest in the use of patents to claim rights over discoveries in this field.

Second, the growing demand for biological or genetic resources, due to their demand in the biotechnology, pharmaceutical, cosmetics, agriculture and other industries, has seen a rise in bioprospecting activities in many countries in the biodiversity-rich South. Bioprospecting activities have been accompanied by the problem of biopiracy, whereby traditional or indigenous knowledge is employed to assist in the search for plants or other biological materials with commercial potential but without any authorization or compensation. The incidence of biopiracy has been facilitated, to an extent, by the patents applied for by foreign individuals or companies over the biological resources and their genetic components.

Finally, developing countries are now obliged to implement Article 27.3(b) of the TRIPS Agreement, which requires World Trade Organization (WTO) members to provide for the patenting of certain life forms and processes within their national laws. The transition period for developing countries to complete their implementation of TRIPS came to pass on 1 January 2000. As such, many developing country members have had to tackle the issue of how to incorporate the obligations under Article 27.3(b) into their national legal frameworks.

Article 27.3(b) of TRIPS

Article 27.3(b) has aroused significant public controversy and has become one of the more contentious topics in the WTO TRIPS Council. Upon analysis, it can be said that Article 27.3(b) deals with four different aspects, as follows:

1 the option to exclude from patentability certain living organisms but not others;
2 the option to exclude from patentability certain processes but not others;
3 the requirement to protect plant varieties either by patents or an effective sui generis system or a combination of the two; and
4 a review process for this subparagraph.

These aspects have practical consequences almost exclusively for developing countries, because developing countries have typically retained exclusions for living organisms in their patent legislation. In addition, most developing countries usually do not have plant breeders' rights (PBR)-type legislation for plant varieties.

For these and other reasons, questions are being raised as to the appropriateness of patents on life forms and about the implications of such patents for developing countries. These are some of the questions to which I will try to provide some answers.

Implications for developing countries

The use of IPRs (particularly patents) in the context of living organisms and biological resources is a relatively new phenomenon. The patent system was originally intended for the protection of mechanical and non-living inventions. In the 1980s however, a number of industrialized countries began to move beyond the original tenets of patent law by allowing patents on living organisms, although there were numerous differences in the extent of patentability in each country's patent laws.

With Article 27.3(b), minimum standards of patent protection for living organisms are now prescribed for WTO members, both developed and developing countries. With advances in biotechnology and genomics, a very large number of patents are being applied for on genes, cells and DNA sequences of plants, animals and even humans. Many of these applications are from private corporations. The granting of such patents raises the question of who will have access to, and control over, the technologies, knowledge and discoveries covered under the patents.

This question is pertinent, especially when one considers that the great majority of patents are granted to corporations, institutions and individuals from the North. For example, almost all biotechnology-related patents originate from industrialized countries with 37 per cent coming from the US, 37 per cent from Japan and 19 per cent from Western Europe.

These figures have led some commentators to argue that such patents are likely to lead to transfer of income from developing countries to developed countries, and eventually affect the competitiveness of smaller firms and less technologically advanced countries. Such patents are also a cause for concern for scientists, doctors and smaller research firms, where in some cases patents have had the effect of restricting research and preventing the use of diagnostic tests. Even in the US, some unease has been expressed over the US Patent and Trademark Office's practice of allowing ever-broader patents.

Some patent experts have argued that the patent system may not be appropriate for protecting and rewarding discoveries in biotechnology and genomics. The patent system, originally designed to protect mechanical inventions, makes a distinction between mere discoveries and inventions. It seems only logical that biological materials are naturally occurring and can only be discoveries and not inventions.

However, Article 27.3(b) distinguishes between plants and animals on one hand and micro-organisms on the other, and between essentially biological processes on the one hand and microbiological and non-biological processes on the other. Some scientists argue that such distinctions should not be drawn, and consequently all living organisms and living processes cannot be patentable. They also call for a ban on certain patents, such as those that are really biopiracy, and those on discoveries (micro-organisms, cell lines, genomes, genes, including human cell lines and human genomes and sequences), transgenic techniques and transgenic plants, animals and micro-organisms, and nuclear transplant cloning.

Patents or other IPRs on plants and agricultural crops also raise the fundamental question of whether or not there should be private ownership of plants or their genes. A very small number of staple crops – rice, wheat, maize and potato – form the basis of 70 per cent of the world's food supply. Patent laws in many developing countries still do not allow the patenting of such plants and plant varieties, the rationale being that these form the backbone of crop production, plant breeding and, ultimately, food security. However, through stronger plant breeders' rights and the extension of patent protection to plant genes and cells, and even whole plant varieties, a number of agricultural or food crops have come under private ownership. This is an issue currently under intense negotiation at the Food and Agriculture Organization (FAO).

As can be seen from the discussion above, Article 27.3(b) is rich with implications for a wide range of issues. Concerns have been raised in terms of the effect of patents on life forms with regard to developing countries' sovereignty over their genetic resources, to agriculture and food security, as well as raising ethical and moral issues.

Article 27.3(b) has been discussed in the context of other international agreements such as the Convention on Biological Diversity (CBD) and the FAO International Treaty on Plant Genetic Resources for Food and Agriculture. The questions raised in these forums include the impact of Article 27.3(b) on the nature, evolution and ownership of knowledge in the use of biodiversity, the sharing of benefits derived from the use of biodiversity, the nature of 'invention' in matters relating to nature and biological processes and products, the rights of local and farming communities, and the ecological, social and ethical impacts of modern biotechnology, in particular genetic engineering.

THE ARTICLE 27.3(B) REVIEW PROCESS

Due to its controversial nature, Article 27.3(b) stipulates that a review of the provision should be undertaken before the end of 1999. A review process was commenced in December 1998 under the TRIPS Council. However, the scope of the review is not clearly defined within the provision. This has led to a debate within the TRIPS Council as to the nature of the review. The developed countries, led by the US, had argued that the review process should be confined to examining the extent to which the provision has been implemented. The developing countries, on the other hand, maintained that the review should be of a substantive nature, and have called for amendments to TRIPS in connection with this review.

Although the review process commenced before 1999, it has not concluded. During the review process, WTO members had also begun preparations for the WTO's Third Ministerial Conference, held in Seattle from 30 November to 3 December, 1999. As part of these preparations, developing countries submitted a number of proposals for the reform of TRIPS.

The African Group proposal on Article 27.3(b)

In July 1999, as part of the preparatory process for the WTO's Seattle Ministerial Conference, Kenya, on behalf of the African Group, submitted a detailed paper to the General Council on the TRIPS Agreement, which proposed clarification of, and changes to, Article 27.3(b). This paper garnered wide support from developing countries, as well as civil society movements around the world.

In its proposal, the African Group questioned the artificial distinction made by Article 27.3(b) between plants and animals on the one hand, and micro-organisms on the other, and also that between essentially biological processes for the production of plants and animals, and microbiological and non-biological processes. In the light of these artificial distinctions, the proposal called for a revision of Article 27.3(b) so as to prohibit the patenting of all life forms and natural processes.

The African countries also proposed clarification on the requirement for protection of plant varieties under Article 27.3(b), namely, that countries in so doing could still adopt measures to protect farmers' and communities' knowledge and innovations in farming, agriculture and health, as well as to prevent anti-competitive practices. This was an attempt to rebut the assertion (put forward by some WTO members) that the International Union for the Protection of New Varieties of Plants (UPOV) system is the only sui generis system recognized under TRIPS. The UPOV regime, particularly the UPOV 1991 version, has been criticized for granting rights almost akin to patents, with adverse effects for traditional breeders and farmers, and for food security, in developing countries.

According to the paper:

> *There is a lack of clarity on the criteria/rationale used to decide what can and cannot be excluded from patentability in Article 27.3(b). This relates to the artificial distinction made between plants and animals (which may be excluded) and micro-organisms (which may not be excluded); and also between 'essentially biological' processes for making plants and animals (which may be excluded) and microbiological processes. By stipulating compulsory patenting of micro-organisms (which are natural living things) and microbiological processes (which are natural processes), the provisions of Article 27.3 contravene the basic tenets on which patent laws are based: that substances and processes that exist in nature are a discovery and not an invention and thus are not patentable. Moreover, by giving Members the option whether or not to exclude the patentability of plants and animals, Article 27.3(b) allows for life forms to be patented.*

Therefore, the African Group proposed that the review of the substantive provisions of Article 27.3(b) should clarify the following:

- Why the option of exclusion of patentability of plants and animals does not extend to micro-organisms, as there is no scientific basis for the distinction.
- Why the option of exclusion of patentability of 'essentially biological processes' does not extend to 'microbiological processes' as the latter are also biological processes.
- That plants and animals as well as micro-organisms and all other living organisms and their parts cannot be patented, and that natural processes that produce plants, animals and other living organisms should also not be patentable.

The Like-minded Group proposal

The Like-minded Group of developing countries (comprising Cuba, Dominican Republic, Egypt, El Salvador, Honduras, India, Indonesia, Malaysia, Nigeria, Pakistan, Sri Lanka and Uganda) also highlighted the conflict between their commitments under the Convention on Biological Diversity (CBD) and under TRIPS. The CBD stipulates that IPRs must be supportive of the Convention's objectives, but TRIPS makes no reference to the key objectives of the CBD, namely the conservation and sustainable use of biological resources, and fair and equitable sharing between the providers and users of such resources of the benefits arising from their use.

Post-Seattle and implementation issues

Since the Seattle Conference came to an inconclusive end, these proposals have yet to be considered. They remain on the agenda of the TRIPS Council. At the TRIPS Council meeting in September 2000, a submission from India urged a proper hearing for these proposals (which form part of the numerous proposals for addressing problems of developing countries in implementing the WTO agreements, put forward for consideration at the Seattle Conference, collectively referred to as 'implementation issues'). The Indian paper also called for a clarification of how the objectives and principles of TRIPS, namely technological innovation, transfer of technology and promotion of public interests, could be effectively put into operation.

At the same meeting, Mauritius, on behalf of the African Group, also submitted a proposal which, among other things, called for the review of the link between Article 27.3(b) and development, and specifically, to address whether the appropriate balance has been struck between the protection of IPRs and the protection of key socio-economic interests such as food security, health and the conservation and sustainable use of genetic resources. The proposal also reiterated the African countries' earlier proposal on the review and revision of Article 27.3(b) (see Chapter 1).

Kenya, in supporting the Mauritius proposal, added that the amendment of Article 27.3(b) should 'prohibit or exclude from patentability all biological and living organisms (these include plants, animals, micro-organisms and parts thereof, such as cells, cell lines, genes and genomes) as well as any processes making use of, or relating to, such biological and living organisms'. Such prohibition or exclusion, said Kenya, was justifiable on legal, scientific, developmental, moral and ethical grounds. In addition, the exclusion of plants from patentability would mean no patents should be allowed on plant varieties. Therefore, the amendment may only require sui generis systems of protection for plant varieties. In this regard, Kenya called for a clarification that such sui generis systems should include the effective protection and promotion of the rights of farmers, indigenous and local communities over their genetic resources and their knowledge relating to the use of such resources.

The US also submitted a paper outlining its views, asserting that for the purposes of Article 27.3(b) a dictionary definition of a (patentable) micro-organism was sufficient. This view attracted some critical comment from developing countries and commentators. In response to the US position, Brazil said that a more precise and scientific definition was required, for the purposes of clearly defining the scope of exceptions to patentability set out in Article 27.3(b). A clear definition of micro-organisms and the criteria for patentability would also prevent broad patents on micro-organisms (including those that are mere discoveries), which would have the effect of restricting research, thereby undermining the patent system. The Brazilian legislation excludes from patenting all or part of plants and animals, except for transgenic micro-organisms provided the requirements of patentability – novelty, inventive step and industrial application – are met.

Status of review process

In the meantime, the deadline for implementation of Article 27.3(b) has arrived without concrete conclusions being reached as to the review process. The review process of Article 27.3(b) remains uncompleted and is still on the agenda of the TRIPS Council. It should also be noted that WTO members had agreed during the December 1999 (post-Seattle) General Council meeting that members would exercise 'restraint' in dealing with the implementation deadlines.

Consultations on how to resolve the outstanding issues arising from the Seattle Ministerial Conference are still ongoing. In July 2000, the General Council of the WTO held a Special Session to consider the complaints of developing countries about the imbalances and inequities of the WTO agreements, including the TRIPS Agreement. Prior to and during the Seattle Ministerial Conference, developing countries had said that unless these implementation issues were addressed and rectified, they would be unable to undertake more obligations (whether under the existing agreements or through negotiation of new agreements in a new round).

This implementation process has identified a number of issues in relation to the TRIPS Agreement (raised in the developing country proposals for Seattle), including the need to harmonize TRIPS with the CBD, the implications and review of Article 27.3(b), and the exclusion of essential drugs from patentability. However, the General Council process has yet to yield concrete results.

However, the position adopted by the majority of the developing countries seems clear:

- They are opposed to the patenting of life, and seek clarification and revision of Article 27.3(b) to that effect.
- They also regard the provision to be inconsistent, or in conflict, with the provisions of the Convention on Biological Diversity and the FAO International Treaty on Plant Genetic Resources; specifically, with regard to the protection of indigenous and local community knowledge, and farmers' rights. The developing countries propose that measures be taken to ensure that the TRIPS provisions are consistent with, and supportive of, these international obligations.

Mindful that the TRIPS Agreement requires implementation of Article 27.3(b) by the 1 January 2000 deadline, the developing countries had proposed that the deadline for implementation be extended by another five years. Developing countries have argued that the review, if it was only on implementation, would not be effective (or make sense) if it were carried out before the developing countries had implemented the provision. Similarly, if the review were to be a substantive one, it would also not make sense for them to implement the existing provision, given that the review process could well result in its being revised.

THE ROLE OF NATIONAL AND REGIONAL INITIATIVES IN THESE DEBATES AND NEGOTIATIONS

While the review of Article 27.3(b) is ongoing, developing countries are faced with the prospect of implementing Article 27.3(b) (since the deadline for implementation was January 2000) without knowing the eventual result of the review process.

In these circumstances, a cautious approach is recommended, which should ideally preserve the basic premise of non-patentability of all naturally occurring living organisms (including naturally occurring micro-organisms) and their parts, as well as all natural processes. The specific reference to micro-organisms raises the issue of whether genetically modified or transgenic micro-organisms must be patentable. For example, the approach of the Brazilian legislation excludes from patenting all or part of plants and animals except for transgenic micro-organisms provided the requirements of patentability are satisfied. There is also the question of consistency and coherence of the TRIPS requirements with other international obligations, such as the Convention on Biological Diversity and the FAO International Treaty on Plant Genetic Resources for Food and Agriculture.

A number of African regional and national initiatives to implement international obligations have played a role in defining the African Group's position on the review of Article 27.3(b). Of note is the Organization of African Unity's (OAU's) initiative in developing a Model Law for the Protection of the Rights of Local Communities, Farmers, Breeders, and Regulation of Access to Biological Resources, which is described in Chapter 24. The African Group position on the review of Article 27.3(b) reflects the approach that has been adopted in the model law. Aspects of the model law have been adopted by a number of African countries, the most recent example being Namibia, which is currently undergoing a national drafting process to incorporate the model law into the national legal framework. It can therefore be said that the OAU model law reflects the common understanding of African countries in relation to their obligations under international agreements, including TRIPS and the CBD.

It is important that any regional or national processes relating to Article 27.3(b) remain linked to the Geneva process. Africa has stated its position, and it is crucial that in all instances this position be consolidated, especially now as the African Group seeks ways of moving the process forward and to convince its developed country negotiating partners to amend the TRIPS Agreement.

I would further suggest that African members keep each other informed of attempts from some quarters to weaken the African Group position. Believe me, there are many such attempts. If any African policy coordinating processes allow themselves to be adversely influenced, then this makes things difficult for the African Group in Geneva.

Chapter 10

The Revised Bangui Agreement and Plant Variety Protection in OAPI Countries

Jeanne Zoundjihekpon

INTRODUCTION

Since the dawn of history, local communities have been using biological resources to cater for such daily needs as food, traditional medicine, housing or cosmetics. In Africa, these biological resources have been managed by village communities for many centuries. Thus seeds and medicinal plants are exchanged among peasants and traditional healers within and between communities, the main concern being to meet the daily requirements for survival. In this situation, the food supply of the greater part of the population is produced by traditional, family-based farming methods, despite many difficulties. Seeds, for instance, are passed on from generation to generation and are exchanged among peasants, relatives or friends, or sold in local markets.

But with modern agriculture and colonization, African agricultural products have been ushered into international trade. The Convention on Biological Diversity (CBD) recognizes the sovereign right of states over biological resources. In its Article 8(j), moreover, the convention stipulates that each contracting party shall:

> *subject to its national legislation, respect, preserve and maintain knowledge, innovations and practices of indigenous and local communities embodying traditional lifestyles relevant for the conservation and sustainable use of biological diversity and promote their wider application with the approval and involvement of the holders of such knowledge, innovations and practices and encourage the equitable sharing of the benefits arising from the utilization of such knowledge, innovations and practices.*

TRIPS obliges all member countries to recognize intellectual property rights (IPRs) over plant varieties. Since IPRs do not cover farmers' rights, however, even though these are recognized by the Food and Agriculture Organization (FAO), nor the local community rights highlighted in Article 8(j) of the CBD, a conflict arises between biodiversity and the world trade rules. Annex X on plant variety protection added to the Revised Bangui Agreement Establishing an African Intellectual Property Organization (OAPI) is merely one illustration of this conflict.

THE MAIN CHALLENGE OF AGRO-BIODIVERSITY IN AFRICA: FOOD SECURITY

Like the other inhabited continents of the world, Africa contributed to the birth of agriculture some 12,000 years ago. For millennia, African peasants created food crops by domesticating the wild varieties of plants offered by nature. Examples of such food plants include: yam, millet, fonio, sorghum and oil palm in West Africa; coffee and yam in Central Africa; coffee, teff or sorghum in East Africa; and date palm, wheat and artichokes in North Africa. As a result of this collective approach to farming, genetic resources are considered to be shared and to belong to everyone. Right across the continent, since food is based on traditional family-based agriculture, cultivated plants are exchanged among relatives and friends, or sold on local markets, far removed from any notion of monopoly such as underlies intellectual property rights or breeders' rights. Nowadays in Africa, subsistence farming accounts for the bulk of agricultural activity, with food crops that are specific to each region and each country, so that a large proportion of small farmers grows more food crops than non-food cash crops.

Despite the natural constraints arising from drought and bouts of famine that occur in some countries of the subregion, local communities use their traditional knowledge to practice subsistence agriculture. Seeds for food crops are therefore managed by local communities. In several countries of the subregion, depending on the ethnic groups and local socio-cultural customs, seed selection is the responsibility of the head of the family and is sometimes related to socio-cultural or religious rituals. African farmers therefore act as breeders and their main objective is to ensure the food security of their families. In other words, the breeding of traditional varieties is conducted without any idea of material gain.

In June 1999, in an official memorandum addressed to the governments of French-speaking Africa, the International Union for the Protection of New Varieties of Plants (UPOV) drew attention to the main advantages of introducing legislation on the protection of plant varieties in Africa. UPOV maintained that the protection of plant varieties enhanced the well-being of the population by contributing above all to food security (by increasing the quantity, quality and diversity of food products). And yet there is no provision in the UPOV Convention to directly link plant breeding to food security. The situation in Africa is that food security is mentioned only in the preambles of systems governing breeders' rights. Moreover, the only criteria applied to the protection of breeders' rights are novelty, distinctness, uniformity and the stability of a variety. The system does not even require that varieties should be 'improved'. Hence even 'discoveries' may be protected, even though no effort of breeding has been made.

A 1999 report by Genetic Resources Action International based on research in three African countries with breeders' rights systems clearly showed that they are in no way linked to 'food security' (Genetic Resources Action International, 1999). In Kenya, for example, not a single application filed and verified since the start-up of its system of breeders' rights until May 1999 had concerned a crop of any significance for the country's food security: 135 breeders' rights applications had been filed for industrial crops and only one for a food crop, a variety of green bean cultivated for the European market. In Zimbabwe, from 1973, when the law on plant breeders' rights was enacted, until 1999, 534 applications were filed for industrial crops, and 208 for food crops, while in South Africa, out of 1435 breeders' certificates granted from 1977 to the end of 1998, as many as half concerned industrial crops. It would appear, therefore, that the system of protecting agro-biodiversity with breeders' rights encourages breeders to concentrate their work on industrial crops rather than food crops.

THE REVISED BANGUI AGREEMENT AND TRIPS

With the industrial society and its underlying profit motivation, mechanisms have been developed to protect all types of intellectual creations. Thus if individuals or companies can prove that they have created or invented something new, they are given the right to protect it, subject to the currently established procedures. In accordance with this system, patents allow inventors the exclusive right to prevent any other persons or companies from exploiting their creations or inventions. The protection period, which generally lasts 20 years, is intended to be sufficient to enable inventors to recover their costs before their invention enters the public domain. This is the case for a number of products and production techniques.

The Bangui Agreement, which is legislation common to all the OAPI member states, was signed in 1977 to protect intellectual property in 16 countries of West and Central Africa (Table 10.1).

In order to meet WTO requirements, UPOV and the World Intellectual Property Organization (WIPO) convinced OAPI to revise its basic text by adopting rules similar to those of UPOV. These rules are contained in Annex X of the Revised Agreement. In spite of this, two-thirds of OAPI's membership are least developed countries (LDCs), who according to TRIPS do not have to provide plant variety protection until 2006. The problem is that the UPOV Convention serves the interests only of multinationals and those involved in industrial agriculture, whereas in Africa the food consumed by most people is produced by family-based traditional agriculture.

The Revised Agreement was signed in February 1999 by 15 French-speaking African countries (at the time, Equatorial Guinea was not yet a member),

Table 10.1 *Date of ratification or accession of OAPI member countries to international instruments concerning biological diversity and trade*

Country	*CBD ratification date*	*WTO entry date*	*Revised Bangui Agreement ratification date*
Benin	30 June 1994	22 February 1996	–
Burkina Faso	2 September 1993	3 June 1995	8 June 2001
Cameroon	19 October 1994	13 December 1995	9 July 1999
Central African Republic	15 March 1995	31 May 1995	–
Congo	1 August 1996	–	–
Côte d'Ivoire	29 November 1994	–	24 May 2000
Gabon	–	1 January 1995	27 December 1999
Guinea Bissau	27 October 1995	31 May 1995	–
Guinea	7 May 1993	25 October 1995	13 July 2001
Equatorial Guinea	–	–	23 November 2000
Mali	29 March 1995	31 May 1995	19 June 2000
Mauritania	16 August 1996	31 May 1995	5 July 2001
Niger	25 July 1995	13 December 1996	–
Senegal	17 October 1994	1 January 1995	9 March 2000
Chad	7 June 1994	19 October 1996	24 November 2000
Togo	4 October 1995	31 May 1995	29 November 2001

establishing an IPR system for seeds and plant varieties. The problem is that the agreement was prepared between 1995 and 1999 without consulting the peasants and local communities or even the general populations of the OAPI member countries. The agreement entered into force on 28 February 2002. Annex X concerning plant variety protection, however, did not enter into force, officially because certain measures needed to be taken for its application.

Yet in 1999, the African Group in the WTO had made appropriate proposals to the WTO secretariat. One of the proposals was headed: 'Deadline for the implementation of the provisions of Article 27.3 (b)…'. After recalling that issues concerning that article were being debated in related forums, such as the FAO or the Convention on Biological Diversity (CBD), the proposal went on: 'the members of the African group consider it would be appropriate to postpone the implementation deadline until Article 27.3 (b) has been examined in detail. The time allowed for the implementation of the provisions should be the same as that provided for paragraphs 1 and 2 of Article 65, namely five years starting from the date when the examination will be completed. This delay is to allow the developing countries to set up the infrastructure required by implementation.' It seems clear, therefore, that the OAPI member countries should not have rushed to revise the Bangui Agreement. The haste with which WIPO and UPOV drove the OAPI to implement the TRIPS Agreement appears all the more dubious, now that the WTO members have delayed the provisions of the agreement on pharmaceutical products for the least developed countries until 2016.

As in the case of UPOV, the new Bangui Agreement grants exclusive commercial rights (monopolies) to breeders of plant varieties that are new, distinct, uniform and stable. Although constituting the very basis of new varieties, traditional varieties and the related knowledge are ignored. This means that farmers will have to pay royalties on new seeds and will be entitled to keep part of their crop for future sowing only subject to certain conditions. Thus the new agreement restricts the rights of farmers to stock seed and introduces a system whereby life forms are privatized.

While the Revised Bangui Agreement protects new or improved plant varieties, it offers no protection for traditional varieties developed by local communities because of the fact that traditional knowledge is not new, and because the holders of such knowledge are neither individuals nor commercial entities. Yet it is the traditional varieties that provide the basis for improving varieties, whether by conventional or biotechnological means. So the rights of local communities are not protected by this supranational agreement. The OAPI, in conjunction with UPOV and WIPO, protects the interests of breeders and multinationals, but not those of peasants, traditional healers or local communities.

The application of the Bangui Agreement will have serious consequences for present and future generations in the OAPI member countries. One of these is that farmers will become completely dependent on multinationals and foreign scientific research institutes. This is because peasants and local communities are forbidden to reproduce IPR-protected seeds without a licence. This could have dangerous consequences for food security in Africa. Another consequence will be the loss of crop diversity, which will leave both producers and consumers extremely vulnerable. This is because the Revised Bangui Agreement protects only uniform varieties. Another issue of concern is the plunder of African biological resources. And with regard to health, one can expect a further increase in the prices of basic medicines which are already out of reach of our populations. This is because the agreement prohibits the parallel importation of cheaper generic medicines from countries outside the group of OAPI member countries.

Under Annex X of the Revised Bangui Agreement, breeders may use protected varieties to develop new varieties, but they may not work these new varieties if they are similar to the initial varieties. Farmers are allowed to stock, use and exchange (though never to sell) the seeds they have gathered of protected varieties subject to the conditions that: (i) they own their own land; (ii) no fruit varieties are involved; (iii) no forestry varieties are involved; (iv) no ornamental plants are involved; and (v) they have paid royalties on the initial variety.

Since 1992, the African countries have not taken any national measures to ensure 'the fair and equitable sharing of the benefits arising from the utilization of biological resources'. The conclusion must be that the gathering of biological resources and bioprospecting in Africa by multinationals and foreign research institutes amounts to 'biopiracy'.

SOME EXAMPLES OF PATENTS FILED ON WEST AND CENTRAL AFRICAN PLANTS

The Revised Bangui Agreement with its Annex X on plant variety protection amounts to an official licence to plunder African biological resources, to the detriment of farmers and local communities. There are many examples of African plants on which patents have been filed and that yield enormous financial gains but without provision for the sharing of benefits. Worse still, once the patent has been filed, parallel supply circuits are usually established, with the help of genetic engineering. Since transgenic plants are also plant varieties, they are protected by the Revised Bangui Agreement, whereas the wild varieties from which they were derived are not.

The case of West African thaumatin

Thaumatin is a natural sweetener extracted from the fruit of *Thaumatococcus daniellii*, which grows in the forests of West Africa. The fruit has been used for centuries as a sweetener by a number of local communities. The protein, which is 2000 times sweeter than ordinary sugar, was discovered by researchers at Ife University in Nigeria. For years, thaumatin has been marketed as a low-calorie sweetener and has been used by the food and confectionery industries in several developed countries. Since the plant yields fruit only in its original surroundings, for several years the British sugar producer, Tate and Lyle, imported the fruits from Ghana, Côte d'Ivoire, Liberia and Malaysia, and marketed the product under the name of Taline.

In the US alone, the low-calorie sweetener market is estimated to amount to US$900 million a year. As it is expensive to extract the substance, genetic engineering has been resorted to by several companies. Beatrice Foods obtained a patent in the US for the process of cloning the gene in yeast. According to estimates, the company may obtain royalties worth US$25 million. Researchers of the Lucky Biotech Corporation and the University of California have filed an American patent on all transgenic fruits, seeds and vegetables containing the gene that produces thaumatin. Thanks to this, the companies will no longer need the fruits from West Africa.

The case of brazzeine in Central Africa

Brazzeine, a protein that is 500 times sweeter than sugar, is derived from a berry that grows in Gabon and Central Africa. Unlike other sweeteners, brazzeine is a natural substance that does not lose its sweetness when heated. This makes it a favourite with the food industry. This plant drew the attention of an American researcher, who observed animals and people consuming the fruit in their natural habitat. In the US, four patents were filed (Table 10.2), and one patent in Europe (No 684 995) concerning the extraction of a protein from the *Pentadiplandra brazzeana*, the establishment of the genetic sequence coding for this protein and transgenic organisms. It later became possible to produce brazzeine in the laboratory with transgenic plants, making it unnecessary to purchase plants from Africa.

Since the world market for sweeteners is estimated to be worth US$100 billion per year, it is easy to imagine how important this plant is. According to the University of Wisconsin, brazzeine was 'invented by one of its researchers' and there is no plan to share benefits with the peoples of Central Africa who discovered and looked after the plant for centuries. 'Nektar Worldwide and

Table 10.2 *Some patents on West and Central African biodiversity*

Varieties	*Patent Number*	*Patent Owner*	*Origin*	*Utilization*
Dioscorea dumetorum Yellow yam	US 5 019 580	Shaman Pharmaceuticals M Iwu	West Africa	Treatment of diabetes in West Africa. The patent applies to the use of dioscoretin for the treatment of diabetes.
Thaumatococcus daniellii	US 4 011 206 US 5 464 770	Tate & Lyle (UK) Xoma Corp (US)	West Africa	Scientists at Ife University were the first to identify its potential as a sweetener. Since then, a gene has been cloned and used as a sweetener for confectionary. The people of West Africa have received no compensation.
Prunus africana Pygeum	US 3 856 946 FR 2 605 886	Debat Lab (France)	Mountain forests in Africa, especially Central Africa	Medicinal plant. The wood of the tree is used for sculpture. For the treatment of prostate disorders, gross overexploitation has been observed in many areas, with sales amounting to US$150 million per year.
Pentadiplandra brazzeana Brazzeine	US 5 527 555 US 5 326 580 US 5 346 998 US 5 741 537	University of Wisconsin (US)	Gabon	Traditionally used as a sweetener. The patent applies to the sweetening protein compound, the brazzeine gene and transgenic organisms carrying the gene. Again, this means the developed countries can bypass the gathering or commercial growing of this African plant. The US company ProdiGene is currently introducing the gene into maize.
Eupenicillium shearii Mushroom	US 5 492 902	US Department of Agriculture, Research Foundation of the University of Iowa, Biotechnology Research and Development (US)	Côte d'Ivoire	To be used as an insecticide.
Dioscoreophyllum cumminisii	US 3 998 798 JP 5 070 494	University of Pennsylvania (US) and Kirin Brewery Ltd (Japan)	West Africa	Used to sweeten foods and drinks for centuries.

Source: Wynberg, 2000

ProdiGene, a branch of Pioneer Hi-Bred International, the largest seed company in the world, have now modified maize genetically, in order to produce large quantities of brazzeine. They estimate that demand in future can be met with a million tons of genetically modified maize, replacing any other supply coming direct from Central Africa' (Genetic Resources Action International, 2000).

CONCLUSION

The signing and ratification of the Revised Bangui Agreement are tantamount to granting legal authorization to plunder African biological resources by OAPI member states. The only redeeming feature is that Annex X on plant variety protection has not yet entered into effect. It is now time for the farmers' organizations and local communities to mobilize, calling the whole world to witness.

Within the framework of the implementation of this convention and of observance of the WTO's provisions (Article 27.3(b)), support must now be given for the initiatives of the African Union, in order to find an alternative to patents or plant breeders' rights, by proposing model legislation for the protection of the rights of local communities, farmers and breeders. All national and international organizations working in Africa in the area of biological diversity, food and agriculture should help to make this model law better known and have it adopted as part of the legal arsenal of every African country in the interest of their farmers and local communities.

Also, the African Group within the WTO should urgently renew and strengthen its 1999 position on Article 27.3(b) which is still under review. In the light of the experience gained in Francophone Africa and in OAPI member countries, where pressure to comply with UPOV on account of that article's requirements has been successful, the African Group should call for the removal of any reference to plant varieties. In other words, just as it is unacceptable to grant patents on life forms, which constitutes the first part of the African Group's position, it is equally unacceptable to impose IPR protection of plant varieties. New and existing plant varieties represent the very basis of world food security and monopoly systems are definitely not the answer to their management.

REFERENCES

Genetic Resources Action International (1999) *Plant Variety Protection to Feed Africa? Rhetoric versus Reality*, Barcelona: GRAIN.

Genetic Resources Action International (2000) *Of Patents & Pi®ates: Patents on Life: The Final Assault on the Commons*, Barcelona: GRAIN.

Wynberg, R (2000) *Privatising the Means of Survival: The Commercialization of Africa's Biodiversity*, Cape Town, Barcelona and London: Biowatch, GRAIN and Gaia Foundation.

Chapter 11

The World of Biotechnology Patents

Silvia Salazar

INTRODUCTION

During the past decade, the world economy has undergone profound changes. The new trend is towards a more globalized economy through the liberalization of markets and free trade agreements between countries and, above all, between trade blocks. Although the beginnings of the international intellectual property rights (IPR) regime predate these changes, discussion on the subject had been confined to specialists. In fact, intellectual property was of interest only to a small circle of people who had a direct interest in the regime, such as inventors, authors and lawyers. However, with the internationalization of the economy and the advent of free market agreements, the subject of intellectual property rights is now an obligatory topic of discussion and negotiation in free market agreements worldwide.

Prior to these economic changes, the worldwide panorama with respect to intellectual property protection was unbalanced. While in most developed countries intellectual property was strongly protected and the trend was towards ever stronger protection, in developing countries the situation was very different. In these latter countries, little protection was available at all, and where there was it was often ineffective, and some industrial sectors were excluded. During the 1960s, opposition to patenting among many developing countries resulted in their reforming their patent laws to exclude certain sensitive areas, such as pharmaceuticals, foods and agrochemicals. These are precisely the areas of greatest interest to the developed countries and, above all, to the transnational companies that commercialize products in these fields.

BIOTECHNOLOGY

Before continuing, it is good to explain some basic issues regarding biotechnology. Biotechnology holds much promise as a new set of tools for increasing the efficiency and sustainability of agricultural production and assuring the safety, quality, variety and quantity of food products. These tools enable scientists to understand and manipulate life processes at the molecular level in ways that were unknown and unattainable just a few years ago.

Biotechnology refers to methods of using plants, animals and microbes either wholly or in part, to produce useful substances or improve existing species. More specifically biotechnology is the use of technologies based on living systems to develop commercial processes and products.

Although the word biotechnology is relatively new, the subject has an ancient history. For thousands of years, yeasts, moulds and bacteria have been used to make fermented foods and beverages like bread, wine and beer. Biotechnology is around us every day, just as it was for our ancestors. But what was often mysterious to them can now be understood through the discoveries of biotechnology. To differentiate these older techniques from the modern ones, I refer to 'the new biotechnologies'.

The new biotechnologies include recombinant DNA, gene transfer, embryo manipulation and transfer, plant regeneration, tissue culture, monoclonal antibodies, and bioprocess engineering. These new technologies allow scientists to genetically improve animals and plants, to control diseases and pests, and to increase productivity and quality. For example, scientists are now able to develop plants with improved resistance to insects and environmental stresses such as drought or cold.

FORMS OF PROTECTION

Intellectual property developed in these technological fields can be protected in several ways, depending on the type of subject matter for which protection is sought.

Plant variety protection

Several developed nations enacted plant variety protection (PVP) legislation during the post-Second World War period. In addition, the EU created a Europe-wide PVP system in 1994. A number of developing nations are now adopting parallel legislation in order to comply with the requirements of TRIPS relating to protection of plant varieties. Such legislation, also known as plant breeders' rights, provides an IPR system adapted to the needs of traditional plant breeders and is designed to give these breeders an increased incentive to develop new varieties while respecting the traditions of breeding.

These laws typically grant protection to varieties that are novel, distinct, uniform and stable. Novelty requires in particular that the variety was not sold previously, typically with a grace period of one to several years depending on the country and the species. Distinctness requires that the variety be clearly distinguishable from previous varieties, while uniformity and stability require that the plant be uniform and that it breed true to type, but is typically defined in such way as to allow for the protection of hybrids.

The protection is by means of a certificate granted most typically by an office of the ministry of agriculture upon receipt of a relatively simple and inexpensive application. The certificate entitles its holder to be the exclusive marketer of the relevant variety and also of the product of the variety. This right may be licensed to others. The certificate does not prevent others from using the protected variety in efforts to breed further varieties.

The PVP laws are generally adopted in accordance with an international treaty called the International Convention for the Protection of New Varieties of Plants, or UPOV for short (after the French acronym of the union made up of the convention's contracting parties). The convention's most recent acts were adopted in 1978 and 1991. Countries are members either of the 1978 Act or the 1991 Act. Any country that wants to join the treaty will have to adapt its laws to the 1991 Act, which is slightly different from the earlier act. For example, the 1978 Act requires parties to allow use of protected material for the breeding of additional varieties, as already mentioned. It also implicitly permits farmers to replant their harvested seed. The 1991 Act permits both but with some differences. First, it does not require that the 'farmers' privilege' be recognised, treating it as an optional provision. As for the 'breeders' exemption', this is slightly modified in response to the development of the new biotechnologies. The 'essentially derived variety' provision states that a breeder remains free to use a protected variety and to make any change in such variety, but this is subject to the rights of the owner of the initial variety if that change is so small as to leave the new variety essentially derived from the earlier one. One of the examples listed in the article is any transformation by genetic engineering. So if a biotechnologist takes a protected variety and introduces a resistance gene, he will have to ask for a licence to commercialize that new variety from the owner of the original variety.

It is also important to note that a biotechnological breeder will not acquire enough protection for transformed plants under the PVP system. If a transgenic variety is protected under PVP, another breeder can purchase the variety, cross it with his material, develop a new variety containing the gene, and market it without infringing any PVP right.

Patent protection

In some countries it is now possible to patent biological materials such as plants, animals, genes and micro-organisms. Utility patents provide broad protection subject to fulfilment of the criteria of novelty, utility and non-obviousness. The patent itself includes both a description of how to practice the invention and a statement of claims, which precisely define the exclusive rights defined by the patent. Obtaining a patent is both slower and more expensive than PVP certificates. The patent owner has also to be able to enforce his rights in the courts against infringements, which can also be expensive.

Patents, like PVP certificates, are territorial, meaning that they give rights in the country where they were granted for a limited time in accordance to specific national laws. Just because a gene is patented in the US does not mean it is also protected in Trinidad and Tobago. The patent holder will have to seek protection in every country in which he wishes to commercialize the invention.

Patents are not granted in order to protect secrets or withhold scientific and technical information. On the contrary, patents require the disclosure of pertinent information surrounding the inventions. They are published and anyone can have access to them. Nowadays one can even access patent databases through the internet.

Utility patents do not normally contain provisions specifically allowing farmers to save seed for replanting (although the EU Directive on the Legal Protection of Biotechnological Inventions is an exception). However, from a practical perspective, preventing farmers from saving seed may be difficult to enforce. It is known that some seed companies in the US sell seeds with labels indicating possible infringements and are also forcing farmers to sign contracts to prevent infringement precisely to avoid these problems.

It is clear that patents are more restrictive than PVP certificates. Because patents do not allow the free use of the invention to develop another one, and provide the ability to protect genes and traits, as well as products, utility patents provide the strongest form of statutory protection for unique germplasm.

Trade secret protection

Some intellectual property is not suitable for protection under any statute. In other cases the developer may simply elect not to seek statutory protection. Trade secret laws can provide protection in these situations. A trade secret can be any kind of information that is not common knowledge and that gives its owner some form of business, technological or trade advantage over competitors. The strength of the protection depends on the ability to keep critical enabling information secret.

Intellectual property owners wishing to protect their property through secrecy must actively take steps to maintain the secrecy. If the secret information becomes known, the protection is lost. Certain types of property are very poor candidates for trade secret protection simply because the enabling information is evident and disclosed by the product. Some biological materials fall into this category.

Some forms of biological material are readily protectable as trade secrets because of the inherent nature of the subject matter. An example is hybrid corn. Because hybrids cannot be reproduced without access to the parent inbred lines, protecting the parent lines as trade secrets is not seriously compromised by the sale of the hybrid seed to farmers.

This form of protection has been sufficient to provide the incentives needed for research investments in the hybrid corn industry for many years. In addition, farmers are unable to grow their own seed without suffering significant yield losses. This form of biological protection, in concert with strict control of parent inbred lines, has provided excellent intellectual property protection.

Contracts

Agreements and contracts can be in the form of licence agreements, sales contracts and restrictive use provisions or labels. Combinations of more than one form can be used. With each approach the owner attempts to restrict or control the manner in which other parties may use the intellectual property.

The effectiveness of various contracts in controlling the unauthorized use of intellectual property depends, to some extent, on the strength of the underlying IPRs. A contract backed by a patent or plant variety protection certificate affords the best protection. Written agreements signed by both parties are the most desirable because they help assure that both parties understand and agree to the contract terms.

One of the most used types of contract in biotechnology-based breeding is the material transfer agreement (MTA) used to exchange genetic materials and information. An MTA is a simple contract, formalized under relevant national contract law principles, providing for an allocation of rights in the materials. The precise terms may vary from case to case, but may, for example, permit the recipient to use the material only for research purposes, or require the recipient to negotiate a royalty arrangement should it identify commercial applications for the material or a product derived from it. Clearly the most important and difficult issue is how far the supplier's rights should run under such an agreement.

The precise terms of this agreement may vary from context to context. Universities exchanging material at the relatively basic scientific level are most likely to allow the material to be used freely for research but with a protection for their interests should there be a commercial application. The private sector may exchange material only after a careful negotiation that actually sets royalties or profit shares in resulting inventions and varieties. Developing nations with an interest similar to that of the universities may seek to protect a right to a share of profits in the material (a genetic resource) and their concern clearly becomes significant in any situation in which biotechnological methods are applied to materials derived from such nations.

THE PATENTING OF LIFE FORMS

Developments in the field of biotechnology have been accompanied by changes in the patent system. Hitherto, the patent system protected machines, articles, tools and devices, but not living products and processes. However, the assumption that living organisms are unpatentable because they are products of nature has changed profoundly in the last decades.

It is important to bear in mind that even though discussions on the desirability of intellectual property protection systems for developing countries remain unresolved, international rules in this area have been established in the form of TRIPS, which requires patents to be available for all fields of technology. There are some exceptions like plants, animals and essentially biological processes to produce them, but patents must be available for micro-organisms like bacteria and viruses, which are so important in biotechnology, and microbiological processes. TRIPS obliges WTO members to protect plant varieties by means of the patent system, a sui generis system, or a combination of both.

TRIPS does not require WTO members to go as far as the US, Japan and Europe in the area of patenting living organisms. Indeed, Article 27.3(b) is currently being reviewed, and many developing countries are using this as an opportunity to voice their opposition to the patenting of life forms.

The US pioneered the extension of patents to cover life forms and goes further than any other country. It is possible there to patent, for example, plants, animals, micro-organisms, genes, gene sequences, methods of localizing genes, genetic engineering technologies for the manipulation of genes, and cellular sequences. This broad view, for example, has meant that within the agricultural sector, the private sector has had incentives to invest in research. On the other hand, the possibility of patenting these inventions, together with the wide research capacity of the transnational enterprises, has meant that nowadays it is difficult to carry out agricultural biotechnology research without the risk of trespassing on a patent.

Before going further, however, it is important to bear in mind as before that patent rights are territorial, which means that they are valid only in the country in which they were granted. This means that if a person obtains a patent for a plasmid in the US but nowhere else, this plasmid is not protected anywhere other than in the US. If a researcher has access to this plasmid in a country where it is not protected and uses it, he would not infringe the patent.

It should also be noted that most patent systems have what is called the research exemption, which means that whenever the plasmid in the above example is protected in a second country, if the law of that country allows the research exemption, the researcher can use it for research without infringing the patent.

Any commercial use of the plasmid without authorization by a third party in the territory of the country protecting it is considered an infringement of the patent. This is important in the context of the use of the plasmid, for example, in order to transform a plant, which later may be introduced into the country where the plasmid is protected. It is still not clear whether a product derived from a plant transformed and cultivated in a country where the plasmid is not protected infringes on the patent in the country where it is protected. An example could be a banana from a genetically modified plant resistant to black Sigatoka.

As mentioned above, protection of life forms started in the US. Although in 1873 Pasteur was granted a patent involving a yeast culture as a manufacturing process, it was not until 1930 that protection for a life form as such was granted in the US. The Plant Act of 1930 provided alternative intellectual property protection for certain types of asexually reproduced plant materials. In 1970, the Plant Variety Protection Act was passed and a protection system for sexually reproduced plants was granted. In 1977 a new step was taken when the US Patents and Trademarks Office (USPTO) ruled that any product of nature isolated from its natural form can be patented. That allowed the patenting of products found in nature in a compound form when man intervenes and isolates it and identifies its utility.

Another crucial step was taken in 1980 in the Diamond versus Chakrabarty case when the US Supreme Court ruled that any invention, including a life form, was patentable under the utility patent law. The Chakrabarty case involved the development of a genetically engineered bacteria with a unique trait. This new organism was clearly the result of human scientific intervention. The court's decision, however, did not single out inventions created using specific techniques, such as genetic engineering techniques, nor did it limit patent protection to genetically engineered biological materials. Rather it extended protection to any biological material with uniqueness contributed by scientists or inventors, without regard to the techniques used to achieve and perfect uniqueness.

The Chakrabarty decision did not immediately result in the patenting of plant and animal materials, but an important appeal decision held that plants and parts of plants, including genes and fruits, could be patented under the utility patent law even though the plant material had previously been afforded protection under the Plant Variety Protection Act. This decision opened the door for protection of plant materials via utility patents. A related ruling in 1987 clarified that animal inventions could be protected under the patent law. The first patent for a plant was granted to a maize variety with a higher concentration of an amino acid called trytophan. The first animal patent was granted to Harvard University for their famous oncomouse.

In 1989 the US Patent and Trademark Office granted a patent on human genetic material, specifically a cell line from an organ of John Moore. Nowadays it is possible in the US to obtain a patent in the biomedical area for gene therapy techniques, cloning techniques, ex vivo gene therapies and human cells. In the agricultural biotechnology area it is possible to obtain a patent on a gene and its application in a plant, diagnostic probes, transformation processes and materials, and finished varieties.

PROTECTING GENES

With regard to the protection of genes there is a lot of controversy. Some have used the concept 'as found in nature' to create an opposition to 'manipulated by man' in order to differentiate between a discovery and an invention. It has been maintained that the patenting of genes and sequences in the USPTO, for example, is incorrect, because the genes have not been modified by man and have simply been discovered. It is a generally accepted principle that scientific discoveries are not patentable.

The reasoning behind the patenting of genes in the US is, first, that genes are considered as chemical substances, and these have been patentable for a very long time. And second, genes are not found isolated in nature but form part of a molecule called DNA. It has been said, therefore, that if substance X is found in nature, which is composed of A, B, and C, when A, B, and C are not found alone in nature, only together in compound X, if compound B can be isolated and it is useful, it could be patentable, because the hand of man would be present in the isolation. This same reasoning applies in the case of genes.

For the USPTO the isolation of a product that did not exist by itself in nature may be deemed as sufficiently non-obvious for a patent to be granted, even though it is accepted that the compound was not created by man. This same reasoning applies in the case of genes. The USPTO argues that genes do not exist as themselves in nature, but are parts of the DNA molecule. Man's contribution is the possibility of isolating or purifying them, and assigning them a function, that is to say, demonstrating that they have utility. This sole contribution is enough for a patent to be allowable. Clearly, this reasoning is contrary to the view that genes already exist in nature and are simply discovered by man. But another fact that has to be taken into account around this debate is that the US Constitution grants protection to discoveries, which is contrary to the majority of laws in other countries which specifically declare that discoveries are not inventions. A worldwide debate has been raised around this issue. Each country has to decide its own interpretation since TRIPS allows for different interpretations.

CONCERNS

The protection of life forms has been subject of a huge debate all over the world. Despite the progress made in the biotechnological research field, the legal protection of biotechnology has caused much controversy. There are ethical, philosophical, religious and political considerations that have added to the debate on the advisability of protecting biotechnological inventions through IPRs.

Some of the concerns regarding the protection of biotechnology are ethical and philosophical in nature, questioning the morality of transferring genes from one species to another and manipulating what God has created. There are questions regarding the right to place bad genes with good genes, and who decides which are bad genes and which are good ones. The possibility of someone owning life or part of it is highly criticized. In this context, it is worth mentioning that recently the Vatican issued a press release supporting biotechnological research in agriculture but expressing concern about human cloning and the integrity of life from the stage of fertilization of the egg.

Another concern is the fact that the agriculture industry, which is essential to the survival of humanity, is concentrated in a few firms or transnational corporations, and that all inputs needed for agriculture are concentrated in those same companies. This situation creates potential obstacles for poor and subsistence farmers to access technology and affordable agricultural inputs.

Another controversial issue arising from the increased patenting of biotechnological inventions around the world is the possibility of obtaining patents with very broad claims that cover a very broad group of plants. Famous examples are cotton and soybean-related patents granted during the 1990s to Agracetus that were later acquired by Monsanto. The USPTO granted this company patents covering all transgenic cotton and transgenic soybean. In practice this meant that if a person succeeded in genetically transforming cotton with another characteristic, that would infringe the original patent.

Since it is possible to protect hybrids in the US, it is impossible for another plant breeder to use the material as a parental line. This has been severely criticized because of the restrictions it imposes on the improvement of varieties, as opposed to the possibilities offered by plant breeders' rights.

Another topic of debate, which has yet to be resolved, refers to the scope of the rights granted by the patent. In particular, there are questions regarding whether the by-products or the offspring of protected plants and animals fall under the scope of protection provided by the patent, which, depending on interpretation, could provide the holder with an extremely wide range of protection.

These uncertainties are yet to be resolved by the courts and a lot of litigation is still going on relating to biotechnology patents. Some companies have avoided litigation by acquiring their competitors and in consequence their intellectual property. But there is still a lot of insecurity and many of these patents are thought not to be strong enough to survive litigation.

The relationship between access to genetic resources and protection of life forms has been the subject of a lot of debate. The regulation of access to genetic resources is based on states' sovereign rights over their natural resources. These rights were recognized in the Convention on Biological Diversity (CBD). A lot of concerns have arisen due to the possibility that transnational companies will access genetic resources in developing countries and apply for patents derived from them without sharing any benefits. However, it is important to clarify that the problem of access to genetic resources is not a patent matter, and can best be solved in forums like the CBD or others dealing with genetic resources. Patent systems cannot be blamed just because countries are unable to effectively regulate access to their resources.

Finally protection of living organisms has also received the same criticism that is given to patents in general. Among the criticisms are that patents are an obstacle for accessing technologies, that they increase prices, that they are expensive to acquire or license, and that they create abusive monopolies.

RECOMMENDATIONS

In order to allay concerns related to the IPR protection of living organisms, this chapter closes with some recommendations. First, it is very important to accurately define terms. For example, legislation that states that micro-organisms are patentable requires a clear definition of the term. Second, policy-makers must adopt a wide perspective encompassing the need to provide incentives for education, research, and scientific and technological development, including for industry. IPRs are a tool but they are not the solution to the problem of underdevelopment. Third, public sector research must be encouraged so that technologies and inputs needed by farmers are available as well as those of transnational companies. It is worrying that in some countries public sector agricultural research is in decline as governments cut their research budgets. Fourth, laws must be enacted to regulate monopolies. It is necessary to prevent a situation in which only five companies are doing most of the agricultural research. One approach may be to enact an international anti-monopoly code. Unfortunately, there is little discussion about this in intellectual property negotiations. Fifth, prices must be controlled. If a country considers that patents are prejudicial in terms of prices, they can introduce price controls. But such measures must be used carefully because these procedures can discourage companies from distributing their products in that country. Sixth, incentives need to be created. We cannot expect people to breed new plant varieties with enhanced productivity and disease resistance without the incentive of legal protection enabling them to recover their investment. Seventh, more training on IPRs is essential. Finally, access to technological improvements must be promoted. IPRs encourage innovation and investment, while farmers and society need access to new technologies and products. That is why a balance is needed. Sometimes it is necessary to give a little to receive something in return.

Chapter 12

The Implications of Intellectual Property for Agricultural Research and Seed Production in West and Central Africa

Oumar Niangado and Demba Kebe

INTRODUCTION

The signing of the agreement establishing the World Trade Organization (WTO) in April 1994 passed unnoticed in most West African countries. Few institutions were aware of its contents outside the offices of the ministries of trade. When it was signed, a new term, intellectual property, was added to the experts' jargon. Previously used only among inventors and artists, the term became established in the life sciences.

The race to appropriate life forms began in 1980 when the Supreme Court of the US authorized the first patent on a gene. The work done since on unravelling the genome has led to many patents being filed and the question of intellectual property has become a major economic issue affecting not only food and farming but also the medical and pharmaceutical industries. The patentability of genes came as a real shock, as it made genetic resources, which until then had been considered part of the common and freely accessible human heritage, especially with respect to plant breeding, into a major trade issue.

Nowadays, knowledge is the most important factor as far as a country's standard of living is concerned. No less than 90 per cent of commercial research and development activities take place in the industrialized countries, which hold a similar share of scientific publications. The gap between North and South, with respect to knowledge, is bound to increase as the means of acquiring knowledge are privatized. While the introduction of stricter intellectual property regimes and their extension to biological materials open up prospects for the North, they merely generate concern for developing countries. Is it not more than likely that globalization in combination with intellectual property rights (IPRs) will adversely affect agricultural research and seed production in West and Central Africa? In this chapter, we review the situation of agriculture and seed production in West and Central Africa. We then consider the implications of IPRs for biological diversity and agricultural research.

The context of traditional agriculture

In West and Central Africa, agricultural production follows a pattern of itinerant farming. With the growth of population, however, sedentary habits have been gaining ground. Crop rotation varies according to different areas. Usually the fertility of the soil is exhausted within five to eight years. This fertility must then be restored by leaving the land fallow for periods that vary according to the initial degree of fertility of the soil, the surface area and the pressure of cultivation and population. The dominant method of cultivation is a combination of crops. Quite often, for instance, millet is combined with other crops such as niebe, groundnut, sorghum, Guinea sorrel, sesame or maize. The combination might also consist of two varieties of the same species. In some regions of Mali, early millet is often planted alongside late millet. This habit of combining crops is so widespread that it is even doubtful whether single crops are ever grown. The average area under cultivation, for instance in Mali, varies between five and eight hectares. Yields are low, averaging between 600 to 800 kg/ha for millet and sorghum.

From the point of view of land cultivation, there are two types of fields in Mali. The '*soforos*' or 'home fields', which are generally well fertilized (with household refuse, park compost, etc). These in-fields are used chiefly to grow early varieties to cover food requirements in the transition period between crops. Early maize is much used for this purpose in the south of the country.

Further out there are the '*koungo foro*' or 'bush fields', which produce relatively low yields. These are used more to grow late varieties. Field activities take up much of the agricultural calendar. As winter approaches, time is spent gathering straw and clearing new fields of tree stumps. When trees are cleared, the peasants tend to leave some of the useful trees standing, like the karite, balanzan, baobab and nere. Only bushes are cut back to ground level.

Even when ploughing begins, the balanzan and karite trees tend to be left standing. Farmers find they can manage with the trees in the fields. Very early on, the balanzan trees were found to have a fertilizing effect. Also from very early times, the significance of karite, baobab and nere for human food became established. As in the case of the balanzan, however, the way they affect pedoclimatic factors and crop yields has not yet been studied.

Biodiversity in West and Central Africa

The region of West and Central Africa is a major centre for diversity. It is the main source of diversity for African rice, millet, yam, sorghum, niebe, fonio and others. The peasants have helped develop diversity within these different crops. Local genetic resources provide a solid base for the improvement of varieties.

Long years of cultivation practice and/or cohabitation have produced many local cultivars that are well adapted to their environment. The farmers' preference for these cultivars, despite the widespread introduction of new elite varieties, has attracted the attention of breeders and raises the question of the continued management of these genetic variations.

After the drought of the 1970s, a large-scale programme to gather plant genetic resources was implemented in West and Central Africa under the patronage of the Food and Agriculture Organization (FAO). From the collected material, the International Agricultural Research Centres were able to build up many gene banks. Yet in Africa at present few of the national research institutes possess any of the material gathered during the programme. In many countries the farmers are the only source of material. According to estimates, 40 per cent of the world economy is based on biological products and processes. In Africa in general, and in West and Central Africa in particular, which is little industrialized, the population depends on biodiversity for 85 to 90 per cent of their basic needs.

The socio-economic background of production and marketing

Most of the grain production is consumed domestically. A very small percentage is marketed. From 1960 to 1994, the producer price of a kilo of millet rose from 5 CFA francs to 60 CFA francs, while the price of a kilo of combined cotton fertilizer rose from 26.5 CFA francs to 120 CFA francs. During the same period, the price of a multi-purpose cultivator rose from 6500 CFA francs to 69,205 CFA francs. In those conditions, peasants can hardly be expected to intensify their system of production. The only easily accessible input is seed. This is either produced on the land itself or is derived from exchange with neighbours. Any attempt to intensify through inputs, equipment or seed in this case is simply unrealistic. We are in a situation, it should not be forgotten, in which people live on less than US$2 a day.

The farmers' purchasing power is so weak, and as a consequence also their ability to purchase equipment and external inputs, that in many regions the *daba* (hoe) is the only tool they have available. They have to combat weeds manually and with great difficulty, an activity which causes delays in the farming cycle.

Little income is derived from the sale of agricultural products, especially grain, being rarely enough to undertake investments in better production. There are no proper credit facilities which would enable farmers to acquire inputs and equipment or to share the risk of bad harvests. The farmers are reduced mainly to using resources produced on the land itself (manure and seed) and hand tools (such as the *daba*). They do their best in the circumstances to optimize all local resources.

With the growth in population, however, needs have been increasing, with greater pressure being brought to bear on resources. As a result, traditional systems become inadequate and harmful for the environment unless appropriate solutions are found. In the unfavourable environment of the Sudano-Sahelian region, producers have developed different strategies. They face a variety of risks, of which external actors are often unaware. As a result, they use different strategies to reduce the impact of those risks on their activities. One such strategy is to limit the effects of risk. This involves practices requiring relatively low investments in terms of labour and capital. An example is the widespread preference for combined crops. To offset the effects of uncertain rainfall, producers grow different varieties. Another strategy is to circumvent risks, such as through diversifying agricultural and non-farming activities. In practice, farmers often prefer to opt for less costly combinations.

The seed system in West and Central Africa

Seed constitutes the most important production factor and the cheapest production input in sub-Saharan African. The seed system is made up of two parts, which overlap in many areas.

The first is the formal system, which exists in practically all countries, is generally state-run, and is based on the Western model of production and distribution. The formal system may involve such bodies as the research unit in charge of creating (prospecting, introducing and selecting) and producing prebase or base seed, and the national seed service in charge of producing certified seed. The seed itself may come from government-run institutions, such as state farms, seed farms or seed reproduction centres, or networks of seed farmers. Seed quality is checked and certified by a specialized service that is independent of the research unit, the seed service and the dissemination service.

Generally speaking, formal systems do not operate satisfactorily despite considerable investment in them by the state and its partners. Among the reasons put forward for this are the difficulty in estimating supply and demand in the seed market, the low incomes of farmers, the poor yield levels of the varieties available, the lack of qualified personnel, and the lack of outlets for any surplus production.

The second is the informal system, which is fairly widespread throughout the area. Peasants gather inflorescences in their fields (ears, panicles or pods), which they keep as seeds until the next sowing period. In this way the peasants supply their own seed from what their land produces. It is only in the event of a disaster (such as drought, floods or war) that seeding poses a serious problem. Quite often peasants exchange seed among themselves. Seed acquired in this way is first assessed over a small area before being applied to larger plots. Little seed is traded. In some areas, seed is considered as a divine gift and peasants often say that selling it brings bad luck. There is no quality control, or rather the recipient himself checks the quality of the seed when he uses it. If the seed is not of good quality (especially from the point of view of germination), the peasant will stop using it. In this sort of system, the peasants attach little importance to particular varieties. They may well mix a number of varieties or even different species as mentioned above. Homogeneity is not considered to be a sign of quality.

In the case of integrated supply networks (such as cotton or groundnut companies), the seed distributed by the controlling organization must satisfy homogeneity and purity requirements in order to meet the standards laid down by the state's regulatory and supervisory bodies. In fact, it is the companies which produce certified seeds from the base seed supplied by the research units, which also distribute the seed together with other inputs (such as fertilizers and pesticide). In some cases, the controlling company buys up the whole output (especially cotton producers).

Demand for seed

According to some authors, the seed sector in West and Central Africa, given its importance in relation to other sectors such as agricultural research and dissemination, has received little attention. With regard to demand for seed, Tripp notes that in Kenya, Malawi, Zambia and Zimbabwe, various reasons are given for a request for seed (Tripp, 2000). In West and Central Africa, farmers order seed either following a disaster, or because of the poor performance of their variety, or to try out new strains of a seed after seeing it advertised or after attending an open day at the research centre.

From the 1980s onwards, the seed sector was liberalized in many countries as a result of sectoral adjustment. In some countries, however, the sector still remains in the public domain. Because of these shortcomings and the excessive degree of centralization, non-governmental organizations (NGOs) have taken over the distribution of seed in many countries from the state.

An estimated 120 million tonnes of seed is used each year. In the developing countries, about 80 per cent of the seed for foodstuffs is derived from farm production. Table 12.1 shows that two West African countries, Niger and Senegal, are typical in this regard.

Most of the seed used in Africa is produced by farmers and distributed according to traditional systems of exchange. Very little seed is distributed via the market.

The private sector plays very little part in the process. The main reasons given are the low prices available and poorly organized supply channels. In West and Central Africa, as pointed out above, production systems are very varied and one might go as far as to say that each area of land has its own range of varieties. Considering also the variability of the start of the rainy season, it is likely that the farmer might change varieties at any time. It is therefore practically impossible to plan the supply of seed in advance. Many private companies, which are very active in the pesticide market in West and Central Africa, are generally little involved in the seed market. These companies are much more active in Southern and Eastern Africa, especially in Zimbabwe and South Africa, where the system of production and dissemination of hybrids is well advanced.

THE IMPLICATIONS OF INTELLECTUAL PROPERTY RIGHTS

Does the IPR system encourage innovation and the spread of knowledge? Can it lead to an increase in biodiversity? Can IPRs be used to protect the knowledge and biological resources of local communities? These questions are being asked nowadays and are discussed below.

Table 12.1 *Sources of millet and groundnut seed in Niger and Senegal (%)*

Source	*Niger*		*Senegal*	
	1996	*1997*	*1996*	*1997*
Millet				
– Own production	93	82	66	57
– Family and friends	2	7	0	1
– Village market	5	9	31	39
– Seed sector	0	2	2	3
Groundnut				
– Own production	89	82	54	36
– Family and friends	3	4	0	1
— Village market	8	14	28	38
– Seed sector	0	0	18	25

Source: WCA-ICRISAT Survey 1997, see Ndjeunga et al (2000)

For agricultural research

Agricultural research first made a formal appearance in French-speaking sub-Saharan Africa before independence. But the first research institutions specializing in tropical agriculture appeared during the Second World War and gradually spread throughout the colonies. When they became independent, most countries made an effort to set up their own specialized agricultural research institutions according to their own methods and systems.

However, despite the considerable role of indigenous and rural communities in developing local crop varieties, research programmes initially focused on introduced genetic material from the US or Asia. But after several years of experimenting, it was found that the new varieties did not suit the tastes of consumers and were ill adapted to the region. After these setbacks, the importance of local varieties was brought home to breeders operating in the continent. In these circumstances, one may wonder who should be entitled to the plant variety certificates if the farmers also contribute to developing new varieties.

The traditional free exchange of genetic material and related information has contributed a great deal to the dissemination of varieties. An example of the frequency of these exchanges in West Africa is the spread of the mango tree and the neem. So while exchanges have never been subject to constraint, IPRs might seriously restrict the freedom to innovate and to operate. In a region where most of the people live on less than US$1 a day, it becomes meaningless and unacceptable to try to prevent such people from selling part of their production in the form of seed, especially if the farmers draw no distinction between the use of land for foodstuffs or for seed. It is also most unlikely that this prohibition will encourage the national or international private sector to invest in the seed system.

Agricultural research in West and Central Africa is to a large extent financed from public funds, and its results are made available to farmers free of charge. But nowadays publicly funded agricultural research is short of funds. The decline in public sector funding has given rise to new partnerships with the private sector. Such interactions could contribute to the development of knowledge and the transfer of know-how as long as the rules are clearly set out beforehand. In particular, the private sector may have a part to play in the area of cash crops, such as cotton and groundnut, where selection criteria are determined industrially. But in our opinion, traditional food crops have never been attractive to the private sector, and there is no reason to believe that the existence of IPRs will encourage the development of seeds of such crops. Moreover, an IPR regime could lead to a breeders' monopoly. Producers would then be excluded from the system and there is no certainty that the private sector will fill the gap.

For the preservation of agro-biodiversity

Do IPRs aggravate genetic erosion or does diversified breeding add to genetic diversity? Opinions in this respect are divided. Although the direct effects of IPRs on genetic erosion may be minimal, the indirect effects might be considerable. IPRs could stimulate the breeding of commercial plants by diverting efforts to the development of the most marketable varieties, that is, crops which are generally cultivated over large areas and whose characteristics are perfectly adapted to the requirements of commercial farmers and the processing industries. Crops offering less marketing potential, but which may be suited to specific ecological niches or to the needs of small farmers, may then be neglected and gradually abandoned altogether.

We take the view that IPRs may have the effect of excluding farmers and restricting them to using local varieties. This may be beneficial for the conservation of genetic resources, but could raise an acute problem of food security in a rapidly growing demographic environment. However, if farmers were allowed to take part in plant breeding programmes, this could help to marry enhanced productivity with conservation. Producers should not be limited to merely preserving biological diversity. In the world of farming, there is no such thing as conservation in the strict sense. It is more a matter of constantly and gradually improving genetic material in a situation where there is a substantial exchange of genes between varieties.

In view of the agricultural and ecological diversity available in West and Central Africa, it would be a good idea to include farmers in the breeding team, where they would be considered as breeders on an equal footing with others. In many countries, farmers have been increasingly involved in plant breeding activities. The necessary rules and regulations would still remain to be decided on such matters as rights and remuneration.

REFERENCES

Tripp, R (2000) 'Strategies for seed system development in sub-Saharan Africa. A study of Kenya, Malawi, Zambia and Zimbabwe', *Working paper series* 2, Bulawayo: ICRISAT.

Ndjeunga, J, Anand Kumar, K and Ntare, B R (2000) *Comparative Analysis of Seed Systems in Niger and Senegal*, Working Paper Series no 3, Socio-economics and Policy Program, ICRISAT, Hyderabad, India

Chapter 13

Access to Medicines and Public Policy Safeguards under TRIPS

K Balasubramaniam

THE HEALTH NEEDS OF PEOPLE IN SOUTH AND SOUTHEAST ASIA

It needs to be underscored that access to medicines is a means to an end and not an end in itself. The end is health for all. It is therefore very important not to discuss access to medicines in isolation, but in the wider context of health for all, which is our final goal.

Poverty is the deadliest disease of all and the commonest cause of ill-health in the world. The biological manifestations of this socio-economic disease are referred to as 'diseases of poverty' and are the common communicable diseases. The consequences are very low standards of health characterized by unacceptably high infant, maternal and general mortality rates, and high prevalence of malnutrition of children under five years. A majority of South and Southeast Asian countries are poverty stricken.

In spite of special UN programmes to arrest and reverse the deterioration in the socio-economic situation of the least developed countries (LDCs), these countries are lagging further and further behind and are in some cases moving backwards. In addition they are growing in numbers. The list began with 24 countries in 1971. The most recent review was done in April 2000. At present there are 49 LDCs with a population of 620 million. The original list in 1971 had four LDCs in South and Southeast Asia. They were Bhutan, Lao PDR, Maldives and Nepal. Three more have been downgraded to LDCs. They are Bangladesh, Cambodia and Myanmar. The UN Committee for Development Policy has identified India, Indonesia, Pakistan, Sri Lanka and Vietnam as countries that meet some but not all of the criteria for inclusion on the list of LDCs.

If the economies of these countries continue to deteriorate prompted mostly by rising debt, falling commodity prices and sharp declines in development aid and foreign investments, the ranks of LDCs will continue to grow during the next decade. The future, therefore, looks very bleak unless realistic poverty eradication measures are put into effect. Unfortunately it would appear that responsibility for poverty eradication has been given to the rich countries. Although the G8 governments have committed to halving world poverty and reducing child mortality by two-thirds by 2015, the reality seems to be different. The 2001 Human Development Report warns that the goal of reducing infant and maternal mortality is nowhere near this target. Ninety-three countries with almost two-thirds of the world's population will miss the target to reduce mortality of children under five by two-thirds.

About 600 million people in the region live below the poverty line. The population in the region is 1735 million and constitutes about 30 per cent of the world's population and approximately 50 per cent of the world's poor. The higher incidence of poverty in the region is due not only to low GNP but also to the high maldistribution of income among population subgroups in these countries.

The only source of access to medicines for the poor is the public sector, where medicines are given free. But the public sector health expenditure in countries of the region is very low. The public sector drug budgets are minimal. This is the reason why over 2 billion people have no regular access to essential medicines. Indeed, in 6 out of the 15 South and Southeast Asian developing countries, public health expenditure is less than 1 per cent of the GDP, and in 13 countries it is less than 2 per cent. Bhutan and Maldives, both LDCs, are the only two countries that spend 5.1 per cent of their GDP each on public health.

According to the World Health Organization (WHO) nearly 90 member states have national drug policies in place or in preparation. Three out of four countries, over 140 in total, have adopted national essential drug lists. These national lists are widely used for drug purchases, training and public education about medicines. Nearly 100 governments have developed national treatment guidelines. There seems to be an apparent contradiction between the success of the WHO Essential Drugs Programme and the fact that more than half the world's population has no regular access to essential drugs. Essential drug lists and national drug policies apply only to the public health sector in all developing countries and not to the private sector. Essential drug lists and national drug lists are irrelevant to the private sector, which controls about 50 to 90 per cent of the pharmaceutical market in these countries.

Among the further constraints to regular access to medicines are the absence of national health insurance systems in any of the countries in the region, and of effective price regulatory and control mechanisms for drugs in these countries, except India. Yet despite the constraints to access, one redeeming feature is the relatively low prices in the region due to the generic manufacture and competitive national drug industry in India. This is possible because the Indian patent system still does not provide patent protection for pharmaceutical products. However, when India changes its patent law to provide product patents in conformity with the TRIPS Agreement in 2005, the national generic drugs industry may collapse and drug prices will rise, depriving more people of regular access to essential drugs.

TRIPS AND THE IMPACT OF PATENTS ON DRUG PRICES

Several studies based on critical analysis of empirical data have reported on the negative impact of strong pharmaceutical protection on public health, specifically on the prices of medicines. TRIPS requires that developing countries have to allow 20 year patent protection for pharmaceutical products. Of the 15 South and Southeast Asian developing countries, all are WTO members except Bhutan, Cambodia, Lao PDR and Nepal, which are observers.

According to a World Bank economist the minimum welfare loss to a sample of developing countries (Argentina, Brazil, India, Mexico, Korea and Taiwan) would amount to a minimum of US$3.5 billion and a maximum of US$10.8 billion, while the gains to foreign patent owners would be between US$2.1 billion and US$14.4 billion (Nogues, 1990). A 'national health disaster' has been anticipated by the Indian Drug Manufacturers Association (IDMA) as a result of the implementation of the TRIPS Agreement in that country, where only 30 per cent of the population can afford modern medicines in spite of the fact that drug prices in India are among the lowest in the world. A comparison of prices of drugs between India and countries where patent protection exists indicate that in some cases they are up to 41 times costlier in countries with patent protection (National Working Group on Patent Laws, 1993). A study by an IMF economist reported that drug prices in Malaysia, where patent protection exists, were from 20 to 760 per cent higher than in India (Subramaniam, 1990). Further studies by the same author looked at the likely impact of pharmaceutical product patents in small and large countries, in cases where either a perfectly competitive market or a duopolistic market becomes a monopoly under patents. Welfare and price effects were found to be negative for a number of Asian countries. Price increases estimated for patented drugs ranged from 5 to 67 per cent. Annual welfare losses for India ranged between US$162 million and US$1261 million and annual profit transfer to foreign firms between US$101 million and US$839 million (Subramaniam, 1995a,b). Price increases of drugs resulting from the introduction of product patents in Egypt were estimated to be five to six fold as compared to non-patented products (El Shinway et al, 1997). A study conducted in Argentina estimated that the introduction of pharmaceutical product patents in the country would imply an annual additional expenditure of US$194 million with a reduction of 45.5 per cent in the consumption of medicines as a result of price increases of around 270 per cent (Challu, 1991).

Table 13.1 gives the retail prices of 100 tablets of Zantac (ranitidine) manufactured and marketed by the same manufacturer, showing that these vary from US$2 in India to US$183 in Mongolia, a least developed country. It is noteworthy also that Bangladesh, India and Nepal do not provide product

Table 13.1 *The retail prices in US$ of 100 tablets of 150mg Zantac in two developed and nine developing countries in the Asia-Pacific region*

	Minimum daily wage US$	GNP per Capita US$	Zantac tablets 150mg US$
Australia	46	18,720	23
New Zealand	32	14,340	21
Bangladesh	2.1	240	9
India	1.3	340	2
Indonesia	0.5	980	41
Malaysia	na	3890	55
Mongolia	0.8	310	183
Nepal	1.6	200	3
Pakistan	2.2	460	22
Philippines	5.0	1050	63
Sri Lanka	1.4	700	61

Source: Bala, K, Lanza O and Rani Kaur S (1998)

patents and have the lowest prices. Also, Australia and New Zealand have policies of regulating drug prices. In the other countries there is price discrimination and profit maximization. Evidently, prices are determined by what the markets can bear.

Initiatives by the WHO

At a meeting held in Bangkok, Thailand in February 2001, the WHO initiated a process to monitor and analyse the impact of multilateral trade agreements on access to drugs in partnership with four WHO collaborating centres in Brazil, Spain, Thailand and the United Kingdom.[1] The meeting was in response to the mandate the World Health Assembly gave to the WHO in its Resolution WHA 52.19 on the Revised Drug Strategy in May 1999. The main emphasis of the meeting was to develop a framework of operations for a nascent Network for Monitoring the Impact of Globalization and TRIPS on Access to Medicines. The meeting established that the network would undertake research through the individual and collective work of the four collaborating centres, and shed light on four questions: (i) how is patenting affecting drug pricing? (ii) how are patents and enhanced intellectual property protections affecting the rate of introduction of generic drugs? (iii) are TRIPS and expanded intellectual property protections spurring development of drugs for neglected diseases? and (iv) are TRIPS and expanded intellectual property protection contributing to an increase or decrease in the transfer of technology and direct foreign investment in developing countries? Critical analysis of the questions will hopefully provide adequate justification for a review and revision of TRIPS.

Implementing TRIPS for access to essential medicines

WTO members must implement the minimum standards set by TRIPS. Nonetheless, there are opportunities to develop appropriate national strategies within its framework. The impact of TRIPS will therefore depend on how individual countries choose the strategies best suited to their technological, commercial and economic development and thereby achieve the country's policy goals. The major policy goal in the pharmaceutical sector is to ensure regular access to essential drugs to meet the real health needs of all the people.

The two possible options to ensure regular access are national production by state-owned firms, national companies, subsidiaries of foreign companies or joint ventures, and imports. These are not mutually exclusive. A country's stage of technological development will determine the options. India is the only country in the region which is self-reliant and can meet its total requirements with national production. The smaller LDCs, Bhutan, Cambodia, Lao PDR and Maldives, may have to import their total requirements. All other countries will use both options. Having selected the policy options, a country needs to create appropriate legal structures and provisions, and design administrative measures required to implement the legal provisions taking TRIPS into account and the clarifications provided in the Doha Declaration (see below). Unfortunately, the technical assistance given by the World Intellectual Property Organization (WIPO) and the World Trade Organization (WTO) to developing countries with respect to creating national intellectual property rights (IPR) legislation seems to be more concerned with how to comply with TRIPS but not to make best use of the agreement's safeguards.

TRIPS, like all other WTO agreements, is an agreement on a legal framework. Its implications will be decided by the resolution of disputes. That makes case law and the power of the parties involved of great importance. A single set of minimum rules may seem to create a level playing field, since one set of rules applies to all. But the game is hardly fair when the players are of such unequal strength economically and institutionally. The US spends about US$1 billion to maintain its patent office. Even this office grants faulty patents that were subsequently revoked or invalidated in the courts. For a large number of developing countries, enacting, implementing and enforcing an efficient and effective intellectual property regime will put stress and strain on the very limited resources and administrative skills available to them. Moreover, the very high costs of disputes with the world's leading nations are frightening and discourage these countries from asserting their rights. Very few developing countries have enacted appropriate national legislation including the safeguards provided in TRIPS. There is at present very little if any empirical evidence available on the effects of such legislative changes.

Compulsory licensing

Until quite recently, it was not only developing countries that refused to provide patent protection on pharmaceutical products. Many of today's advanced economies refused to grant such patents throughout the 19th century and much of the 20th, or found legal and illegal ways of circumventing them. They formalized and enforced IPRs gradually as they shifted from being net users of intellectual property to net producers. Several European countries including France, Germany and Switzerland offered what is now standard protection only in the 1960s and 1970s.

During the 1970s India, Brazil, Argentina, Mexico and the Andean Pact countries introduced laws with weaker patent protection in the pharmaceutical sector. India passed its Patents Act in 1970 following the German system of allowing process patents but not product patents. Protection was for seven years. This law became the foundation for a highly successful generics industry. A country with some of the highest drug prices became, within about two decades, a country with the lowest prices.

A study undertaken by WIPO in 1988 for the negotiating group that was dealing with TRIPS in the Uruguay Round revealed that of the 98 state parties to the Paris Convention, 49 excluded pharmaceutical products from protection (Mills, 1985). Developing countries and generic manufacturers became a threat to the Western pharmaceutical cartels that had dominated the international pharmaceutical industry. Following the recommendations by UNCTAD for a revision of the Paris Convention, the negotiations began in 1980. The fiercest debates took place on compulsory licensing. Attempts to revise the Paris Convention broke down and no revision was ever agreed. Negotiations on international IPR standards then proceeded instead under the auspices not of WIPO, which was responsible for administering the Paris Convention (as well as several other IPR treaties), but of the General Agreement on Tariffs and Trade (GATT), in which the US was a highly influential actor. TRIPS removed those very provisions that enabled the development of the pharmaceutical industry in developing countries, namely exclusions of pharmaceuticals from patentability and remedies against non-working of patents.

Many industrial countries include compulsory licensing and parallel importing in their law and practice, as part of their national strategy for using IPRs for achieving their policy goals. Yet under intense pressure from some leading countries to introduce legislation beyond that required by TRIPS ('TRIPS-plus'), many developing countries have legislated themselves into a position of disadvantage. Since the adoption of TRIPS, Canada, Japan, the UK and the US have issued compulsory licences for pharmaceuticals. In contrast, not one compulsory licence has been issued south of the equator. What developing countries in South and Southeast Asia need are alternative legislative models that will avoid emphasis on litigation and create provisions suited to their needs. Unfortunately, Article 31(f) of TRIPS limits the use of compulsory licensing by developing countries by stipulating that a compulsory licensee's use of the patent must be 'predominantly for the supply of the domestic market of the Member authorizing such use'. The requirement that the licensee must 'predominantly' supply the local market limits the capacity of many members to use this provision because at most only ten developing countries have the capacity to copy patented pharmaceutical products. Moreover, the smaller importing members will find it increasingly hard to source these products, while the diminishing number of exporter countries may find themselves with limited capacity to establish economies of scale that would make supply cost-effective. Perhaps one solution is to propose amending the TRIPS Agreement to delete 31(f). This would permit compulsory licensing predominantly for export and eliminate the most serious obstacle to manufacture and trade in public health-related products. In view of the time constraints, a waiver of Article 31(f) might be adopted pending such an amendment.

The Human Development Report 2001 offers some recommendations towards the creation of a legal structure to include compulsory licensing suited to developing countries. First, the best option is an administrative approach that can be streamlined and procedural. Overly legalistic and expensive-to-administer systems should be avoided. Second, TRIPS gives governments broad powers to authorize the use of patents for public, non-commercial use and this authorization can be fast-tracked without usual negotiations. No developing country should have public use provisions weaker than German, Irish, UK or US law on such practice. Third, legislation should permit production for export when (i) lack of competition in a class of drugs has given the producer global market power that impedes access for alternative drugs, or (ii) when the legitimate interests of the patent owner are protected in the export market. Fourth, compensation needs to be predictable and easy to administer. Royalty guidelines reduce uncertainty and speed decisions. For example, Germany has used rates from 2 to 10 per cent, while in Canada, the government used to pay royalties of 4 per cent. The onus should be on the patent holder to back up claims that the royalty is inadequate. This will promote transparency and discourage intimidating but unjust claims.

At a 2002 workshop on TRIPS and Public Health, which was organized by the Third World Network and held in Geneva, a draft discussion paper on issues in formulating appropriate national legal provisions and procedures on patents and public health was presented. The following was a suggested model provision for parallel imports:

> *It shall not be an infringement of a patent to import, offer for sale, sell or use:*
>
> - *any patented product;*
>
> *or*
>
> - *any product obtained directly by means of the patented process or to which the patented process has been applied, which has been put on the market in any country outside of .... (name of country), by the patent holder, or with his consent or by another party authorized by a compulsory licence given on grounds to correct anti-competitive practice.*

Compulsory licensing and parallel imports are measures to improve access to essential drugs. But these are not permanent sustainable solutions completely under the control of individual countries. Strengthening the technological, economic and commercial development of the pharmaceutical sector will enable developing countries to build and strengthen their pharmaceutical manufacturing capacities. This is the only way to ensure a truly competitive market for pharmaceuticals. The smaller developing countries, about 60 of them, do not have the resources to set up domestic pharmaceutical industries or to administer an IPR system designed to make use of compulsory licensing and parallel importing.

The TRIPS Agreement prevents developing countries from enacting national legislation, which can be policy instruments in developing and strengthening their pharmaceutical industry. In this respect, the 2001 Doha Declaration on the TRIPS Agreement and Public Health only clarifies TRIPS, but does not address some of the problems developing countries face. One may refer here to the faulty patent granting systems that fail to adequately screen applications for novelty and inventive step. While this is an issue even in the US, the inadequate capacity of developing countries to process large numbers of applications disclosing obscure and very lengthy specifications is clear. To illustrate this concern, it has been reported that in 2000, WIPO received 30 patent applications over 1000 pages long with several reaching 140,000 pages.

NOTES

1 Network for Monitoring the Impact of Globalization and TRIPS on Access to Medicines. Health Economics and Drugs EDM Series No 11, Report of a Meeting, February 2001, Bangkok, Thailand. World Health Organization, 2002.

REFERENCES

Bala K, Lanza O and Rani Kaur S (1998) 'Retail drug prices: The law of the jungle', *HAI News* 100.

Challu, P (1991) 'The consequences of pharmaceutical product patenting', *World Competition* 15(2).

El Shinway, Assa, Sala, Hassan, Hassan, Ibrahim Ali and El Sawly, Tayseer (1997) *On the Egyptian Pharmaceutical Sector (mimeo),* Cairo.

Mills, D M (1985) 'Patents and exploitation of technology transferred to developing countries (in particular those of Africa)', *Industrial Property* 24.

National Working Group on Patent Laws (1993) *Patent Regime in TRIPS: Critical Analysis*, New Delhi.

Nogues, J (1990) 'Patents and pharmaceutical drugs: Understanding the pressure on developing countries', *Journal of World Trade Law* 24(6).

Subramaniam, A (1990) 'TRIPS and the paradigm of GATT: A tropical temperate view', *The World Economy* 13(4).

Subramaniam, A (1995a) 'Putting some numbers on the TRIPS pharmaceutical debate', *International Journal of Technology Management* 10(2/3).

Subramaniam, A (1995b) 'Trade-related intellectual property rights and Asian developing countries: An analytical view', paper submitted to the Conference on Emerging Global Trading Environment and Developing Asia, International Monetary Fund, Manila.

Chapter 14

Intellectual Property Rights and Public Health in the Revised Bangui Agreement

Rosine Jourdain

MAJOR PUBLIC HEALTH CHALLENGES FOR AFRICAN COUNTRIES

The African countries are facing major challenges in the area of public health. Generally speaking, the health situation appears to be closely related to the country's socio-economic circumstances. A very high prevalence of poverty combined with a very low level of literacy correlates with alarming health indicators in such areas as infant mortality and life expectancy. Priority health problems to be overcome include generally high morbidity and mortality, high incidence of HIV/AIDS, poor geographic or financial access by the population to health services, poor quality of healthcare, and inadequate inter-sectoral coordination, collaboration and human resource management.

In the case of AIDS, UNAIDS estimates that out of a total of 40 million infected people, 36 million who live in developing countries have no access to anti-retroviral drugs, which could prolong their lives. In fact, access to anti-retroviral drugs is denied to 96 per cent of HIV carriers, totalling between 5 and 7 million persons, who are in need of immediate treatment. In 2001, AIDS killed 3 million persons and now tops the list of causes of mortality in Africa.

REVISION OF THE BANGUI AGREEMENT

In French-speaking West Africa, patents are issued by a regional office, the African Intellectual Property Organization (OAPI), whose headquarters are in Yaoundé, Cameroon. Until 1962, patents were issued by the French National Industrial Property Institute, which served as a national office for all the countries then belonging to the French Union. When they became independent in the early 1960s, the French-speaking African countries decided to set up a common structure, which would act as a National Industrial Property Office for each country. The OAMPI (African and Malagasy Industrial Property Office) was set up as a result in September 1962 under the Libreville Agreement.

Subsequently, the OAMPI was replaced by the OAPI when a new agreement, the Bangui Agreement, was signed in 1977. The OAPI now has 16 members: Benin, Burkina Faso, Cameroon, Central African Republic, Chad, Congo (Brazzaville), Côte d'Ivoire, Equatorial Guinea, Gabon, Guinea, Guinea Bissau, Mali, Mauritania, Niger, Senegal and Togo. Among these countries, four are classified as developing countries (Cameroon, Congo, Côte d'Ivoire and Gabon), while the rest are least developed countries (LDCs).

In OAPI member countries, patents are now issued under the terms of the Bangui Agreement, which has the force of national law for all member states. The OAPI receives all patent applications and issues regional patents, which automatically take effect in all 16 countries. Once they have been issued by the OAPI, patents are then managed by individual states at national level. All matters concerning existing patents (such as infringements and voluntary and compulsory licences) are dealt with by the civil courts in individual countries.

The establishment of the World Trade Organization (WTO) led in 1999 to a revision of the 1977 Bangui Agreement. Under the terms of its Article 43, the Revised Bangui Agreement of 1999 was to enter into force two months after the deposit of instruments of ratification by at least two-thirds of the member states, which occurred on 28 February 2002. Annexes 1 to 8 entered into force at that date by decision of the Administrative Council, while Annexes 9 and 10, concerning layout designs of integrated circuits and plant variety protection respectively, were left for a later date.

THE ORIGINAL BANGUI AGREEMENT OF 1977

According to the 1977 Bangui Agreement, a patent could be granted for any invented product (including a pharmaceutical) or process, provided that the invention was new, involved an inventive step and had an industrial application. A patent was granted for a period of ten years from the time the patent application was filed. The Bangui Agreement reflected a desire to secure a balance between the public interest and the rights granted to patent owners. Thus, a number of clauses were aimed at offsetting the monopoly created by patents. Thus, the duration and validity of patents depended on the way they were worked locally and the benefits they brought to the population.

According to the agreement, an invention was considered new 'if it has not been anticipated by prior art'. This meant that the invention should not have been made available to the public, in any way whatever, in any country of the world, before the filing date of the patent application. It was therefore theoretically impossible to obtain a patent for a drug that was already on the market. However, in practice, the OAPI granted patents without detailed examination of applications and without checking the novelty or the inventive quality of inventions. This was due to the shortage of human and technical resources. The implication of this was that any patent granted by OAPI might be contested and annulled by the civil courts of an OAPI member state if it could be shown that the patented invention was not really new or inventive at the time the application was filed.

The life of the patent could be extended at the request of the owner for two successive five-year periods. The owner had to submit proof of the local industrial working of the invention to OAPI, in other words, of the fact that the patented product was being manufactured, or that the patented process was being worked on the territory of one of the OAPI member states, unless there were legitimate reasons for not doing so. The purpose of this clause was to ensure that patents made an effective contribution to the industrial development of countries of the region and not merely to grant a monopoly to their owners. If within five years following the grant of the patent the owner had not worked his invention or caused it to be worked locally, without legitimate reason, then no action for infringement could be brought before a court. This clause was particularly important in the pharmaceutical sector, where the supply of medicines in the region often depends on imports. It therefore appeared that, if a patented invention was not worked locally, the owner would lose his exclusive rights over the patented invention. It would then be possible to import the same medicines manufactured by others without incurring any penalty.

Any person resident in an OAPI member state could file an application for a compulsory licence. The request could be made only after the expiration of a period of four years (from the date of the filing of the patent application), or three years (from the date of the grant of the patent). In addition, certain conditions had to be met. First, the applicant had to have previously applied unsuccessfully for a licence under contract from the patent owner. Second, the patented invention had not been industrially worked on the territory of a member state. Third, local working of the patented invention had not 'on reasonable terms' met 'the demand for the protected product', or had been prevented or hindered by importation of the protected product. Fourth, a refusal of the owner to grant a voluntary licence was prejudicial to 'the establishment or development of industrial or commercial activities' in the country. Fifth, the petitioner was able himself to work the invention locally in such a way as to remedy the insufficiencies that justified the grant of a compulsory licence. These clauses emphasized the fact that a patent granted by the OAPI conferred not only rights on its owner but also obligations in regard of the public and could not impede access to patented products. However, a compulsory licence could not be granted to import a patented product.

If the compulsory licence was granted, the civil court dealing with the case specified what rights were conferred by the licence, its scope and the period for which it was granted. It is worth noting here that decisions concerning compulsory licences took effect only on the territory of the state where the decision was delivered.

Ex officio licences could be obtained only from the state, 'for the exploitation of a patented invention of vital importance to … public health', while compulsory licences were open to everyone. At the request of the ministry of health, the minister in charge of intellectual property could notify the owner of a drug patent that his invention had to be worked in order to satisfy the needs of public health. If the summons was not followed by action within 12 months, or if the working of the patent undertaken was seriously prejudicial to public health, the Bangui Agreement recognized the government's right to work the patented invention or cause it to be worked.

These provisions could serve as a legal basis for improving access to vital medicines whenever a patent constituted the main obstacle to such access. Moreover, the 1977 Bangui Agreement specified that an ex officio licence could be obtained for the purpose of importing the patented product, which was particularly important for countries that had no pharmaceutical industry.

In conclusion, the 1977 Bangui Agreement recognized the rights of inventors and encouraged innovation, while at the same time, through some of its provisions, ensuring that benefits accrued to the population at large.

THE REVISION OF THE BANGUI AGREEMENT

Following the creation of the WTO, the OAPI members were obliged to comply fully with TRIPS by 1 January 2000 if they were developing countries, and by 2006 if they were LDCs. The main changes to be introduced related to the duration of patents, their nature and the withdrawal of the local working condition.

The revised agreement specifies that a patent may henceforth be granted not only to protect a product or a process, but also to protect 'a use thereof'. In the pharmaceutical area, this means that patents may be granted for the use or therapeutic prescription of a medicine. This sort of patent will constitute a further obstacle to access to medicines in cases where the patent application, for instance for different prescriptions, has not been lodged at the same time as the patent covering the basic molecule of the medicine. When the first patent protecting the molecule expires, the use of that molecule for unpatented prescriptions remains forbidden until the second patent has expired.

The Revised Bangui Agreement extends the term of protection of patents automatically to 20 years from the application's filing date. Such protection is no longer subject to the local working of a patented invention. Moreover, the revised text specifies in its transitional provisions that any patent granted or recognized prior to the signing of the agreement shall remain in force for a period of 20 years as from its filing date. This means that patents granted for an initial term of ten years are automatically extended. For example, a patent on the azythromicine molecule, marketed under the trade name of Zythromax and used to treat various infections including trachoma, was granted by the OAPI to Pfizer in 1988 for a period of ten years. When the patent expired in 1998, the generic version manufactured by Wockhardt brought the price down from US$2.5 to US$0.175, which meant that 14 times more patients could be treated (200,000 patients were treated in Mali for trachoma by Médecins Sans Frontières in 2002).

The revised version of the agreement introduced some limitations on the rights conferred on patent owners. Parallel imports are admitted only among

OAPI member countries. This means it is possible for an OAPI member country to import a patented medicine which is sold more cheaply by the same laboratory in another OAPI member country. Also, 'acts in relation to a patented invention that are carried out for experimental purposes' do not constitute a violation of the patent owner's rights. Experiments performed on products patented by manufacturers of generic medicines, if any, are recognized as legitimate.

The conditions governing the grant of a compulsory licence, which becomes a non-voluntary licence under the terms of the revised version, remain the same, except for the fact that the need for working the patented invention may henceforth be satisfied by importation. In other words, the failure to work a patented product locally may no longer give rise to a non-voluntary licence if the market is covered by importation. On the other hand, the obligation of local industrial working remains for the beneficiary of a non-voluntary licence.

Under the terms of the Revised Bangui Agreement, ex officio licences may be granted 'when certain patents are of vital interest to ... public health ... or where non-working or insufficient working of such patents seriously compromises the satisfaction of the country's needs'. However, ex officio licences are no longer covered by special rules and are subject to the same conditions as non-voluntary licences. Such licences may therefore no longer be granted except for purposes of local industrial working and not importation, which deprives the provision of any meaning for countries which have no pharmaceutical industry of their own.

The WTO adopted the Declaration on the TRIPS Agreement and Public Health at the Doha Ministerial Conference in November 2001. The declaration recognizes the seriousness of public health problems, particularly those due to the HIV/AIDS pandemic, tuberculosis, malaria and other epidemics. But it states that the TRIPS Agreement must be part of a broader effort to deal with these problems. It also encourages health authorities to take appropriate protective measures, especially with regard to ex officio licences.

This raises a difficulty with respect to the 1999 Revised Bangui Agreement, since ex officio licences are subject to the same conditions as non-voluntary licences, which excludes resorting to importation. In this context, it is worth noting that Article 17 of the Revised Bangui Agreement states that: 'in the case of discrepancies between the provisions of this Agreement ... and those of the international conventions ..., the latter shall prevail'.

SOME RECOMMENDATIONS

The 1999 Revised Bangui Agreement strengthens the rights of patent owners by extending the duration of patents, by recognizing that importation is sufficient for the purpose of working a patent, and by laying down stricter conditions for the granting of non-voluntary licences. These provisions are unlikely to encourage the technology transfers required to develop a pharmaceutical industry in the OAPI area, so that the dependence of member countries on imports of medicines is bound to increase still further. Bearing these points in mind, this chapter closes with some recommendations. First, the revised version needs to be reviewed in the light of new international tendencies, particularly in regard to parallel imports and the need for specific measures concerning ex officio licences that include the possibility of importing without the obligation to undertake prior negotiations with patent owners. Second, the extension of the transitional period for LDCs to 2016 for making patents available for medicines, as agreed at Doha, should be implemented by the OAPI through an official amendment to the Bangui Agreement. Third, measures favouring the transfer of technologies to the LDCs in order to equip them with a pharmaceutical industry should be implemented. Fourth, information concerning the prices of medicines and the competitive pricing of generics should be collated and disseminated. Fifth, following the recommendations of the Director-General of OAPI, immediate imports under non-voluntary licences of the medicines needed to treat thousands of patients should be allowed, as is the practice already in some countries such as Cameroon, Mali and Côte d'Ivoire.

Chapter 15

The TRIPS Agreement and Generic Production of HIV / AIDS Drugs

Narendra B Zaveri

Like the traditional patent system, the TRIPS rules on patents are founded on the 'quid pro quo' principle. While providing inventors/owners of patents with the exclusive right to exploit the invention for a fixed term with statutory protection to support it, TRIPS also seeks to promote scientific and technological research and development (see Articles 7 and 8). In return for the patent grant, the owner is obliged to disclose the invention to enrich the pool of technical knowledge, and also to use the invention, or to permit the government/third parties to do so (see Article 31). The patent holder is also expected to help in meeting the demands of the community for the patented product on fair and reasonable terms (as in Article 5A of the Paris Convention).

Article 31 is of vital importance, providing the means to achieve the objectives enshrined in Articles 7 and 8. Though represented to be restrictive, Article 31 actually recognizes the government's right, not only to use, but also to authorize use by a 'third party', if his 'efforts to obtain authorization from the right holder on reasonable commercial terms and conditions ... have not been successful within a reasonable period of time'. To avail himself of this benefit, a third party is required to first seek such authorization from the right holder. This necessarily implies that the exclusive right, that is, the right to prevent or exclude others, provided as per Article 28, is not an absolute right. It is subject also to the rights of the government, and third parties to use the invention during the patent term, on 'reasonable commercial terms and conditions' as per Article 31.

Despite these clear provisions, there have been considerable confusion and controversies about the scope and terms of use permissible under Article 31. The different requirements prescribed by Article 31 for such use have been interpreted as preventing, rather than permitting, government or third-party uses. Though some of the requirements are apparently intended for public interest or for the benefit of consumers or third parties, these are also being misread as conditions preventing such government or third-party uses.

Unfortunately such confusion has enabled some multinational pharmaceutical companies holding patents in different countries in respect of drugs required for treatment of HIV/AIDS, to threaten or raise legal disputes to prevent governments and NGOs in some of the sub-Saharan African countries procuring such drugs from generic sources, even as millions of the poor in such countries are dying without treatment.

Among the contentions raised by them are that parallel imports from unauthorized generic sources and exports to other countries of the licensed products by generic manufacturers are prohibited by Article 31, particularly by clause (f). This presentation is intended to show, first, that on correct interpretation of Article 31 including clause (f) (briefly set out below), it will be observed that such contentions are not tenable; and secondly, that even if such an interpretation is to be accepted, having regard to the over-riding human rights considerations, access to medicines cannot be denied. It would be convenient to first take up the human rights aspect.

The Declaration on the TRIPS Agreement and Public Health, adopted by the World Trade Organization (WTO) Ministerial Conference at Doha on 14 November 2001, provides an official interpretation which, by virtue of Article IX of the Agreement Establishing the WTO, is binding on the members. The full legal significance of reference in the declaration to 'customary rules of interpretation of public international law', of which the Vienna Convention on the Law of Treaties is the accepted authority, can be appreciated by reference to Article 3.2 of the WTO Dispute Settlement Understanding, giving official status to these rules for interpreting WTO agreements, particularly in the context of dispute settlement.

References in the declaration to objects and purposes of TRIPS provisions, and also to the wider national and international action, are based on Article 31 of the Vienna Convention. The mandates in the declaration about healthcare priorities are founded on the principle of 'jus cogens' enshrined in Article 53 of the Vienna Convention, which, being of vital importance, is reproduced here:

> *A treaty is void if, at the time of its conclusion, it conflicts with a peremptory norm of general international law. For the purposes of the present Convention, a peremptory norm of general international law is a norm accepted and recognized by the international community of States as a whole as a norm from which no derogation is permitted and which can be modified only by a subsequent norm of general international law having the same character.*

The peremptory norms of general international law, which would have the effect of over-riding any restrictive trade rules of TRIPS, are brought out, among others, in the UN Declaration of Commitment on HIV/AIDS and the Universal Declaration on Human Rights. These and other related treaties have been accepted as more fundamental treaties or conventions, and the TRIPS provisions have to be interpreted and implemented to support and not defeat these more fundamental human rights and international law obligations. In this context, reference can also be made to the provisions relating to human rights to life, better standard of living and health as set out in the Preamble, and Articles 1, 2 and 55, and the binding obligations as per Articles 53 and 103 of UN Charter.

The declaration has thus provided official interpretation, removing many of the doubts, controversies and disputes on the subject, which have prevented or obstructed such production and supplies.

The declaration expressly recognizes that the public health crisis relating to HIV/AIDS 'can represent a national emergency or other circumstances of extreme urgency' (Paragraph 5c), and also that 'Each Member has the right to grant compulsory licences and the freedom to determine the grounds upon which such licences are granted' (Paragraph 5b). This reaffirmation facilitates production and supplies of generic drugs required for treatment of pandemics like HIV/AIDS, malaria and tuberculosis.

The declaration leaves nothing to chance. First, it recounts that TRIPS is part of the 'national and international action to address these problems'. Second, it reaffirms that 'the TRIPS Agreement does not and should not prevent Members from taking measures to protect public health', and 'that the Agreement can and should be interpreted and implemented in a manner supportive of WTO Members' right to protect public health and, in particular, to promote access to medicines for all'. Third, it reaffirms that each provision of the TRIPS Agreement, shall be read applying the 'customary rules of interpretation of public international law' and 'in the light of the objects and purposes of the Agreement, as expressed, in particular in its objectives and principles'. And fourth, it accepts 'the right of WTO Members to use, to the full, the provisions in the TRIPS Agreement, which provide flexibility for this purpose'.

The implications of these declarations are that the reference to 'national and international action to address these problems' is obviously intended to stress the gravity of the problem and to refer to the 'Global Crisis – Global Action' spelt out in the 'Declaration of Commitment on HIV/AIDS', unanimously adopted by the UN General Assembly on 27 June 2001. As this declaration of commitment expresses it:

> *Deeply concerned that the global HIV/AIDS epidemic, through its devastating scale and impact, constitutes a global emergency and one of the most formidable challenges to human life and dignity, as well as to the effective enjoyment of human rights, which undermines social and economic development throughout the world and affects all levels of society – national, community, family and individual; and needs urgent and exceptional national, regional and international action.*

The declaration of commitment also mandates that by 2003:

> *Also, in an urgent manner make every effort to provide progressively and in a sustainable manner, the highest attainable standard of treatment for HIV/AIDS, including the prevention and treatment of opportunistic infections, and effective use of quality-controlled anti-retroviral therapy in a*

> *careful and monitored manner to improve adherence and effectiveness and reduce the risk of developing resistance; and to cooperate constructively in strengthening pharmaceutical policies and practices, including those applicable to generic drugs and intellectual property regimes, in order further to promote innovation and the development of domestic industries consistent with international law.*

As a direct and immediate consequence of the guidance and assurance provided by the declaration, member nations can now adopt much simpler and quicker procedures to permit 'other use' by government or third parties, 'without authorisation of right holder' (commonly referred to as compulsory licences) in terms of Article 31 for generic production of HIV/AIDS drugs. Prevention, control or treatment of HIV/AIDS can now be statutorily accepted as a ground for the granting of compulsory licences. This eliminates the need for each intending generic producer to plead or prove justification for the grant, and also limits the patentee's right to raise objections or disputes for lack of justification.

Recognition of the HIV/AIDS crisis as 'national emergency' or 'circumstances of extreme urgency' implies that the requirement of TRIPS of first approaching the right holder as a condition for such authorization, can now be dispensed with in the case of HIV/AIDS drugs. The procedure for the grant can be greatly simplified, and the scope of patentees' objections and resulting delays and uncertainties for the grant, can be virtually eliminated. It is now for the member nations to frame their patent laws to take fullest advantage of this benefit.

The declaration has direct and immediate implications also in respect of Article 31(a) requiring 'authorisation of such use shall be considered on its individual merits'. Whether each case should be considered individually or collectively is merely a matter of procedure. It is well established that matters of procedures have to yield to substantive provisions, such as the objects and purposes of the law. Procedures can certainly not prevail over the more fundamental and substantive provisions which are accepted as matters of national emergency or extreme urgency as in the case of the HIV/AIDS crisis.

Article 31 provisions have to be interpreted in a manner supportive of, and not antithetical to, the objects and principles of the TRIPS Agreement. Article 31 provides for 'other use . . . without the authorization of the right holder, including use by the government or third parties authorized by the government'. This would include commercial and non-commercial use by the government; and by third parties. The three exceptions referred to in clause (b), which are 'national emergency', 'extreme urgency', and 'public non-commercial use', only go to show that the expression 'other uses' contemplated by Article 31 is of wide amplitude, extending to all uses of a patent by the government, including commercial uses and uses undertaken by it for sovereign and non-sovereign functions, and not falling within the scope of Article 30. Barring three specific exceptions of 'national emergency'; 'extreme urgency' or 'public non-commercial use', in all other cases of 'other uses' as per Article 31, clause (b) requires that the right holder should be first approached for his authorization for the intended use and for reasonable commercial terms for such use, and only if the right holder fails to authorize such use on 'reasonable commercial terms' and within a 'reasonable period of time', recourse can be taken to authorization as per Article 31.

In a recent case at the WTO, the Dispute Settlement Body panel interpreted the words 'third parties'. 'Third parties are by definition parties who have no legal right at all in being able to perform the tasks excluded by Article 28 patent right.' The only condition required to be satisfied by a third party for being permitted to use the patented invention, is that 'prior to such use, the proposed user has made efforts to obtain authorization from the right holder on reasonable commercial terms and conditions and that such efforts have not been successful within a reasonable period of time'. However, since the HIV/AIDS crisis is accepted as matter of national emergency or extreme urgency, this requirement of prior approach to patentee and his non-response is waived for third parties also.

The scope of Article 31(a) inquiry can and should be limited in national law by specifically accepting the HIV/AIDS crisis as constituting national emergency or extreme urgency. The consideration of individual merits would therefore be restricted to: (i) the applicant's capability and facility to undertake such production; (ii) reasonableness of the commercial terms and conditions to be fixed for the grant; (iii) adequacy of remuneration and economic value of authorization; (iv) 'consumers affordability'; and (v) the nation's financial resources, the national objectives and priorities for prevention and control of the HIV/AIDS crisis.

Each of these matters, not having been defined in Article 31, is flexible. Excepting item (i), the remaining other matters can be covered by common statutory guidelines applicable to all such cases. This would considerably reduce the scope of inquiry, delay, uncertainties and disputes. So far as item (i) is concerned, the production facilities of the applicant vis-à-vis drug control regulations, good manufacturing practice (GMP) and quality control standards etc, are matters for which certification/licences and verification by drug control regulatory authorities can be accepted as sufficient and conclusive.

The expressions 'reasonable commercial terms' and 'reasonable period of time' in Article 31(b) are not defined or specified. The necessary implication is that each country is left free to specify or define these according to its own economic and technological development, national priorities and the nature of goods, and possibility of indigenous production and availability.

The Article 31(h) requirement of adequate remuneration, taking into account the economic value of the authorization, is normally understood as referring to reasonable royalties. If the parties mutually agree upon a rate of royalties, such a rate may be accepted for the granting of licences, otherwise royalties may be fixed on the basis of the statutory guideline. A statutory guideline can be established providing for maximum and minimum royalties payable on the ex-factory sale price of the patented product in bulk, taking into consideration the nature and extent of invention and the degree of technological innovation achieved.

The rates of royalty generally prescribed by different countries in their patent laws, range from 1 to 4 per cent of the sales turnover, depending on the nature of the goods. Having regard to the potential of a vast market and opportunities being opened up and the longer patent term available under the WTO and TRIPS regimes, remuneration on the basis of even 1 per cent royalty may provide a very fair return to the right holder.

The principle of differential or tiered pricing has recently been evolved and is proposed for ensuring availability of vital drugs at affordable prices in developing nations. The scheme contemplates that manufacturers of patented pharmaceutical products may maintain high prices in advanced countries, but should supply such products at lower prices to developing nations having regard also to the capacity of the consumers to pay. In fact most often the prices fixed by patent holders themselves vary from country to country and generally also reflect such economic differences.

However, it would be advisable that the national law should provide for the immediate issue of the compulsory licences on satisfaction of the drug regulatory requirements pending inquiry about remuneration, royalty or other commercial terms and conditions for the grant, if the intending user undertakes to pay the royalty which he concedes, and agrees to deposit the maximum statutorily permissible royalty. Consumer interests also require that the products of invention be made available to them without delay. Clauses (i) and (j) of Article 31 provide for review of the decision relating to authorization as well as remuneration, by judicial authority or by independent and distinct higher authority. This would involve further delay. Here, the maximum periods for filing applications for such review, as well as for disposal of the case, should be fixed. There is no requirement that, pending any such appeal against grant of authorization, the compulsory licence should be withheld or suspended. It is therefore possible to allow the licensee to operate the licence pending such appeal. The requirement of termination need not be applied as it is difficult to predicate with any certainty the total elimination of HIV/AIDS.

Article 31 specifically requires that for 'use by the Government', its provisions 'shall be respected'. As worded, Article 31 provisions would certainly apply to state/crown use provisions. However, a study of the state use provisions in patent laws of different countries reveals that most of them do not satisfy the requirements prescribed by Article 31. In fact, ignoring these requirements, most countries, including members of the G7, have reserved very wide, unlimited and over-riding powers for state uses, which do not 'respect' any of the terms prescribed by Article 31, except that patent laws of most countries provide for payment of compensation to the right holder to be determined as per statutory provisions. Section 1498 of the US Patent Act is an example of such a provision. State use may be made directly by the concerned government department, or it may employ some agents or contractors to do the job.

Compulsory licenses can also be provided on the basis of Article 8(2) of TRIPS read with Article 5A(2) and (4) of the Paris Convention to prevent or control abuses of patent protection. Article 5A(2) enables member countries to grant compulsory licences to prevent or control such abuses. Article 5A(4) provides special remedy for abuse of non-working or insufficient working. It has been common universal experience that patents for drugs and medicines are grossly abused by right holders by fixing and maintaining outrageously high prices of such drugs during the entire patent term, and also by preventing and obstructing production or imports of generic drugs. As recently observed in sub-Saharan Africa, less than 1 per cent of the population suffering or dying from HIV/AIDS was able to receive treatment by such drugs; 99 per cent of the population was denied such treatment. This situation needs to be remedied urgently.

Chapter 16

International Legal Protection for Genetic Resources, Traditional Knowledge and Folklore: challenges for the intellectual property system

Weerawit Weeraworawit

Introduction

The 1883 Paris Convention for the Protection of Industrial Property and the 1886 Berne Convention for the Protection of Literary and Artistic Works, including their respective revisions and related agreements, have for the past 100 years established the international protection of innovation and creativity with their clearly defined sets of rules and standards. Those rules and standards have been adopted and reinforced by the TRIPS Agreement. However, they have been increasingly perceived as being unresponsive to the growing demand especially in the developing world that innovation and creativity in the forms of traditional knowledge (TK) and folklore should be accorded international legal protection, and that sovereign rights over genetic resources be respected. Many assert that the present intellectual property system has not been geared to protect genetic resources, TK or folklore. Some argue that intellectual property concepts and mechanisms exist that could and should be applied to give sufficient legal protection to these categories. Some contend that there is a need to create a sui generis system for them. In any case, traditional knowledge and folklore have become emerging global issues that are here to stay and will not go away. The run-up to and the outcome of the Fourth Session of the 2001

World Trade Organization (WTO) Ministerial Conference clearly shows that the importance and value of these new global issues have been recognized in the context of international trade albeit in the wording that is broad enough to satisfy both the member countries that are keen supporters of the setting up of the international legal protection for these issues and those that are yet to be converted. The ministerial declaration adopted at the WTO Ministerial Conference made a special reference[1] to the work to be undertaken by the TRIPS Council concerning the relation between TRIPS and the Convention on Biological Diversity (CBD), in particular having in view the protection of TK. The latest development in the WTO is not an isolated incident. There have been efforts at the domestic, regional, and international levels to deal with these global and emerging issues. The rate of progress greatly varies, ranging from the making of international agreements such as the CBD and the International Treaty on Plant Genetic Resources for Food and Agriculture under the Food and Agriculture Organization (FAO).

The World Intellectual Property Organization (WIPO) has carried out a series of studies and consultations among the member states on the global and emerging intellectual property issues, notably in terms of genetic resources, TK and folklore. The new global issues were incorporated in the agenda activities of WIPO with the endorsement of the General Assembly in 1999.

It is clear that the so-called global and emerging issues involve the works and concerns of other international and regional organizations regarding the legal means of protection, access and transfer of technology, scientific and technical cooperation in the preservation and sustainable use of biodiversity, as well as benefit sharing. It is also clear that intellectual property has an indispensable role in the formulation of an internationally acceptable regime on the global and emerging issues.

Intellectual property has to be studied in relation to other international agreements and instruments especially the CBD, the FAO International Treaty on Plant Genetic Resources for Food and Agriculture, the International Union for the Protection of New Varieties of Plants (UPOV) and TRIPS. It goes without saying that there is a need for WIPO, UNEP, FAO, UNESCO, and the WTO to work closely together.

At the present time, there is no comprehensive regime governing the protection and exploitation of the global and evolving issues mentioned above. However, there have been unequivocal developments underlying the fact that the issues of genetic resources, biodiversity, TK and folklore are being tackled seriously in the international context. These are not just a flash in the pan or merely futile aspirations of the developing countries. The outcome of the WIPO Meeting on Intellectual Property and Genetic Resources, held in April 2000, clearly shows broad international consensus that the issue of genetic resources is not a North–South issue, and recognition of the interrelationship and interdependence between genetic resources and the new global issues of TK, folklore and biodiversity. The meeting reached the consensus that WIPO should facilitate the continuation of consultations among member states in coordination with the other international organizations concerned, through the conduct of appropriate legal and technical studies, and through the setting up of an appropriate forum within WIPO for future work. This led to the setting up of the Intergovernmental Committee on Intellectual Property and Genetic Resources, Traditional Knowledge and Folklore, which has convened several meetings in Geneva since 2001. If things follow their normal course in the WIPO context, it is expected that this intergovernmental committee will follow in the footsteps of other WIPO intergovernmental committees by achieving sufficient international consensus to pave the way for the convening of a diplomatic conference and the adoption of an international agreement or set of agreements on these issues.

In order to determine the desirable international regime for the new global issues, it is crucial to look at the rationale for giving international legal protection to these issues, the present protection afforded by the existing international agreements and arrangements, present problems, and likely solutions.

RATIONALE

From the intellectual property perspective and evolution, the Paris and Berne Conventions of 1883 and 1886 have served to give protection to innovative and creative works respectively. Patents afford protection to something new without giving regard to the sources of research and development giving rise to such new invention. This emphasis on protection of novelty while ignoring the sources has become more pronounced with the progress of biotechnological innovations making use of genetic resources and giving rise to complaints by developing countries about 'biopiracy'. In the case of copyright, expressions of folklore do not benefit from the copyright regime due to the simple fact that copyright gives a limited period of protection to new expressions thus excluding most expressions of folklore handed down from generation to generation and practised as an integral part of people's everyday lives. Article 19 of the Berne Convention allows members to provide additional protection to that which the convention expressly requires. But such protection would only have domestic effect. Some argue that lack of novelty and a limited period of protection do not automatically preclude legal protection for works of TK such as indigenous designs and expressions of folklore. Some intellectual property rights (IPRs) such as trade secrets or undisclosed information, trade marks especially certification marks, copyright and related rights, geographical indications, and even patents, as well as competition law could, they claim, be used to afford adequate legal protection. They also suggest that the word 'tradition' should not mean 'old' but 'the manner of producing such knowledge, and not to the date on which the knowledge was produced'. Thus, TK is knowledge that has been developed based on the traditions of a certain community or nation. Following such definition, TK and folklore would not be barred on the ground of lack of novelty. However, there have been no internationally accepted definitions of the terms 'traditional knowledge' and 'folklore'.

The rationale for giving international special legal protection to TK and folklore is to depart from the individual-focused rights of the mainstream international agreements on intellectual property, and instead to emphasize communal rights. It is the community which benefits from the protection not any single individual, since it is the community that keeps TK and folklore alive, and conserves genetic resources in their in situ conditions. Critics argue that it is impossible to identify the traditional knowledge, folklore or genetic resources. This argument could be easily defeated by pointing to the ongoing work of international organizations such as UNESCO in collecting data on expressions of folklore in the global context, and the efforts of various countries in preserving their national cultural heritage. These efforts have been much facilitated by advances in information technology. The same goes for genetic resources. The CBD promotes the conservation of biodiversity by stating that such conservation is a common concern of mankind and that states have sovereign rights over the biological resources in their territories. Article 1 defines the objectives of the CBD as 'the conservation of biological diversity, the sustainable use of its components and the fair and equitable sharing of the benefits arising from the use of genetic resources, including by appropriate access to genetic resources and by appropriate transfer of relevant technologies, taking into account all rights over those resources and to technologies, and by appropriate funding'. The stage has been set for a new kind of rights, which have an uneasy coexistence with the long-established concept of patents at the moment.[2]

It could also be argued that even the traditional rationale for IPRs could be used in support of the legal protection of TK and folklore. The concept of reasonable reward for the inventor or creator could be applied to genetic resources, TK and folklore, since the people or communities which have a role in the preservation and maintenance of such materials have the right to reasonable reward as well, at least on a par with the inventor or creator who enjoys protection in the form of industrial property and copyright, as well as other new rights as stipulated in TRIPS. The granting of benefits seems to be more readily accepted in the field of genetic resources used in agriculture as shown in the International Treaty on Plant Genetic Resources for Food and Agriculture as adopted by the 31st Session of the Conference of the FAO on 3 November 2001 which clearly acknowledges farmers' rights.

Genetic resources, traditional knowledge and folklore

The very concept of traditional knowledge is clearly stipulated in Article 8(j) of the CBD in connection with in situ conservation of biological diversity. The provision is not mandatory due to the terms 'as far as possible and as appropriate', which give member states a high degree of leeway. However, it has given rise to some regional arrangements, notably, those of the Andean Community (see Chapter 25). It should be mentioned here that Thailand, though not a party to the CBD, has passed the Protection of Plant Varieties Act 1999, providing legal protection not only to new plant varieties along the lines of UPOV but also indigenous plant varieties, with clearly defined provisions on the rights of the local community concerned, authorization, access and benefit sharing. The effect of this law was very much debated during its passage in the Thai parliament as to whether it would favour multinational companies which have accumulated new plant varieties, some of which are believed to be developed from indigenous plants, or the local plant breeders who have been consistently prolific. At the end, a balance was struck with the dual approach of giving protection to both new and indigenous plant varieties.

With regard to the identification of sources of genetic material and TK used in patent applications, there seems to be consensus across the board that this would be a desirable measure. However, there is no consensus on what to do in the case of non-compliance. The EU has Recital 27 of its Directive on the Legal Protection of Biotechnological Inventions, which stipulates that 'whereas if an invention is based on biological material of plant or animal origin or if it uses such material, the patent application should, where appropriate, include information on the geographical origin of such material, if known; whereas this is without prejudice to the processing of patent applications or the validity of rights arising from granted patents'. It should be noted that the factor of knowledge plays an important role. This factor puts an onus on the countries owning TK and genetic resources to have clear information on what they have alone and in common. The biotechnology sector in the developed countries often raises the problem of how to identify accurately the source of materials they use. This problem is not difficult to overcome because comprehensive databases could be provided in the near future. It should be further noted that in the case of the EU, the non-disclosure of source does not give rise to any erosion of the granted rights.

TRIPS is silent on genetic resources, TK, folklore and biodiversity, but it does have certain provisions which could be interpreted in favour of the concept of access and transfer of technology. Article 7 stipulates that 'the protection and enforcement of intellectual property rights should contribute to the promotion of technological innovation and to the transfer and dissemination of technology, to the mutual advantage of producers and users of technological knowledge and in a manner conducive to social and economic welfare, and to a balance of rights and obligations'. These provisions are broad and subject to interpretation by WTO members. They provide the safeguard, but not the direct protection of genetic resources, TK and folklore. The same thing could be said for Article 27.2 on the exclusion from patentability on the ground of public order or morality, including prejudice to the environment. This could be used to prevent unfair or abusive exploitation of genetic resources, but does not confer legal protection on these or TK. Article 67 deals with technical cooperation from the developed countries to the developing and least developed countries. It also refers to assistance in the prevention of abuse. So these TRIPS provisions are either remedial or preventive in nature, and do not confer rights on genetic resources or TK.

In any case, the issue of access will not simply go away just because international uniform practice is lacking. An important development at the FAO is the adoption on 3 November 2001 of a binding agreement known as the International Treaty on Plant Genetic Resources for Food and Agriculture. This international treaty incorporates farmers' rights and the Multilateral System of access and benefit sharing. This development has complemented the CBD in a way beneficial to those actually involved in the use and maintenance of genetic resources.

Although the concept of access is deemed desirable, it has not made much headway into the established patent regime judging from the response to the questionnaire sent out by WIPO's Working Group on Biotechnology to the organization's member states. Of the 50 countries that responded, only five countries gave a positive response to the question 'does your legislation include any special provisions to ensure the recording of contributions to inventions (such as the source of government funding, the source of generic resources that originate or are employed in biotechnological inventions, the grant of prior informed consent to have access to those resources, etc)?' Thirty-five countries replied that they did not plan to introduce legislation to ensure the recording of such contributions.

However, the aforementioned WIPO Meeting on Genetic Resources established a strong consensus for WIPO to set up an appropriate forum for future work on genetic resources and related issues. It also shows that many countries have not made up their minds on the question of reforming the patent regime to give international legal protection to genetic resources and traditional knowledge. In any case, it underlines the importance of these new global issues which continue to generate debates and discussions far beyond the confines of the patent regime.

Expressions of folklore are not protected by copyright. However, according to TRIPS and the Berne Convention, new works derived from them can be, as can collections of them on the basis of being compiled works.

WIPO and UNESCO have for over two decades carried out joint activities relating to the international legal protection for expressions of folklore. One of the early results of such collaboration was the 1982 Model Provisions for National Laws on the Protection of Expressions of Folklore against Illicit Exploitation and Other Prejudicial Actions. Due to the over-broad nature of the availability and scope of protection, the model law was not widely adopted and little further work was conducted in this area for several years. The lull was broken with the WIPO-UNESCO World Forum on the Protection of Folklore, which took place in April 1997 in Phuket, Thailand. The forum's Phuket Statement requested that WIPO and UNESCO work together to find an appropriate protection for expressions of folklore. As a result, four regional consultations were organized in 1999. They all emphasized the importance of expressions of folklore and related issues in the modern economy.

In the world of information technology, satellite broadcasting and the internet, expressions of folklore have gained more economic value due to their very own creativity preserved and refined by the indigenous or local communities. The merchandising business associated with copyright works and expressions of folklore has become more prominent. A clear example of such merchandising is associated with the 2000 Sydney Olympics, where products inspired by or based on Aboriginal folklore and traditional knowledge generated huge income. The fast increasing popularity of entertainment on the internet means greater demand for creative works. Expressions of folklore have become an obvious attraction, as they are free of charge due to the lack of international legal protection.

The same expressions of folklore may exist in more than one country. This points to the need to catalogue existing expressions of folklore to facilitate identification and to acknowledge the fact that in several cases regional countries have to share benefits. The very exercise of cataloguing and identification will help preserve expressions of folklore which are a valuable national heritage in the face of the onslaught brought about by Western values and lifestyles. The process of seeking to share benefits from shared expressions of folklore will help to strengthen mutual appreciation and respect, an important factor contributing to regional peace and stability.

Critics of the international legal protection of folklore often argue that expressions of folklore are already in the public domain, and that any attempt to create special protection would cause confusion and uncertainty as well as undermining the very concept of copyright. It could be countered that expressions of folklore are not copyright protected. Moreover, the EU now gives special protection to non-original or non-copyrightable data in databases if they have been collected with substantial financial investment and if they constitute a substantial part of the database. Such practice is clearly a departure from the very concept of copyright.

SOLUTIONS

At this stage, it is clear beyond doubt that there is no unified international legal protection of genetic resources, TK, folklore and biodiversity, although there is a general consensus that such new global issues should be tackled together in a comprehensive manner and in connection with intellectual property to produce an internationally acceptable regime. This is being done at the moment by the WIPO Intergovernmental Committee on Intellectual Property and Genetic Resources, Traditional Knowledge and Folklore. Parallel efforts have been launched by the Fourth Session of the WTO Ministerial Meeting in November 2001 to the effect that there will be serious consultation on the expansion of the scope of Article 23 of TRIPS beyond wines and spirits and on TK and related issues, as well as greater flexibility in approaching patents on life-saving medicines.

There is no international consensus on the substance of an internationally acceptable regime of protection. This is to be expected given that the countries endowed with genetic resources, traditional knowledge and folklore seek to secure protection for such resources, while the user countries are bound to be reluctant to submit to additional restraints on innovating and creating in ways that conform to existing intellectual property agreements. However, such perceived resistance may not be long-lasting once a clearer form and substance of the internationally acceptable regime emerges. Besides, the user countries are at the same time the holders of genetic resources, traditional knowledge, and folklore, and vice versa. Australia and Canada are clear examples of developed countries with an interest in giving legal protection to traditional knowledge and folklore, especially the products of indigenous cultures, through the existing intellectual property system. Consequently, these are not North–South issues. Developed and developing countries alike share the desire to find an appropriate mechanism or arrangement to give adequate protection, although they may not superficially seem to have common interests.

It would be extremely unrealistic to expect the international community to agree on the substance of the protection of the new global issues overnight. To achieve international consensus on the form and substance of such a regime needs serious and continuous consultations among the members of the international community aided by studies produced by WIPO and other international agencies. The future is not as pessimistic as many critics believe. The horizontal cooperation among the international organizations is producing results, as can be seen from the harmony between the new International Treaty on Plant Genetic Resources for Food and Agriculture and the CBD, which has greatly improved farmers' rights at the domestic and international levels.

It is also crucial for the developing country owners of genetic resources to agree among themselves on the best possible model. They could start by collecting and sharing information on their respective resources, perhaps through the development of electronic prior art TK databases, facilitating the retrieval of information, identifying the problems involved, exploring options without predetermined results, forging regional and international consensus, and having sufficient political will to establish a fair, convenient, and practical multilateral system. The multilateral system could be multi-tiered, starting from the national authority and a national fund to manage TK for the various communities, the regional authority and a regional fund to manage TK at the regional level, especially on the sharing of benefits for materials that exist in several regional countries, and ultimately, the international authority and a global fund to manage benefit sharing between countries from different parts of the world. The respective authorities could be run by committees of representatives of the concerned parties. This multi-tiered system could be based on a compulsory licensing basis, namely, by payment of fixed rates for specific uses of certain materials without any need to seek approval from the national, regional, or international authority concerned beforehand. This compulsory licensing approach has worked in Japan in the case of the use of sound recordings for commercial reproduction.

There is a greater need for educating and making the public understand the issues involved in order to facilitate their maximum use of the present intellectual property system to legally protect, whenever possible, their genetic resources, traditional knowledge and folklore, while regional and international consultation on the protection of these new global issues is going on. Improved understanding will, on the one hand, help avoid confrontation, and on the other hand, encourage continuous and balanced consultation and negotiation, as the present IPR system is perceived as being biased toward the developed countries and multinational corporations.

To sum up, there must continue to be a distinct forum, whatever its designation, for consultations among the regional countries and on the global basis. The WIPO Intergovernmental Committee seems to be the appropriate forum at the moment due to its broad mandate and participation of both governments and concerned groups. It should enhance cooperation with other international and regional organizations to ensure a comprehensive approach that is perceived as convenient, fair and equitable by all the parties concerned, and to make the best use of the ongoing efforts to find the most appropriate mechanism to give adequate international legal protection to the global and emerging issues of genetic resources, TK and folklore. There will be many obstacles on the way, but these are to be expected as the new global issues are complex and intertwined, involving not only IPRs but also other major concerns such as environmental and human rights. Now is the time for a holistic approach to dealing with these potentially controversial issues as we move closer to the development and adoption of an international agreement.

NOTES

1 See Paragraph 19 of the Doha Ministerial Declaration: 'We instruct the Council for TRIPS, in pursuing its work programme including under the review of Article 27.3(b), the review of the implementation of the TRIPS Agreement under Article 71.1 and the work foreseen pursuant to paragraph 12 of this Declaration, to examine, inter alia, the relationship between the TRIPS Agreement and the Convention on Biological Diversity, the protection of traditional knowledge and folklore.'

2 Colombia tried to introduce into the Patent Law Treaty a requirement to identify the genetic or biological resource in a request for patent, but the consensus is to tackle this issue under a separate agenda as it involves a very important issue of access and benefit sharing, not just a procedural matter.

Chapter 17

Indigenous Knowledge and its Protection in India

Suman Sahai

Indigenous knowledge (IK)[1] has been used for centuries by Indian indigenous and local communities, and has been the mainstay of their existence, especially in the key sectors of food and health. In addition, IK plays a vital role in the conservation of biodiversity.

The Indian Systems of Medicine (ISM) have a central place in the official Indian healthcare system. Doctors trained in Ayurveda, Siddha and Unani are part of the formal system. The government of India has recently created a Department of Indian Systems of Medicine in the Ministry of Health to oversee policy and research in this area. India has also set up National Institutes of Homeopathy and Ayurveda. Similar institutions exist for the Unani and Siddha traditions. There are colleges teaching ISM and training doctors all over the country. The ISM tradition is stronger in South India where it is the preferred option for many people.

The use and continuous improvement of farmers' varieties (landraces) is essential in many agricultural systems. In India, as in many other countries, seed supply fundamentally relies on decentralized local systems of seed production. These systems operate on the basis of the free diffusion of the best seed available within a community, with local farmers ensuring that the local community is supplied with planting material. The knowledge of farmers about crop varieties and their special characteristics has been central to the development of new plant varieties and for global food security.

As for conservation of biodiversity, tribal populations have created and maintained sacred groves in forest areas. These are found all over India in the tribal zones. They represent some of the few surviving examples of climax vegetation. Such virgin forests are usually located at the origins of forest water springs and in the catchment areas of river basins. A sacred grove is usually dedicated to a deity or a 'mother goddess' who is supposed to protect and preside over it. It is believed that such sacred groves date back several thousand years. The degree of sanctity of these sacred forests varies. In some forests even the dry foliage and fallen fruits cannot be touched. In others, the dead wood may be picked up, but never the live trees or their branches. The animals and the birds are not disturbed. The Garo and Khasi tribes of Northeastern India completely prohibit any human interference in their sacred groves. The Gonds of Central India prohibit the cutting of trees but allow fallen branches to be used.

The sacred groves of ancient times have become, in many cases, the 'biosphere reserves' of today and are found throughout India. The states with large tribal populations have the highest number of biosphere reserves in the form of wildlife sanctuaries and national parks.

In some parts of the country, especially where soils were poor and agriculture alone could not sustain the communities, the hunting of animals and gathering of wild edible plants was critical for survival. Here again, indigenous communities developed strategies to ensure that critical species were not over-hunted or over-collected.

For example, the Onges of the Little Andaman Island in the Andaman and Nicobar group, who love to hunt wild pigs, developed a technique to ensure that pigs were not over-hunted in any particular location. Every time an Onge killed a pig, he half broke a branch of the largest tree in the area. This branch then hung half broken from the tree and was a signal to all other Onges that a pig had been killed there recently. No one else would then hunt a pig in that locality, but move elsewhere. After a sufficient period of time had passed, the branch would totally dry up and fall off, once again opening the area for hunting.

The Cholanaickan tribals of Kerala devised elaborate social procedures to conserve and sustainably exploit natural resources by, for example, demarcating the ranges from which individual families can collect various resources. Resources can be extracted from common lands but users must comply with certain rules, according to which rights to a particular honeycomb or tree go to the first person who spots it and reserves it. The person or the party who has first sighted the beehive, and accordingly marked the tree where it is located, has the sole right to collect honey at that time and also in subsequent years from the same tree. This rule is never transgressed.

The Cholanaickan have well-defined principles that allow the members to gather and extract non-timber forest produce within their respective region. There is no restriction on gathering edible tubers, roots, fruits and leaves for self-consumption. One is free to move in the entire forest region and to collect tubers, roots and fruits as and when required. But people usually gather edible products only in their own area. However, there are rigid norms regarding the collection of non-timber forest produce. Trespassing in the territory of another Cholanaickan to collect non-timber forest produce is considered an offence.

THE MISAPPROPRIATION OF INDIGENOUS KNOWLEDGE

Western science has recently begun looking at IK as a source of new drugs, especially since the cost of putting new drugs on the market is becoming very high. The growing phenomenon of biopiracy shows the somewhat hypocritical attitude of Western scientists towards IK, scavenging it on the one hand and claiming patents on all kinds of products derived from IK, like neem, yet refusing to acknowledge its economic value and ownership.

Despite the growing recognition of IK as a valuable source of knowledge, Western intellectual property law continues to treat it as part of the 'public domain', freely available for use by anybody. Moreover, in some cases, diverse forms of IK have been appropriated under intellectual property rights (IPRs) by researchers and commercial enterprises, without any compensation to the original creators or possessors of the knowledge.

A large number of patents have been granted on genetic resources and knowledge obtained from developing countries without the consent of the possessors of the resources and knowledge. There has been extensive documentation of IPR protection being sought over resources 'as they are' without further improvement. These include a US patent on quinoa, which was granted to researchers of the Colorado State University, a US plant patent on ayahuasca, a sacred and medicinal plant of the Amazon region, and other patents on products based on plant materials and knowledge developed and used by local and indigenous communities, such as those relating to the neem tree, kava, barbasco,[2] endod[3] and turmeric, among others.

Some of these patents have been revoked by the competent national authorities following challenges by interested parties, including NGO campaigns. Thus, the Council for Scientific and Industrial Research (CSIR) of India requested the re-examination of US patent No 5 401 5041 granted for the wound healing properties of turmeric. The US Patent and Trademark Office (USPTO) revoked the patent after ascertaining that there was no novelty, the 'invention' having been used in India for centuries. In early 2000, a patent granted to W R Grace Company and the US Department of Agriculture on neem (EPO patent No 436257) was revoked by the European Patent Office on the grounds of its use having been known in India. The most important use of the neem tree is as a biopesticide. In this respect, neem has more than 60 valuable compounds, which include the widely used azadirachtin A. According to Grace, azadirachtin was being destroyed during traditional processing. This is highly misleading. The extracts were indeed subject to degradation but this did not amount to any wastage since farmers put such extracts to use as and when required. The problem of stabilization arose only when it needed to be commercially packaged for a long time. The 1992 patent application was filed by Grace on the principle that the process supposedly invented by them paved the way for additional extraction in the form of water soluble neem extracts, and hence is an add-on rather than a substitute to the current neem industry in India. In short, the processes are supposedly novel and an advance on the Indian techniques. However, the idea that any of this is novel is born of ignorance. A re-examination request for the patent on basmati rice lines and grains (US patent No 5 663 484) granted by the USPTO was also made by the CSIR. The patent owner, RiceTec, responded by withdrawing 15 of its 20 claims.

PROTECTION OF IK THROUGH EXISTING IPRS

Apart from patents, other IPRs could be used to protect IK. Copyright can be used to protect the artistic manifestations of the holders of indigenous knowledge, especially artists who belong to indigenous and native communities, against unauthorized reproduction and exploitation of those manifestations. But it is unlikely that copyright protection can be applied to IK related to bioresources unless presented in written form. New plant varieties could be protected through plant variety protection (see the section on Indian Plant Variety Protection and Farmers' Rights Act below). The design and shape of utilitarian craft products such as furniture, receptacles, garments and articles of ceramics, leather, wood and other materials may qualify for protection as industrial designs. Trade marks can assist in the effective marketing of indigenous products, including agricultural and biological products. Such goods and also services offered by manufacturers, craftsmen, professionals or traders from native and indigenous communities, or by associations representing them, may be differentiated from each other by the use of trade marks and service marks, and this could help to generate significant income. Geographical indications may be used to protect products of a special region, like basmati rice, Darjeeling tea, alphonso mangos, Kolhapuri slippers. Other World Trade Organization members are also interested in protection similar types of product, such as Bulgarian yoghurt, Czech Pilsen beer and Hungarian Szatmar plums.

The importance of IK has gained growing recognition in international forums. In 1982 the WIPO-UNESCO Model Provisions for National Laws on the Protection of Expressions of Folklore against Illicit Exploitation and other Prejudicial Actions were adopted. Ten years later, the Convention on Biological Diversity (CBD), which specifically addressed the issue (in Article 8(j)), was opened for signature at the Earth Summit. In 2000, WIPO established its Intergovernmental Committee on Intellectual Property and Genetic Resources, Traditional Knowledge and Folklore.

However, international conventions and treaties dealing with IK are characterized by the fact that the provisions they contain are not self-executing, and therefore do not establish clearly binding legal obligations on governments. Even where benefit sharing clauses exist, their meaning is contested and many governments refuse to implement or support them. The International Labour Organization Convention 169 Concerning Indigenous and Tribal Peoples in Independent Countries, which only 14 countries have ratified, has much to say about legal standards for indigenous and tribal people, but does not cover their rights over knowledge. The draft UN Declaration on the Rights of Indigenous Peoples recognizes their intellectual property and cultural rights. But even if the UN General Assembly agrees to adopt it, it will still only be a non-binding document. This means it cannot be legally enforced. As for the International Treaty on Plant Genetic Resources for Food and Agriculture, developed nations successfully blocked the international-level recognition of farmers rights, leaving them for national governments to implement. The CBD's provisions on IK cannot be fully implemented because of the US's continued refusal to ratify the convention.

Legal and other initiatives to protect IK in India

In India, special constitutional rights are given to the aboriginal tribal peoples (Adivasis) and include the so-called Scheduled Areas. Accordingly, tribal land cannot be sold to non-tribals and only tribals can be agents of development. The affirmative action policy, guaranteed constitutionally, ensures reservations in education, employment and political representation by reserving political constituencies. A third protection is by Special Provisions (as in the case of Nagaland), where tribal-dominated states have been given constitutionally guaranteed rights. Apart from land ownership, these rights include rights over all natural resources including forests. Although not brutalized like their New World counterparts, tribal societies in India and Asia have often been exploited. The rights that were given to them by post-colonial, independent governments are being eroded by domestic industry and the forces of globalization.

India has had a proactive approach to drafting national legislation pertaining to bioresources and indigenous knowledge. A number of legal initiatives have taken place. One of these is the passage of the Geographical Indications of Goods (Registrations and Protection) Act, 1999. This legislation aims to protect traditional Indian products like basmati rice and Darjeeling tea. The process of compiling the list of products for which India will seek national and international protection under this IPR category is underway.

The Plant Variety Protection and Farmers' Rights Act, 2001, is the sui generis legislation required to fulfil the conditions of TRIPS. India has decided to include farmers' rights in its legislation apart from the mandatory plant variety protection that TRIPS demands. Farmers' rights include the right of farmers to save the harvested seed of protected varieties, and also to sell it as long as they do not market it under the protected brand name. To protect the knowledge of farmers and enable a share of benefits to be derived from new varieties, there are provisions for a national gene fund into which breeders will have to pay revenues for using farmer varieties. The legislation requires full disclosure of the source and origin of varieties and complete passport data from breeders. The penalty for non-disclosure is a heavy fine and/or a jail term. Other elements of farmers' rights are provided by the act. The first of these is the explicit and detailed disclosure requirements in the passport data, which have to be submitted at the time of applying for a breeders' certificate. Passport data refers to the data about the parentage of the new variety. In this case it includes details like name and location of any farmer varieties used. If any concealment is detected in the passport data, the breeders' certificate stands to be cancelled. The second element is the prohibition from using sterile seed technologies in breeding. Breeders will have to submit an affidavit that their variety does not contain a genetic use restriction (or 'terminator') technology. Third, if farmers wish to examine documents and papers or receive copies of rules and decisions made by the various authorities, they will be exempt from paying any fees. Fourth, there is protection from innocent infringement. And fifth, in providing a liability clause in the section on farmers' rights, the farmer in principle is protected against the supply of spurious or bad quality seed.

The Patents Amendment Act of 1999 provides an exclusion for drugs based on ISM, keeping them out of the purview of the patent system. This exclusion has been carried into the Patent Second Amendment Act, 2002 (see Chapter 27 for further details of this legislation). The Biodiversity Bill, which asserts national sovereignty over biodiversity and recognizes the rights of communities, is also described in more detail in Chapter 27.

The Convention of Farmers and Breeders (CoFaB) is an alternative model to the International Union for the Protection of New Varieties of Plants (UPOV) that was jointly drafted by the Gene Campaign along with the Centre for Environment and Agriculture Development (CEAD). It aims to provide developing countries with another way to implement farmers' and breeders' rights that is appropriate for them. The CoFaB treaty seeks explicitly to fulfil the following goals: (i) to provide reliable, good quality seeds to the small and large farmer; (ii) to maintain genetic diversity in the field; (iii) to provide breeders of new varieties with legal protection for their varieties without prejudice to public interest; (iv) to acknowledge the enormous contribution of farmers to the identification, maintenance and refinement of germplasm; (v) to acknowledge the role of farmers as creators of landraces and traditional varieties which form the foundation of agriculture and modern plant breeding; (vi) to emphasise that the tropical countries are germplasm-owning countries and the primary source of agricultural varieties; and (vii) to develop a system wherein farmers and breeders have recognition and rights accruing from their respective contribution to the creation of new varieties.

The salient features of CoFaB are as follows:

- *Farmers' Rights.* Each contracting state will recognize the rights of farmers by arranging for the collection of a farmers' rights fee from the breeders of new varieties. The farmers' rights fee will be levied for the privilege of using landraces or traditional varieties, either directly or through the use of other varieties that have used landraces and traditional varieties, in their breeding programme.
- *Breeders' Rights.* Each member state will recognize the right of the breeder of a new variety by the grant of a special title called the Plant Breeder's Right. The plant breeders' right granted to the breeder of a new plant variety is that prior authorization shall be required for the production, for purposes of commercial and branded marketing of the reproductive or vegetative propagating material, as such, of the new variety, and for the offering for sale or marketing of such material.

DOCUMENTATION OF INDIGENOUS KNOWLEDGE

Substantial work is going on in India to document indigenous knowledge. One of these is the Peoples' Biodiversity Registers programme described in Chapter 20. In this section, we look at a few other examples.

The preparation of village Community Biodiversity Registers (CBRs) for documenting all knowledge, innovations and practices has been undertaken in a few Indian states. The State Plan for Kerala has also actively promoted documentation of local knowledge regarding biodiversity in people's biodiversity registers. One pilot project on this has been completed in Ernakulam district. The Tropical Botanic Garden and Research Institute (TBGRI) and the Kerala Forest Research Institute have initiated two other projects at a single *panchayat* (village council) level.

Gene Campaign has undertaken work on documentation of indigenous knowledge among three tribal populations: the Mundas and Oraons in South Bihar (in the Chotanagpur region), the Bhils of Madhya Pradesh, and the Tharus of the Terai region. Medicinal plants and knowledge of their use for human and veterinary care was documented with the help of educated tribal youth. Elders in the village, medical practitioners and traditional healers were consulted in the collection and understanding of the information.

The documented knowledge has been made into manuals for the tribal people who now use them as practical healing guides. During the data collection exercise, Gene Campaign also conducted a public education programme, telling the community about the new national and international developments and the growing biopiracy which steals their knowledge and their materials. Gene Campaign has made them aware of their rights so that the people are now fully aware that this knowledge belongs to them and cannot be used without their permission, even by the government of India.

Gene Campaign has also been working to conserve indigenous knowledge though its field projects. These include: (i) the collection of local medicinal flora and the establishment of a herbal garden in Jharkhand and Madhya Pradesh; (ii) the development of a genetic diversity centre in Kishanpuri, Madhya Pradesh; (iii) the collection of landraces and traditional varieties of rice, millets and pulses and the setting up of medium-term gene banks in Uttar Pradesh and Bihar; (iv) the survey and mapping of wild relatives of important crop plants in the Upper Western Ghats; (v) a study on agro-biodiversity and farmer perceptions about genetic diversity in the states of Uttar Pradesh and Bihar; and (vi) an inventory of genetic diversity in Indian trees and their known characteristics.

The Beej Bachao Aandolan, in collaboration with the villagers of Jardhar of the Terhi Garhwal district of Uttar Pradesh, initiated an exercise in 1995 to document the various bioresources used by the community and their conservation practices. The members of the Beej Bachao Aandolan, which is a network of local farmers, have been involved for a number of years now in reviving and spreading indigenous crop diversity.

The Traditional Knowledge Digital Library (TKDL)

To prevent biopiracy, the government of India is developing a digital database of public domain traditional knowledge related to medicinal plants. It is proposed to make this digital database available to patent offices all over the world so that examiners are aware of the prior art relating to a particular medicinal plant. This should hopefully prevent the mistaken granting of patents like those on turmeric and neem-derived products. The TKDL project will save huge costs involved in fighting legal battles against such patents. The cost of contesting a patent at international level over a three to five-year period can be very high. And conservative estimates indicate that about 2500 patents have already been granted in error. The addition of 500 new 'wrongful' patents every year will keep adding to the overall cost of such legal challenges.

A joint project of the National Institute of Science Communication (NISCOM) and the Central Department of Indian Systems of Medicine and Homeopathy, the TKDL is based on an innovative software program which facilitates the classification of traditional knowledge, making it compatible with the International Patent Classification. An interdisciplinary team of 30 Ayurvedic experts, five patent examiners and five IT experts have already transcribed about 8000 formulations of the 35,000 *slokas* pertaining to Ayurveda. The information will be made available simultaneously in English, Spanish, German, French, Japanese and Hindi. With each *sloka* yielding four pages of transcription, about 140,000 pages will be available in each language. Thirty-five languages are targeted including all major Indian and foreign languages. Plants that are not in the public domain and knowledge the use of which is to be protected are not placed in the database.

In addition, a National Innovation Foundation has been set up. This foundation, with an initial funding of 200 million rupees (US$4,120,000) is intended to build a national register of innovations, mobilize intellectual property protection, set up incubators for converting innovations into viable business opportunities, and help in nationwide dissemination. It has established four centres across the country to incubate innovation into enterprises, protect IPRs, and mobilize venture capital for the commercialization of local innovations.

ELEMENTS OF A SUI GENERIS SYSTEM FOR PROTECTING IK

There is a lot of debate on the systems of protection that can be adopted to provide legal protection for the intellectual property of indigenous people and communities. Most of these discussions have tried to adapt the existing forms of IPRs like patents, trade secrets and copyrights to the field of IK and bioresources. This is not likely to work because of the inherent mismatch between the protection that was created for finite, inanimate objects coming out of industrial activity, and the flowing, mutable and variable properties of biological materials and associated IK.

An approach that has been strongly advocated by some academics and many NGOs is the development of a sui generis regime, that is, a legal regime 'of its own kind' which is specifically adapted to the nature and characteristics of IK. Though this approach has received considerable attention in the literature, little progress has been made in terms of actually implementing this kind of protection. The establishment of a sui generis regime poses many complex conceptual and practical issues, including the following: (i) how to define the subject matter of protection; (ii) what the requirements for protection should be; (iii) what should be the nature of the rights to be conferred; (iv) who should be the title holders; (v) how the rights should be acquired; (vi) how long the rights should last; and (vii) how the rights should be enforced.

RECOMMENDED ACTIONS TO PROTECT THE RIGHTS OF INDIGENOUS PEOPLES OVER THEIR KNOWLEDGE AT THE NATIONAL LEVEL

Policy and legal measures are needed at the national level to protect indigenous knowledge. Some features that should be included in national legislation are included below:

- Disclosure of origin of materials or knowledge used in patent and plant variety protection applications, including, for example, information on the use of a farmer variety in breeding a new variety or the use of a medicinal or aromatic plant to make products or extracting vegetable dyes from certain minerals and plants.
- Evidence of prior informed consent (in standard format) before using the bioresource.
- Evidence (in standard format) of the nature (monetary, non-monetary), mode and method of sharing benefits derived from using IK.
- Applications for use of IK should be published in all major newspapers, especially the vernacular press.
- Proof of IK should be presented in both written and oral form and in the form of community knowledge conveyed by third parties.
- The onus of proving compliance (burden of proof) should be reversed. In the case of a dispute, the user agency should be required to prove that all conditions of disclosure and benefit sharing have been met.
- The penalty for infringement should be severe enough to be an effective deterrent.
- Access to bioresources should be linked to the provisions of Article 16 of the CBD relating to transfer of technology. The Material Transfer Agreement needed for access to bioresources should be linked to an agreement to transfer technologies in various categories related to biodiversity, including biotechnology.

NOTES

1 Editor's note: Although the term 'traditional knowledge' is used elsewhere in this volume, the author prefers to adopt the term 'indigenous knowledge'.
2 Barbasco is a plant from Latin America whose root contains a natural insecticide and a substance used in the production of synthetic steroids.
3 Endod is a plant from Africa whose berries have molluscicidal properties.

Chapter 18

Access to Genetic Resources and Protection of Traditional Knowledge in Indigenous Territories[1]

Grethel Aguilar

The purpose of this chapter is to set out a legal framework for access to genetic resources and the protection of related traditional knowledge (TK) among indigenous peoples, with the aim of achieving a fair sharing of the benefits obtained from their commercial utilization.

Biodiversity has assumed growing importance not only in the natural sciences but also in the economic and social sphere. For instance, according to the UN Environment Programme (UNEP, 1993), foods, fibres, ornamental plants and raw material of biological origin make up practically half the global economy. This means that biological resources are a form of capital with considerable economic potential. To exploit these resources commercially, it is often necessary to deploy biotechnology, defined in Agenda 21 as 'a set of enabling techniques for bringing about specific manmade changes in deoxyribonucleic acid (DNA), or genetic material, in plants, animals and microbial systems, leading to useful products and technologies'.[2]

Previously, owners of modern biotechnology were not required to share the benefits derived from the genetic resources they used with the countries of origin or with indigenous communities. At present this issue is being discussed, especially in developing countries, which are in the process of developing national laws to implement the Convention on Biological Diversity (CBD).

Historical practice, with few exceptions, has been that the countries and indigenous peoples possessing the genetic resources and related TK have not obtained any direct economic benefits. This being so, we tend to take the view that the developing countries must work on ways of acting as the 'guardians' of biodiversity at the place where these genetic resources are located and of creating 'tools' that will allow them to define the rights and obligations of the different actors involved with respect to access to genetic resources and the related TK.

This set of rules could lead to sustainable use and an equitable sharing of benefits arising from genetic resources and TK. They could also contribute globally to the search for better health and better food security.

THE CONVENTION ON BIOLOGICAL DIVERSITY

The Convention on Biological Diversity (CBD) lays the preliminary foundations for the negotiation and creation of legal solutions to benefit sharing with indigenous peoples at the national level through Article 8(j). While acknowledging the article's recognition of the value of the knowledge of local communities and indigenous peoples and the need for an equitable sharing of benefits, it must be said that the language is weak. It uses, for instance, the expression 'as far as possible', which releases states from any clear legal duty. It reduces national legislation to a responsibility to respect, preserve and maintain knowledge and to encourage the equitable sharing of benefits. This means that without national legislation to implement the article, this is merely an expression of goodwill.

The state may be seen as the political organization overseeing the interests of its citizens including by regulating activities carried out inside its territory whether by nationals or by aliens. Thus, when we consider that one of the CBD's objectives is the equitable sharing of benefits obtained from access to genetic resources, the state must ensure that the knowledge related to these resources is recognized, even in relations between states, as part of its role to protect the interests of its citizens.

However, we may go further in adopting a broader conception of 'the state', according to which all members of a society (including private companies, communities and inhabitants in general) constitute the state. The implication is that all of these 'parts' of the state must play a role in fulfilling the CBD's objectives, which include the equitable sharing of benefits, and not just governments or national regulatory institutions. While Article 8(j) depends on effective national legislation, this does not negate the duty of states to respect the principle of equitable sharing of benefits or to recognize TK. In any case, the sharing of benefits will take place according to mutually agreed terms, which implies that each individual case is negotiated, so that a definition will be agreed among the parties regarding what is fair and equitable.

Despite the CBD's shortcomings, it does give a special position to the protection of TK related to genetic resources. The CBD applies to contracting parties, that is to states. This implies that when the parties engage in a transaction in which access is negotiated to genetic resources, they must also negotiate (with the prior consent of the communities or indigenous peoples) the value of the TK related to those resources, ensuring that the benefits obtained are equitable.

CONCERNS OF THE INDIGENOUS PEOPLES

Undoubtedly these concerns are many and they vary in degree of priority according to the particular people involved or the region or continent we are referring to. What we have done in this section is to collate some information obtained from organized indigenous groups, rather than attempt to give a general overview of the situation.

According to Darrell Posey (1996), the main claims of indigenous peoples may be summarized as follows: (i) self-determination, which includes claims related to property rights over land and resources; (ii) prior informed consent; (iii) human rights; (iv) cultural rights, which encompasses the right to express and maintain different cultures, the right to religion, language and access to sacred sites; and (v) respect for treaties. Of these, the most important, as identified by a survey of statements by indigenous organizations around the world, were self-determination and territorial rights.

The main rights claimed by indigenous peoples with respect to access to natural resources and protection of traditional knowledge are: (i) rights of communal ownership of lands and territories; (ii) rights of self-determination; (iii) the right to exercise customary law in accordance with their social and cultural practice; (iv) the right to be legally and politically represented by their own institutions; and (v) the right to control the ownership of traditional knowledge (International Alliance of Indigenous-Tribal Peoples of the Tropical Forests, 1996).

All these rights are interrelated and play an important role with regard to access to genetic resources and the protection of TK. Thus for example, the recognition of self-determination will give communities in many cases the possibility not only of exercising control over their knowledge, but also over genetic resources located on their territories. Being represented politically and legally by their own institutions will give communities a legal status, enabling them to conclude their own contracts for access to genetic resources and related traditional knowledge.

The above serves to illustrate the fact that these claims are undeniably interlinked in practice. It is not possible to deal with the issues of TK protection and access to genetic resources as if they have no relation to the other rights claimed by indigenous peoples.

PROPERTY RIGHTS AND EQUITABLE BENEFIT SHARING

At the heart of the debate on the equitable sharing of benefits arising from the use of traditional knowledge is the matter of who is the owner. In this respect, a distinction has to be drawn between different types of ownership, which are (i) ownership of territories, (ii) ownership of genetic resources, and (iii) ownership of traditional knowledge, innovations and practices.

The connection between territories, land tenure and access to the natural resources located within them is of great importance, and has been since colonial times when the division of traditional indigenous lands into administrative parcels, combined with differential treatment between them, made it possible to maintain a system of subjection for over three centuries.

Local communities and indigenous peoples are faced with a complexity of legal practice when it comes to ownership, tenure, and use of resources and access to them. Some communities have no ownership titles, others have only usufruct rights, and some have no rights and lose their lands after many years of possession. There are communities which divide up the land into personal holdings, and there are others that have systems of communal ownership. There is a wide range of situations which are sometimes hard to distinguish.

Where the use of natural resources is concerned, the situation is even harder to unravel. There are countries that recognize rights of ownership over land, but not over subsoil, that is, not over minerals. For example, if oil is found, this would be the property of the state and not of the landowners. Sometimes ownership of land includes property rights related to biological resources. In other countries, land ownership does not guarantee property rights over the biological resources. Others consider that natural resources belong to the public domain, that is to say, they belong to all and not to the landowner, which is problematic as far as the issue of access to genetic resources is concerned. This is not to mention protected areas, which in some cases have been established where these communities live, denying or disregarding their rights. Yet faced with this wide range of situations, the communities themselves often have no choice but to depend on and live off the land.

Land claims are closely and inseparably linked to struggles for territorial independence and for self-government, to the rights to food and cultural preservation, and to rights to recognition of traditional knowledge. International Labour Organization (ILO) Convention 169 concerning Indigenous and Tribal Peoples in Independent Countries tried to establish obligations in relation to ownership rights. Although the convention has been generally looked upon as a weak instrument, it does provide a few significant measures for the protection of indigenous rights and in particular for the recognition of lands, territories and the use of natural resources.

The convention states that the rights of ownership and possession of the peoples concerned over the lands which they traditionally occupy must be recognized. In addition, governments must take steps as necessary to guarantee effective protection of those rights of ownership and possession. With regard to access to natural resources, ILO 169 states that the rights of the peoples concerned to the natural resources pertaining to their lands must be safeguarded, including the right to participate in the use, management and conservation of those resources. It also draws attention to the obligation of governments to consult the peoples concerned before undertaking any programmes for the exploration or exploitation of mineral or subsurface resources that are owned by the state but located on the lands of the peoples concerned.

Most of these undertakings ratified by governments, however, run into problems of implementation. This is shown by the endless number of court cases concerning problems of ownership, or the struggle waged by groups like the Congreso General Gnobe-Bugle of Panama, who have been fighting for 20 years to stop the exploration contract between the state-run mining enterprise and a transnational corporation. It should be added that local communities are combating not only the seizure of lands which have belonged to them historically, but also the negative effects on the environment which may be produced by works, such as oil operations without environmental planning, logging or water contamination.

It is worth mentioning the efforts made by the UN Working Group on Indigenous Populations in 1993, when it presented its final draft of the Declaration on the Rights of Indigenous Peoples. Although this document is still in draft form, it constitutes a fundamental reference where indigenous populations and the recognition of their rights are concerned. It asserts the rights of indigenous peoples to control access to natural resources and to the ownership of plants, animals and minerals that are vital to their cultures. It also recognizes their right to own, develop, control and use their lands and territories, including the total environment of the lands, air, waters, coastal seas, flora and fauna and other resources which they have traditionally owned or otherwise occupied or used. They should be entitled to special measures to control, develop and protect their sciences, technologies and cultural manifestations, including human and other genetic resources, seeds, medicines, knowledge of properties of fauna and flora, etc. It is precisely on account of the failure by governments to recognize these claims that the issue of rights over lands, territories and access to resources has increasingly become a priority.

According to Article 15 of the CBD, 'recognizing the sovereign rights of States over their natural resources, the authority to determine access to genetic resources rests with the national governments and is subject to national legislation'. Despite the fact that the wording appears to suggest that the states own the genetic resources within their territory, the interpretations which have been given of this article tend rather to take the view that the state has unique and exclusive authority to regulate access to genetic resources. This means that the responsibility for exercising this authority rests within the national domain.

Here too a distinction needs to be drawn between 'common ownership' of biological resources, an idea which was rejected, and the 'common interest' of humankind, an idea which has been maintained, recognizing an international interest in the conservation of biological diversity.

As the regulation of access to genetic resources depends on national jurisdiction, there are countries, for instance, where genetic resources belong to the owner of the land, while in other countries, such as Costa Rica and Colombia and many developing countries, the state owns a land's genetic resources, even though that land may be privately owned.

According to Costa Rica's Biodiversity Act, the state exercises full and exclusive sovereignty over the elements of biodiversity, while the biochemical and genetic properties of wild or domesticated elements of biodiversity are in the public domain. The Wildlife Act had already established that wild flora and the development of wild genetic resources which constitute genetic reserves are of public interest. In that case, the resources do not belong exclusively to those who have the right of ownership over the land.

The terms of the Biodiversity Act state that the technical office must notify those concerned that any application for access to biodiversity elements must be accompanied by prior informed consent, issued by the owner of the property where the activity is to take place, or by the authority of the indigenous community when it is located within their territories, and the director of the conservation area.

This law recognizes the right of local communities and indigenous peoples to oppose access to their resources and related knowledge, for cultural, spiritual, social, economic or other reasons. The basic requirements for access also include the conditions of technology transfer and equitable sharing of benefits, if any, agreed in the licences, agreements and concessions, as well as the type of protection of related knowledge required by the representatives of the place where access is to materialize.

But despite the fact that in spirit the purpose of this law is to protect TK and to recognize the indigenous peoples' right to ownership over land and territories, the wording is weak in that there is some confusion between 'ownership' rights over genetic resources and rights over traditional knowledge related to those resources. The case might well arise that access to genetic resources might be granted, but not access to the related TK.

In other words, there is a thin line between the concepts of ownership of lands, territories and genetic resources, and the ownership of traditional knowledge, which belongs exclusively to the communities so only they can decide what becomes of it, regardless of whether access to genetic resources is authorized or not. The importance of this distinction is apparent especially in indigenous territories which have fallen into the category of protected areas or national parks, like the International Friendship Park in Costa Rica. Before long there is sure to be a debate about who gives consent in such a situation. Should it be the state in such protected areas, or the indigenous peoples to whom the territory belongs whether or not they have legal title?

Costa Rica's Biodiversity Act was one of the first of its kind in the world. Many of these issues are still being discussed within the local communities and indigenous peoples, and what happens in practice is sometimes different from what the law intended. One approach is to require that prior informed consent be given first, before the state allows access to genetic resources in indigenous territories. However, a situation could arise whereby the state would opt to grant authorization despite opposition from the indigenous community on the grounds that the activity is in the public interest. In such case, the community's interest would be considered secondary to the national interest. This tends to happen in the case of oil exploration or exploitation.

Traditional knowledge is subject to ownership claims and as such may be the subject of negotiation. Ideally, TK should be considered an asset which may be protected by a right that remains with its owner, even though the latter may be allowed to transfer it on the basis of an established negotiation. This knowledge can then yield a benefit stream to the owner should it ever give rise to a marketable product.

For this reason, when we think of compensation, this must not be negotiated in terms of a perishable good, but rather as ongoing compensation which may be paid as a percentage of the earnings derived from the discovered product. At the same time the ownership of this knowledge must be preserved and it must be transmissible (without commercial gain) to other communities and to future generations. We could then imagine a marketing technique whereby the user – at the time the product is purchased – also pays a value corresponding to the traditional knowledge related to genetic resources and which made possible the creation of the pharmaceutical product in the first place.

This point is controversial and open to discussion. Some believe that it is not fair on the buyer. The problem resides, however, in the fact that this cost was never contemplated in the pharmaceutical companies' accounts. Few users ever query the cost of a product or the income of pharmaceutical companies. This is not to say that the pharmaceutical companies should not make a profit, but rather that all should benefit. If the cost of using technology is chargeable, then the cost of the TK used should also be charged.

The notion that TK must be used for the benefit of humankind is right. But for humankind to benefit from TK does not mean to say that the latter must be handed over free of charge and with no recognition. There is no doubt that the CBD's objective of achieving the equitable sharing of benefits becomes meaningless if we start from the assumption that TK is freely available.

On the other hand, the view that TK is part of the public domain has also been the subject of debate. It has been suggested that no protection should be considered for knowledge that has become part of the public domain. Nevertheless, it is still true that knowledge always comes from an original source and the fact that it is in the public domain does not necessarily mean to say that the source has disappeared.

PROTECTION OF TRADITIONAL KNOWLEDGE

Patents and other intellectual property rights (IPRs) are not really suitable for protecting TK for both practical and cultural reasons. Nonetheless, non-Western systems of innovation exist independently of scientific laboratories, such as the informal collective innovation systems of developing country farming communities, whose seeds are manifestations of their ingenuity. Indigenous communities are also innovative in the ways they select plants and prepare extracts and mixtures to cure illnesses. However, the protection of these people's intellectual property rights has no place in TRIPS. In effect, we are accepting that the only form of knowledge deserving of legal protection is that generated in laboratories.

There is a strong current of opinion favouring a sui generis system separate from the IPR system, to protect traditional knowledge related to genetic resources. Unless we begin to look for viable alternatives, we shall continue being the victims of knowledge piracy. There is an urgent need to establish equal recognition for the creativity of indigenous peoples.

According to Costa Rica's Biodiversity Act, the state expressly recognizes and protects, under the common name of sui generis community intellectual rights, the knowledge, innovations and practices of indigenous peoples and local communities, related to the use of biodiversity elements and related knowledge. This right exists and is legally recognized merely on the basis that the cultural practice or knowledge related to the genetic and biochemical resources exists. It does not require any prior declaration, express recognition or official registration, and as such may include practices which acquire that status in future. Such recognition implies that none of the forms of IPR protection may affect these historic practices.

In order to determine the scope and nature of sui generis community intellectual rights, the act establishes that within 18 months following the act's entry into force, a participatory procedure must be established with the indigenous and peasant communities for this purpose. The act further provides for an inventory to be drawn up of specific sui generis community intellectual rights which the communities wish to protect, while the possibility must remain open for the registration or recognition of others meeting the same criteria in the future. Recognition of these rights will be voluntary and free of charge.

Clearly, much still remains to be done and the real challenge will be how to regulate the content of the law, since it does not define the ownership title of knowledge, the way in which benefits are to be shared or even the scope of 'rights and obligations' that the community intellectual rights involve. In other words, the act provides the basis and principles on which to develop a sui generis system, but the process is still incomplete.

CONCLUSIONS

Indigenous peoples need new instruments to protect their genetic resources and associated traditional knowledge. Better protection is needed against the piracy of their knowledge and intrusion on their territories. A sui generis system tied to the framework provided by the CBD and Article 27.3(b) of TRIPS is urgently needed. This would provide a means of calling the attention of major pharmaceutical companies, researchers, developed countries and developing countries to the rights of indigenous peoples and local communities. Why is this? Simply because it would bring the matter within the sphere of commercial interests.

National policies and legislation provide a key tool for ensuring that the objectives of the CBD are met, and especially to ensure that the equitable sharing of benefits obtained from genetic resources and related traditional knowledge becomes a reality. To these ends, national policy-makers must start to recognize the rights of indigenous peoples to sovereignty, self-determination, the ownership of land and natural resources, and to enjoy their own customary rights. All these concepts are inseparably linked to the protection of traditional knowledge. There are many ways of achieving this, but it has to be borne in mind that there must be effective and transparent participation in the process of decision-making whenever decisions are taken.

NOTES

1 Paper presented at the International Conference on Trade, Environment and Sustainable Development: Prospects for Latin America and the Caribbean. Mexico City, 19–21 February 2001. UN Environment Programme, Regional Office for Latin America and the Caribbean.

2 The Convention on Biological Diversity (CBD) defines biotechnology as 'any technological application that uses biological systems, living organisms, or derivatives thereof, to make or modify products or processes for specific use'.

REFERENCES

International Alliance of Indigenous-Tribal Peoples of the Tropical Forests (1996) 'The Biodiversity Convention: the concerns of indigenous peoples', *Submission of the International Alliance to the CBD Secretariat.*

Posey, D A (1996) 'Identifying commonalities and divergencies between indigenous peoples and farmers groups', *Bulletin of the Working Group on Traditional Resource Rights* 3.

UNEP (1993) *Report of Panel I, Priorities of Action for Conservation and Sustainable Use of Biological Diversity*, UN Doc. UNEP/Bio. Div/N5-inc.3/3.

Chapter 19

Traditional Knowledge and the Biotrade: the Colombian experience

Ana María Hernández Salgar

Applied traditional knowledge (TK) has preserved and improved plant and animal species and in doing so has made a substantial contribution to the lives of all humans. The great majority of traditional communities show a willingness to share knowledge which is beneficial to humankind. But despite this, the cultural wealth of communities is being seriously depleted by Western-style methods of acquiring knowledge that may be characterized as misappropriation. Clearly the need has now arisen to establish mechanisms for protecting this knowledge.

In recognition of the importance of preserving TK for the sake of present and future generations, the international community has tried to identify strategies for appropriate action. Negotiations have been taking place in major forums, such as the Convention on Biological Diversity (CBD), to find the best mechanisms and means for ensuring the protection of TK. Meanwhile UNCTAD, through its Sustainable Biotrade Initiative, has undertaken projects to assess the viability of business transactions involving the wider use of TK, while at the same time preserving biodiversity and sustainably utilizing its components.

This chapter describes a pilot project launched in Colombia by the Sustainable Biotrade Programme of the Alexander von Humboldt Institute, which aims to devise possible mechanisms for protecting knowledge, innovations and traditional practices relating to the use of medicinal plants. The project involves a local association called Centro de Investigaciones y Servicios Comunitarios (CISEC), whose members include several chiefs of the Paez del Cauca indigenous community and a plant pharmacology laboratory called Labfarve. These two parties have decided to undertake a joint project for the commercial development of two plants with medicinal properties.

The Humboldt Institute is assisting the project by developing guidelines for protecting the TK relating to the use of the medicinal plants provided by the association to Labfarve, and to ensure that benefits derived from the use of these plants are shared in the fairest and most equitable way possible. Such benefits are envisaged as being both financial and non-monetary in nature.

To develop these guidelines, it was necessary for the institute to clarify the existing national and international rules governing intellectual property and TK, and identify areas where such rules may be lacking. Based on this information, the institute would try to come up with benefit sharing standards or guidelines, as well as basic proposals for establishing mechanisms for the protection and recognition of TK. It emerged in the course of the enquiry that no set answers were to be found in existing national or international legislation or policies in the areas of intellectual property rights (IPRs) and TK. It was also found that while basic guidelines were needed, each individual community approaches negotiations of this kind with different priorities. We therefore concluded that attempting to draw up rigid inflexible programmes for TK protection would be mistaken. It would be preferable to settle for 'framework' programmes or strategies allowing the commercial use of biodiversity and related TK to be conducted on a case-by-case basis. The next part of this chapter deals with the specifics of the institute's analysis.

BENEFIT SHARING

The institute found that the benefits which may be derived from the use of biodiversity or knowledge associated with genetic resources may be manifested in various forms. Benefits could be as financial remuneration, but could also include education, training or health provision. There are no international rules at this time which establish specifically just when and to what extent the reference to a 'fair and equitable sharing' is applicable. But it is clear that fairness and equity are directly related to the participation of the users and owners of a resource, and this must be mutually agreed among them. Thus, benefits constitute a voluntary agreement between the parties.

The community's participation in the traditional medicinal use of the plants must be recognized, and one way of doing this is by means of labelling. When the medicines come onto the market, the labels directly indicate that research was carried out on the basis of information provided by the chiefs of the Paez Community concerning the beneficial properties of the plants, and the fact that their marketing or use has been endorsed by them. This benefit would accrue both to Labfarve and to the association. The former would benefit because the laboratory is shown to be a pioneer in joint activities of such a kind with traditional communities, and because it may achieve greater credibility, both for the product if it is shown to be related to TK, and for the laboratory itself. The latter would benefit because the association gets publicity and the medical community is better informed of the association's readiness to exchange knowledge. This could lead to further mutually beneficial arrangements.

Benefit sharing could also be achieved through contracts. Labfarve and the association could enter into a contractual relationship according to which a certain portion of sales revenues could be shared. Although Labfarve does not itself engage in marketing for profit, account must be taken of the fact that the knowledge associated with the use of medicinal plants carries an intrinsic value in every sale. Such a contract should also provide for purchase prices specifically related to the raw material, taking account of the added value attributable to the TK input. It would not be appropriate in this respect to apply market prices for the plants without taking into account the traditional knowledge component, which is what gives use value to the medicinal plants. This added value should also be negotiated between the parties in order that the communities do not feel that their moral rights over their knowledge are being infringed.

A number of other approaches might be adopted. For example, an agreement could be made between Labfarve and the association to provide: (i) technical training for members of the community working directly with traditional medicine; and (ii) education and information workshops for the community on research processes pursued by the laboratory with a view to detecting and using other plants with active components having medicinal properties.

TRADITIONAL KNOWLEDGE PROTECTION

In view of the lack of existing mechanisms that are likely to work in this particular case, the institute made seven recommendations. First, Labfarve must undertake not to protect the results of its research as intellectual property, unless it has obtained the prior consent of the chiefs belonging to the association, and such consent must be given in writing. It must also be accompanied by a proposal for the sharing of benefits, together with a recognition of the moral rights of the association as provider of the knowledge.

Second, a 'list' may be drawn up of the items of traditional knowledge of the chiefs belonging to the association which may be used by Labfarve. This list should be produced in accordance with criteria agreed with the chiefs, handled by the association and made public, especially among the medical community. The items of knowledge included on the list should not be withdrawn except for justifiable reasons acceptable to both parties, and any withdrawal should not be applicable to retroactive use of the information. The purpose of the list would be to establish which items of TK are to be given broad dissemination and use, while the use of other knowledge which the chiefs believe should be kept secret will be left to their discretion.

Third, Labfarve must expressly recognize that the results of research on the medicinal plants imply an intellectual contribution from the indigenous peoples. This recognition should be mentioned in publications resulting from the research and on labels attached to any resulting products. Other forms of recognition may be established by mutual agreement between the parties.

Fourth, in case the parties commit to commercial exclusive exploitation of the medicinal plants concerned, Labfarve would not be able to purchase raw material from other suppliers, and the association would agree not to offer its product to any other user than the laboratory. This would be an optional commitment, if considered desirable by the parties.

Fifth, the fact that the association has disclosed its TK on medicinal plants to Labfarve does not imply a transfer of the rights involved. In other words, the members of the traditional communities belonging to the association continue to maintain their rights over the knowledge, and to disseminate and protect them in whichever manner they consider most convenient.

Sixth, it must be borne in mind that the protection of traditional knowledge has not yet been specifically regulated. This means that any agreement reached between Labfarve and the association must contain a clause providing that, in the event of regulations governing TK being issued in the future, any transaction between the parties will have to be conducted within that framework, so that, if appropriate, any existing commitments would need to be adjusted accordingly.

Seventh, the legal representative of the association must consult the chiefs belonging to the association and agree among themselves on how TK should be protected. If such agreement is not forthcoming, decisions would not be considered representative and would on those grounds be inapplicable.

RESPONSES FROM LABFARVE AND THE CISEC ASSOCIATION

Negotiations between the parties towards agreement on the joint development of projects relating to research and marketing of products derived from the two medicinal plants have not yet been completed. Despite general agreement regarding TK protection and benefit sharing, some remaining points await a resolution. So far, Labfarve has agreed to undertake a number of activities.

First, it has offered to provide the association's producers with training and advice concerning raw material processing, standardization and pharmaceutical production techniques to enable environmentally, socially and economically sustainable production, and quality control in processing and manufacture. Second, Labfarve has agreed to conduct academic research into plant pharmacology, toxicology, pharmacognosy and phytochemistry, and clinical handling. However, it is favourable to the idea of joint publications describing the results of both traditional and academic research (indigenous and Western knowledge), if the community so wishes. Third, Labfarve will conduct market research through the training programme undertaken by medical staff enrolled in the health and research programmes of the Labfarve Foundation. Fourth, Labfarve will offer training in its laboratories to individuals registered with CISEC. Fifth, it has proposed a sum higher than the normal purchase price of raw material as recognition of the intrinsic value of the related traditional knowledge. Sixth, Labfarve recognizes that, in some specific cases, an added value might be offered, corresponding to a fair trade stamp which would be placed on the label, or as an insert, in order to express the participation in the production processes of the chiefs belonging to the association and the recognition of their intellectual contribution. Seventh, Labfarve wish to retain its freedom to choose other producers and buyers of raw materials. Eighth, Labfarve undertakes not to protect as intellectual property the results of research arising from studies without the prior consent of the chiefs belonging to the association. Labfarve leaves it to the association's discretion to obtain patent registration, as appropriate, or other sui generis forms of protection of traditional knowledge. Ninth, Labfarve undertakes not to make gainful or unilateral use of information derived from research on the medicinal plants, nor on any other plant which might subsequently enter into the process, without the consent of the indigenous chiefs represented by the association. Tenth, it proposes that both parties should sign a parallel exclusivity agreement stating that only they are authorized to conduct the marketing of the finished products.

For its part, the CISEC Association made the following responses in pursuing its interest in TK protection and fair and equitable benefit sharing. First, it stipulated the recognition of the communities' rights over their resources and knowledge in any type of negotiation, and the duty of the parties to obtain the prior informed consent of the indigenous communities before proceeding to any type of marketing. Second, it required that communities belonging to the association be fully informed about the social and cultural effects of the works carried out and the results of the research and marketing of products. Third, it stressed that any agreement should involve a commitment to undertake and foster traditional research into bi-cultural forms of medical diagnosis and treatment. Fourth, the association requested that communities be provided with training and advice regarding standards and techniques of agricultural production allowing environmentally, socially and economically sustainable production, as well as in raw material processing, standardization and pharmaceutical production techniques, quality control, and preparation of protocols for quality control at the different stages of production. Fifth, in joint development activities, the laboratory should allow members of the association to take part in activities related to the research processes concerned, through visits or training programmes. Sixth, any publication resulting from traditional and academic research regarding the use of the medicinal plants must be undertaken jointly with the consent of the communities involved and subject to joint authorship by the parties. The consent of the communities would be given through the association. Seventh, the association preferred that, for marketing purposes, the parties should agree on the basic traditional and scientific information required, to include the name of the association and mention of each of the participating indigenous communities. A mention should also be made of the added value of the raw material used, related, among others, to the contribution of the associated indigenous communities. Eighth, Labfarve should undertake not to protect the results of its research as intellectual property except with the prior consent of the associated chiefs, given in writing. For all effects of patents and other intellectual property rights, all existing and future standards issued for the specific protection of traditional knowledge must be taken into account. In case protection is obtained, the amount of compensation agreed in favour of the association should be subject to negotiation, taking into account the fact that in any event the community will appear as the innovator owning the information used to develop the product. Ninth, the association may also initiate procedures to obtain suitable protection for TK, subject to the prior informed consent of the communities, and will take all necessary steps to defend the protection granted. Finally, the results of the research should not be supplied to third persons without the consent of all the parties.

FINAL CONSIDERATIONS

Through its Sustainable Biotrade Initiative, the Humboldt Institute continues to act as a facilitator in the process. Unfortunately, it appears that both of the parties involved in the negotiation are trying to extract economic gain from the negotiation. While it must be clear that the objective of biotrade initiatives is to maximize economic benefits from the sustainable use of biological resources, it must also be understood that a component such as traditional knowledge which is so intrinsic to the handling of biodiversity cannot be seen merely from the point of view of the value added to the product which is to be marketed. The biotrade must take account of the fact that beyond the search for added value the negotiation affects the cultural wealth of a people and that every effort should be made therefore to ensure the respect and preservation thereof.

The legal vacuum and the political sensitivity connected with any biotrade initiative that includes traditional knowledge constitute a formidable obstacle when it comes to establishing a transparent negotiation. It is essential, therefore, to try to establish clear rules in this respect, both nationally and internationally. Moreover, while undoubtedly efforts have been initiated on all sides to arrive at an approved proposal in this respect, insufficient heed has been paid to the traditional communities, who are the people most directly affected. One common mistake biotrade actors often make is to think for the communities. In fact, the general outlook of traditional peoples is very far removed from Western ways of thinking. On the other hand, the standards governing biotrade initiatives are usually based on Western ways of thinking, not traditional ones.

Chapter 20

Documentation of Traditional Knowledge: People's Biodiversity Registers

Ghate Utkarsh[1]

Globalization and its attendant impacts such as commercialization, monopolization and economic inequity raise numerous concerns. One of the most important of these is that knowledge and other public goods are rapidly being appropriated, transformed and marketed by commercial concerns, without any benefits being shared with the original producers. The infamous patents relating to neem, turmeric and basmati are good evidence of this process, which is being accelerated by the TRIPS Agreement. It is a major challenge to provide physical access to biodiversity and related traditional knowledge while retaining intellectual property rights (IPRs) and ensuring equitable benefit sharing. Beyond this, we need to find ways to make benefit sharing encourage the sustainable use of bioresources and the maintenance of biodiversity-friendly livelihoods at a time when biodiversity forms an indirect and shrinking economic axis of rural livelihoods.

Documenting traditional knowledge (TK) in a participatory fashion can lead to protection of the IPRs of knowledge contributors, and benefit sharing thereof can promote sustainable utilization of biodiversity. This is demonstrated by India's People's Biodiversity Registers (PBRs). PBRs are village-level documents of people's knowledge of biodiversity including conservation and sustainable utilization, and their perceptions relating to use and commercial exchange. The PBRs are often developed by local school teachers, students and NGO researchers along with the villagers (but rarely by educated villagers themselves). Biodiversity registers from villages can also be assembled at the level of *talukas* (counties) and also districts, states and the whole nation, in the form of computerized databases, thereby proving important information to the people, government and industry. PBRs have been recognised by the Indian Biological Diversity Bill as a way to ensure equitable access and benefit sharing, by recognizing such registration as prior art to scrutinize related IPR applications as well as the basis for sharing resultant benefits equitably. Similar provisions for recognizing these registers through a consolidated Indian digital database at the global level will help to reconcile equity and conservation concerns with globalization.

PRIOR INFORMED CONSENT, ACCESS AND BENEFIT SHARING

The Convention on Biological Diversity (CBD) makes access to genetic resources and knowledge contingent upon prior informed consent (PIC) and mutually agreed terms of benefit sharing. However, in reality, there is little scope for such agreements to precede access due to the ready availability of much of the public domain material and knowledge, including through digital databases. Further, modern technology can extract genetic information from international museums and collections that store many of the biodiversity specimens that are easily available to commercial interests. Thus, corporate interests can easily access the material and information without the consent or even knowledge of its country or community of origin, forfeiting any chances of benefit sharing. This happened, for example, with neem, turmeric and basmati. Benefit sharing through PIC thus appears limited to yet untapped traditional knowledge or folk innovations or crop varieties that are confined to remote villages.

To cover public domain resources, the benefit sharing system must de-link PIC from physical access and impose it prior to commercialization. Thus, benefit sharing agreements must precede approval of IPR applications, even if such PIC was not sought prior to physical access to material or knowledge. Secondly, benefits must be interpreted in more ways than mere cash compensation. While benefits relating to knowledge could be as royalty or awards, or in kind as public acclaim, benefits relating to physical access to material include resource usage or regulation rights. The monetary benefits could include upfront or initial payments, for collecting samples, milestone payments from when product development and marketing starts appearing feasible, and long-term payments, which may come from public funds consisting of direct payments from industry including to those communities that are not parties to any contract.

THE RATIONALE FOR REGISTRATION

Global efforts for access and benefit sharing (ABS) have generally focused on monetary benefits. These efforts are concentrated in tropical developing countries. Unlike India, these countries harbour ethnic groups with strong and discrete territorial resource claims over forests and water, and whose local economies depend greatly on forest products. The isolation of many of these groups from urban society and modern education systems suggest that substantial biota and related knowledge remain to be discovered. Thus, legislation in these countries has sought to encourage contractual arrangement for monetary benefit sharing.

The Indian situation differs due to the lack of any community rights over forests and waters, substantial territorial overlap between ethnic communities, substantial traditional knowledge being available publicly, and the minimal economic importance of forest produce. Thus, a review of the existing Indian legal and policy framework reveals the lack of any benefit sharing system even within the nation for public lands, except joint forest management areas or on private lands such as for agro-biodiversity conservation. There is also no system of registering stocks and transactions of material and knowledge at subnational levels in any legislation. Such a system is needed to ensure that equitable benefit sharing complements access to resources and knowledge, by recognizing and rewarding efforts to sustainably use and conserve biodiversity and related traditional knowledge and practices.

Under the above-mentioned system of PBRs designed to address this, registration and supportive activities involve:

- Documentation of people's knowledge and practices relating to use and conservation of bioresources, both wild and domesticated.
- Participatory planning for sustainable and equitable use of TK and biological resources.
- Local government approval and use of the PBR in contributions to resource management.
- Public acclaim for folk healers, traditional farmers or fishermen and others to accord them with respect, and enthuse the younger generation.
- Publicizing the PBRs programme to attract wider interest and adoption, stimulate discussion, and exchange ideas on improvement.
- Building electronic databases containing information in the registers as proof of prior art and as a basis for sharing benefits resulting from commercialization.

In contrast with similar experiments elsewhere in the world, PBRs do not block access to knowledge. In addition, our programme embraces a much broader range of practices concerned with the managing of biological resources at the village and community level.

PBR SCOPE AND DEVELOPMENT

The preparation of biodiversity registers involves various activities, namely: (i) clarifying the project rationale and obtaining people's approval for the documentation; (ii) identifying different biodiversity user groups; (iii) identifying knowledgeable individuals; (iv) interviewing members of different user groups and knowledgeable individuals; (v) field visits to various land and water elements, along with some user groups and knowledgeable individuals, to document their biodiversity, its uses and history; (vi) mapping the landscape of the study site; (vii) discussions with the entire village assembly on management planning; (viii) discussions with outsiders related to resource use such as nomadic shepherds or artisans, traders and government officials; (ix) village council meeting to approve consensus management plans; and (x) village meetings in the presence of the media to honour and give publicity to TK practitioners and biological resource conservers.

The PBRs at this stage comprise the following modules:

- *The 'peoplescape'.* This comprises different occupational segments of society such as farmers, fishermen, labourers, forest produce collectors, medicine men, etc.
- *The landscape.* This involves noting and mapping the mosaic of land and water habitats from which the concerned people acquire most living resources, thereby helping to understand the biomass resource flows, and serving as a benchmark for monitoring future changes.
- *The 'lifescape'.* This refers to levels of abundance, harvests and uses of different elements of biodiversity known to people, and their distribution in different land and water elements.
- *Ecological Changes.* These are ongoing changes in the local landscape, waterscape and lifescape. The forces driving these changes are studied, such as the impacts of land reform legislation in triggering deforestation during the 1960s.
- *Conservation Practices.* These are local practices of sustainable use, conservation and restoration of biodiversity resources. For example, sacred groves or ponds or sacred plants and animals are recorded besides people's perceptions of ongoing conservation and development efforts.
- *Developmental aspirations.* These comprise people's choices in such areas as housing, roads, water, electricity, healthcare, education and other amenities, and how these may be reconciled with conservation in order to minimize damage.
- *Conflicts and Consensus.* Conflicts arising out of differences in choices of various segments of society are investigated. Ways to minimize such friction and enhance cooperation are also explored.
- *Management Options.* Local people's options for development and management of the natural resource base in a biodiversity-friendly fashion are articulated, such as to prioritize farms and cost–benefit measures for traditional varieties, harvest quotas, cultural festivities at sacred sites to promote conservation, cultivation of medicinal plants for own use, and regulation of trade by local people's committees.

The programme originated with the 'Community Register' (CR) concept launched by the Foundation for Revitalization of Local Health Traditions (FRLHT) in a meeting of Southern Indian NGOs during 1994. It systematically documented the traditional knowledge and skills of the villagers and recognised them as 'prior art' to contest the related, fraudulent IPR claims. CRs differed from similar initiatives in focusing on communities rather than individuals and on traditional rather than emerging knowledge or practices. In 1995, the phrase 'Community Biodiversity Register' (CBR) was adopted instead, making the programme more closely linked to the principles of the CBD. Spearheaded by the Indian Institute of Sciences (IISc) in Bangalore, this phase documented not just species but also their habitats, thus embracing the landscape as a whole. However, the costs and efforts multiplied due to the greater involvement of external researchers.

The next phase married traditional conservation practices such as sacred groves with the modern ones, especially the protected areas such as wildlife sanctuaries, national parks and biosphere reserves. Facilitated by the World Wide Fund for Nature–India (WWF) and coordinated by IISc, this phase formed a part of a nationwide exercise called the Biodiversity Conservation Prioritization Project. Costs and efforts needed per register skyrocketed due to external researchers and their wide travel. However, this phase also facilitated compromise between conservation and development at the village level through its involvement of external users and not just local communities. Numerous publications had re-christened the effort by now as 'People's Biodiversity Registers', thereby dispensing with the academic debate on the community versus the individual in the TK context.

Innovative approaches in the next phase included a focus on private lands and on documenting local cultivation practices. Hundreds of PBR initiatives were started up all over Andhra Pradesh state that were promoted by the Deccan Development Society and in Western Karnataka by the Nagarika Seva Trust. Costs were kept down by placing responsibility for the documentation work on educated village youths and only rarely resorting to technical translations by urban experts. An NGO called Kerala Shastra Sahitya Parishad inspired 80 such registers in the Ernakulam district of Kerala state, using government funds under the 'people's planning' campaign for decentralized governance. This popularization phase attracted publicity and ultimately influenced law and policy-making.

LESSONS

The development of the concept of People's Biodiversity Registers offers several important lessons for South Asian and other countries. First, much of the traditional knowledge can be better protected, both from erosion and biopiracy, through publicity and not secrecy, as there is little danger of biopiracy. Second, unique knowledge may best be registered in full through refereed databases, while PBRs may be used just to make claims to such knowledge alongside public domain knowledge and resources. Third, PBRs help in promoting sustainable local use and trade, as much as in staking claims on prior art to protect traditional knowledge from biopiracy. Third, local teachers and NGOs can help in compiling the PBRs along with the villagers, and also help in follow-up activities. Fourth, it is important to publicly recognize the role of PBRs both in the target villages and at higher spatial scales as an official instrument of biodiversity planning and revitalization of local traditions in the area of biodiversity. Fifth, registration can be followed up with social incentives to preserve and share knowledge such as public acclaim of knowledgeable individuals or conservers. Sixth, PBRs need to be computerized at higher spatial scales as a record of prior art in the scrutinization of IPR claims. Seventh, computerized databases also help in recognizing and rewarding grassroots innovations and unique traditional knowledge for further value addition. Finally, another advantage of computerized databases is they can assist decisions of how to allocate a fair share of financial or other benefits that may be generated from use of information in the PBRs.

NOTES

1 Numerous villagers, including forest produce collectors, farmers, fisherfolk and medicine men helped to shape this chapter. Various Indian government departments, such as the Ministry of Environment and Forests and Department of Biotechnology, have variously supported the initiative. The evolution of the ideas presented were greatly helped by discussions with R V Anuradha, Kamal Bawa, Ashwini Chhatre, Sachin Chaturvedi, Suprio Dasgupta, Biswajit Dhar, Preston Devasia, Graham Dutfield, Madhav Gadgil, K N Ganeshaiah, Yogesh Gokhale, N S Gopalakrishnan, Anil Gupta, Ashish Kothari, G Natarajan, P R Seshagiri Rao, R S Rana, Dwijen Ranganekar, P V Satheesh and Darshan Shankar. I am indebted to them all.

2 http://ces.iisc.ernet.in/hpg/cesmg.

Chapter 21

Requiring the Disclosure of the Origin of Genetic Resources and Traditional Knowledge: the current debate and possible legal alternatives

David Vivas Eugui[1]

INTRODUCTION

The Convention on Biological Diversity (CBD) has three main goals, which are the conservation of biological diversity, the sustainable use of its components, and the fair and equitable sharing of benefits from the use of genetic resources. Within this framework, a key topic is the existence of transparent regimes to regulate access to genetic resources and traditional knowledge (TK) as a means for achieving those objectives. Currently, the number of cases of 'biopiracy'[2] or illegal access and use of genetic resources and traditional knowledge are still increasing. That is to say, individuals, companies and research institutions are accessing and using genetic resources and traditional knowledge originating in biodiversity-rich countries for commercial intent without the existence of prior and informed consent and mutually agreed terms as required by the CBD. Consequently, there is a need to establish legal measures to reduce or to stop this behaviour nationally and internationally.

The CBD has been ratified by more than 180 countries and implemented through national legislation or biodiversity action plans. The Bonn Guidelines on Access to Genetic Resources and Fair and Equitable Sharing of the Benefits Arising out of their Utilization, which were adopted in 2002 by the Conference of the Parties (COP) to the CBD, include a precise set of options for developing procedures for the access and benefit sharing process, clarifying the relation with traditional knowledge, identifying practical mechanisms for monitoring, and opening space for legal remedies. The guidelines also deal with some aspects of the role of intellectual property in the access and benefit sharing (ABS).

Article 15 of the CBD clarifies that authority to determine access to genetic resources for all uses, including research and commercialization, rests with national governments, and that access to genetic resources shall be subject to prior informed consent of the contracting party providing such resources. However, in order to guarantee that genetic resources and/or traditional knowledge used or incorporated in particular inventions are legally acquired and in compliance with the CBD, it is necessary to design appropriate monitoring or control mechanisms in the intellectual property filing process.

A number of mechanisms have been proposed to ensure that the acquisition of intellectual property rights (IPRs) complies with the principles and objectives of the CBD. Two of these, which are closely related, are: (i) certification of origin of biological or genetic material in the process of acquisition of IPRs; and (ii) voluntary or mandatory disclosure of origin of the same material. A variant of both proposals is to require IPR users to supply information relating to traditional knowledge.

Certificates of origin are normally used in trade as a way to guarantee that goods supposed to come from a country that enjoys a particular tariff privilege genuinely originate there. The certificate of origin works as an official recognition of the legal origin (legal access) of a particular sample of a genetic resource or piece of information linked to traditional knowledge. In the case of the disclosure of the origin, the objective is that the origin of the genetic resource or traditional knowledge used or incorporated in an invention or a creation is expressly indicated in intellectual property filing procedures so as to assure compliance with the CBD and national access legislation. Disclosure of origin is considered by some to be an adequate way to prevent illegal access and use of genetic resources by non-authorized third parties within the intellectual property system.

This chapter briefly describes the debate surrounding the requirement for the disclosure of the origin of genetic resources and traditional knowledge and its relationship with the TRIPS Agreement. It explains the legal nature of the mechanism, describes the treatment of the disclosure of the origin in the Bonn Guidelines, identifies the main legal arguments for and against such a mechanism, and presents a list of possible legal options that could be used by policy-makers when implementing mechanisms for assuring legal access in intellectual property filing procedures.

THE CONTEXT: WHO WANTS WHAT AND WHY?

Mechanisms to assure the existence of prior informed consent and benefit sharing in patent filing and granting procedures have been developed in different national and regional legislations. Proposals for their inclusion have also been submitted before various international organizations. The most controversial of those mechanisms is the mandatory disclosure of origin of biological or genetic resources and the traditional knowledge as a condition for acquiring a patent.

For developing countries, disclosure of origin is seen as an important tool for implementing the objectives and obligations of the CBD. Also, some international forums have called for changes at the national law and policy level, as well as in international accords, to recognize this mechanism. The Conference of the Parties (COP) to the CBD, at its sixth meeting, adopted the Bonn Guidelines, which requested countries with users of genetic resources under their jurisdiction to consider 'measures to encourage the disclosure of the country of origin of the genetic resources and of the origin of traditional knowledge, innovations and practices of indigenous and local communities in applications for intellectual property rights'.

Nevertheless, some members of the COP are unconvinced about the need for certification and disclosure of origin, and a few are opposed. Such countries include Australia and Canada. The US, which is an observer in the CBD, is also highly sceptical that either is workable. At COP-6, one of the two working groups set up to discuss this and other issues recommended that the COP gather information and carry out further analysis with regard to the feasibility of the certification of origin system and the efficacy of disclosure.

In June 2002, 11 developing countries, namely Brazil, China, Cuba, Dominican Republic, Ecuador, India, Pakistan, Thailand, Venezuela, Zambia and Zimbabwe, tabled a document in the TRIPS Council which recommended that the Trade Negotiation Committee take a decision to initiate negotiations to amend the TRIPS in light of the objectives and principles of the CBD. The proposal recalls relevant provisions of the Bonn Guidelines and proposes that TRIPS be amended to provide that WTO member states must require:

> *that an applicant for a patent relating to biological materials or to traditional knowledge shall provide, as a condition to acquiring patent rights: (i) disclosure of the source and country of origin of the biological resource and of the traditional knowledge used in the invention; (ii) evidence of prior informed consent through approval of authorities under the relevant national regimes; and (iii) evidence of fair and equitable benefit sharing under the national regime of the country of origin* (World Trade Organization, TRIPS Council, 2002).

In the same year, various developing countries negotiating the text of the Substantive Patent Law Treaty (SPLT) at the World Intellectual Property Organization (WIPO),[3] presented a proposal to ensure full flexibility to implement measures in the patent filing or granting process related to biodiversity and environment. Under the heading of 'general principles', the proposal states that:

> *Nothing in this Treaty and the Regulations shall limit the freedom of a Contracting Party to take any action it deems necessary for the preservation of essential security interests or to comply with international obligations, including those relating to the protection of genetic resources, biological diversities, traditional knowledge and the environment* (World Intellectual Property Organization, Standing Committee on the Law of Patents, 2002).

Brazil has also submitted a set of proposals to guarantee flexibility in the relevant articles of the SPLT to ensure responsiveness to public interest concerns, among which are biodiversity and environmental issues. The Brazilian proposal in the SPLT negotiations is broader in scope than the two above-mentioned proposals. This difference between the proposals is due to the wider scope of patent negotiations in WIPO, which includes all substantive patent law aspects, while TRIPS Council discussions under Article 27.3(b) have been rather limited to patentability of life, the meaning of 'sui generis system', the relationship between the CBD and TRIPS, and the protection of traditional knowledge. The Brazilian proposal in the SPLT indicates the following, also in the section on general principles:

> *(3) [Public Interest Exceptions] Nothing in this Treaty or Regulations shall limit the freedom of Contracting Parties to protect public health, nutrition and the environment or to take any action it deems necessary to promote the public interest in sectors of vital importance to its socio-economic, scientific and technological development.*

Under Article 13, which deals with grounds for refusal of a claimed invention, Brazil proposed the following text:

> *(2) [Compliance With Applicable Law on Other Matters] A Contracting Party may also require compliance with the applicable law on public health, nutrition, ethics in scientific research, environment, access to genetic resources, protection of traditional knowledge and other areas of public interest in sectors of vital importance for their social, economic and technological development.*

Several developed countries are reluctant to support these amendments, claiming that disclosure of origin is incompatible with TRIPS. The US has expressed the view that such a measure 'would be complicated' and 'create a legal and administrative nightmare' for national patent systems.

The disclosure of the origin of genetic resource and associated TK is a common procedure in various national laws and is based on the principle of good faith and the fair behaviour of the applicant. The disclosure does not mean that the applicant has to investigate the entire chain backwards to the origin or that it is a burdensome activity. A good faith applicant must only show the best information available or known to him. If he does not have any knowledge of the origin of the genetic resource or the TK, the applicant may just indicate that the information sought is not available. Also it must be borne in mind that in any bioprospecting activity or anthropological investigations, researchers always include in their basic data collections the geographical coordinates and the particular environment where the sample was taken or where the investigation was carried out. This situation makes the geographical origin of genetic resources or TK in the case of inventions that result from bioprospecting activities or anthropological investigations a necessary part of the available information.

The disclosure requirement is mainly applicable to inventions and discoveries in the field of biotechnology where specific requirements in patent filing procedure, such as the deposit of a sample of the genetic material, already exist. Applicants should not consider this particular requirement as burdensome. On the contrary, it contributes to the description of the invention. The costs associated with a disclosure requirement could be even lower than the deposit of the genetic materials where cooling facilities are needed to preserve them. Similar procedures can be found in the Budapest Treaty on the International Recognition of the Deposit of Micro-organisms for the Purposes of Patent Procedure.

As mentioned earlier, the basic objectives of the disclosure requirement are to ensure compliance with the principle of prior informed consent, and with fair and equitable benefit sharing. This requirement can be seen as being complementary to the obligation in TRIPS to disclose the invention in a manner sufficiently clear and complete as to be carried out by a person skilled in the art, and also to identify the best mode to carry out the invention. This becomes relevant when the origin of the genetic resource or the traditional knowledge is directly linked to the replication of the invention, such as in the case of endemic genetic resources or the particular medicinal properties of a local plant already identified and used by traditional communities.

Legal arguments for and against disclosure

The pre-eminence of rights: public interest vs private rights

For biodiversity-rich countries, the CBD's reaffirmation of sovereign rights over biological resources implies a subordination of private rights, of which IPRs are an example, to public interest-related measures such as prior informed consent and fair and equitable benefit sharing. States cannot be forced to grant private rights if a potential title holder is in violation of national norms or principles of public interest. Also, the CBD clearly requires states to ensure that the exercise of patents and other IPRs does not violate the objectives of the CBD. TRIPS also recognizes members' rights to formulate or to modify their laws to promote the public interest, as long as these laws do not directly violate the other parts of the agreement.

Those countries opposing this interpretation rely on Article 22 of the CBD, which establishes that the provisions of the CBD shall not affect the rights and obligations of any contracting party deriving from any existing international agreement, except where the exercise of those rights and obligations would cause a serious damage or threat to biological diversity. At the same time, they consider that the last phrase of Article 8.1 of TRIPS ('... provided that such measures are consistent with the provisions of this Agreement'), limits any freedom to establish the type of measure being discussed in this chapter, as it must be compatible or specifically authorized by the TRIPS Agreement within its text. According to this view, a mandatory requirement of the disclosure of the origin will be TRIPS incompatible.

The compatibility of the requirement of the disclosure of the origin with the TRIPS Agreement

Different arguments rejecting or supporting the disclosure mechanism have been used in discussions at the TRIPS Council and in WIPO. Arguments against the requirement of disclosure have been based on the incompatibility of such a requirement with Articles 27.1, 29, 30 and 62 of TRIPS and because it places a new condition on patent filing procedures that is not allowable. Arguments in favour consider that an interlinked and reasonable interpretation of Articles 1, 8.1, 27, 30 and 62 of the TRIPS allow the use of this type of measure.

Several countries believe that the requirement of disclosure is incompatible with the TRIPS Agreement because of its effects on the freedoms of patent applicants and holders. This viewpoint is based on four arguments. The first of these is that the disclosure requirement is incompatible with Article 27.1 of TRIPS because it adds another substantive condition to the traditional ones of novelty, inventive step and industrial application. It is possible that non-authorized access or use of genetic resources could violate civil and/or criminal regulations, but member states could not turn non-disclosure into a violation of the law of patents.

Second, the disclosure requirement would not be compatible with Article 29 of TRIPS, which establishes the formal conditions for granting a patent, and specifically the obligation to disclose the invention in a clear and complete manner so an expert in the field can replicate the invention. The indication of origin of genetic resources or TK in the description would not be necessary or relevant in the majority of cases for this replication.

Third, according to an interlinked interpretation of Articles 27.1 and 32, a patent may only be revoked for failure to fulfil one or more of the elements of the patentability criteria (novelty, inventive step and industrial application).

Fourth, the disclosure requirement would not be compatible with Article 62, which establishes the conditions for the acquisition or maintenance of IPRs. This article does not allow requirements beyond the ones related to the substantive conditions for the acquisition of the right or the payment of certain tariffs. According to this argument, the only substantive requirements of the patent are those contained in Article 27.1. This article also establishes that the proceedings for acquisition and maintenance of rights should be 'reasonable'. In that sense, some argue that the disclosure requirement will impose heavy and exaggerated administrative costs, and therefore be unreasonable.

These arguments, however, do not take into consideration all principles and aspects of TRIPS. Countries asserting that the disclosure requirement is compatible with TRIPS find support in several of its provisions.

First, according to Article 1, members can freely establish a method to apply the provisions of the accord within their own system and legal practice. Additionally, other TRIPS provisions, such as the preamble and Articles 7 and 8, can support a flexible interpretation of the agreement allowing measures related to development and the public interest.

Second, although Article 27.1 controls the substantive requirements in the process of having a patent granted, other type of requirements could be involved in the patent filing process, such as payment of fees or presentation of power of representation. The differentiation between substantive and formal requirements is an artificial one since in both cases the failure to fulfil those requirements will have the same effect, which is that of not granting the patent or revoking it as the case may be.

Third, in relation to the question of discrimination as to field of technology, the WTO panel decision in Patents of Canada vs EU (World Trade Organization, 2000) has affirmed that Article 27.1 does not prohibit exceptions destined to solve problems that only exist in certain product sectors. Arguably, the requirement to disclose the origin of genetic resources or TK would be acceptable according to this interpretation. The panel made clear that conduct prohibited by Article 27.1 is 'discrimination', and 'discrimination' is not the same as 'differentiation'. The panel suggested that governments are permitted to adopt different rules for particular product areas or locations of production, provided that the differences are adopted for bona fide purposes. The panel did not attempt to provide a general rule regarding what differences could be considered bona fide.[4] There may, however, be bona fide reasons for drawing distinctions, such as assuring that compelling public interests are satisfied.

Fourth, Article 29 of TRIPS is not *numerous clausus*. That is to say, its enumeration of formal requirements does not exhaust the conditions that might be imposed on patent applicants. As mentioned above, requirements like payments of fees and presentation of documents related to corporate capability (legal incorporation of an entity) within the process of patent granting is a normal part of many national patent systems.

Fifth, some consider that disclosure of origin is not linked to the technical solution of a particular problem, and is therefore irrelevant to the description. Nevertheless, in cases where the genetic resource is endemic or only available in a particular environment, the geographical origin becomes relevant for the description as it helps to identify an important raw material necessary to replicate the invention. In the case of traditional knowledge and the description of the invention, some consider that traditional knowledge is a value added to genetic resources and could have an important effect on the novelty examination.

Sixth, Article 32 of the TRIPS Agreement does not establish a list of causes for revocation/forfeiture of patents. WTO members are free to establish the causes for revocation according to their own national legislation. Although some countries are of the opinion that TRIPS establishes limited causes for revocation/forfeiture, discussions during the negotiations of the agreement on a list of causes for revocation, reinforce the thesis that this matter was deliberately omitted and is therefore left open to member determination. Examples of this situation in the legal practice are revocation or forfeiture on such grounds as: (i) non-payment of fees, taxes or annuities; (ii) the grant of the patent to a person who was not entitled to it; (ii) the extension of the patent's subject matter beyond the subject matter in the application as filed; and (iv) the failure of the applicant to disclose the invention clearly enough and completely enough for it to be performed by a person skilled in the art. None of these is explicitly mentioned in TRIPS.

Seventh, the 'rationale' required by Article 62.1 is a subjective concept, and it has to be determined in the context of a specific case. In the case of the disclosure requirement, countries seeking enforcement defend the need to avoid costly legal disputes in international courts each time there is a case of wrongful appropriation or an illegal use of genetic resources or traditional knowledge. In this sense, this requirement seems to be absolutely rational and indispensable.

Eighth, in the continental law system, the state can pass legislation to limit the private rights of third parties in order to preserve the patrimony in conformity with the public interest. This is relevant to tangibles and intangibles. Therefore, a state would have the right to revoke a patent for genetic information acquired illicitly in order to protect the compliance of the law and the sovereign rights of the same state.

POSSIBLE LEGAL OPTIONS FOR THE DISCLOSURE OF ORIGIN

There are various options for the disclosure of the origin of genetic resources that could be identified in the comparative legislation and by commentators. These are described below.

Mandatory disclosure requirement

The existence of such a mechanism would seek not only to enforce CBD principles but also to clarify the description of any biotechnology inventions. In this particular case, the option implies that disclosure of all information available about the genetic resource will be obligatory. There are three possible legal consequences for the failure to meet such requirement: abandonment of the procedure; relative nullity and suspension of the process; and revocation.

Taking the first consequence, if there is no disclosure or presentation of the access contract or the agreement of the traditional communities, the process of applying for an IPR will be considered deserted based on the case.

As to the second, in the case of a patent application without the disclosure of origin of genetic resources, the administrative process will be temporarily suspended (not generating legal effects) until the procedural vices are corrected. The application of nullity should be accompanied by a presumption that allows for the derivative rights from the date of the patent application not to be affected, like the right of priority.

With respect to revocation, this applies only after the patent has been granted, and its basis is that of demonstrating insufficient disclosure or fraud. This option has been chosen by India in its Patent Act of 2002. It includes two new grounds for revocation, which are that patents may be revoked on the ground

> *that the complete specification does not disclose or wrongly mentions the source or geographical origin of biological material used for the invention,*

and

> *that the invention so far as claimed in any claim of the complete specification was anticipated having regard to the knowledge, oral or otherwise, available within any local or indigenous community in India or elsewhere.*

Similarly, the Andean Community applies a general conditionality for granting industrial property rights subject to the legal acquisition of the genetic resources or associated TK. Andean Community Decision 486 includes two ex ante mechanisms to implement this conditionality in the patent chapter, which are the presumption of desertion and relative nullity in case of lack of disclosure, and one ex post mechanism, which is revocation in the case of patent granted under fraudulent omission of disclosure or illegal procurement of genetic resources or associated TK.

Also the Brazilian provisional measure 2.186-16 of 2001 indicates that:

> *the grant of industrial property rights by the competent bodies for a process or product obtained using samples of components of the genetic heritage is contingent on the observance of this Provisional Measure, the applicant being obliged to specify the origin of the genetic material and the associated traditional knowledge, as the case may be.*

Voluntary disclosure requirement

This is the system applied in the EU in its 1998 Directive on the Legal Protection of Biotechnological Inventions, where disclosure of genetic resources within the patent filing process is voluntary. The directive indicates in its preamble that:

> *Whereas if an invention is based on biological material of plant or animal origin or if it uses such material, the patent application should, where appropriate, include information on the geographical origin of such material, if known; whereas this is without prejudice to the processing of patent applications or the validity of rights arising from granted patents.*

In this case, there is no legal sanction for non-disclosure. This option puts a burden on the countries or the communities concerned in providing the necessary evidence and assuming the costs of legal procedures when they suspect any illegal access use or incorporation in a particular invention or discovery in the context of a patent application.

Ex posteriori mechanism of unfair competition: the clean hands doctrine.

According to this approach, the disclosure of origin is not by itself a violation of TRIPS (Carvalho, 2000). The violation occurs only when a patent is revoked for a failure to disclose. This view is based on the 'clean hands theory' from common law, and exists in the area of competition where legal authorities in some jurisdictions have powers to prevent the enforcement of an IPR when the right has been obtained in an abusive way. According to the clean hands theory, if an entity or individual has committed fraud in violation of competition rules, this entity or individual will have the right to a patent without the derivative rights (exclusive rights) until the vices are corrected (until the hands are cleaned).

Effective and parallel follow-up of the patent

This option is followed in Norway and Denmark. Disclosure of origin of genetic resources is requested on a voluntary basis, and without the effects of nullity produced by insufficient information. However, the intellectual property authorities, in conjunction with the environmental authorities, investigate the composition and source of compounds claimed in relevant patent applications, and if these turn out to have been used illicitly, sanctions established in civil, environmental or criminal law may apply. Some consider that this option should be complemented with the charging of payment of an additional fee to cover the appropriate monitoring or tracking of the use of genetic resources or TK in patent filing procedures.[5] The payment of the fee would allow the 'spot checking' of patent applications from those who have chosen not to disclose.

CONCLUSIONS

Encouragement of mechanisms like disclosure of the origin of the genetic resources and traditional knowledge or other similar ones[6] in patent filing procedures as proposed by developing countries would create mutual supportiveness between IPR and access and benefit sharing regimes. Mutual supportiveness of the TRIPS and CBD objectives would generate less complex or burdensome access regimes and increase confidence between private enterprises or research centres and biodiversity-rich countries and indigenous communities. Countries should be allowed to explore the options that could be supportive of both IPRs and the CBD's objectives. Nevertheless, it seems that some of the opposition to these proposals is not related to the search for mutually supportive solutions, and is preventing any advance towards positive outcomes in the international arena.

NOTES

1 The author would like to thank Christophe Bellmann, Graham Dutfield, Maria Isabel Moya, Anne Perault and Christophe Spenemann for their comments and suggestions.
2 There is no commonly accepted definition of 'biopiracy'. Instead of this word, some experts are starting to use the terms 'illegal access' and 'use', both of which are used in the recently adopted Bonn Guidelines.
3 These countries are Brazil, Chile, Colombia, Cuba, Ecuador, Dominican Republic, Honduras, Nicaragua, Peru and Venezuela.

4 See UNCTAD/ICTSD (2002) TRIPS and Development: Resource Book (chapter on nature of obligations, principles and objectives). See http://www.ictsd.org/ipronline/
5 This idea has been proposed by Anne Perault from the Center of International Environmental Law.
6 Brendan Tobin has proposed the adoption of a certification of origin system as an alternative to disclosure. See Tobin, B (1997) 'Certificates of origin: a role for IPR regimes in securing prior informed consent', in J Mugabe, C V Barber, G Henne, L Glowka, and A La Viña (eds), *Access to Genetic Resources: Strategies for Sharing Benefits*, Nairobi: ACTS Press.

REFERENCES

Carvalho, N P de (2000) 'Requiring disclosure of the origin of genetic resources and prior informed consent in patent applications without infringing the TRIPS Agreement: the problem and the solution', *Washington University Journal of Law and Policy* 2.

World Intellectual Property Organization – Standing Committee on the Law of Patents (2002) *Proposals by the Delegations of the Dominican Republic and Brazil concerning Articles 2, 13 and 14 of the Draft Substantive Patent Law Treaty. Document prepared by the International Bureau,* [SCP/8/5].

World Trade Organization – TRIPS Council (2002) *The relationship between the TRIPS Agreement and the Convention on Biological Diversity and the protection of traditional knowledge.* Communication from Brazil on behalf of the delegations of Brazil, China, Cuba, Dominican Republic, Ecuador, India, Pakistan, Thailand, Venezuela, Zambia and Zimbabwe, [IP/C/W/356].

World Trade Organization (2000) *Canada – patent protection of pharmaceutical products. Complaint by the European Communities and their member States. Report of the panel,* [WT/DS114/R].

PART THREE

IMPLEMENTING THE TRIPS AGREEMENT

Regional Initiatives

National Legislative Reforms

Chapter 22

Formulating Effective Pro-development National Intellectual Property Policies

Carlos Correa

Developing countries face significant challenges for formulating an intellectual property policy compatible with their production structure, cultural values and development needs, and for translating such policy into laws and regulations consistent with international obligations. This chapter reviews those challenges and makes preliminary suggestions about ways in which developing countries can deal with human, institutional and financial constraints to ensure the coherence, sustainability and effectiveness of their policies.

Intellectual property as a policy instrument

The purpose of intellectual property rights (IPR) policy is often described, in a simplistic way, as a means to reward inventors and creators for their contributions to the state of the art. IPRs, however, have been designed to benefit society by providing incentives to introduce new inventions or creations. Their purpose is not the exclusive benefit or advantage of individuals or corporations, but of the public or community at large through the activities of inventors and creators.

Intellectual property is an instrument for achieving specific objectives, which have historically evolved and varied across countries. How the rationale for IPR protection has changed over time in developed countries is well documented, particularly in the area of patents. The available evidence clearly suggests that the role of IPRs vary significantly in accordance with productive structures and levels of development. As the World Bank has noted, in the area of intellectual property 'one size does not fit all' (World Bank, 2001).

In the US, for instance, weak copyright protection during the 19th century was deliberately aimed at promoting the development of the domestic printing industry. One century later, the promotion of domestic industry is still present in US law. Under Section 204 of the Bayh-Dole Act, a preference for US industry for the exploitation of publicly funded inventions is granted. Similarly, many European countries only strengthened patent protection (particularly for pharmaceuticals) as their industries developed, or until they were forced (like in the case of Spain and Portugal) by other partners in trade agreements.

Ideally, an IPR policy should be designed in any particular country having in mind its broad impact on society, both in the short and long term. There is no universal model of IPR policy that suits all countries. Different industrial structures, modes of agricultural production, availability of natural and human resources, and development strategies, call for different types and extent of intellectual property (IP) protection. The objectives that an IPR policy may pursue include, inter alia:

- promoting the disclosure and exploitation of innovations;
- fostering R&D activities;
- promoting foreign direct investment and the importation of foreign technology;
- inducing local manufacturing (such as through compulsory licensing in cases of non-working);
- providing incentives for the transfer and commercial exploitation of knowledge (eg in the case of university R&D results and traditional knowledge); and
- protecting investments made (such as databases and protection of undisclosed data submitted for approval of agrochemical and pharmaceutical products).

What objectives are pursued, and how possible tensions among them are to be dealt with, should be a matter of national policy in the context of broader development strategies.

DESIGNING IPR POLICY IN DEVELOPING COUNTRIES

A major challenge for developing countries is to effectively integrate development policies (in the areas of industrial development, public health, food security, education, etc) into IPR policies. A development assessment of different components and levels of IPR protection needs to be undertaken for that purpose.

This is not a simple task, since on the one hand there are several components of intellectual property (patents, trade marks, copyright, designs, etc) which play different roles. Therefore, any generalization about the impact of IPRs is of very little practical value. Thus, patents impose significant losses in static efficiency by diminishing access to medicines and seeds, while patents' dynamic efficiency effects may be insignificant or non-existent in poor countries. At the same time, they may benefit from the use of trade marks to identify and promote quality products. Some countries also have considerable expectations about the use of some components of intellectual property, such as geographical indications.

On the other hand, IPRs differently affect firms and consumers across sectors and even within a given sector. For instance, in India some domestic pharmaceutical firms, which have reached significant productive and technological capacity, are reported to be potential beneficiaries of the introduction of pharmaceutical patents, while smaller pharmaceutical firms may face substantial problems to survive in the new legal context. Similarly, copyright protection may favour authors and artists (eg musicians in the Caribbean) while adversely affecting access to educational materials, especially for the poor.

Assessing the development impacts of intellectual property requires a deep understanding of IPR institutions and appropriate knowledge about strengths and weaknesses in different sectors. It also calls for a forward-looking approach and the capacity to foresee possible scenarios. There are, in fact, no easy-to-apply methodologies for this purpose. This task is particularly difficult in developing countries for various reasons.

First, developing countries have little analytical capacity to undertake a sound cost–benefit assessment of the impact of IPR protection in different productive sectors and on consumers. Unlike the situation in developed countries, firms and consumers in developing countries generally lack the organization to articulate their interests in the area of intellectual property (an important exception may be the domestic pharmaceutical industry where it exists). Moreover, the design of IPR policy, including the participation in international negotiations on the matter, is often left in the hands of trade departments and industrial property offices, without or with limited participation of representatives from public health, agriculture and other areas of government.

Second, developing countries have been strongly lobbied or subject to political pressures to adopt IPR legislation that responds to the interests of industries from industrialized countries. Some of such industries – as illustrated by pharmaceuticals and computer software – have a significant capacity to lobby developing countries' as well as their own governments. Industrialized countries' governments have championed the cause of their industries in bilateral, regional and multilateral agreements involving IPRs. In contrast, developing countries' governments often lack sufficient knowledge on and interaction with their domestic industries.

Third, in many instances the adoption of high IPR standards of protection by developing countries has been the price paid in return for expected trade benefits in other areas (such as agriculture and textiles). This was notably the case in the Uruguay Round, though it is questionable whether such benefits have actually materialized. There are also indications that Free Trade Area of the Americas negotiations may follow a similar pattern.

Fourth, even if developing countries had the expertise to design their IPR policy and draft their own IPR laws accordingly, many of them face the constraints imposed by over-protectionist bilateral or regional treaties that include obligations on IP. Examples of agreements which impose 'TRIPS-plus' obligations are the US bilateral agreements with Cambodia, Laos and Jordan, the cooperation agreements established between the EC and Bangladesh, Nepal, Laos, Cambodia and Yemen, and the 'Cotonou Agreement', which replaced the Lomé Convention, between the 77 countries of the African, Caribbean, and Pacific region and the European Community. Another example is provided by the 'Bangui Agreement' entered into between the 16 French-speaking African countries (eight of which are least developed countries – LDCs) that make up the African Intellectual Property Organization (OAPI), under which the contracting parties declined their right to use the flexibilities that the TRIPS Agreement recognizes in relation, for instance, to parallel imports, compulsory licences, farmers' right to save seeds, and the protection of data submitted for the registration of pharmaceuticals and agrochemical products.

This vast array of agreements has been negotiated without any development assessment, and ties the hands of developing countries who are parties to them to design IPR policies more suitable to their own levels of development. Due to the application of the most favoured nation clause, in addition, those countries who are World Trade Organization (WTO) members are bound to grant the same level of IPR protection to other WTO members who are not parties to said agreements. Thus, 'TRIPS-plus' standards established under agreements with the US also benefit right holders in the EU, while US right holders benefit from the standards negotiated by the EU.

ASSESSING NEEDS AND PRIORITIES

As mentioned, assessing the development impact of IPRs is not a simple task. Relevant data need to be collected and analysed at the national level. Box 22.1 presents some of the issues to be addressed.

An IPR development assessment should examine the possible impact of IPRs on local production and the development and diffusion of technologies in

BOX 22.1 MAPPING NATIONAL INTERESTS

1. Industrial structure (contribution to GNP and trade of different sectors, productivity indicators, firms' size, etc).
2. National innovation system (scientific capacity, industry–academy linkages, main areas of research, technological performance of various sectors, patterns of innovation, etc).
3. Current and potential role of foreign direct investment (FDI) (resource-oriented, domestic/export market-oriented) and technology licensing.
4. IP-sensitivity of foreign trade.
5. Public health situation (access to medicines, coverage of social security systems, epidemics, etc).
6. Supply of seeds (formal and informal systems), systems of exchange and distribution, farmers' practices.
7. Supply of and access to educational materials, software and other copyrightable works.
8. Traditional knowledge, extent of its use and commercialization.
9. Importance of regional production.

Table 22.1 *Subject matter and main fields of application of IPRs*

Types of intellectual property right	*Subject matter*	*Main fields*
Patents	New, non-obvious, indigenous applicable inventions	Chemicals, drugs, plastics, engines, turbines, electronics, industrial, control and scientific equipment
Trade Marks	Signs or symbols to identify goods and services	All industries
Copyright	Original works of authorship	Printing, entertainment (audio, video motion pictures) software, broadcasting
Integrated Circuits	Original layout designs	Microelectronics industry
Breeders' Rights	New, stable, homogeneous, distinguishable varieties	Agriculture and food industry
Trade Secrets	Secret business information	All industries
Industrial Designs	Ornamental designs	Clothing, automobiles, electronics, etc
Geographical Indications	Geographical origin of goods and services	Wines, spirits, cheese and other food products
Utility Models	Functional models/designs	Mechanical industry

different sectors. For instance, the analysis of item 1 may lead to important conclusions for framing an IPR policy. As noted, the relevance of different kinds of intellectual property significantly varies according to the types of industries involved, and the rate and nature of their innovative activities (see Table 22.1).

As Table 22.1 suggests, the implications of IPRs will substantially depend on what kind of IPRs are involved and what the nature of the covered activities is. It is well documented that the R&D intensity significantly varies across sectors.[1] In a country where high-intensity R&D sectors (eg aerospace, computers, pharmaceuticals) are significant, an IPR policy may provide powerful incentives to undertake costly R&D. But in countries where the dominant sectors are agriculture, textiles and other low-intensity R&D industries, and where 'minor' or 'incremental' innovations derived from the routine exploitation of existing technologies prevail, IPRs may have little or no effect on innovation, while reducing the diffusion and increasing the cost of foreign products and technologies.

Another important aspect is firms' size. Small and medium enterprises (SMEs), particularly in developing countries, may benefit little from the IPR system, as illustrated by the case of patents. Their innovations often concentrate in products and processes with a short life cycle, while obtaining patent protection often takes a long time (from two to six years depending on the country). In addition, obtaining a patent and maintaining it in force are generally quite costly, unaffordable to most SMEs. Most importantly, defending a patent against validity challenges by third parties, or enforcing it against infringers are extremely expensive, and risky, operations. This explain why the patent system has been found to be 'at best an irrelevancy' for SMEs even in industrialized countries (Coleman and Fishlock, 2002).

A comprehensive development assessment cannot be limited to the impact on production and innovation. It also needs to consider other crucial dimensions, such as public health, nutrition and food security. There exists a tension between high levels of IPR protection and public interest in those fields. The normal effect of IPRs is to allow the title holder to charge prices above marginal cost, thus reducing the diffusion of the protected innovations and reducing access thereto. While many developing countries are likely to benefit little, if at all, from the dynamic efficiency effects of IPR protection, they will surely suffer losses in static efficiency. Therefore, a sound IPR policy should evaluate and try to minimize the short-term social costs of introducing or increasing IPR protection.

DRAFTING IPR LAWS

Several difficulties also arise in relation to the drafting of IPR legislation in developing countries. Government officials in the executive branch and law makers generally lack expertise in IPR law. Such expertise can only be domestically provided, in some cases, by lawyers who have been trained in foreign universities and represent or advise foreign IPR holders. There are often conflicts of interests that are not apparent to policy-makers. There is anecdotal evidence about policy-makers being grossly misled in the process of drafting IPR laws.[2]

Intellectual property is a 'cross-cutting issue' involving several government departments. Quite often, however, departments with a substantial interest in the matter do not participate in decision-making. This has typically been the case of health authorities, which were absent in the Uruguay Round negotiations. The World Health Organization has actively promoted in the last three years awareness on IPR issues among such authorities, but their actual influence in decision-making is still limited.[3]

Due to their limited domestic capacity, developing countries are strongly dependent on technical assistance, and rely for expert advice and commentary on new draft legislation on the World Intellectual Property Organization (WIPO) and the WTO, especially to confirm consistency of draft legislation with international obligations. WIPO has had a prominent role in providing technical assistance to developing countries for drafting IPR laws. This is reflected in WIPO Secretariat reports as well as in the extensive use by developing countries of the 'model laws' developed by WIPO. WIPO's advice has emphasized the benefits and largely ignored the costs of IPR protection, and has generally failed to present the range of options that developing countries may have to pursue their own interests, including the flexibilities allowed by the TRIPS Agreement.[4]

Developing countries have received significant support from WIPO, the European Patent Office and other agencies to 'modernize' their IPR administration systems, including activities by police and custom authorities.

These actions directly benefit IPR applicants. They generally involve training in industrialized countries, and transmit the concepts and values prevailing in those countries.

In some cases, advice has also been provided by industrialized countries' international cooperation agencies for drafting IPR laws. For instance, the US Agency for International Development has had a relevant role in shaping IPR legislation (not surprisingly encompassing high levels of IPR protection) in some Arab and Central American countries. A law adopted in Guatemala provided for a 15-year exclusive protection of data submitted for the registration of pharmaceutical products, three times the period available in the US.

CAN CONSTRAINTS TO DESIGNING IPR POLICIES BE OVERCOME?

The design of IPR policy and drafting of IPR legislation in developing countries has largely failed to consider their productive structures, cultural values, and development needs. Such legislation has been generally based on the models applied in industrialized countries, with little or no adaptation to the circumstances and development needs of developing countries. Moreover, developing countries have been coerced to adopt standards of IPR protection in the context of bilateral and regional agreements that go even beyond the TRIPS Agreement.

Though (as history shows) industrialized countries did enjoy freedom to design their IPR regimes as they developed, the room left to developing countries has been significantly limited, though not totally suppressed, by TRIPS and other bilateral and regional agreements.

There are outstanding examples of the design of IPR policy that reflects national conditions and needs, developed with the active participation of different branches of government and civil society. The adoption of the Indian Protection of Plant Varieties and Farmers' Rights Act provides one such example (see Chapter 27).

Hence, IPR policy can be modelled, to a certain extent, to respond to different social and economic conditions prevailing in developing countries. There is some room to do so, but it has already been limited and it is continuously narrowing down as new bilateral and regional agreements on IPRs are negotiated.

The constraints that developing countries face to formulate pro-development IPR policies may be addressed by a number of actions, which are only presented here for further discussion. They may include actions to increase the 'freedom to operate', as well as to improve policy-making and drafting of legislation.

Increasing the freedom to operate

- Avoiding new IPR commitments under bilateral and regional agreements (including as trade-offs for concessions in other trade areas);

- Carefully considering the implications of accession to existing IPR treaties and of other current negotiations;
- Promoting the revision of bilateral and regional agreements that establish TRIPS-plus standards;
- Undertaking the review of national legislation from a development perspective, in the light of the flexibilities allowed by the TRIPS Agreement;
- Reviewing national legislation in the light of the Doha Declaration on TRIPS and Public Health.

Improving policy-making and drafting

A national IPR policy that integrates development objectives should not only be defensive, that is, aimed at minimizing the costs of introducing IPR protection in different areas. It should also actively explore whether new modalities of IPR protection may be established to respond to development needs. For instance, the possible impact of a second-tier form of protection for non-patentable innovations needs a deeper consideration. The issue of the protection of traditional knowledge also requires careful analysis. However, such analysis should not only include the possible benefits for right holders, but the possible implications of protection for public health, food security and other public interests.

The implications of IPRs are too important to leave policy and drafting in the hands of lawyers, foreign consultants or officials in international organizations. Actions to be taken to improve policy-making and drafting may include:

- Establishing inter-agency governmental committees to address IPR policy issues, including bilateral, regional and international negotiations, with the participation of the private sector and civil society;
- Undertaking interdisciplinary studies on the implications of IPRs on different sectors (such as pharmaceuticals, software) and activities (such as education);
- Training government, academy and NGO professionals (including but not limited to lawyers) in IPR policy-making and drafting;
- Redirecting technical assistance on IPRs to policy formulation rather than IPR administration;
- Monitoring technical assistance activities of international organizations, such as WIPO, so as to ensure unbiased advice that presents all options available to developing countries.

NOTES

1 See for example, OECD (1992) *Technology and the Economy: The Key Relationships*, OECD, Paris.

2 In one country, for instance, health authorities claimed that a 'Bolar exception' had been introduced into their patent law. However, a more careful analysis of the adopted law indicated that registration procedures before expiration of the patent

had been exempted from criminal sanctions, but not from the ordinary civil or commercial legal actions that the patent holder could exercise.

3 As noted in the CIPR report, there is evidence indicating that 'some countries have established mechanisms to improve the coordination of policy-making and advice, with the main participants being the key ministries most involved ie health, justice, science, environment, agriculture, education or culture (for copyright and related rights). However, these mechanisms are often only embryonic and their degree of effectiveness is yet to become apparent – particularly in respect of integration of IP issues with other areas of economic and development policy. In many cases, this may reflect the fact that such coordinating bodies are not able to draw readily on a supply of the necessary technical advice and expertise, but it also reflects divergent interests within government (see Commission on Intellectual Property Rights, 2002).

4 See, for example, the recently published WIPO's model laws, available at http://www.wipo.int.

REFERENCES

Coleman, R and Fishlock, D (2002) *Background and overview of the intellectual property initiative*, available at http://info.sm.umist.ac.uk/esrcip/background.htm.

Commission on Intellectual Property Rights (2002) *Integrating Intellectual Property Rights and Development Policy*, Report of the Commission on Intellectual Property Rights, London: CIPR

World Bank (2001) *Global Economic Prospects and the Developing Countries 2002*, The World Bank, Washington DC.

REGIONAL INITIATIVES

Chapter 23

Implementing the TRIPS Agreement in Africa

Francis Mangeni

INTRODUCTION

The first standard point that should be made on preparing and adopting laws, especially laws in quite involved areas like TRIPS, is this: use precedents, though not quite in the same sense as the nine year old the teacher caught copying from the next pupil, who leapt to his defence saying, 'I am only looking for a precedent!'. But in three senses; first, that developing countries need to adopt coherent and convincing state practice to pit against any efforts to put adverse meanings to certain provisions of the TRIPS Agreement, especially meanings that reflect only the practice, experience and interests of developed countries based on their domestic laws and their court and administrative decisions; second, that a common regional understanding and approach to TRIPS obligations will facilitate cooperation among intellectual property offices and between governments at large; and third, that the building of expertise at the regional level through training and basic teaching will be greatly facilitated through real equivalence in courses of learning that cover more or less the same subject matter and through making the establishment of regional training facilities meaningful and useful as a result of similar legal and policy regimes on the subject.

We need African precedents for preparing and adopting laws to implement obligations under TRIPS. This must indicate the important role that African economic communities and think tanks, including the African Union, the regional economic communities like the Common Market for Eastern and Southern Africa, the Southern African Development Community and the East

African Community, and the African Centre for Technology Studies, stand to play as forums for cooperation among the member states in establishing appropriate legal policies on TRIPS, in terms of both the drafting methodology and the content of the laws.

The standard rider, again, is that member states will obviously act in their best interests. There should be little to differ about, as developing country interests and concerns relating to TRIPS have attracted plenty of helpful literature, debate and programmes which together have resulted in fairly common positions on basic issues, reflected for instance in submissions and statements of World Trade Organization (WTO) developing country delegates and particularly the African Group of ambassadors in Geneva. At the continental level, trade ministers have issued declarations at their formal meetings, and the African Union and the UN Economic Commission for Africa have hosted preparatory workshops and meetings, to develop common positions ahead of WTO Ministerial Conferences. These regional initiatives will provide very valuable perspectives and content to the preparation and adoption of laws implementing TRIPS.

The importance of African perspectives and initiatives on WTO matters including TRIPS cannot be overemphasized. It is not just that 40 of the 140 members of the WTO are African countries, a substantial voting clout that has never been used in the WTO due basically to yielding to the practice of decision-making by consensus, which in practice has replaced the weighted voting system used in the World Bank and the IMF consistently to the benefit of two or so developed countries and almost invariably to the prejudice of anything close to three-quarters of humankind. But also, it is perhaps in Africa that some of the worst consequences of TRIPS have been felt and experienced, both in the impact on access to medicine and ensuring food security, and in the impact on development prospects in a region that now features as the tattered face of poverty and international marginalization.

The absolute importance of active and effective engagement in international rule making has received satisfactory priority from some African countries through their participation in the WTO, but much more is still to be done to lead the process of setting the agenda and the interests of the WTO.[1] Having said this, the giant strides African delegates to the WTO have made in championing the concerns of Africa need due recognition. Africa is generally considered the leader on developing country perspectives on TRIPS. Africa has prepared a comprehensive model law on regulating access to genetic resources and protecting the rights of plant breeders, farmers and local communities, which, in appropriately addressing the essential concerns of developing countries in this area, may indeed be a developing country model (see Chapter 24). In 2001, African ambassadors chaired both the Council for TRIPS and the Committee on Trade and Development.[2] The African Group and individual African countries have made comprehensive proposals, submissions and statements raising key issues for debate around TRIPS. These gains are to be supported and promoted by African regional and subregional organizations and think tanks, in addition to celebrating them.

TRANSITION AND APPLICATION

TRIPS became fully applicable to developing countries on 1 January 2000 and will become fully applicable to least developed countries from 1 January 2006. Developing countries still have till 1 January 2005 before beginning to extend patent protection to products formerly not patentable under their laws but which TRIPS now gives patent protection, for instance pharmaceutical products, micro-organisms, and micro- and non-biological processes for the production of plants and animals. Before the agreement becomes applicable, a country does not have to provide the standards of intellectual property protection required or comply with the rules in the agreement.

These transition periods for developing and least developed countries were included in TRIPS in exchange for the transition periods that developed countries got in the agreements on agriculture and on textiles and clothing. It may in passing be pointed out that developed countries remain reluctant to open up their agricultural and textile and clothing sectors, which are of particular export interest to developing and least developed countries.

There are significant exceptions to the transition periods for developing and least developed countries. The obligations to accord national and most favoured nation treatment to nationals of other WTO members became applicable on 1 January 1996. Also, members were required to provide in their laws procedures and permit applications for patents on pharmaceutical and agrochemical products as from 1 January 1995, and to grant exclusive marketing rights in the country for up to five years if some other member had granted a patent and marketing approval for that product. But there was no requirement to grant any patents on these products in the country before the expiry of the transition periods, that is till 1 January 2005 for developing countries and 1 January 2006 for least developed countries.[3] If patents are eventually granted on these applications, the duration of the term is counted from the date of filing the application.

A clear distinction between exclusive marketing rights and patents is necessary, so exclusive marketing rights do not become de facto patents and defeat the provisions for transition periods for developing and least developed countries. A patent gives rights to prevent others from making, using, offering for sale, selling, or importing for purposes of making, using, offering for sale or selling the patented product or product obtained directly by a patented process; and gives the right to prevent others from using the patented process. Exclusive marketing rights do not cover all the rights a patent gives, and do not extend to making, using and importing a patented product, process or product made directly from the process. Exclusive marketing rights are subject to domestic licensing procedures and approval. If marketing approval is not granted, exclusive marketing rights need not be granted. If marketing approval is granted, exclusive marketing rights may still be granted subject to appropriate conditions, for instance, conditions to prevent anti-competitive practices and to secure the public interest.

Of Africa's 53 countries 34 are least developed according to the UN classification. It is less than accurate when one travels from one African country to another; the conditions on the ground hardly show any distinction between developing and least developed countries. It is a story of uninterrupted and absolute poverty and deprivation. Developing African countries might wish to follow the Senegalese lead and get reclassified as least developed. Or, they might consider striving for the use of other criteria in classifying countries, for instance the use of UNDP's social indicators rather than per capita gross domestic product, which does not reflect the huge disparities in incomes nor the actual living conditions of the overwhelming majority usually in the poorest strata of society. Alternatively, if other members agree, developing and least developed countries should invoke the provisions of Article 72 on reservations, so that provisions they object to do not apply to them.

The experience so far with WTO transition periods is that they have been set in an arbitrary manner and have proved inadequate and inappropriate as periods for adjustment and preparation. Developing countries could seek extensions of the expired periods. Least developed countries would do well to support this, as their own transition periods will similarly soon expire with nothing to show for them. Transition periods need specific and appropriately funded programmes to systematically phase in stages of adjustment and preparation. In future, developing countries should not agree to any transition periods that lack a concrete plan and schedule, and specific funds availed and secured as part of the obligations of the agreements to ensure the implementation of any necessary adjustment and preparation.

NON-DISCRIMINATION OBLIGATIONS

Like other WTO agreements, TRIPS requires members to give national and most favoured nation (MFN) treatment. This time, though, the treatment is accorded to persons who are nationals of other members, and not products. The nationals get treatment that is no less favourable than that which the member gives its own nationals in the protection of intellectual property rights – national treatment; and they get treatment that is no less favourable than the best treatment accorded nationals of any other country – MFN treatment.

There are insubstantial exceptions to the MFN, and not the national, treatment obligation. The MFN obligation does not extend to benefits accorded nationals of other countries under agreements for general judicial assistance or law enforcement, and international agreements on intellectual property rights (IPRs) that entered into force before 1 January 1995, predating TRIPS, and that are notified to the Council on TRIPS, and further, that 'do not constitute arbitrary or unjustifiable discrimination against nationals of other members' – a very difficult clause designed to rein in these other agreements particularly of a regional nature like the African Regional Intellectual Property Organization and the Organisation Africaine de la Propriété Intellectuelle (OAPI). The MFN obligation does not extend to rights not provided in TRIPS for performers, producers of phonograms and broadcasting organizations, and to certain benefits relating to copyrights under provisions permitting non-national treatment.

These obligations are complied with by provisions that do not draw distinctions to favour a member's own nationals or to favour nationals of some other member over nationals of another member. The provisions of the law implementing TRIPS – on objectives, rights protected, enforcement of those rights, etc – should not favour nationals of the country over non-nationals; and as between nationals of other WTO members, the provisions should not be more favourable to some than to others. In drafting terms, these obligations are complied with by omitting reference to nationality of applicants and holders of rights, and including any favourable treatment for a country's nationals or products only in provisions on exceptions that the agreement permits members to have in their laws. In policy terms, the provisions on objectives should aim for a socio-economic environment that effectively promotes domestic innovation and dissemination of technology.

It will remain an interesting question whether the agreement should instead have been based on according MFN treatment for listed categories of intellectual property rights – that is, dealing with trade in rights in intellectual products – and then contained a few related transparency and notification obligations, developmental obligations towards developing countries, and balancing exceptions including general exceptions.

DEVELOPMENT OBJECTIVES IN THE LEGISLATION IMPLEMENTING TRIPS

While it is important that the provisions and obligations that TRIPS imposes on members should be very clear in order to prevent the possible increasing or enlargement of the obligations through the dispute settlement system and superpower arm-twisting,[4] developing countries would do well to adopt the conscious strategy of deliberately having broad and flexible development goals in legislation to implement TRIPS. After the patentability criteria are satisfied, the goals should set the parameters for the administrative decision whether or not to grant the application. This administrative power and step must explicitly be provided for as a condition for the grant of patents, making it a mandatory requirement in the procedure for processing and evaluating applications.

The country will then be able to point out that its law may allow any patents as required by TRIPS, but strictly in accordance with the country's development goals of ensuring technological innovation and a sound and viable technological base; the transfer and dissemination of technology in a manner conducive to social and economic welfare, and to a balance of rights and obligations, and the protection of public and nutritional health; and the promotion of the public interest in sectors of vital importance for socio-economic and technological development. For, as the old woman said, while the sun does not discriminate, the moon and the rain do. But above all, these are the objectives of protecting and enforcing intellectual property rights as spelt out in TRIPS.

The problem with these broad goals is that corruption and more arm-twisting might tilt the balance in practice in favour of developed country applicants probably to the prejudice of important national interests like access to seeds, medicine and scientific research tools. If administrative mechanisms in developing country patent offices ensure that applications are properly processed and granted, the broad context provided by domestic laws can be an effective means for ensuring the application of development goals, protecting the national interest and ensuring that the country's patent policy is duly implemented on the ground in taking decisions on applications.

The administrative mechanisms established by the laws should additionally be given a clear and accountable mandate to follow up provisions in TRIPS on technical assistance and technology transfer from developed countries, severally or collectively with other countries in view of any existing regional framework for harnessing support and assistance. The relevant provisions of the agreement include Articles 7, 8, 66.2 and 67.

MINIMUM STANDARDS

TRIPS provides detailed compulsory obligations on seven categories of IPRs. Articles that specify the rights to be granted protection may be incorporated in domestic laws. As TRIPS is unbalanced against society and overly emphasizes the private rights of the IPR holders, a developing country would be keen to qualify the rights with appropriately balancing exceptions. A few exceptions will be found in the provisions of the agreement, which may be incorporated in domestic laws. A good knowledge of the practice and laws of other countries will provide an array of sources to draw on for other exceptions and rights of society against IPR holders as well as obligations that may be imposed on the holders.

The method or form that the implementation takes may vary from country to country. It is possible to incorporate TRIPS in the domestic order by a short statute giving it the force of law in the country. But such a statute would still have to sort out the purely administrative and transitional provisions of the agreement and exercise the options provided in the agreement on various matters; and this would be the same position in cases or for those countries where international obligations are directly applicable. The common approach is to have a full and comprehensive statute adopted in accordance with the constitutional order of the country, that precisely sets out the objectives of granting and protecting IPRs, the rights protected, the criteria and procedure for acquiring the rights, the exceptions to the rights and the obligations of holders of the rights, methods of enforcing the rights and the applicable remedies, the organs or government departments established to administer the law, and other provisions connected with these matters. In any case, any provisions in domestic laws will still be subject to interpretation and application in the processing of IPR applications, which is a necessary and essential way of building a body of practice and interpretation, and of case law, on the country's intellectual property laws and policies. It may always be borne in mind that under TRIPS, 'members shall be free to determine the appropriate method of implementing the provisions of this Agreement within their own legal system and practice'.

PATENTS

Of the various categories of intellectual property rights covered by TRIPS, the provisions on patents have received the widest international attention especially since 1995 when the agreement entered force, and properly so as evidenced by the very savage impact of the provisions on farming and sick low-income populations, and on the development prospects of developing countries.

Patents are to be available for products and processes in all fields of technology including for micro-organisms, and for non- and micro-biological processes for the production of plants and animals. The criteria for patentability are that the invention should be new, involve an inventive step and be capable of industrial application; and that the invention is clearly and completely disclosed in the application. There is some scope here for members to further define the meaning of the criteria, for instance what amounts to novelty or to inventive step, to define appropriate disclosure perhaps bearing in mind their training and teaching facilities for their scientists, or to require the applicant to disclose other patent applications and grants. Other disclosure requirements may derive from the Convention on Biological Diversity, for instance the disclosure of the country of origin of any genetic resources and traditional knowledge used in the invention sought to be patented (see Chapter 22).

Members may exclude from patentability: (i) certain inventions in order to protect ordre public and morality; human, animal and plant life or health; or to avoid serious prejudice to the environment; (ii) diagnostic, therapeutic and surgical methods for human or animal treatment; (iii) plants and animals, and essentially biological processes for the production of plants and animals; (iv) plant varieties, but if excluded from patentability they should be protected by sui generis systems. Members may in addition provide for (v) other 'limited exceptions [which] do not unreasonably conflict with the normal exploitation of the patent and do not unreasonably prejudice the legitimate interests of the patent owner, taking into account the legitimate interests of third parties'; and (vi) for other use without authorization of the patent owner or compulsory licensing, but this is regulated by numerous conditions listed in Article 31.

The conditions in Article 31 include the following: a member must have a law on compulsory licensing or other use; each licence is considered on its own merits; commercial terms and conditions must first be proposed to the holder of the patent and considered; the licence is for a specific purpose; for semi-conductor technology the use must be non-commercial or to remedy anti-competitive practices; the use is to be non-exclusive and non-assignable, for supplying the domestic market and to cease when circumstances that necessitated the licence no longer exist; adequate remuneration is to be paid; there is to be judicial review of the licensing and the remuneration; and so on.

However, Article 31 does not apply to other use authorized by the government 'before the date this Agreement became known'. Some WTO jurisprudence on this exception would be quite interesting if handed down by a panel not hostile to developing country interests.

A broad exception covering TRIPS is that parallel imports are not prohibited. Once a product has been put on the market with the consent of the

IPR owner, for instance sold by it or under its licence, the owner's exclusive rights expire, for instance rights to prevent third parties from making, using or selling the product. The benefit of this principle, in respect of patents, is that there may be other, cheaper or better, sources of the patented product than the owner of the patent. It is based on the idea that selling the product on the market to a buyer is the remuneration the IPR owner is entitled to, whereupon the property passes to the buyer and subsequently to further buyers or those who acquire it, who may therefore deal with it as they deem fit as the product becomes their property. The rights of the patent holder expire at the first sale when the product becomes the property of the buyer.

Members may take measures and impose conditions to prevent anti-competitive practices. Small economies may be particularly vulnerable to the debilitating effects of anti-competitive practices of powerful global companies or monopoly owners of important intellectual property in fact created by the agreement.

The security exceptions make exception for measures taken 'in time of war or other emergency in international relations', and measures taken as UN obligations for maintenance of international peace and security. In June 2001 the UN General Assembly issued a Declaration on HIV/AIDS following the special session held on access to essential drugs for HIV/AIDS and other killer diseases held by the WTO Council on TRIPS. Whether the prevalence on epidemic proportions of specific diseases, killing off entire populations of several nations, should be construed as constituting an international emergency, and a threat to international peace and security, does deserve some serious attention by WTO members and bodies.

As pointed out earlier, a member may make reservations to certain provisions of TRIPS if other members consent. Developing and least developed countries need to keep this option effectively on board, and it should not be too late particularly for obligations that do not yet apply, by setting out to study possibilities of being permitted by other members to enter reservations on some provisions that are clearly adverse to their development prospects.

Without any intention to downsize the importance of rights and obligations on patents nor to remove attention from patents, it needs to be indicated that the other categories of intellectual property rights – copyrights, performers, trade and service marks, geographical indications, industrial designs and integrated circuits – do require urgent attention on the part of African countries given their far-reaching socio-economic impact and in view of the expiring transition periods and the review of TRIPS under Article 71.1.

TRADITIONAL KNOWLEDGE

Fortunately, the concern over patent provisions has raised and brought in the important area of traditional knowledge (TK), but with the onerous disadvantage that TK has been subordinated to a manner of prioritizing that is subjectively deemed appropriate by the champions of balancing and ensuring development-friendly patent rights. Developing country governments need to reclaim their prioritizing of issues from the invisible hand of developed country media; and to adopt conscious and deliberate, rather than default, strategies to ensure that civil society organizations – they have been decisively instrumental in shaping international public opinion on some major patent issues – always duly give the area of TK the seriousness it more than deserves. Further, African countries should wish to ensure that the regional issues in this area – which in certain respects would be different from those of India and Brazil, the WTO protagonists in this field – are duly taken on board.

In Africa, TK does not yet have the degree of commercialization, standardization and documentation it does in other regions; but the immense knowledge and vast resources of Africans are steadily helping innovations in developed countries and are a goldmine for patents taken out in developed countries that are based on the knowledge and resources of unremunerated and unrecognized local communities in developing countries. TK as a resource remains largely untapped by owners who continue to be blissfully careless about the very huge global market for traditional knowledge products, already put in the neighbourhood of US$50 billion way back in 1985, and projected to be astronomically increasing.[5] As an important economic area, traditional knowledge has not appropriately in terms of emphasis been mainstreamed into national development programmes. The World Bank has a project in Africa for documentation of the knowledge and assisting its use, but this does not address the area of protecting this knowledge and enforcing the rights of its holders.[6] There therefore have to be several fronts for addressing issues of traditional knowledge – domestic, international and of course regional.

At the domestic level, rights of local and farming communities should be protected, and access to genetic resources regulated. The Organization of African Unity (OAU), now the African Union[7], has produced a comprehensive and well-thought-out draft model law on regulating access to genetic resources and on protecting the rights of breeders, farmers and local communities (see Chapter 24). Some African countries have already used the draft model law in preparing and adopting domestic laws on protecting plant varieties as required by Article 27.3(b) of TRIPS and on implementing the Convention on Biological Diversity. At the regional level, the African Union needs to expedite the completion and dissemination of the model law and of current programmes on intellectual property rights in general and traditional knowledge in particular.

African regional economic communities have largely been dormant as partners in this task of adopting regimes on traditional knowledge, and on the whole lack divisions within their secretariats devoted to programmes on TK, an embarrassing shortcoming given their avowed objectives of speeding up economic development and the economic emancipation of the peoples of Africa. African economic communities should be urged to establish and manage concrete and substantial programmes for developing TK as an important economic resource.

African intellectual property organizations are unfortunately either Anglo- or Franco-phone; a divide that already has been devastatingly exploited by alien interests, and one that needs appropriate priority by the African Union in terms of speedy and focused efforts to remedy. For instance, Francophone Africa was perhaps rushed or unduly influenced into adopting an instrument to more or less replicate the provisions of the 1991 Act of the International Convention on the Protection of New Varieties of Plants, which developing countries had and have unanimously objected to as hostile to their farmers, food security policies and measures to protect the public interest (see Chapter 10). In the WTO negotiations and review of provisions on plant varieties under Article 27.3(b), African positions have lacked cogency or even appropriate presentation in part due to this divide, which has also contributed to delays in finalizing work on the draft model law.

It is the international level that can effectively deal with the problem of mischief abroad, when unruly persons and companies take out patents and breeders' rights, inconsistently with domestic laws and regulations or procedures in place in developing countries, and sometimes even inconsistently with internationally recognized standards of patenting such as the criterion of novelty of inventions. TK is an invention of the mind just like other categories of intellectual property, and in terms of the history and practice under geographical indications as protected in TRIPS, intellectual property can belong to entire regions and communities and may significantly be helped by geographical conditions such as those of Africa that have necessitated and produced the immense stock of knowledge and resources that can positively serve humankind.

Some solutions at the international level include the use of the WTO compulsory jurisdiction and enforcement mechanisms to require all WTO members to recognize and protect TK for the persons and traditional communities that hold it. The place in the WTO for locating this obligation would be in TRIPS, by including TK as an additional section or category of IPRs in Part II of TRIPS, allowing sui generis systems of protection in order to take into account the versatility of TK, but, at the same time, unequivocally requiring all members to recognize and protect it as an economic resource of countries and communities that hold it and as knowledge that defeats the novelty requirement in patenting and that must be duly rewarded where it contributes to inventions that satisfy novelty tests as applied and recognized by the laws of WTO members.

ENFORCEMENT OF INTELLECTUAL PROPERTY RIGHTS

The agreement imposes on members the obligation to provide, in their domestic laws, fair and equitable procedures for enforcement of IPRs as well as expeditious and effective remedies against infringement, but to do so without creating barriers to trade. The law should require that decisions on the merits of the case be written and reasoned, based on evidence the parties have an opportunity to respond to, and promptly made available to the parties. And it should provide for judicial review of final administrative decisions and for appeal from lower courts. However, there is no obligation to establish a distinct judicial system for enforcement of IPRs. In many cases, existing civil and criminal procedural laws will already have provisions on many of the agreement's requirements on enforcement. A few amendments may be necessary to introduce some of the remedies required, as indicated below. Still, this bold attempt to include a 'TRIPS Procedure Code' in TRIPS seems an excess if the WTO is a trading body.

In the proceedings, the parties are to be entitled to notices and representation by lawyers, and are to be able to fully present their case. Courts should be able to order discovery of evidence, as well as provision of information on any other infringers. The courts should be able to award costs to the party in whose favour they decide the matter.

The courts are to have power to make orders for provisional measures preventing infringement including entry into the channels of commerce or preserving relevant evidence. But the law should require prompt notice of provisional orders to the other party, adequate security to protect the defendant, and ending of provisional measures if proceedings for determining the matter on the merits are not started within a reasonable period of time.

Regarding substantive remedies, courts should have power to grant injunctions and damages, to prevent infringing products entering the domestic channels of commerce, as well as to order the disposal outside the channels of commerce of the infringing products including materials and implements for making the goods. Unaffixing counterfeit trade marks is not to be sufficient to permit release of the goods into the channels of commerce. Public authorities and officials are to be immune from liability in protecting or enforcing IPRs only for actions taken or intended in good faith.

Customs authorities are to have the power, acting at their own instance or on application by a right holder, to suspend releasing counterfeit trade mark or pirated copyright goods, where infringement is adequately shown at that stage. But the applicant is to start proceedings within ten days unless the period is extended, and to provide adequate security. The authorities are to have the power to destroy the infringing products or dispose of them outside the channels of commerce.

Criminal procedures and penalties are to be available for wilful trade mark counterfeiting or copyright piracy on a commercial scale. The penalties are to include imprisonment, fines, seizure, forfeiture and destruction of the goods and the materials and implements for making the goods.

FURTHER RESEARCH

The exceptions in TRIPS are far out of step with comparable exceptions in the other WTO agreements. While TRIPS has a security exception just like the other agreements, unlike the other agreements it does not have general exceptions. This anomaly can only go uncorrected in contradiction of and against universal practice.

In the security exception provision is made for measures in situations of war or other international emergency. A question here is whether international emergencies can be constituted by killer diseases affecting entire populations, for instance in cases of epidemics and plagues like HIV/AIDS. Recent UN practice, for instance the UN Declaration on HIV/AIDS, needs to be built upon to establish a basis for taking certain health measures within the scope of this security exception.

The TRIPS Agreement was in essence written by developed country industry lobbies. It would appear however that they missed an obvious and peculiar point, that they need a growing and vibrant market for their products. On Earth and for the foreseeable future, developing countries will continue to make up about three-quarters of humankind. Developing countries are here to stay and to develop. The fate of humankind is inextricably tied up with the fate of developing countries. They make up a vast market potential and it would only be in the best interests of industry to have them firmly on board and to develop this huge market. Impoverishing and leaving destitute entire populations in developing countries is economic suicide for developed countries and industry lobbies.

The nuisance that industry lobbies and developed countries have made of themselves, influencing developing countries to forfeit their WTO rights and to adopt positions that harm them, must now get serious attention with a view to ending this situation. In the case of Africa, this matter is not just about trade disputes threatened or started far away in Geneva at the WTO. It is a matter that touches upon any aspect of dealings with the developed countries, in areas of economic cooperation, debt, technology transfer, environment, culture, and so on. What Africa must have at national, subregional and the continental level, are sharp teams rearing to challenge any assault on the rights and integrity of African countries. For purposes of the WTO, recent efforts to establish legal aid and technical support, including the provision in Article 4 of the WIPO-WTO Agreement for legal-technical assistance to all developing countries having membership in either organization, still fall far short of targeting and decisively dealing with the particularly weak position of Africa in international economic and trade relations. Africa must have its own spears.

Were an African country to win a case at the WTO, for instance against the EU or the US or Japan, and the Dispute Settlement Body to go ahead to authorize it to take retaliatory measures against the other country, the African country would simply be unable to exercise that option for practical considerations – its trade would be negligible and closing up might hurt it more than the countries exporting to it. It has therefore been obvious that Africa and other developing countries do not have any retaliatory sanctions to talk of for purposes of backing up any actions they might contemplate against countries that breach their rights. You might say it is not as bad as that, for African countries could always join any African country that started a case, as co-complainants or interested parties and then collectively threaten sanctions if they won, sanctions such as withdrawing the protection of IPRs of owners based in defendant countries. This is an area that needs careful thinking to build on work that has already started.

Other research areas include gender aspects of TRIPS, taking TRIPS out of the WTO and some of it to WIPO, alternative models for TRIPS based on development and strictly trade perspectives, the non-application of non-violation complaints to TRIPS, the comprehensive set of obligations that IPR holders should have to the general public particularly in developing countries, TRIPS vis-à-vis the African Union, and finally Africa's economic emancipation.

NOTES

1 Many African countries do not have missions in Geneva, many do not have a consistent internet connection to the WTO, and many have only tiny or skeletal missions in Geneva to cover the entire UN system, with the result that effective and consistent participation in WTO proceedings and activities is compromised.
2 Ambassador Boniface Chidyausiku of Zimbabwe and Ambassador Nathan Irumba of Uganda, respectively.
3 Article 65(4) allows developing countries to delay the application of the agreement to new areas where patenting is introduced, for an additional period of five years from 1 January 2000.
4 The unfortunate fact of more or less persecuting developing countries around the world on the basis of Section 301 of the US Trade Act, is real and well established, and should be kept high on the reform agenda of strengthening the multilateral trading system. The dispute settlement system, despite Article 23 of the Dispute Settlement Understanding clearly prohibiting unilateralism, has been somehow able to find that the US provisions and practice are not inconsistent with WTO obligations – on the basis of an administrative undertaking to still act consistently with WTO obligations.
5 Mugabe cites statistics putting the OECD market at US$43 billion in 1985 (see Mugabe, J 'Intellectual property protection and traditional knowledge'. *Biopolicy International*, no. 19. Nairobi: African Centre for Technology Studies Press. The WHO estimates that 80 per cent of the world's population depends on traditional medicine. According to UNCTAD's Biotrade Initiative, the annual global market for genetic resources-based products is between US$500 billion and $800 billion. Some sources estimate that the global market for herbal products will reach US$5 trillion by the year 2020.
6 The documented knowledge has been posted on the World Bank website for anybody to access. Perhaps this can already help in the application of novelty tests in patent offices around the world but that remains to be seen. What needs to be done urgently is ensure that this publication does not instead facilitate biopiracy as the information is not adequately protected. [www.worldbank.org]
7 The act establishing the African Union entered force on 26 May 2001 and the Union was formally launched in Lusaka by the OAU Assembly of 39 heads of state and government at the 9–12 July 2001 summit.

Chapter 24

The African Union Model Law for the Protection of the Rights of Local Communities Farmers and Breeders and the Regulation of Access to Biological Resources[1]

Johnson A Ekpere

THE OAU INITIATIVE: RATIONALE AND ESSENTIAL FEATURES

The Organization of African Unity (OAU) Model Law was developed as a direct response to the decision taken and the directive given by the OAU Council of Ministers in 1988. As its title suggests, it is an effort to create a sui generis system of protection of the rights of local communities, farmers and breeders and for the regulation of access to biological resources. It was developed through a process of regional, subregional and national consultation of stakeholders, and informed public debate. The objective of the resultant legislation is to give reasoned attention to the conservation of biodiversity, sustainable use of biological resources, maintenance of food security, protection of community rights, equitable sharing of benefits consistent with the provisions of the Convention on Biological Diversity (CBD), and the concept of national sovereignty. It is intended to provide OAU member states with a framework for the formulation of legislation relevant to their national interest and the protection of new plant varieties as required by the TRIPS Agreement.

In adopting the model law and recommending it as a framework for the development of TRIPS-compliant legislation at the national level, African governments shared several fundamental viewpoints. First, the concept of intellectual property rights (IPRs) as expressed in TRIPS is alien to Africa's understanding of property and rights. It is therefore inappropriate for the protection of community rights, traditional knowledge, technology, innovations and practices in the African cultural context. Second, Africa is committed to the basic tenets and fundamental principles of the Convention on Biological Diversity, and the inalienable rights of local communities to assume ownership of and regulate access to their biological resources. The TRIPS Agreement does not recognize community rights. Third, there is no empirical evidence or practical experience that the prescribed patent regime will improve the economic welfare of Africans. Fourth, Africa fears that patent protection will hurt the small farmer, aggravate the food security situation and increase Africa's dependence on external food aid and markets. This is because of the limitation placed on the free exchange of farm-saved seed and other planting materials through the monopoly ownership conferred on the patent holder. Fifth, the debt burden of the continent will be exacerbated through royalty payments to the North where over 90 per cent of the patents for improved agricultural inputs, including seeds and other biological resource-based innovations, are held. Sixth, the issue at stake for the continent is the appropriation of the knowledge, innovations, technologies and practices of local communities and their associated biodiversity without equitable sharing of benefits and consideration for their sustainable use.

The second component of the OAU initiative in this whole area is the coordination of an African common position on TRIPS in general and the review of Article 27.3(b) in particular. Most African countries were not active participants in the negotiations leading to the final agreement even though they became signatories to TRIPS. The need for a common position was informed by a better understanding of the agreement and its obvious contradictions with the relevant provisions of the CBD. Consequently, the OAU initiative provided the conceptual framework and empirical evidence for the formulation of the African Common Position that was discussed at the OAU Council of Ministers Meeting in Algiers (July 1999), the meeting of African Ministers of Trade in Algiers (September 1999) and at the meeting of African Ministers of Trade in Cairo (September 2000).

The 1999 communication to the Council for TRIPS by the government of Kenya on behalf of Africa, the submission by the Southern African Development Commission to the World Trade Organization (WTO), and the ongoing negotiations by the African trade missions in Geneva are all reflections of the OAU initiative in pursuance of Africa's common position on TRIPS and the review of Article 27.3(b).

The primary objective of the model law was to ensure the evaluation, conservation and sustainable use of biological resources, including plant (agricultural) genetic resources as well as associated tradition knowledge, in order to improve their diversity as a means of sustaining life support systems. The rationale derives from the need to: (i) recognize, protect and support the inalienable right of local communities, including farming communities, over their biological resources, crop varieties, medicinal plants, knowledge, technologies and practices; (ii) recognize and protect the rights of breeders over varieties developed by them; (iii) provide a mutually acceptable system of access to biological resources, community knowledge, technologies and practices, subject to prior informed consent (PIC) of the state and concerned local community; (iv) ensure and promote the supply of good quality seed and planting materials to farmers; and (v) ensure that plant genetic resources are utilized in a sustainable and equitable manner in order to guarantee national food security.

The law was crafted with specific reference to the CBD and Article 27.3(b) of TRIPS. It does not address the various other contentious issues of TRIPS, but it can be applied in the formulation of legislation on access and benefit sharing, sui generis legislation on the protection of new plant varieties, and protection of traditional knowledge and the rights of local communities including farmers.

The model law is unique in other ways because it addresses the following issues in a holistic way: (i) food security in terms of access to planting materials and food at all times for an active and healthy life; (ii) the sovereign and inalienable right of states over their biological resources, access and benefit sharing; (iii) community rights as guaranteed by the state; (iv) the importance of community knowledge, technologies, innovations and practices to the life support systems of the human kind; (v) participation in decision-making and essence of dialogue in governance; (vi) regulation of access to biological resources as entrenched in the CBD; (vii) prior informed consent as an essential pre-condition for access; and (viii) fair and equitable sharing of benefits as required by CBD.

The model law is specific in its enunciation and amplification of the African common position against patents on life forms. It acknowledges the pivotal role of women in the conservation of biological diversity and gender equality in decision-making.

THE RELATIONSHIP BETWEEN THE MODEL LAW AND OTHER INTERNATIONAL INSTRUMENTS

The OAU model law may be described as an eclectic document. It was developed with full awareness of the best practices implicit in other international instruments, but fashioned with the best interests of Africa in mind. It was developed with due knowledge, consideration and commitment to the spirit, philosophy and overall objective of the CBD. Consequently it emphasizes the requirements of Article 8(j) of that convention.

The proponents of the model law were fully aware of the dangers of implementing most international instruments as separate entities and in isolation from each other. Consequently, even though the model law rejects the concept of protection by patents, it accepts the notion of protection through a sui generis option. You may ask, what is the difference? Think about it objectively. The model law is completely at variance with the patenting of life forms, but supportive of breeders' rights. There are areas of convergence between TRIPS and the OAU model law, but there are also several areas of disagreement.

The OAU model law was crafted in anticipation of the conclusion and outcome of the negotiations on the revision of the International Undertaking on Plant Genetic Resources and Agriculture, which resulted in a new treaty (see Chapter 6). It therefore integrates the concept of farmers' rights which was then under discussion and negotiation at the Food and Agriculture Organization (FAO), and advocates them as a counterbalance to breeders' rights.

The International Union for the Protection of New Varieties of Plants (UPOV) Convention was extensively consulted in the design of the OAU model law. There is a substantial relationship in concepts, though there are differences in interpretation. The historical development of plant variety protection in Europe before the first adoption of the UPOV Convention in 1961, as well as the experiences gained during its evolution into more recent versions (most recently in 1978 and 1991), were very informative. However the model law differs in that UPOV does not guarantee the rights of farmers, which is fundamental in Africa, to exchange farm-saved seeds. UPOV does not recognize community rights and only rewards individual monopoly rights to the exclusion of others.

CURRENT STATUS OF IMPLEMENTATION

Substantial progress has been made in Asia and South America to develop and enact appropriate legislation compliant with the CBD and TRIPS. Most of these countries have chosen the sui generis option for obvious reasons. In Africa, however, prior to the adoption of the model law by the OAU member states, there was very little effort in the formulation of such legislation. The OAU initiative was a major factor in ongoing discussions in various national parliaments on the development of legal instruments.

However, the development of national laws based on the model law has been slow even though the idea of the sui generis option has been accepted. A review of African countries in the process of developing legislation and adopting the model law framework suggests that they can be classified into four categories. The first category comprises countries with several variants of sui generis systems, embodying components of the model law and having internal capacity for their implementation. This group includes South Africa, Egypt, Namibia and Zimbabwe. The second category consists of countries having enabling legislation pending in parliament, such as Kenya, Uganda and Nigeria. The third group are countries of French-speaking West and Central Africa that are members of the Organisation Africaine de la Propriété Intellectuelle (OAPI), and which through revision and ratification of the Bangui Agreement are adopting the sui generis system based on the UPOV 1991 model (see Chapter 10). Finally, there are those countries without legislation that are only now contemplating the possibility of developing a sui generis system of protection fashioned after the OAU model or other forms of legislation. The majority of African countries belong to this category and are seriously considering the use of the model law. However, they face external pressure not to do so.

MAJOR PROBLEMS IN ADAPTATION TO NATIONAL LAW

The most important challenge for adapting the OAU model through the design and implementation of appropriate protection laws is that of having sufficient capacity, skill and expertise in legal drafting and full knowledge of its implications for national development and international cooperation. Most countries have had problems in adapting various articles of the model law to national priority objectives.

There are problems of definitional equivalence of terms, common meaning and interpretation of the provisions of the law. For example, the World Intellectual Property Organization (WIPO) is working hard to provide a better understanding of traditional knowledge (TK) and how best it can be protected. Governments are not well informed on the utility of traditional knowledge protection even though they now recognize that their TK is being misappropriated. There are problems of scope. There are arguments in support of framework laws to protect all components of TK, ranging from plant varieties and biological resources, to the rights of local communities. Others suggest the development of separate legislation for specific components to which sui generis legislation is applicable. There are constraints of implementation capacity, public awareness, advocacy and civil society participation to ensure action. There are also several intangible constraints that impede an objective debate of the OAU Model Law as an important factor in national development.

SUGGESTED SOLUTIONS TO MITIGATE CONSTRAINTS

The OAU Model Law as a form of sui generis system of protection can be effective if it is adequately adapted in time and space specific to the subject to be protected and the socio-economic environment in which it is to be implemented. But perhaps the most important constraint presently is the lack of awareness about the model law. The problem of capacity building can be allayed through specialized training, confidence building and dialogue with relevant stakeholders. There is a need for careful planning and extensive advocacy work to explain the essence of the model law, not only to legislators, policy-makers and government functionaries but also to members of civil society groups and the general public.

National governments and the international community should learn to be more participative, strategically patient and democratic in their decision-making processes. They should ensure that those most likely to be affected by these legislative imperatives not only understand the issues involved, but actually get a fair hearing and participate in the whole process.

There is a need for more widespread discussion of the Model Law at national, subregional and regional levels on the continent to more realistically elicit the reaction, support or otherwise of Africa. Finally, there is a need to commission studies to better understand the constraints to the implementation of the OAU Model Law at national level to enable a more objective suggestion of solutions.

HOW TO PROMOTE IMPLEMENTATION OF THE MODEL LAW

It is an understatement that most Africans are not aware of the OAU Model Law. The need for promotion as a pre-condition for effective adaptation and implementation is therefore self-evident. The poor knowledge of the existence of the model law is further accentuated by the fact that most Africans are not even aware of the reasons for its development. There is poor knowledge of patent protection, TRIPS, Agenda 21, the CBD, the Biosafety Protocol and the FAO International Treaty on Plant Genetic Resources for Food and Agriculture by scientists, government functionaries not directly involved in the negotiations, and the general public. Consequently, there is neither the urge nor the motivation to acquire, read and understand the OAU Model Law. There is therefore a need to develop some innovative methods to promote the law and disseminate the information embodied in it. For purposes of this discussion, I suggest, first, mass production and dissemination, free of charge, of copies of the model law, in all African countries. Second, the document should be placed on the website of interested organizations and institutions. Third, special workshops, conferences and sensitization seminars on the protection of biological resources and traditional knowledge should be organized for stakeholders using the OAU Model Law as the medium of information sharing and dialogue. Fourth, other forms of mass media and advocacy should be used to popularize and promote the model law. In all these efforts, national governments should play the lead role with supportive activities from civil society, NGOs and international organizations.

NOTES

1 Acknowledgement is made to the OPEC Fund for International Development for financial support. The opinions expressed in this paper are those of the author and not necessarily those of the African Union.

Chapter 25

The Andean Community Regimes on Access to Genetic Resources, Intellectual Property, and the Protection of Indigenous Peoples' Knowledge

Manuel Ruiz

Introduction

The Andean region is, arguably, where the most intense and extensive debate has taken place regarding the issues of access to genetic resources, intellectual property rights (IPRs) and their impact on biodiversity and the protection of indigenous peoples' knowledge. These discussions and their progression into regional policies and regulations in the Andean Community of Nations started in 1992, the year the Convention on Biological Diversity (CBD) was opened for signature, and at the same time as a regional legal regime for the protection of new plant varieties was being drawn up.

The consequence of this debate was the development by the Andean Community of Decision 391 on a Common Regime on Access to Genetic Resources (adopted in 1996), Decision 486 on a Common Regime on Industrial Property (2000), Decision 523 on a Regional Biodiversity Strategy and Decision 524 which established an Indigenous Peoples Regional Working Group (both in 2002). These are all binding instruments which are in force in all five member states (Venezuela, Colombia, Ecuador, Peru and Bolivia). At the national level these issues are now also well established in national policy agendas.

Notwithstanding these developments at the conceptual, policy and legal levels, there remains much to do regarding implementation and verifying practical results from these different instruments. This chapter offers a brief overview of the progress made in the region and some perspectives as to the challenges and problems which might lie ahead during implementation, including some suggestions on how to confront these successfully in the near future.

ACCESS AND BENEFIT SHARING IN THE ANDEAN COMMUNITY: A LONG ROAD AND STILL LOOKING FOR ANSWERS

The always controversial and complex issues of access to genetic resources, IPRs and indigenous peoples' knowledge emerged in the region during the development of the 1993 Decision 345 of the Andean Community on a Common Regime on Plant Breeders' Rights.

As a countermeasure to balance the granting of IPRs over life forms, in this case exclusive rights over seeds and new plant varieties, and to ensure genetic resources used in research and development processes were legally obtained and benefits shared, in accordance with the CBD, access to, control of and legal rights over genetic resources became part of regular policy and legal debate during this period.

When as part of the process of negotiating Decision 345 an explicit reference was made to plant breeding as implying 'the use of scientific knowledge in hereditary breeding of plants', certain institutions openly questioned whether this meant the exclusion of other forms of knowledge, such as indigenous peoples' knowledge and techniques which might contribute to the breeding of new plant varieties. As a result, indigenous peoples' knowledge, innovations and practices as they relate to biodiversity also came to occupy an important place in regional and national debates.

Decision 345 incorporated a Third Transitory Disposition which called on member states of the Andean Community to develop a regional common regime on access to genetic resources and biosafety in accordance with the CBD. This provision was quite ground-breaking at the time. Indeed, for the first time, an IPR regulation incorporated a specific reference to access to genetic resources, thereby highlighting the emerging and complex relations between these two issues.

Three years later, and after a technical and political process within the Andean Community which involved the participation of a wide range of stakeholders, Decision 391 was enacted in July 1996. Decision 391 establishes the regional legal regime on access to genetic resources and benefit sharing. Key aspects of this regulation are: (i) the definition of 'access', which implies access to and use of genetic resources or their derivatives for commercial, industrial or scientific purposes; (ii) the objective of the common regime, which is to ensure benefit sharing, enhance scientific and technical capacities, promote conservation and strengthen negotiating capacities of member states; (iii) the scope of the regime, which applies to genetic resources and their derivatives of which member states are countries of origin; (iv) the legal status of genetic resources, which is that they and their derivatives are patrimony of the state, but biological resources can be subject to private rights; (v) that indigenous peoples have the right to decide over the use of their knowledge, innovations and practices as they relate to genetic resources; and (vi) that contracts are the main instrument through which access and benefit sharing will be regulated.

Progress in implementing Decision 391 in the various member states has been uneven. Venezuela decided to apply Decision 391 directly and, to date, eight or nine access contracts have been actually signed. Colombia also decided to apply it directly, but to date, limited implementation has taken place. Bolivia enacted a national implementing regulation in 1996, but no access applications have yet been processed. Ecuador and Peru have drafted implementing regulations which are still to be formally approved.

From accumulated and partial evidence over the last few years, it seems clear that Decision 391 has had limited impact in achieving its most important objectives. Reasons for this are varied but it is worthwhile to mention at least four. First, at the time of negotiating Decision 391, there were high expectations of the monetary and economic returns that would result from bioprospecting. Second, there is still the need to carefully analyse and understand the nature of genetic resource markets and industrial demand in order to respond with adequate policy and regulatory measures. Third, the availability of genetic resources and their 'physical' nature also have a bearing on how practical a legal regime should be. As a consequence of these, a fourth reason, or rather an effect, is that transaction costs for implementing Decision 391 seem particularly high.

The effect of such a limited amount of formal bioprospecting activities taking place in the region is that very few benefits exist to be shared. In this circumstance, there is a need to undertake an overall review of Decision 391. The review should take into account how incentives (and which particular incentives) might most effectively promote bioprospecting and thereby generate benefits. It may also be necessary to modify Decision 391 by incorporating 'partnerships' and 'collaborative agreements' as key components of any regional strategy for bioprospecting, and in this regard focus on further engaging national research and scientific institutions in the development of these agreements. These reforms might lead us towards a simpler and more effective regulatory approach, that in turn will ensure that bioprospecting activities actually take place and generate benefits, such as technology and knowledge transfer, training and enhanced national research.

LINKING INTELLECTUAL PROPERTY RIGHTS TO ACCESS AND INDIGENOUS PEOPLES' ISSUES IN DECISION 486

Closely linked to Decision 391, although adopted almost four years later, is Decision 486 on a Common Regime on Industrial Property. Many experts openly question the IPR system in general, including Decision 486. Indeed, their arguments go beyond the actual content of this particular law and focus more on the overall IPR system and TRIPS in particular, as mechanisms which have been imposed (fundamentally by the US) on developing countries and, ultimately, only favour commercial interests of industrialized nations. In doing so, they also stress how the important, but often sidelined, moral and ethical argument against patenting of life forms is seldom discussed.

However, Decision 486 does contain various explicit and ground-breaking provisions and self-executing articles which seek to protect member states' interests in genetic resources and biologically derived materials, as well as the interests of indigenous peoples. A national, let alone a regional, IPR regulation containing a single reference to access or indigenous peoples' issues would have been unthinkable only a couple of years ago anywhere in the world. With Decision 486, an important step has been taken to find ways in which IPRs, access and benefit sharing (ABS) provisions and the CBD's principles can be reconciled to ensure that biodiversity components are sustainably used and, especially, the benefits derived thereof can be equitably shared.

Article 3 of Decision 486 (Biological and Genetic Patrimony and Traditional Knowledge), establishes that '... Member States will make sure that protection provided through elements of industrial property [not only patents] is provided safeguarding and respecting their biological and genetic patrimony as well as the traditional knowledge of their indigenous, Afro-American and local communities. In this regard, patents concerning materials obtained from this patrimony or knowledge, will be subject to those materials having been obtained in conformity with international, regional and national regulations.'

Basically, what Decision 486 is proposing is that since biotechnological inventions may directly or indirectly derive from genetic resources from member states or related indigenous knowledge, applicants for patents must also make sure they comply with pertinent access and indigenous peoples' knowledge regulations (in this particular case with Decision 391 provisions). In this regard, Decision 486 seeks to be supportive of CBD principles and recognise member states' interests in their genetic resources as well as the interests of indigenous peoples.

Article 15(b), on the other hand, excludes from patentability living organisms or their parts as they are found in nature, biological material which is found in nature or is isolated including parts of the genome of living organisms. Clearly, the principle of non-patentability of discoveries is being expressly specified and clarified.

Decision 391 already incorporated a clear and unmistakable linkage between access to genetic resources and IPRs. Although this is true in a regional and international context, strictly speaking the first legal instrument to establish some linkage between access and IPRs was really Decree 533 of Colombia of 1994, which regulated the plant breeders' rights regime. Article 10(f), regarding the application to obtain a breeders' certificate, establishes that the application should disclose the genetic origin of the material, while paragraph (h) refers to the need to disclose geographical origin of the material used for the new variety.

Peru's Regulation for the Protection of Plant Breeders Rights[1] of May 1996, which is complementary to Decision 345, is even more specific and clear in its linkage of plant breeders' rights with ABS. Article 15(e), when referring to the application for a plant breeder certificate, establishes that the application should indicate '...the geographical origin of the plant material used as raw material by the breeder in his new variety, including, if it be the case, the document which proves the legal origin of the genetic resources contained in the variety as provided by the National Competent Authority on Genetic Resources'.

Paragraph (f) goes further in requiring the application to indicate '... the genetic content and origin of the variety and include all known detail regarding the source of the genetic resources contained in the variety or for its development, as well as all information regarding knowledge related to the variety if it be the case'. In some cases, such 'knowledge' could be indigenous knowledge. If an application is not complete or is missing these requirements and the applicant fails to provide it in due time, the National Institute for the Defence of Competition and Protection of Intellectual Property (INDECOPI), which is the governmental authority dealing with patents and plant breeders' rights, can declare it as abandoned.

Based on Article 16(5) of the CBD and a general consensus among negotiators that mechanisms should be developed to ensure that IPRs are supportive of the CBD objectives, Decision 391 included two extremely important provisions for member states and the region, which have gone as far as to dramatically influence negotiations and the adoption of Decision 486. These types of measures have also been incorporated into legislation in Brazil, Costa Rica and other countries.

The Second Complementary Disposition of Decision 391 established that '... Member States will not recognize rights, including intellectual property rights, over genetic resources, derived or synthesized products and intangible associated components, obtained or developed based on access activities which do not comply with this Decision'. Additionally, '... Member States are entitled to request the annulment of or present the corresponding actions in countries which might have conferred rights or protection titles'. In principle, this provision seeks to ensure the interests of member states as countries of origin. It is worth noting the reference to 'synthesized products', which are essentially new technologies over which Decision 391 seeks to extend its scope.

The Third Complementary Disposition establishes that 'national intellectual property offices shall, in cases where they have reasonable or concrete evidence that the product or processes for which protection is being requested have been obtained or developed from genetic resources or their derived products for which any of the Member States is a country of origin, require the applicants to submit the registration number of the access contract and a copy of it, as a prerequisite for the granting of the corresponding right'. This provision continues by establishing that IPR offices and access authorities will develop mechanisms to exchange information regarding access contracts and IPR applications.

In accordance with these dispositions and further specifying their scope, Article 26(h) of Decision 486 requires patent applications to include, if applicable 'a copy of the access contract, when products or procedure whose protection is requested have been obtained or developed based on genetic resources or the derived product of which any of the Member State is a country of origin'. Paragraph (i) goes on to establish that, if applicable, a copy of the licence or authorization for the use of indigenous knowledge will also be requested. Critical here is the 'if applicable' qualifier. National authorities will have to determine under what circumstances and regarding what inventions they will request these documents. For example, they may act on the basis of evidence that a biotechnological invention is based on genetic resources of which member states are countries of origin.

This approach is clearly one innovative mechanism to ensure that when using genetic resources or traditional knowledge in an invention for which an IPR is requested, applicants have complied with all regulations related to ABS and indigenous knowledge protection before the rights are granted. There are some constraints, though, including jurisdictional limitations in the sense that this mechanism can only be applied in member states. There could also be practical problems in, for example, identifying the exact geographical and legal origin of genetic resources contained in a biotechnological invention for which an IPR is requested.

However, if adequately implemented, not only in member states but throughout the world, this mechanism could: (i) provide a means for all parties to the CBD, providers and users of genetic resources alike, to promote compliance with its general ABS, technology transfer and IPR provisions; (ii) act as a measure to safeguard the interests of mega-diverse countries which provide Northern biotechnological sectors with genetic resources; and, most importantly; and (iii) create a system which encourages mega-diverse countries to make their ABS regimes more flexible and thus more effective. If industrialized nations adopt these measures and include them in their own IPR regimes, this could pave the way to a process of mutual confidence building among those traditionally supplying resources and those using them, and positively influence international negotiations, research and development initiatives and bioprospecting endeavours in general.

PROTECTING TRADITIONAL KNOWLEDGE: DEVELOPING A SUI GENERIS MODEL OR AN INTEGRATED SYSTEM OF PROTECTION

Decisions 391 and 486 do not specifically protect indigenous peoples' knowledge. However, they do address this issue and certainly contain provisions oriented to ensuring indigenous interests are taken into account. It should be noted that Decision 391 did include an Eighth Transitory Disposition which calls on member states to initiate a process to develop a regional regulation for the protection of indigenous peoples' knowledge. The Regional Biodiversity Strategy (Decision 523) and, especially, Decision 524 (which establishes a regional working group for indigenous peoples) offer an ideal opportunity and scenario to comply with these mandates and develop the said legal regime.

In the short term, it is highly unlikely that a single legal mechanism or instrument will achieve protection of all traditional knowledge and its manifestations, such as a new plant variety, the use of a medicinal herb or single plant, a culinary recipe, a cultivation technique, the use of combined medicinal extracts, at least until a decision is taken at the international level to negotiate an all-embracing international agreement for the protection of indigenous intellectual property. Not even a regional Andean regulation will ensure indigenous peoples' knowledge is effectively protected at the international level although it will be a great step forward.

However, through a series of existing legal and non-legal instruments and mechanisms, three basic objectives of a regime to 'protect' indigenous peoples' knowledge might be achieved. These are control over the use of knowledge, compensation, and maintenance of traditional knowledge. These could be achieved without the need to develop a completely new legal regime. Indigenous peoples' knowledge, innovations and practices could be protected by existing legal and non-legal instruments and modified hybrids of these integrated into a comprehensive system.

In this regard, it is necessary to integrate a series of instruments and mechanisms to form the basis for a comprehensive approach to the protection of indigenous knowledge, innovations and practices. Under this notion, protection might extend to native crops, indigenous knowledge per se, and any other type of innovation generated by indigenous peoples. Depending on the objectives sought by the protection regime, several measures could be considered. These include control over the use of resources, protection of innovation in the area of plant variety breeding, prevention of biopiracy, equitable benefit sharing, maintenance of indigenous knowledge, such as through the development of national or regional registers or databases, conservation of areas identified as centres of biological and cultural diversity, and the identification and assistance of conservation-minded indigenous people.

It is important to briefly comment on what the notion of 'integral' means in the context of a system. It is proposed that for the system of protection to be effective and efficient, it is necessary that the instruments and mechanisms which have been proposed are integrated and articulated. For this, it is necessary that the system has: (i) permanent and necessary coordination among institutions who are responsible for administering or managing each of the elements which are part of the system; (ii) permanent flows and generation of information among institutions, and (iii) an institution which is responsible for ensuring the efficient operation of the system. If one of these elements is weakened the system in its integrity becomes weakened and protection as such will be considerably affected.

The Andean Community countries have taken important steps in this regard. In terms of conceptual developments and approaches, much progress has been achieved. In terms of policy and regulation, there have also been important developments. In August 2002, Peru enacted Law 27811, which establishes a system for the protection of indigenous peoples' collective knowledge associated with biodiversity (see Chapter 30). The Andean Community has also been actively participating in the Free Trade Area of the Americas negotiation. The agreement on IPRs contains a complete section on genetic resources and indigenous peoples' knowledge that is currently under negotiation.

FINAL COMMENT

There are certainly some very complex linkages between access to genetic resources, IPRs and indigenous peoples' knowledge-related issues. It becomes increasingly difficult to address each issue in isolation. For the IPR system to ensure the interests of countries of origin and indigenous peoples are taken into account, there need to be smooth connections with the access regime. In turn, a regulation or system which seeks to protect indigenous peoples' knowledge will have to be positively connected to the access regime and certainly to the IPR system. This overlap makes the challenge of implementing effective rules even more interesting. In sum, there will probably not be a single answer or response to ensure effectiveness of the access or IPR system or the protection of indigenous knowledge.

NOTES

1 Supreme Decree No 008-96-ITINCI.

Chapter 26

The Central American Regional Protocol on Access to Genetic and Biochemical Resources

Jorge A Cabrera Medaglia

The Central American Protocol on Access to Genetic and Biochemical Resources was negotiated by the member states of the Central American Commission on Environment and Development (CCAD), which are Belize, Costa Rica, El Salvador, Guatemala, Honduras, Nicaragua and Panama. The process of developing the protocol required each state to consult internally with civil society. This chapter makes reference to the main issues addressed during discussions on the protocol. The protocol has been signed by the seven members of the CCAD and is awaiting ratification before the national parliaments.

The biological wealth of tropical countries, including Central America, and the potential utilization of genetic and biochemical resources and related traditional knowledge are nowadays an unmistakable reality. The possibilities offered by the 'new biotechnologies' have opened the door to a new consideration of the 'hidden' value of our resources and traditional knowledge. Agrochemical, seed and pharmaceutical companies are increasingly expressing an interest in prospecting our natural wealth and in using traditional knowledge as a guide for their research. However, under the legal provisions which we shall comment on below, such access to our resources and knowledge must comply with a number of requirements. The first is to obtain the prior informed consent (PIC) of states and other title holders of knowledge or of the biological, genetic or biochemical resource. The second is to negotiate the sharing of benefits arising from access to biodiversity and the related traditional knowledge, by means of an agreement or contract setting out 'mutually agreed terms' according to which such access is conducted. The third is to preserve biodiversity and create a national capacity for adding value to the natural resources pertaining to each country.

These new legal requirements are contained in the Central American Protocol on Access to Genetic and Biochemical Resources. Basically, once fully implemented, the regime will function through agreements or contracts concluded between the companies conducting research of this type, including intermediaries, and any collaborators in the country of origin of the resource, such as the government, scientific institutions, or members of local or indigenous communities. The latter would thus be assured some type of compensation in exchange for the germplasm or traditional knowledge, such as upfront payment on specimens, royalties on net income from potential results, technology transfer and training. Part of this compensation would be used for the conservation of biological diversity. In this way, criticisms that genetic resources are obtained freely and products based on them are patented and sold would be addressed, and the benefits arising out of the utilization of biological diversity would be equitably shared.

It is not a question, however, only of monitoring access to biological, genetic and biochemical resources. Within such regulatory frameworks, protection must also be afforded to the knowledge, innovations and practices of local communities and indigenous peoples. The fact that for centuries the indigenous peoples and peasants have developed their own systems, practices and knowledge for the purposes of agriculture, pest control, handling of natural resources, traditional medicine, etc, is recognized by present-day societies. This knowledge is valuable and useful for social sectors other than those that created and developed it through their intellectual effort. In this way, the use of these traditional practices has brought huge economic and social benefits to the rest of the population of each country and even to other countries in the world. And yet, what has happened to these indigenous peoples and local communities? Have they received any form of compensation for their work and their science? The answer to this question has to be no. For a time, biological diversity, the traditional work of improving crops and animals and the indigenous knowledge thereof were considered as a non-exclusive type of public good, access to which was open and free of charge. It was considered as a 'common heritage of humankind'. And yet, from those genetic resources obtained at no cost, products of different kinds were developed, such as new plant varieties, pharmaceutical products or pesticides, which were then labelled as private property, and subject to intellectual property rights. They were then made available to the developing countries for a price. The asymmetry of this relation between genetic resources supplied free of charge by the South and end products acquired for a price paid to Northern businesses had to be justified in some way. To do this, a concept was invented as a means of extracting the genetic wealth of our countries without offering any offsetting compensation. According to this concept, biological diversity was a common heritage of humankind, that is to say, a public good, which may be enjoyed at no cost. The derived pesticides, medicines and improved seeds, however, are placed under the cover of another notion, namely private property.

At the same time as the international community began to reject the concept of the common heritage of humankind, the new third generation biotechnologies (basically recombinant DNA and cell fusion) and the advances made in the field of microelectronics and testing techniques for biological materials revived the interest of pharmaceutical, chemical, biotechnological and seed companies in both genetic resources in their natural state, and in the traditional knowledge of indigenous peoples and local communities.

A further factor to be taken into account is the alarming disappearance of biological diversity, as well as of indigenous communities and all their knowledge and traditions. Despite this, there are many instructive data and examples of benefits derived from germplasm and traditional indigenous knowledge by the biotechnological industry, especially in the food, pharmaceutical, agrochemical and seed sectors. In a study by the Rural Advancement Foundation International (Rural Advancement Foundation International, 1994), commissioned by the UN Development Programme, they give a hundred examples of contributions by both wild and domesticated biological resources, with or without related traditional knowledge, which have constituted a significant input by our countries to the well-being of the planet, including that of our own peoples. While there are many other studies and articles we could mention to demonstrate the importance of informal and cooperative innovation systems, the above-mentioned study and a few data we shall refer to here provide a good illustration of the value involved.

The Convention on Biological Diversity (CBD), which was opened for signature at the Earth Summit in Rio de Janeiro in 1992, attempted to change the situation. Any such change, however, will depend in the end on individual countries and cooperation between them, if they are to establish policies and legislation regarding access and the sharing of benefits, subject to regional harmonization where appropriate.

The convention reaffirms that states have sovereign rights over their own biological resources, and establishes as one of its objectives, alongside the conservation and sustainable use of biological diversity, the fair and equitable sharing of the benefits arising out of the access to and utilization of biodiversity. This sovereignty entails the possibility of regulating access to these resources and the related knowledge, making it subject to the provisions of domestic legislation and to the need for a fair and equitable sharing of benefits among the various actors.

These articles demonstrate a concern to establish more concrete measures for the fair and equitable sharing of benefits arising from the utilization of biological diversity, especially the technology, output of research and benefits derived from the use of genetic resources, between those who produce them and those who benefit from them.

The CBD constitutes a source of international environmental law, with implications for flows of materials, intellectual property rights (IPRs) and due compensation for those who contribute them (the providers) by those who use them (the users). Again according to the convention, all countries should share the economic and other benefits between those who provide genetic resources and those who benefit from them. Moreover, it is required that the country that provides genetic resources should do so by prior informed consent, a necessary condition for the user to access the resources. It is also presumed that this requirement of prior consent and the sharing of benefits applies equally within the country's borders, that is with respect to local communities, indigenous peoples and in general individuals living within those borders. This informed consent should lead to a contract containing the mutually agreed terms mentioned in the convention.

Although in some parts of the convention it is clear that the emphasis is placed on relations between a developed country (or enterprise belonging to that country) and a developing country, it is equally clear that the obligation to share benefits arising from the use of materials (regardless of whether they have been improved or not, of whether they are wild or cultivated, whether they have been improved by breeders or indigenous peoples, etc) must also apply between developing countries. Exactly how benefits are to be shared and in general terms what is fair and equitable is something which still remains to be defined, since the convention only provides very general guidelines. In practical terms, the convention[1] assumes that if institution A holds genetic resources and transfers them to institution B, this transfer must be regulated in such a way that it allows the equitable sharing of all the different benefits which institution B might obtain from the transfer. Presumably a country might opt not to exercise that right to share the benefits; it may also not issue specific legislation regarding access to its genetic and biochemical resources.

Despite the economic importance of this diversity and related knowledge, however, concerns have been expressed with regard to the relatively unrealistic expectations concerning the return for conservation which may arise from 'bioprospecting', either from the sale of specimens or from the vertical integration of research. Barton and Christensen calculate that the commercial value of biological resources for the agricultural industry amounts to as much as US$100 million a year (Barton and Christensen, 1988). However, these figures are much higher in the case of the chemical and pharmaceutical industries.

Others, like Sedjo and Simpson, consider that genetic prospecting may not be much help in the battle to preserve habitats rich in biological diversity, suggesting that the income received from pharmaceutical research is unlikely to generate significant funds for conservation. According to them, this conclusion applies whether the approach adopted is that of contracts signed for prospecting or the vertical integration of research, whereby the developing countries acquire the equipment and technical capacity necessary to conduct research operations. They end up concluding that the importance of contracts and vertical integration may be overestimated as a conservation strategy (Sedjo and Simpson, 1995). Among other reasons, this is because a considerable percentage of the added value in bioprospecting projects accrues outside the country of origin, and until this situation changes it is hard to justify any greater degree of compensation, giving rise to criticism of low rates of royalties and conditions for granting them (for instance, the condition that the active agent should not be in the public domain or should not be known by any other means).

Unfortunately, there is a lack of appropriate legal frameworks in this area (apart from Costa Rica's recent Biodiversity Act, which is still not applied in practice). There are no rules for the sharing of benefits, nor any clear focal points, nor appropriate requirements for the conclusion of access contracts, nor standards on the protection of traditional knowledge or on the compatibility between IPRs and biodiversity conservation objectives, nor any express mention of prior informed consent or mutually-agreed terms.

Despite this vacuum, Central America has recently experienced a growing drive for regional integration as a way of responding to the challenges of economic globalization, and due to an imperative need to achieve sustainable development. As part of this new tendency, many regionally binding legal instruments have been signed and ratified, as well as many declarations related to sustainable development. By way of illustration, we might mention the following agreements: the Regional Agreement on the Handling of Natural Forest Ecosystems and the Development of Forest Plantations; the Central American Agreement on Climate Change; the Regional Agreement on Cross Border Movement of Toxic Waste; the Central American Agreement on the Protection of the Environment; and especially the Agreement on Priority Natural Areas and Conservation of Biodiversity in Central America. In addition to these international environmental instruments and the creation of a significant number of regional bodies responsible for implementing them, important documents have been signed giving expression to the commitment of Central American countries to sustainable development. Particularly worth mentioning are the Central American Alliance for Sustainable Development (ALIDES) and the Joint Declaration of Cooperation between the United States and Countries of the Alliance, known as CONCAUSA.

Alongside this intensive effort in the field of sustainable development, several general regional instruments on integration have referred to the need to harmonize environmental legislation, of which one of the most relevant components is a system of rules governing access to genetic and biochemical resources. In terms of legal precedents for this move towards legal harmonization, we have the Central American Agreement on the Protection of the Environment (1989), the setting up of the Central American Commission on the Environment and Development (CCAD), which specifically establishes an obligation for signatory states to 'favour compatibility between the main lines of national legislation and the region's sustainable development strategies'. The Tegucigalpa Protocol (1992), which modifies and redesigns the Central American Integration System, includes as one of its objectives: 'to establish agreed actions for the preservation of the environment through respect for and harmony with nature, ensuring the balanced development and rational exploitation of natural resources in the area, with a view to establishing a new ecological order in the region'.

The reform of the economic integration sector, under the terms of the Guatemala Protocol, which modifies the Central American Economic Integration System (SIECA), stipulates clearly that 'in the field of natural resources and the environment, the State Parties agree to develop common strategies with the objective of strengthening the capacity of States to protect the natural heritage of the region, to adopt sustainable development practices, to make optimal and rational use of the area's natural resources and to re-establish the ecological equilibrium, amongst others, by improving and harmonizing national environmental legislation at regional level ...'. Furthermore, the Central American Alliance for Sustainable Development

(ALIDES), signed by all the presidents of the region, pursues the specific objective of 'harmonizing and modernizing environmental parameters, legislation and national institutions responsible for environmental management'. Lastly, in the Joint Declaration by the US and Central America, the states of the area undertake 'to promote legislative and political reforms for the elaboration of environmental legislation and standards which are regionally compatible and which afford high levels of protection, as well as effective mechanisms for the application and implementation of environmental legislation'.

In other words, there is a broad legal framework in the region aimed at the harmonization of laws and standards, which would also include aspects related to access to genetic and biochemical resources. On the basis of these and other legal provisions, the Central American Commission on the Environment and Development, through its Biodiversity and Legislation Programmes, and with the support of the Central American Protected Areas System, has undertaken the task of promoting the process of discussion and analysis leading to a future common access system.

For the purpose of establishing mechanisms for the sharing of benefits, most of the options referred to are based on access to resources through regulations and procedures, which mostly stipulate a contract of agreement between the provider of the resource or knowledge and the party interested in access, subject to prior approval (or in some cases participation in the actual contract) of the government. The requirement stipulated in the CBD, whereby access should depend on the prior informed consent of the country of origin of the resource, would be met by this legal system. The underlying idea is to ensure in some form that the use of biological and genetic resources and of related traditional knowledge is compensated, if they are used for prospecting purposes.

Some have suggested that legal access regulations (referring to national and not specifically regional initiatives) should include at least the following headings: principles, objectives and definitions; scope (resources covered by the regulations); access procedure (including the designation of a focal point, prior informed consent, mutually agreed terms, confidentiality, trade marks, etc); restrictions on export and monitoring of materials; sanctions; monitoring and financial aspects. (Glowka, 1998).

Generally speaking, to develop any system of rules, a number of matters need to be clarified.

The first matter is which resources should be subject to the access rules. It is important to bear in mind that natural resources are to a great extent public in nature. This is because they may be located in such places as national parks; in domesticated crops, which are mainly under private ownership, such as plantations; in biological resources not used as a source of genetic resources (for instance, an orange for eating is not the same as one used in the search for useful genetic information); and in human bodies (blood samples, DNA, etc), to give just a few examples.

The second is that of who should apply for access and for what purpose. The issue here is whether access should be applied for only for commercial purposes, or also for purposes of research or teaching, such as in identifying a species taxonomically or including in a public inventory.

The third is that of determining who should be the competent entity to authorize access. This involves determining such questions as whether this should be a national authority or a local-level one, whether the authorization would be the same for marine and for land resources, and also if permission must be requested in the case of access to resources on private lands or only on public lands, etc. In the case of indigenous lands and under the terms of existing legal provisions, such as Convention 169 of the International Labour Organization on Indigenous and Tribal Peoples in Independent States, these peoples must be consulted and must be part of the decision-making process. In view of the strategic character of resources and the fact that the authorization to use them might entail the possibility of forfeiting benefits through a bad agreement, one might choose to request the advice of special committees or consultants before signing an access agreement. While these points all make sense, however, a constant effort must be made to avoid converting the access procedure into a cumbersome and bureaucratic formality.

The fourth matter is that of the conditions according to which access should be granted. The central point of any country's strategy for sharing benefits is this: if access is authorized, what mutually agreed conditions should apply? Examples of such conditions include transfer of technology (equipment, materials, etc), training and instruction, joint research on topics of interest to the country, in addition to the topic of interest to the applicant, percentages of net product sales (royalties), upfront payments, copies of reports, products at non-market prices, infrastructure construction, contracting of local labour, etc. The guidelines for ensuring fair and equitable sharing of benefits must be applied both to the applicant–state relationship and to the applicant–provider (private or indigenous peoples) relationship, whichever is appropriate.

The fifth is that of what access procedures should be employed. Such procedures could be on the basis of public tender or by requests leading to contracts or agreements. Policy-makers might wish to vary procedures according to the motive for requesting access, which may be commercial or non-commercial, or the industrial sector from which the company making the request operates in. Other considerations include whether a register of applications should be drawn up and whether access to it should be public or restricted, what requirements should be met by the applicant (identification data, purposes of access, national counterparts if applicable, funding, guarantees, etc), whether material transfer agreements are to be used instead of contracts and on what occasions. Certainly, such procedures must be transparent and subject to the appropriate administrative and judicial remedies. They must take account of the provisions contained in the Convention on International Trade in Endangered Species of Wild Fauna and Flora (CITES) and must not constitute an unnecessary obstacle to international trade.

The final matter is that of what sanctions should be imposed against illegal access or failure to fulfil the clauses of a contract, monitoring and follow-up.

Beyond these questions, four issues need to be considered in connection with access:

1 *Intellectual property.* One of the ways of linking the issue of access to IPRs consists of a requirement that before any patent or right to a plant is granted and before any product making use of genetic and biological resources has been approved, it should be demonstrated by means of a certificate of origin that the resource was accessed lawfully and that due compensation was paid to the resource's country of origin (see Chapter 21 for a detailed discussion on this proposal).
2 *The role of the state.* The experience of the Andean Community and the somewhat conflicting positions of some of its members show that it must be made clear just how far the role of the state should extend in negotiations for access agreements and what falls within the role of private access providers.
3 *The value of genetic resources.* While there is no doubt that, in view of the advances in genetic engineering, new screening techniques, the search for active components in plants and in general in the chemistry of natural products, biological and genetic resources have regained a strategic role for the pharmaceutical and biotechnological industry. Their value needs to be specified. Unlike mineral prospectors, who have a fair notion of what they are looking for, bioprospectors do not know what they will find in the great chemical factories of forests and reefs. For example, for a long time the US National Cancer Institute has been looking for promising agents to use against cancer, and more recently against AIDS, yet from all the specimens collected at high cost, the results obtained and the agents which have reached a more advanced stage of clinical testing are few and far between. One of the greatest obstacles to the formulation of access policies is the absence of effective methods of valuing biodiversity. The developing countries could increase their ability to derive benefits from biological resources by seeking new forms of adding value to their biological resources. The value of those materials is relatively low. This value could be increased by establishing or developing institutions engaged in identification, collection and screening. This would enable developing countries to share the benefits of biotechnological research and to strengthen their scientific, technological and institutional capacity. For this reason, the value of bioprospecting must not be overestimated, though at the same time its importance should not be denied as part of a broader strategy for the conservation and sustainable use of biological diversity.
4 *The nature of regulations.* One of the greatest lessons learned by the countries of the Andean Community and the Philippines (which was a pioneer in regulating bioprospecting) has been that the consequence of seeking extremely restrictive regulations has been to make them practically inapplicable. This experience should not be forgotten when attempting to build standards governing access to biological and genetic resources.

To conclude, this type of system is based on controlling access subject to prior informed consent, which is to be granted under mutually agreed conditions. This in turn should ensure a real sharing of benefits and the fair compensation referred to in the various legal instruments mentioned above. One hopes that the protocol will succeed in achieving this for the benefit of the Central American nations and their populations.

NOTES

1 I should point out that this is an oversimplification. The CBD mentions only countries as providers and users of genetic resources and not enterprises or institutions. It is presumed that each country should issue laws which apply to the latter and which in the end comply with agreed international obligations. At the same time, although this has more of a legal basis in the text of the actual agreement, the sharing of benefits should reach the custodians and improvers of biodiversity, within each country, such as the peasants and indigenous communities, among others.

REFERENCES

Barton, J H and Christensen, E (1988) 'Diversity compensation systems: Ways to compensate developing nations for providing genetic materials', in J R Kloppenburg (ed), *Seeds and Sovereignty: The Use and Control of Plant Genetic Resources*, Durham and London: Duke University Press.

Glowka, L (1998) *A guide to Designing Legal Frameworks to Determine Access to Genetic Resources*, Gland and Bonn: IUCN.

Rural Advancement Foundation International (1994) *Conserving Indigenous Knowledge: Integrating Two Systems of Innovation. An Independent Study by the Rural Advancement Foundation International*, New York: UN Development Programme.

Sedjo, R A and Simpson, R D (1995) 'Property rights, externalities and biodiversity', in T Swanson (ed), *The Economics and Ecology of Biodiversity Decline: The Forces Driving Global Change*, Cambridge: Cambridge University Press.

Chapter 27

The Indian Experience in the Field of IPRs, Access to Biological Resources and Benefit Sharing

Atul Kaushik[1]

INTRODUCTION AND SCOPE

Due to globalization, population growth and deforestation, biodiversity is declining at a rapid pace. Another factor in the loss of biodiversity and associated traditional knowledge (TK) is the decreased motivation among the local communities to conserve and protect them. This is happening because of changes in their lifestyles as well as misappropriation of their resources and their knowledge. Such misappropriation not only violates the rights of communities who conserve them, but also adversely affects their conservation and sustainable use.

The contribution of knowledge – both traditional and modern – as a factor of production has acquired a dominant role in trade, investment and technological change. But holders of traditional knowledge are generally unaware of or not used to the modern systems of legal protection and part with their knowledge without receiving a fair reward or having a say in its commercial exploitation. However, the misappropriation of such knowledge without returning any benefits may result in the disappearance of the traditional systems of knowledge and the associated resources.

To prevent such a catastrophic situation, measures must be introduced to ensure that the traditional systems of conserving and sustainably utilizing biological resources and associated traditional knowledge are preserved. And for that, the crucial issues being debated are rights, access and benefit sharing.

In this chapter, we explore solutions in the light of the Indian experience. The chapter is divided into five parts. The next part discusses the evolution of the concepts of access and benefit sharing in the area of biological diversity. Part three lists some of the major Indian initiatives on access and benefit sharing (ABS). Part four takes us through the legal mire in the Indian legislative system. The final part identifies the gaps that still remain, and offers suggestions for action at the national and international level.

THE EVOLUTION OF ACCESS AND BENEFIT SHARING IN THE AREA OF BIOLOGICAL DIVERSITY

Like other global commons, biological diversity was treated as a free good until the early 1990s. This was in spite of the inescapable realization that genetic resources have tremendous economic potential, and the fact that much is being done to harness this potential. As explained elsewhere in this volume, the Convention on Biological Diversity (CBD) changed this situation, encouraging governments to frame regulations controlling access to such resources in the interests of the nation and local communities. Consequently, genetic resources and associated traditional knowledge can no longer be treated as free goods. The predominant use of genetic resources in the area of medicine, and the emergence of the biotechnology era, has enhanced the commercial importance of genetic resources. This suggests to some that the CBD was just an attempt to legitimize access to and control of the genetic resources of the gene-rich countries. While this may be an extreme view, the fact that the CBD can be interpreted as anything other than an instrument for the benefit of biological diversity should only further the resolve of the international community to fulfil its objectives by putting in place an effective and operational ABS mechanism for rewarding the local people for their efforts in conserving biological resources and creating and preserving traditional knowledge.

Before putting in place any access regime, the problem of the concept of 'rights' has to be grappled with. The problem is compounded by the fact that discourse on the subject limits itself often to the modern and industrial definitions of rights, which do not necessarily encompass the more traditional forms of right acquisition and exploitation. For example, traditional knowledge in India has been preserved through *smriti* and *shruti*, that is, through the word of the teacher, which is heard and remembered, not documented or converted into a statutory right in favour of the teacher or his disciple. Customary law, of which traditional rights associated with knowledge form a part, is recognized under India's legal system under common law,[2] in which case such rights might be defined in a formal sense through jurisprudence. Alternatively, the rights might be defined and legitimized in a more substantive way by converting them into a part of the statutory law.[3] The problem is that such customary rights are unlikely to be recognized outside the jurisdiction of India.

The CBD provides some guiding principles. Article 15 confers on states sovereign rights over their genetic resources. With respect to ex situ resources, though, this principle is restricted to those which were acquired after the date that the convention entered into force. It obliges parties to provide access to others, but only on mutually agreed terms. This means there has to be a negotiation of the terms of access. In addition, access must be subject to the prior informed consent of the providers. In other words, providers have the right to prevent others from committing acts of biopiracy. It also authorises parties to ensure fair and equitable sharing of benefits arising out of research as well as commercialization of the resources. Similar provisions exist for traditional knowledge under Article 8(j).

The CBD declares that nations have sovereign rights over their genetic resources, but does not clarify who enjoys the rights to the resources within the nation. This could be the state, the community concerned, the individuals, or some association on behalf of the individuals.

With respect to benefit sharing, implementation is also at the national level. The CBD principles assume that the exploitation of the right of the holder, irrespective of the way it is determined, will be ensured through a process of fair and equitable benefit sharing. There is an implicit recognition that outsiders misappropriate resources and associated traditional knowledge, and that a benefit sharing mechanism would address the problem. But determining the value of the resource or knowledge, and the share of the profits earned by the outsider that should be returned to the holder, are no mean tasks. In some of the agreements that have been concluded between developing country right holders and developed country corporations, royalties promised range from 0.1 to 3–4 per cent. This brings us to the negotiating power of the local communities who are right holders but do not have the wherewithal to get their fair share from powerful corporations. It is this realization that has perhaps made countries like India install regimes that provide for state intervention in determining ABS arrangements.

THE INDIAN EXPERIENCE

In the recent past, there have been several cases of biopiracy of Indian TK. First it was the US patent on the wound healing properties of haldi (turmeric), then there was the patent granted on the neem derivatives in the European Patent Office (both of which were revoked through considerable time, effort and expenditure). Since then, patents have been obtained in other countries on, for example, hypoglycaemic properties of karela (bitter gourd) and brinjal. An important criticism in this context relates to foreigners obtaining patents based on Indian biological materials. There is also the view that TRIPS aids the exploitation of biodiversity by privatizing biodiversity expressed in life forms and their knowledge. The time, effort and money involved in getting individual patents re-examined and revoked in foreign patent offices is prohibitive. Hence, an internationally accepted solution to such biopiracy is considered necessary.

Various suggestions have been advanced to extend protection to traditional knowledge, innovations and practices. These are described below.

Documentation of traditional knowledge

In India, a number of TK documentation projects have been undertaken, some of which are described elsewhere in this volume (see Chapters 17 and 20). Documentation of TK is one means of giving recognition to knowledge holders and preventing the patenting of this knowledge in the form in which it exists, but it does not by itself enable sharing of benefits arising out of the use of such knowledge unless backed by other measures.

Benefit sharing models with public/private partnerships

Some limited efforts have been made in India to register claims over biological resources and associated traditional knowledge. For example, the Honeybee database established ten years ago in India is a facility for the registration of innovations by innovators. The database can be accessed for adding value to these innovations and sharing benefits with the knowledge providers and innovators. Thus the Honeybee Network involves documentation, experimentation and dissemination of traditional knowledge. The network has probably the world's largest database on grassroots innovations, having now about 10,000 innovations, with names and addresses of the innovators (individuals or communities). Through the Honeybee Newsletter, grassroots innovations have been disseminated to more than 75 countries.

More important efforts have been made, however, for public/private partnerships to ensure benefit sharing. Despite their criticism on account of inadequacy of the rewards to the innovators, it is a path worth pursuing so that some critical mass of opinion on what should be an equitable reward emerges. The most written-about benefit sharing partnership in India involved the Kani tribe and the Tropical Botanic Garden and Research Institute (TBGRI).[4] TBGRI developed a drug based on the anti-fatigue properties of a wild plant *Trichopus zeylanicus*, which the Kani people informed TBGRI researchers about. TBGRI granted a seven-year licence for the process of making the drug to a pharmacy for 1 million Indian rupees and a royalty of 2 per cent based on the ex-factory price. It shares 50 per cent of the licence fees and royalties with the Kani tribe (Anuradha, 1998).

Recently, UNCTAD and the Research and Information System for the Non-Aligned and Other Developing Countries (RIS) conducted a study of six benefit sharing models. These include the 'payback for collection and cultivation' in the Dabur-India and Dabur-Nepal cases, the 'supply to buyers and redistribution of benefits among primary producers' in the Gram Mooligai Company, and the 'commercialization of private traditional knowledge' by Mr Bommu Shivu Ganga Godwa as some success stories. The study highlights the rich benefit sharing arrangements, mostly by good Samaritans, prevailing in the Indian ethos.

Other initiatives

Another relevant aspect relating to TK is the need for value addition to this knowledge for converting it into economically profitable investments or enterprises. Many of the innovators, however, lack the capacity for value addition. Thus there is a need for providing institutional support through public funding in scouting, sustaining and scaling up of grassroots innovations, and to enhance the technical competence and self-reliance of these innovators, through the establishment of green venture promotion funds and incubators. It was also proposed as part of the 1999–2000 national budget of India that a National Innovation Foundation would be set up (see Chapter 17). Apart from this, the Ministry of Environment and Forests has established a National Biodiversity Strategy and Action Plan (NBSAP), which is undertaking a number of activities including identifying access and benefit sharing methods that are easy to follow and take into account the concerns of the innovators. The NBSAP is being run by a non-governmental organization, showing the extent of civil society involvement in the effort.

STATUTORY PROVISIONS ON ACCESS AND BENEFIT SHARING IN INDIA

The Constitution of India

The Constitution of India confers on its citizens the fountainhead of power. The constitution provides fundamental rights to equality, equal opportunity, right to life and personal liberty and to conserve distinct language, script or culture. The directive principles enjoin the state, inter alia, to direct its policy towards ensuring that the ownership and control of the material resources of the community is so distributed as to serve the common good. The Panchayati Raj (power to village bodies) was introduced in the constitution through an amendment in 1976. Article 243 enables the state to make laws to empower *panchayats* (elected village bodies) to deal with certain matters including schemes of economic development and social justice. The areas in which the *panchayats* could implement such schemes include agriculture, social forestry and farm forestry, minor forest produce and maintenance of community assets.

Laws prior to the CBD

The Transfer of Property Act, 1882, in defining property in Section 2(6) includes intangible assets. Section 47 covers the concept of 'common property' in the scope of the act. The Contract Act, 1972, similarly, defines a contract as valid only when it is between parties who have agreed by their free will, and where there has been an informed acceptance of the offer for a lawful consideration and a lawful object. An agreement without consideration is void under the act.

The Indian Forest Act, 1927 regulates the use of forests and forest produce; its scope includes almost everything that may constitute biodiversity. Once notified, forests come under regulation, in which case the government makes rules for the cutting of trees and collection, removal and manufacture of forest produce (including its import or export), as well as the granting of licences to the local communities to use the forest produce. Rights over forests and forest produce can be acquired either by succession or through a valid contract (for example, a licence) with the government. Village forests have a special place as village communities have the right to govern the forest as well as to administer the forest produce. Forests and wildlife are in the concurrent list; hence many states have passed laws on these subjects.

The Wildlife (Protection) Act, 1972, allows the government to notify certain plants and other living things that need to be protected by state intervention. It prohibits the collection and transfer of such plants or their derivatives, except by the scheduled tribes (indigenous communities), who can collect them for their personal use but not for commercial exploitation. Exceptions to this prohibition can, however, be made on application to the authorities for limited purposes such as education, scientific research, collection, preservation and display in a herbarium of any scientific institution, and propagation by a person or a government-approved institution.

Some regulations exist at the product stage also, insofar as forest produce is concerned. Two such acts are worth mentioning. The Seeds Act, 1966, allows the government to declare any variety of seed to be a notified variety, and controls the sale of such a variety for the purpose of maintaining its purity. It also controls the import and export of seeds of notified varieties by insisting upon conformity with standards of purity and marking/labelling them as such. Under the Drugs and Cosmetics Act, 1940, a manufacturer or seller of a drug has to specify where he got the drug. For Ayurveda, Siddha or Unani drugs (that is, those based upon the various Indian systems of medicine), although quality standards are prescribed, these do not apply to Vaids and Hakims (traditional medicine dispensing doctors).

A common feature of all the laws discussed above is that they regulate access to certain resources, but have nothing to say about benefit sharing. One positive feature of these laws, not discussed above, however, is that most of them have institutionalized systems of regulation and monitoring in the form of committees or boards, which may come in handy once access and benefit sharing mechanisms are put in place through the upcoming biodiversity-related laws, leading to lesser implementation costs than would be incurred for greenfield applications.

Post CBD laws

The Biodiversity Bill, 2000,[5] has the object of providing for conservation of biological diversity, sustainable use of its components and equitable sharing of the benefits arising out of the use of biological resources.

It should be noted that access is granted to citizens only after prior intimation, while it is granted to foreigners after prior approval. The different approaches appear to have been necessitated because, while it might be easy to bring a citizen under the jurisdiction of the competent authorities and the courts, this would be impossible for foreigners. Second, not only access to the resource, but even transfer of research results abroad are prohibited without approval of the competent authority. This appears to be in recognition of the fact that knowledge about the resources is as important as the resources themselves for the purpose of ensuring conservation. Of course, this prohibition does not extend to 'collaborative research'. Thus, research conducted with the approval of the government, and that meets the guidelines to be laid down by the government, is permitted by foreigners also. Third, no-one can apply anywhere in the world for an IPR on knowledge based on a resource obtained in India without approval of the competent authority. This is an important clause for the purpose of the debate on enforceability abroad, as will be seen in the last part of this chapter.

How will the access and IPR application permissions be granted, and by whom? While the answer to the first question will have to await the drafting of detailed rules under the bill, once it is passed and becomes an act, the competent authorities are identified in the bill itself. There will be a National Biodiversity Authority at the federal level, State Biodiversity Boards at the state level, and Biodiversity Management Committees at the local level. The National Biodiversity Authority has to give effect to benefit sharing in any of the following manners:

- grant of joint ownership of IPRs to the National Biodiversity Authority, or where benefit claimants are identified, to such benefit claimants;
- transfer of technology;
- location of production, research and development units in such areas which will facilitate better living standards to the benefit claimants;
- association of Indian scientists, benefit claimers and the local people with R&D relating to biological resources, bio-survey and bio-utilization;
- setting up of venture capital funds for aiding the cause of the benefit claimants; and
- payment of monetary compensation or other non-monetary benefits to the benefit claimants as the National Biodiversity Authority may deem fit.

Corresponding provisions have been added in the Indian Patents Act, 1970 by the Patents (Amendment) Act, 2002,[6] in order to ensure disclosure of the source of origin of the biological resource or associated traditional knowledge used in an invention by an IPR applicant.

Section 3 of the act lists inventions that are not patentable. An invention 'which, in effect, is traditional knowledge or which is an aggregation or duplication of known properties of traditionally known component or components' is added to this section to exclude traditional knowledge from patentability. To ensure disclosure, Section 10 of the act, which deals with contents of the patent application, has been amended to require that the application be accompanied by an abstract to provide technical information on the invention. If the applicant mentions a biological material in the specification, and if such material is not available to the public, the application shall be completed by depositing the material with an authorized depository institution as may be notified by the government.

Similarly, Section 25, which deals with grounds for opposition claims, has been amended to add two more grounds for revocation, which are that the complete specification does not disclose or wrongly mentions the source or geographical origin of biological material used for the invention, and that the invention so far as claimed in any claim of the complete specification is anticipated having regard to the knowledge, oral or otherwise, available within any local or indigenous community in India or elsewhere. Similar provisions have been inserted in Section 64 of the act, which deals with revocation of patents.

The Protection of Plant Varieties and Farmers' Rights Act, 2002[7] also has some access and benefit sharing provisions. As regards access, the breeder has to furnish information on the geographical location from where plant genetic material has been taken for development of the new variety. This legislation is described in more detail in Chapter 17.

CONCLUSIONS AND RECOMMENDATIONS

The most relevant issues regarding conservation and sustainable use of biodiversity and associated TK are prevention of biopiracy and misappropriation, systems of protection, and means of fair and equitable sharing of benefits arising out of utilization of biological resources and associated TK. Efforts are being made in various countries with regard to the above issues, some of which are described in other chapters of this book. However, the actual measures provided or proposed are different in each country. There is no uniformity in the provisions and each country's legislation is developed based on the specific requirements of each individual country, its communities, their lifestyles and types of traditional knowledge and the way it is being protected or held by the communities and the way it is being accessed for modern scientific purposes. It is very clear that a uniform international system for protection of biological resources and associated TK would not be able to cater to the requirements of individual countries. Rather, the need is for a system which recognizes such diversity.

In this context, a recent initiative of biodiversity-rich countries in New Delhi may be a first step. In an international seminar organized by UNCTAD and the government of India with the participation of 14 countries on 3–5 April 2002, the participants agreed[8] that benefit sharing mechanisms installed through national legislation would need to be recognized in user countries. Some of the essential components of a framework for international recognition of various sui generis systems, customary law and others for protection of TK identified include: (i) local protection to the rights of TK holders through national-level sui generis regimes; (ii) protection through registers of TK databases to avoid misappropriation; (iii) a procedure whereby the use of TK from one country is allowed, particularly for seeking IPR protection or commercialization, only after the competent national authority of the country of origin gives a certificate that the source of origin is disclosed and prior informed consent, including acceptance of benefit sharing conditions, obtained; and (iv) an internationally agreed instrument that recognizes such national-level protection.

The participants recommended that their countries would work together in various inter-governmental forums particularly the CBD, FAO, WIPO and UNCTAD, to develop an international framework for the recognition of national systems of protection, including diverse sui generis systems.

The development at New Delhi only gives further focus to what has been experienced by India, as this chapter evidences, that the task ahead is twofold. First, the diversity of approaches for protection of biological diversity and associated traditional knowledge needs to be preserved through national-level systems. Second, action at the national level is inadequate for achieving the stated objectives of CBD unless an international recognition is given to these national systems through an enforceable instrument. The international community now needs to focus on forging such an instrument and deciding the forum where it can be lodged.

NOTES

1 The views given here are the author's own and do not necessarily reflect the views of the government of India.
2 The common law recognizes customary law even without a statute to support it, so long as there is incontrovertible evidence of the existence of such customs.
3 For example, the customary law on marriage and devolution of property through succession was codified through a statute in the 1950s in India.
4 Detailed case study available at the CBD website (http://www.biodiv.org).
5 Available at http://www.envfor.nic.in. The bill was referred to a standing committee of the parliament, which has given its suggestions to the parliament. The government has to accept or not accept these suggestions and move the bill again in the parliament for passage.
6 The Patents (Amendment) Act, 2002 (No. 38 of 2002) is available at http://ipindia.nic.in.
7 Passed in the parliament in 2001, but yet to be notified.
8 See the communiqué at http://www.unctad.org/trade_env/test1/meetings/delhi/CommuniqueTK.doc. Ch 27.

REFERENCES

Anuradha, R V (1998) *Sharing with the Kanis: a case study from Kerala, India*. Published on the website of the Secretariat of the Convention on Biological Diversity (http://www.biodiv.org).

Chapter 28

Intellectual Property Rights and Biological Resources: current policy and legislative developments in South Africa

Rosemary A Wolson[1]

INTRODUCTION

South Africa occupies an interesting position in the global arena as a result of the pronounced disparities in the economic conditions of the citizens found within its borders. The country is faced with the task of formulating policy which on the one hand aims to grow the established economy through exports and foreign direct investment in order to create employment, while on the other hand must improve the lives of the country's poorest citizens and eliminate the inequities which are a legacy of the apartheid regime. While these objectives are not mutually exclusive (and in fact should be complementary), the differing policy interventions called for do not always sit comfortably alongside one another. Creating the right balance between them can at times involve a tightrope act. This is perhaps especially true when considering the questions which arise around areas such as trade, intellectual property and biological resources. South Africa has been grappling with management of these issues for a number of years already, and although there are encouraging signs of progress, the implementation of policy and legislation remains some way ahead.

This chapter summarizes some of the relevant aspects of the country's intellectual property rights (IPR) framework before examining the current status of policy on plant breeders' rights and farmers' rights, access to genetic resources and benefit sharing, and the protection of indigenous knowledge (IK).[2]

Overview of South Africa's intellectual property system

For a developing country, South Africa has a relatively strong IPR framework in many respects, entrenched well before this became necessary for many other countries on acceding to TRIPS. South African IPR legislation has historically been based on British law and, more recently, European law, in particular the European Patent Convention (EPC). Table 28.1 lists the main statutes of relevance and the government departments under which they fall, as well as areas of envisaged legislation under discussion for some of the 'new' forms of IPRs. Despite the South African Companies and Intellectual Property Registration Office (CIPRO) being a registration rather than an examining office, the system is considered to operate effectively for the most part, bolstered as it is by strong legislation upstream and enforced by competent courts downstream. However, South African participation in the international patent system remains limited, as indicated by the low number of patents issued to South African entities by foreign patent offices.[3]

South Africa is a member of most of the international treaties and conventions governing intellectual property rights. The country is not a member of the African Regional Industrial Property Organization (ARIPO), but has observer status. Nonetheless, the levels of patenting activity in South Africa greatly exceed those in ARIPO member countries.

A Standing Advisory Committee on Intellectual Property, consisting of stakeholders from academia and the legal profession, was constituted to advise the Minister of Trade and Industry on IPR policy matters. Sub-committees have been established to investigate certain defined areas, including indigenous knowledge systems (IKS) and the commercialization of IPRs. Some of these areas are also being examined in other initiatives, both in the Department of Trade and Industry (DTI) and other government departments.

Table 28.1 *Relevant South African IPR legislation*

Type of IP	*Statute*	*Department*
Patents	Patents Act No 57 of 1978	Trade & Industry
Copyright	Copyright Act No 98 of 1978	Trade & Industry
Trade marks	Trade Marks Act No 194 of 1993	Trade & Industry
Registered designs	Designs Act No 195 of 1993	Trade & Industry
Plant breeders' rights	Plant Breeders' Rights Act No 15 of 1976	Agriculture
Indigenous knowledge systems (IKS)	Still to be enacted	Science & Technology
Farmers' rights	Still to be enacted	Agriculture
Biodiversity/access to genetic resources	Still to be enacted	Environmental Affairs & Tourism

PATENTS

Patent legislation

Patents are governed by the Patents Act and by regulations made under the act which deal with certain procedural matters. In general, patentability requirements are similar to those in most other jurisdictions. The novelty requirement is absolute, so novelty is destroyed if, prior to filing a patent application, relevant information about an invention is made available to the public, anywhere in the world, in any manner.

An 'invention' is defined negatively, via a list of categories which are not considered to be an invention for the purposes of the act. Excluded from patentability are discoveries; scientific theories; mathematical methods; literary, dramatic, musical or artistic works; schemes, rules or methods for performing a mental act, playing a game or doing business; computer programs; and the presentation of information. Furthermore, inventions which might encourage offensive or immoral behaviour, inventions contrary to well-established natural laws, and medical methods of treatment are not patentable. Medicines and medical devices do, however, constitute patentable subject matter.

A patent is granted for a term of 20 years from the date of filing a complete patent application, subject to the payment of prescribed renewal fees. A Patents Amendment Bill has recently been released for public comment. In addition to proposing certain technical changes, it contains clauses introducing a provision based partly on the US Bolar provision.[4] The idea is that R&D based on patented inventions, but not commercial use, should be permitted during the term of the patent so that competitors can enter the market immediately on expiration of the patent. In the absence of this provision, patent holders are effectively able to extend their patent term due to the time required for others to develop and, where appropriate, register the patented product. The proposed provision would apply to all fields of technology and would not be restricted to the pharmaceutical and agrochemical sectors. The pharmaceutical industry is calling for a further amendment to enable the patent term of pharmaceuticals to run from the date of approval by the Medicines Control Council rather than from the date of discovery, to make up for the regulatory delays which limit the time in which a company may exploit the patented drug exclusively.

Patentability of biological inventions

In dealing with the patentability of biological inventions, the Patents Act adopts similar wording to the corresponding EPC provision, stating that 'a patent shall not be granted for any variety of animal or plant or any essentially biological process for the production of animals or plants, not being a microbiological process or the product of such a process'.

While microbiological processes and their products are therefore clearly patentable, exactly what constitutes a 'microbiological process' or a product thereof, and what the situation is regarding the patentability of other living material, is less clear, because the act does not define key terms such as 'variety', 'essentially biological' or 'microbiological', and the courts have not been called upon to interpret these terms. Guidance is therefore obtained from other jurisdictions whose legislation contains similar provisions, the European Patent Office Guidelines for Examination being a commonly used source. A 'microbiological process or the product of such a process' is thus expected to include micro-organisms as well as processes involving their use and utility. The act therefore appears to offer protection for microbiological organisms and processes, as well as for processes producing transgenic plants or animals, and for the products of such processes (provided there is a sufficient degree of human intervention), unless the plant or animal product of such process is a variety.

South African patents have been granted for various biotechnological inventions, including genetically modified micro-organisms, plants and animals. While none of these patents has been challenged in the courts, and their validity could therefore still be brought into question, it is generally accepted from a practical perspective that at least some of these patents are valid. The fact that biotechnology companies continue to file patents for inventions dealing with living material is evidence that there is a degree of confidence in the protection offered by the legislation.

Deposit of samples

South Africa acceded to the Budapest Treaty on the International Recognition of the Deposit of Micro-organisms for the Purposes of Patent Procedure in 1997. Although prior to this the Patents Act provided for the deposit of samples of micro-organisms, where a complete specification claimed as an invention a microbiological process or product, and the micro-organism concerned was not available to the public, the relevant section was not operative until recently. Nonetheless, in practice it was fairly common for deposit to take place for microbiological inventions in appropriate cases even prior to this requirement being mandatory, in order to satisfy the sufficiency requirement for patentability.

Patent filing

Over 10,000 patent applications are filed annually in South Africa (approximately half of these taking priority from other countries), and about 4000 patents issued per year. The South African patent system offers the option of a two-stage application procedure. A provisional application may be filed up to 12 months before filing a complete application with an additional three-month grace period available. This gives an effective date for the invention, from which priority can be claimed, and allows the inventors to develop the invention further before finalizing the content of the complete specification, and/or filing overseas. Alternatively, a complete application may be filed in the first instance. As a member of the Paris Convention, priority can be claimed for subsequent filings in other convention countries from a South African patent application, within one year of the original filing. It is comparatively cheap to file patent applications in South Africa, with the cost of preparation of a specification and filing by a patent attorney usually coming in below US$1000.

The Companies and Intellectual Property Registration Office (CIPRO)

CIPRO was established in 2002 through a merger of the former South African Companies Registration Office and the South African Patents and Trade Marks Office. It is an independent business agency of the DTI, situated in Pretoria, and managed by a chief executive officer overseen by a board. CIPRO aims to provide a gateway to economic participation, both by South African citizens and foreigners doing business in South Africa. One of its early objectives is to ensure that it becomes more accessible to its users and potential users, by increased use of electronic media, education programmes and a customer contact centre. It also aims to expand the role of South Africa in the IPR sphere and to facilitate improved confidence of international investors by ensuring that South Africa is viewed as a country which gives due recognition to intellectual property.[5]

Patent applications are filed through the IPR Division of CIPRO. The patent filing system is relatively unsophisticated. It is a non-examining office, is only partially computerized, and is equipped with neither the human resources nor the technology required for proper examination of a patent application. The registrar therefore conducts only a formal examination, ensuring that all necessary procedural and administrative requirements have been satisfied. The onus for performing novelty searches therefore lies with the applicant. The lack of examination means that there is less certainty about the validity of a South African patent than there would be for a patent which has undergone examination. Nonetheless, a registered patent is considered prima facie valid. Efforts are underway, in cooperation with international organizations such as the World Intellectual Property Office and the European Patent Office (EPO), to address this, but the first priority is to ensure that existing functions operate optimally, to which end extensive upgrading of the information systems is taking place, to facilitate improved record keeping (including an electronic patent journal), search facilities and online applications.[6] Down the line, options under discussion include the introduction of limited examination (in technical fields where local expertise is available and a critical mass of patent applications are filed at CIPRO), and the acceptance of search reports from other approved patent offices.

The role of the judiciary

The validity of a patent is ultimately determined by the courts, which are generally considered competent in this regard. A party wishing to challenge the validity of a patent bears the onus of proving invalidity in the courts. Patent litigation is instituted in the Court of the Commissioner of Patents. The commissioner is a judge of the Transvaal Provincial Division of the High Court of South Africa (TPD). Appeals to decisions of this court can be made to a Full Bench of the TPD, and thereafter to the Supreme Court of Appeal. The courts have generally adopted a pro-patentee attitude, taking a resolute stand against infringement and copying.

Because litigation takes place at the level of the High Court, it is costly. As a result, small companies can rarely afford to litigate and even large companies with the necessary resources are often reluctant to do so, deterred by the high degree of technical expertise involved and the difficulty in finding expert witnesses.

Compulsory licensing

The Patents Act provides for the granting of compulsory licences in respect of dependent patents and in cases where patent rights have been abused. Situations are listed which give rise to the presumption that an abuse of patent rights has occurred. An interested party may apply for a compulsory licence, which will be granted if the commissioner determines that any of the listed situations exist. Only three applications for a compulsory licence have been made in South Africa, all of which failed due to insufficient evidence of abuse being provided. Partly because of this, in an attempt to ensure supply of affordable medicines, in 1997 the Department of Health proposed a controversial amendment to the 1965 Medicines and Related Substances Act, according to which parallel importation of patented medicines would be permitted, notwithstanding anything to the contrary contained in the Patents Act.

This became the subject of a high-profile lawsuit, which reached the courts in 2001. Thirty-nine multinational pharmaceutical companies instituted legal proceedings against the South African government, challenging the relevant provision, but in the midst of a national public outcry and international condemnation due to the country's high HIV/AIDS infection rates, the lawsuit was dropped. Opinion remains divided over whether the section concerned was necessary to enable the government to protect public health, or whether the provisions of the Patents Act and of TRIPS (such as those dealing with compulsory licensing and allowing countries to adopt measures necessary to protect public health) were in fact adequate. Some argue that this was a political move by the government which could undermine the legal system, but the stance of the South African government and the retreat of the corporations have been hailed throughout most of the developing world as a victory in the ongoing quest for health equity.

Plant variety protection

Legislation

Plant variety protection is governed by the Plant Breeders' Rights Act. Amendments in 1996 brought the act into compliance with the 1991 revision of the International Union for the Protection of New Varieties of Plants (UPOV) Convention, which South Africa has signed, but not ratified.[7] A plant variety is eligible for protection if it is new, distinct, uniform and stable, and its denomination (generic name) complies with prescribed requirements. A new variety is developed when important new characteristics are brought about by alteration of existing characteristics through selection and breeding. The term of protection varies according to the type of plant for which protection is sought, ranging from 20 to 25 years. Varieties which meet the requirements from all plant genera and species may be protected. Prior to the 1996 amendments, the minimum term of protection was 15 years, and regulations under the act stipulated which plant species were registrable.

The owner of a plant breeder's right has the exclusive right to exploit a protected plant variety and can exclude others from producing, selling, importing or exporting its propagating material. Private, non-commercial or experimental use of a protected variety for further breeding do not fall within the ambit of the protection conferred by the act. Changes brought about by the amending act include the introduction of the concept of an 'essentially derived variety', commercial use of which requires the consent of the owner of the initial protected variety, and the extension of protection to harvested material in cases where the breeder is unable to obtain remuneration rightfully on the propagating material.

The act makes provision for a breeder's exemption and farmer's privilege, by providing that certain activities undertaken using legitimately acquired propagating material will not constitute infringement of another party's plant breeder's right. These include development of a different variety, bona fide research, private or non-commercial use, and use by farmers of harvested material.

Application

Plant breeders' rights are administered by the Directorate of Genetic Resources in the Department of Agriculture (DoA). A large proportion of registered varieties is held by South African plant breeders, who also register their varieties in appropriate overseas markets. Plant variety protection has undoubtedly been beneficial to the seed industry and formal farming sector, by: (i) stimulating private investment in plant breeding, which has increased considerably since the introduction of plant breeders' rights; (ii) giving local breeders the opportunity to benefit from wider access to new varieties released internationally; (iii) providing a source of funding from royalties on protected varieties for public research institutions; and (iv) allowing farmers and consumers to benefit from increased crop yield and improved crops resulting from new varieties (Van der Walt, 1996).

Farmers' rights

Current legislation is silent on the concepts of farmers' rights. The DoA, however, acknowledges that recognition of farmers' rights is important for promoting the conservation, management and sustainable use of plant genetic resources for food and agriculture and intends to address this. As yet, little progress has been made in giving substance to these principles in order to integrate them into the legislative framework, but it is possible that a working group of stakeholders will be convened to draw up a discussion paper to serve as the basis for a draft bill.

At a DoA National Workshop on Plant Genetic Resources in 1999, some of the relevant issues which were raised included the following: (i) the need for an international, harmonized, practicable system which South Africa would honour once in place; (ii) the requirement for suitable strategies for collection and conservation of material to be developed, together with the use of databases to allow for actual and potential rights to be traced; (iii) the necessity of promoting exploitation of conserved material, subject to rewarding farmers for material obtained from them which is further developed; (iv) the importance of encouraging traditional healers to cultivate and not only harvest medicinal plants; and (v) caution against the impracticalities associated with centralized national and international funding mechanisms.

ARTICLE 27.3(B) OF TRIPS

South Africa is not advocating the reopening of negotiations on Article 27.3(b), but is in the process of defining how the country's interests can best be promoted and protected if the section were to be renegotiated. Stakeholders, including the DTI, DoA, Department of Environmental Affairs and Tourism (DEAT), civil society and the private sector will be consulted.

ACCESS TO GENETIC RESOURCES AND BENEFIT SHARING

Access to genetic resources is currently controlled by legislation at the provincial level. All provinces have ordinances which govern the movement of non-human biological material via permitting systems. The 1997 White Paper on Conservation and Sustainable Use of South Africa's Biological Diversity, which embodies national biodiversity policy, has put into effect South Africa's obligation under Article 8(j) of the Convention on Biological Diversity relating to traditional knowledge.

The draft Biodiversity Bill

At the national level, legislation is currently being drawn up by DEAT in the form of a Biodiversity Bill. Existing legislative models from around the world were extensively consulted, including the OAU Model Law (see Chapter 24), but the bill is not based on any particular precedent. The legislation has four objectives. The first is to provide within a framework of the National Environmental Management Act for: (i) the management and conservation of biological diversity within South Africa; and (ii) the use of biological resources in a sustainable manner and the fair and equitable sharing of benefits arising from the use and application of genetic resources material. The second is to give effect to international agreements relating to biodiversity which are binding on the country. The third objective is to provide for cooperative governance in biodiversity management and conservation, The fourth is to provide for a National Biodiversity Institute to assist in achieving the above objectives.

The document has been through several redrafts over a couple of years, but it is expected that it will finally be released for public comment early in 2003. The bill will govern activities concerning all South African sovereign biological resources other than human material and exotic animals, plants and other organisms not altered through the use of biotechnology with any genetic material or chemical compound found in any such indigenous animals, plants or other organisms. It will establish a framework for the rights and obligations of both the owners of genetic resources and those desiring access, including the matters of use, access for research purposes, bioprospecting and commercialization. More specifically, it is envisaged that the bill will contain provisions (among other things) for the following:

- Where bioprospecting is involved, approval will have to be obtained at national level, from the Minister of Environmental Affairs and Tourism, subject to an appropriate access and benefit sharing agreement being in place.
- The guidelines for the content of such agreements will be determined at a later stage in supplementary regulations, but will require IK to be protected.
- Applications and agreements will be evaluated by the Biodiversity Institute.
- The right of appeal will be provided for, in the event of an application failing to be approved.
- Existing agreements will be permitted to remain in force for a stipulated window period to allow for renegotiation to bring them into compliance with the new legislative requirements. It must be noted that the element of retrospectivity introduced by a provision such as this could have serious ramifications, by affecting vested rights and inadvertently sending a signal to international investors that contractual obligations assumed and agreed to by a South African contracting party might not be honoured. Enforcement is also likely to be problematic. The length of the window period is not known. If it is long enough to allow a majority of existing contracts to run their course, it is less likely to be problematic. The advantage of having some retroactive effect is that parties will not be able to circumvent the provisions of the proposed legislation deliberately by entering into an agreement which can continue in perpetuity prior to promulgation of the act.
- Principles will be laid down for the development of sui generis community rights, but it is not intended for the Biodiversity Bill to give content to such rights, this being the responsibility of the Department for Science and Technology.

PROTECTION OF INDIGENOUS KNOWLEDGE SYSTEMS (IKS)

The process of enacting legislation to promote, develop and protect IKS in South Africa has been a protracted one. An initial draft bill was tabled in parliament in 1997, with a new draft appearing in 2000, but never tabled. A further draft is currently being prepared, together with a draft policy, but both documents remain embargoed at the time of writing.

The first draft bill was entitled 'The Protection and Promotion of South African Indigenous Knowledges Bill', and was introduced by the parliamentary

Portfolio Committee on Arts, Culture, Science and Technology as a private member's legislative proposal. This was a 40-page document providing for: (i) IKS management principles; (ii) establishment of an IK regulatory authority; (iii) fair decision-making and conflict management; (iv) centres of excellence; (v) community protection; (vi) international obligations and agreements; and (vii) enforcement.

It proposed protecting IK via existing IPRs, by extending the definition of 'intellectual property rights' to include IK, and amending relevant legislation accordingly. The implications of this were either that existing IPRs would have to be modified, most likely in contravention of some of the international agreements to which South Africa is a party, or that many forms of IK would not qualify as they would fail to meet the stipulated requirements for existing forms of IPR protection.

Additional concerns which were raised included definitions and terminology used (invariably problematic), the exclusion of biodiversity from the ambit of the bill, the retrospective effect of certain provisions, and the structure of proposed implementing bodies.

The second draft, the Promotion of South African Indigenous Knowledge Systems Bill, was in contrast remarkably concise. It aimed:

> *to provide for the promotion of indigenous knowledges; to provide for the preservation, development, fostering and extension of IKS in the Republic by planning, organizing, coordinating and providing facilities for the utilization of leisure and for non-formal education; for the development and promotion of IKS relations with other countries; and to confer certain powers upon the Minister in order to achieve those objects; and to provide for matters connected therewith.*

The bulk of this significantly abbreviated version empowered the relevant government minister to perform certain stipulated acts for the purpose of developing and promoting IKS in South Africa and building South Africa's relations with other countries in this area, to delegate powers so given, and to make regulations necessary or expedient to achieving the objectives of the act. It was felt, however, that this draft contained insufficient substance to promote the objectives which the bill aimed to achieve, as a result of which it was not taken further.

In 2000, the Parliamentary Portfolio Committee on Arts, Culture, Science and Technology held public hearings on the initial draft bill in each of the country's nine provinces, to assess the extent to which the bill was able to meet the needs of IK holders in light of critical comments which indicated that further research and review was needed to address the concerns which had been raised. The hearings were intended to obtain feedback from a spectrum of stakeholders on contentious provisions of the bill, and were centred around the responses to a series of questions formulated to assist the committee in its review of the problematic issues. The main concerns which emerged were: (i) the need to confer legal status on IKS as a matter of urgency; (ii) unauthorized use of secret and sacred material; (iii) unauthorized use of IK in the absence of benefit sharing with, or recognition of, the providers of the knowledge concerned; (iv) patenting of compounds derived from IK by pharmaceutical companies; (v) retention of art and implements by universities and museums in the absence of prior informed consent; (vi) misinformation and misrepresentation in research involving IKS, and failure to allow the providers of the IKS to participate in decision-making about dissemination of the knowledge; (vii) exclusion of IK from school and university curricula, and the absence of awareness programmes; and (viii) lack of a cohesive organization to represent the interests of indigenous people.

Those rights considered to be most in need of protection were:

- the right of ownership and control of IK;
- the right to benefit commercially from the authorized exploitation of IK;
- the preservation of the right to cultural autonomy in any system for protecting IK;
- the right to approve or reject commercial use of IK;
- the right to maintain the secrecy and sacredness of IKS;
- the right to prevent distortion or mutilation of IKS; and
- the right to legal assistance for negotiating and enforcing IK contracts.

It was noted that certain types of conventional intellectual property, including certification and collective marks, trade secrets and geographical indications, potentially lend themselves to protecting particular aspects of IK, for example by their ability to recognize collective traditions and to be maintained in perpetuity. It was suggested that a register of well-known IK marks be established in the Patents and Trade Marks Office, to be treated in an analogous manner to well-known marks, which are a recognized concept in South African trade mark law.

The compilation of a directory of inventors was supported, although concern was expressed about disclosure of IK. As an interim measure, it was suggested that holders of IK be listed on a voluntary basis with their area of expertise and contact information, but that details of the knowledge be withheld.

Current developments

A multisectoral task team was subsequently convened to oversee the drafting of a new bill, informed among other things by a draft policy and the submissions to the public hearings. Departments represented include Science and Technology (DST), Arts and Culture, DTI, DEAT, Education, Health, Agriculture and Land Affairs. A draft bill and policy were submitted to DST in June 2001, after which a review team made up of stakeholders, including academics, legal practitioners, IKS practitioners, healers and NGOs, engaged with the task team to come up with a final draft for submission to DST. This is currently under internal review within government in an attempt to reach consensus between the different departments involved. The format of the bill will give DST overall responsibility for the overarching legislation, but management of specific aspects of IKS will be assigned to other departments where appropriate. It is hoped that the bill will eventually be submitted to the cabinet, after which it will be released for public comment and roadshows will be undertaken to provide information to interested parties. Legislation is unlikely to be promulgated before 2004.

The absence of clear policy to direct the earlier attempts at legislation perhaps explains some of the shortcomings of the previous draft bills. It would appear that the pace of these early efforts was accelerated due to the importance ascribed to IKS and an over-enthusiasm to legislate quickly, but that this was too ambitious relative to the capacity available.

Conclusion

Several government departments and other stakeholders have spent considerable time, effort and resources in attempting to shape, develop and implement policy for the protection of biological resources which do not meet the requirements for patentability. As yet, no firm proposals are on the table, but it would appear that headway is being made, and delays are arguably preferable to introducing unworkable or unsuitable laws. It is hoped that the extended processes followed will pay off in the form of effective policy and legislation. The wide disparities which characterize South African society mean that many of the issues which cause conflict between North and South in the global arena are fiercely debated among different constituencies within South Africa. Mechanisms to resolve any of these contentious matters successfully in the South African context would potentially have much wider application.

Notes

1 Due to a lack of available formal documentation and literature on the issues discussed in this chapter, and to the fact that these are areas undergoing change, this chapter is based mainly on informal personal communication with government officials, practitioners and other stakeholders, and in some cases from draft documents which have not been released to the public. Sincere thanks go to all those who were willing to share information or opinions, and apologies are made if this paper inadvertently misinterprets any of the information received. In particular, I would like to acknowledge the following individuals: S Clelland, D Cochrane and G Tribe (patent attorneys, Spoor & Fisher); B Koster (patent attorney, Findlay & Tait); P Krappie and R Williams (DTI); W Loubser (General Manager, South African National Seed Organization); M Matsabisa (Indigenous Knowledge Systems Health Manager, Medical Research Council); S Meintjies, M Rampedi and G Willemse (DEAT); P Pla-Pillans (patent attorney, Adams & Adams); T Suchanandan (Department of Science and Technology); and P van Stavel (CIPRO).

2 No attempt is made here to define and distinguish concepts such as indigenous knowledge, indigenous knowledge systems and traditional knowledge. Where different terminology is used in different parts of the chapter, this is indicative of different usage in the documents referred to in the context.

3 About 100 US patents of South African origin are granted annually in the US Patents and Trademarks Office.

4 Editor's note: this is otherwise referred to as a 'Bolar exemption'. Such an exemption permits certain acts relating (most commonly) to a drug patent performed before the expiry date of a patent that would normally infringe it, as long as the acts were related to seeking regulatory approval and did not constitute commercial use. The Bolar exemption was named after a court case in the US involving Hoffman LaRoche and a generic producer called Bolar, and has been incorporated into the patent laws of several countries in order to allow generic competition as soon as possible after a patent protecting a drug product expires.
5 See http://www.cipro.gov.za
6 This is expected to be in place by 2004.
7 It appears that a political decision has been taken not to ratify UPOV 1991, but this does not seem to have any practical effect because of the legislative amendments which have been implemented.

REFERENCES

Van der Walt, W J (1996) 'Plant breeders rights in South Africa', in *Proceedings of Land and Agriculture Policy Centre Genetic Conservation Workshop*, Johannesburg, 19–20 March 1996.

Chapter 29

Towards TRIPS Compliance: Kenya's legislative reforms

James Otieno-Odek

Kenya became a member of the World Trade Organization (WTO) on 1 January 1995. To implement its patent-related TRIPS obligations, the Attorney General published the Industrial Property Bill in May 2000, which was subsequently passed by parliament, and is now the Industrial Property Act. The act seeks to bring Kenya's intellectual property regime into conformity with both TRIPS and the Patent Cooperation Treaty.

The Kenya Industrial Property Act domesticates most of the TRIPS obligations, specifically by incorporating its provisions relating to the patent protection period of 20 years, forfeiture or revocation of patents, abolition of the obligation to locally work a patented invention, and the obligation to protect inventions in all technological fields.

Further, the act embraces in its entirety the TRIPS provisions on compulsory licensing. At any time after four years from the filing date of an application or three years from the grant of a patent, whichever period last expires, any person may apply for a licence to exploit the patented invention on the grounds that a market for the patented invention is not being supplied on reasonable terms in Kenya. A compulsory licence shall not be granted unless, inter alia, the patent owner has refused to grant a contractual licence on reasonable commercial terms.

Plant variety protection

The Industrial Property Act adopts the provisions of Article 27.3(b) of TRIPS. Section 26(a) stipulates that plant varieties as provided in the Seeds and Plant Varieties Act, but not parts thereof or products of biotechnological process, are not patentable. It is clear from this that plant varieties are excluded from patentability but, recognizing that there is a TRIPS obligation to protect new plant varieties by an intellectual property rights (IPR) system of some kind, Kenya already has in place a Seeds and Plant Varieties Act.

This latter act provides rights in respect of plant varieties of such species or groups as may be specified in a scheme. These rights are for a period not exceeding 25 years, although the protection period varies from species to species. An applicant for plant breeder's rights must be the person who bred or discovered the variety concerned. The conditions for the grant of a breeder's right are that the variety shall be:

- sufficiently distinguishable by one or more important morphological, physiological or other characteristics from any other variety whose existence is a matter of common knowledge at the time of the application, whatever may have been the origin, artificial or natural, of the initial variation from which it resulted;
- sufficiently varietal pure;
- sufficiently uniform or homogenous having regard to the particular features of its sexual reproduction or vegetative propagation; and
- stable in its essential characteristics, that is to say, it must remain true to its description after repeated reproduction or propagation … and the agro-ecological value must surpass, in one or more characteristics, that of existing varieties.

To further implement the TRIPS provisions on plant variety protection, Kenya acceded to the International Union for the Protection of New Varieties of Plants (UPOV) 1978 Convention in April 1999. Kenya delayed accession because UPOV 1991 is more rigid and requires members to adopt its standards and scope of protection. These standards have quite different implications with regard to the breadth and scope of coverage, and utilization of protected material in research and production of propagating materials and crops for sale. For example, the 1978 UPOV requires protection to as many plant genera and species as possible with a minimum protection of five species and genera on a state joining UPOV, and 24 species and genera after eight years. The 1991 UPOV requires minimum protection of five species on joining and protection of all plant genera and species 10 years after accession.

In order to give domestic effect to the 1978 UPOV accession, Kenya published the Statute Law Miscellaneous Amendment Act 2000. The act domesticates the UPOV 1978 provisions. To protect farmers' privilege (the freedom to save and replant harvested seed of the protected variety), the Kenyan position on this issue is that the 1978 UPOV Convention permits member states to decide in its domestic legislation whether to recognize farmers' privilege. Kenya supports this flexibility and under the Seeds and Plant Varieties Act, it recognizes farmers' privilege.

ACCESS TO ESSENTIAL MEDICINES

Kenya, as with many other countries of the world, is severely affected by the global AIDS pandemic. Consequently, the question of access to affordable

HIV/AIDS drugs is a priority for the Kenyan people. The HIV/AIDS pandemic thereby created a national emergency in Kenya in the public health sector within the meaning of Article 31 of TRIPS. For this reason, Section 58(2) of the Kenya Industrial Property Act addresses the issue of access to essential medicines, providing that 'the rights under the patent shall not extend to acts in respect of articles which have been put on the market in Kenya or in any other country or imported into Kenya by the owner of the patent or with his express consent'.

This provision was inserted into the law to enable parallel importation of anti-retroviral AIDS drugs. The aim here is to permit Kenya to source cheap drugs from any part of the world. This in essence allows for the application of the exhaustion of rights principle on a national level. Kenya has adopted a parallel importation approach as opposed to differential pricing. Once the patentee places the patented article on the market, his rights under the patent are exhausted within the boundaries of Kenya. It is important to note that Kenya has declared HIV/AIDS a national disaster.

Section 80 of the act also permits the government in the public interest, or on health grounds, to exploit a patented invention on a compulsory basis. The provisions of Section 58 and 80 of the Kenyan Act are in line with the Doha Declaration on the TRIPS Agreement and Public Health, wherein the ministers agreed that TRIPS should be interpreted and applied in a manner supportive of WTO members' right to protect public health and in particular to ensure access to medicines for all.

COPYRIGHT

In 2001, Kenya enacted the Copyright Act to modernize copyright law and bring it in line with international instruments, in particular the Berne Convention and TRIPS. Section 23 of the act confers copyright on every work by an author by virtue of citizenship or residence in Kenya or by a body incorporated in Kenya. Kenya now expressly protects computer programs and data by way of copyright. Folklore is also included and defined to mean a literary, musical or artistic work presumed to have been created within Kenya by an unidentified author which has been passed from one generation to another and constitutes a basic element of the traditional cultural heritage of Kenya. Included are such categories as (i) folktales, folk poetry and folk riddles; (ii) folk songs and instrumental folk music; (iii) folk dances and folk plays; and (iv) the production of folk art, in particular drawings, paintings, sculptures, pottery, woodwork, metalware, jewellery, handicrafts, costumes and indigenous textiles.

To effectively monitor and enforce the copyright provisions, Section 3 of the act established the Kenya Copyright Board whose mandate includes directing, coordinating and overseeing the implementation of laws and international treaties and conventions to which Kenya is a party and which relate to copyright. The board is empowered to appoint inspectors to enforce the copyright laws and prevent infringement.

A novelty in the act is its reference to 'banderole'. A banderole is defined in Section 2 to mean a serialized identification or authentication adhesive or stamp which is affixed to all genuine copyright works. Section 36 requires a manufacturer of sound and audio-visual works or recordings and publisher of literary works to apply to the board for authentication of copyright works. The provisions of this section seem to introduce a requirement of registration. This is in contrast to the general practice where copyright is not registrable. Significant in this regard is that Section 51 abolishes common law rights relating to copyright.

Section 45 of the act defines works which are in the public domain. These are: (i) works whose terms of protection have expired; (ii) works in respect of which authors have renounced their rights; and (iii) foreign works which do not enjoy protection in Kenya.

For effective enforcement of the act, powers of inspection are given to the Copyright Board. Section 40 permits an inspector appointed by the board to enter any premises at any reasonable time for the purposes of ascertaining whether there is or has been any infringement of the act.

TRADE MARKS

In order to implement the TRIPS trade mark provisions, Kenya adopted a three-pronged approach. First, the Trademarks Act was amended with effect from March 1995 to include protection of service marks. Second, under the Miscellaneous Amendment Act 2000, an amendment to the Trademarks Act was made to bring the act in line to comply with the Madrid Agreement, the Trade Mark Law Treaty and the Banjul Protocol of the African Regional Industrial Property Organization, of which Kenya is a member. The third and more drastic approach was to repeal the existing Trademarks Act. The new Trademarks Act changes the duration of trade mark protection to conform to TRIPS.

INDUSTRIAL DESIGNS

Section 86(1) of the Industrial Property Act provides for the protection of new industrial design. The word 'new' was missing in the old legislation. A design is deemed to be new if it has not been disclosed to the public anywhere in the world. An absolute novelty standard is thus adopted. An industrial design is defined to mean any composition of lines or colours or any three dimensional form, whether or not associated with lines or colours. Such composition or form must give a special appearance to a product of industry or handicraft and be able to serve as a pattern for a product of industry or handicraft.

GEOGRAPHICAL INDICATIONS

To effectively implement the TRIPS provisions on protection of geographical indications, Kenya prepared a Geographical Indications Bill, 2001. The bill was placed before the cabinet for consideration and approval. However, the approval has not been forthcoming since publication in 2001, and the bill has now lapsed. According to Kenya's parliamentary practice, once a bill lapses it must be published afresh. There are several factors that have contributed to the lapse of the bill. These include excessive workload pending at the National Assembly, the general election of 2002, review of the Kenya Constitution, and delays in drafting of the bills due to shortage of technical human resource.

LAYOUT DESIGNS OF INTEGRATED CIRCUITS

Kenya's industrial property office has drafted a bill for the protection of layout designs in integrated circuits. The draft bill is presently with the attorney general for consideration. The draft has not been published. Due to this situation, presently, there is no law protecting layout designs for integrated circuits in Kenya.

OTHER LEGISLATIVE REFORMS TO IMPLEMENT TRIPS

To further implement the provisions of TRIPS, Kenya is proposing to undertake two legal reforms. One of these is to have a new law on unfair competition and counterfeit products. The aim here is to review the existing Trademarks Act, Trade Description Act and the Standards Act, so as to effectively enforce counterfeit laws. Harmonization and effective enforcement of these laws is a primary aim. The second is to amend the Customs and Excise Act to take care of counterfeiting of trade marks and copyright piracy. At the moment, Kenya is using Section 14 and 15 as well as the Eighth Schedule of the Customs and Excise Act to deal with counterfeit goods. These sections enumerated prohibited imports and exports. The above-proposed reforms have been under consideration for over three years.

PROTECTION OF TRADITIONAL KNOWLEDGE

The question of protection of traditional knowledge is problematic. The first predicament is definitional: what is meant by the term? The second pertains to what should be the appropriate legal framework. In principle, Kenya is fully committed to protection of traditional knowledge. Two legal provisions permit this. These are the protection of folklore under copyright law, and utility models to protect indigenous 'inventions' under the Industrial Property Act according to which an 'invention' qualifies for a utility model certificate if it is new and is industrially applicable. The patent requirements for novelty and inventive step are not applicable to utility models. But the major problem with TK protection is categorization. There are various categories of TK, not all of which can be fitted under one system. Thus, copyright law protects folklore, while utility models, trade marks and industrial designs may also be useful. There is need for a wider discussion at the national level to deliberate on how traditional knowledge should be protected in Kenya.

ACCESS TO GENETIC RESOURCES AND BENEFIT SHARING

The Environmental Management and Coordination Act, which was enacted in 1999 and came into force the following year, is the key statutory instrument regulating access to genetic resources in Kenya. Section 7 establishes the National Environment Management Authority as a body corporate with perpetual succession.

Section 53 stipulates that the authority shall issue guidelines and prescribe measures for the sustainable management and utilization of genetic resources for the benefit of the people of Kenya. The guidelines shall specify appropriate arrangements for access to genetic resources by non-citizens, including the issue of licences and fees to be paid for that access. Guidelines shall also be adopted for the sharing of benefits derived from the genetic resources of Kenya. The National Council for Science and Technology has prepared guidelines in line with the mandate of the authority and these guidelines await enactment into subsidiary legislation through gazettement. As of December 2002, the guidelines had not been gazetted.

Section 43 of the act stipulates that the minister may declare the traditional interests of local communities customarily resident within or around a lake shore, wetland, coastal zone or river bank to be protected interests. So far, no such declaration has been made.

KENYA'S WTO TRIPS REVIEW

The TRIPS Council review of Kenya's legislation was carried out on 19 June 2001. During the review, several issues were raised such as: (i) the lack of adequate enforcement procedures for intellectual property protection in Kenya; (ii) the protection of foreign copyright works in Kenya; (iii) the adequacy of Kenya's law in respect of access to essential drugs; (iv) Kenya's compliance with Articles 7 and 8 of TRIPS; (v) clarification of Kenya's rules on geographical indications and trade marks; (vi) Kenya's protection of trade secrets; and (vi) Kenya's protection of traditional knowledge and genetic resources.

In response to these issues, Kenya's position is that, as in the UK, trade secrets are protected by the common law. With respect to the protection of traditional knowledge and genetic resources, the matter is under discussion among stakeholders in Kenya. On access to essential drugs, Kenya's view is that Article 6 of TRIPS permits differential pricing. To this end, Kenya's view is that there is a need for flexibility in interpreting and implementing TRIPS on matters relating to public health. On the other issues raised at the review, Kenya responded that legislative reforms are being put in place to strengthen enforcement mechanisms. As regards protection of foreign works, Section 49 of the Kenya Copyright Act permits the minister to extend protection to works from countries that are parties to treaties that Kenya is also a party to.

CONCLUSIONS

In order to enhance Kenya's public policy objectives in the field of IPRs, community rights, and biological and genetic resources, various reforms are necessary. In a broad sense, there are two options. The first is to do nothing and adopt the IPR regimes as they are. This implies maintaining the status quo. The other option is to do something and find new alternatives. It is to these alternatives that we now turn. But before going further, it is important to note that the existing agreements on IPRs and genetic resources are multilateral in nature. For developing countries, these have a positive feature as compared to bilateral agreements in that they enable them to bargain collectively.

First, there is need for a national or multilateral regime for plant breeders that would guarantee that farmers can continue to breed new varieties and maintain genetic diversity in their communities. Linkages to the scientific community and to the modern patent system would need to be forged. Such a system would promote conservation of the biotechnology raw material base and would create a balance between protection and exchange of genetic resources, thereby ensuring the sustainable use of biological material.

Second, a community IPR law needs to be enacted that recognizes informal and indigenous innovations. The current IPR treaties are not designed to acknowledge the intellectual contribution of informal innovation. This omission calls for an alternative regime that would recognize such innovation by redefining IPRs to encompass collective, incremental innovations, practices and knowledge of local communities, and vest those communities with enforceable IPRs in those innovations. The advantage of this approach is that it will recognize the claim to 'ownership' by indigenous communities over their traditional knowledge. The whole community will be deemed to be the rightful owner of creativity or innovation. This will also mean that innovation cannot be dealt with without regard to the past, present and future owners and beneficiaries of the knowledge. The right will therefore endure in perpetuity and cannot be extinguished. In short, the entire ethos of the industrial patent regime would be excluded from a regime establishing indigenous and local community rights.

The problem with this approach is the expense and bureaucracy that it would entail in terms of registration, documentation and potential for social discord between one community and others. Further, rural communities are not likely to be aware when their protected knowledge is utilized for commercial gain especially in distant countries.

Third, in respect of genetic resources Kenya should consider opting for an IPR scheme, according to which free access would be maintained for unimproved germplasm, while proprietary rights would be maintained for improved or modified germplasm. One possibility worth considering is to extend the scope of IPRs to cover those categories of genetic resources traditionally thought of as 'unimproved'. Such a change would be in line with the fact that 'unimproved' genetic material is often the product of considerable breeding and selection by farmers.

Fourth, a new multilateral biological order can be established. Such an order should consist of the following elements: (i) recognition of local and national ownership of genetic resources; (ii) technology cooperation; (iii) strengthening and increasing investment in biotechnology research; (iv) recognition of informal innovation; and (v) capacity building. It should be consistent with and supportive of the CBD and based on an integrated rights approach guided by the need to conserve biodiversity as the raw material for biotechnology, and to effectively protect traditional knowledge including by recognizing and reinforcing customary laws and practices.

Chapter 30

The Peruvian Law on Protection of the Collective Knowledge of Indigenous Peoples Related to Biological Resources

Begoña Venero Aguirre

In August 2002, the Official Journal of Peru published the 'Law introducing a protection regime for the collective knowledge of indigenous peoples related to biological resources'. This legislation establishes a sui generis protection regime that takes elements of existing protection mechanisms to create a new regime designed to take into account the characteristics of the kind of knowledge it covers. It was deemed necessary to establish such a special protection regime complementing the classic branches of the intellectual property rights (IPR) system because the latter cannot provide adequate protection for this kind of knowledge. The scope of the law does not cover traditional knowledge as a whole, but only the collective knowledge of indigenous peoples relating to the properties, uses and characteristics of biological diversity.

The objectives of the regime are to: (i) promote respect, protection, preservation, wider application and development of the collective knowledge of indigenous peoples; (ii) promote the fair and equitable distribution of the benefits derived from the use of that collective knowledge; (iii) promote the use of this knowledge for the benefit of indigenous peoples and mankind; (iv) ensure that the use of this knowledge takes place with the prior informed consent of indigenous peoples; (v) promote the strengthening and development of the capabilities of indigenous peoples, and of the mechanisms traditionally used by them, to share and distribute collectively generated benefits; and (vi) avoid the patenting of inventions obtained or developed using the collective knowledge of the indigenous peoples of Peru.

The purpose of this law is not to prevent access to this knowledge but to promote its use, provided that some requirements are met, such as the prior informed consent of indigenous peoples, and the fair and equitable distribution of the benefits derived from the use of this knowledge. It is worth making a special reference to the sixth objective of this protection regime, which we may refer to as defensive protection, an issue that will be elaborated on below.

The collective knowledge of indigenous peoples has five characteristics that the protection regime takes into account:

First, it has been developed collectively. It belongs to indigenous peoples as a group and not to individuals. Nevertheless, it should be taken into account that, in most cases, it is possible to identify in each community or people some individuals that hold most of the knowledge, such as shamans, elders, or women. In these cases, indigenous peoples may grant certain rights or benefits to these individuals.

Second, the same knowledge may belong to several indigenous peoples. The fact that knowledge is usually shared by a number of indigenous peoples shall be considered when determining who shall give the authorization, and how the benefits derived from the use of this knowledge shall be distributed.

Third, present generations preserve, develop and manage their collective knowledge for their own benefit and for the benefit of future generations. They have received this knowledge from past generations with the obligation of transmitting it to future generations. Therefore, present generations are the custodians of the collective knowledge they possess.

Fourth, collective knowledge forms part of the cultural heritage of indigenous peoples, the admission of which implies recognition of special rights over their knowledge.

Fifth, as part of their cultural heritage, the rights of indigenous peoples over their knowledge cannot be transferred or prescribed. This is closely connected to the third characteristic mentioned above. Present generations cannot transfer their collective knowledge to a third party, but can only grant licences of use, since they are not the owners but the custodians of the collective knowledge they possess. Recognition of rights with a time limit is not enough, since this collective knowledge is a legacy of past generations to present and future generations. It would imply that rights are granted to favour present generations to the detriment of future generations, given that future generations would probably never have the chance to hold these rights.

Prior informed consent

Prior informed consent is the main condition to be fulfilled in order to have access to collective knowledge under this protection regime. Regardless of the purposes for which access is sought, it is necessary to ask and obtain the prior informed consent to have legal access to this knowledge. This obligation is placed upon anybody desiring to access collective knowledge. Indigenous peoples possessing this knowledge may choose not to give their consent. Without their consent, it is impossible to have legal access to this knowledge. According to this law, prior informed consent is to be obtained through the representative organizations of indigenous peoples who possess the collective knowledge to which access is sought. The legislation defines prior informed consent as:

> *Authorization given, under this protection regime, by the representative organization of indigenous peoples who possess the collective knowledge, in accordance with the rules recognized by them for the execution of a particular activity that entails access to and use of the said collective knowledge, subject to the previous supply of sufficient information on the purposes, risks and implications of such activity, including the uses that may eventually be made of the knowledge and, be it the case, its value.*

Prior informed consent may be requested and obtained from one representative organization of indigenous peoples. In other words, if the collective knowledge is shared by several indigenous peoples, it is not necessary to obtain the prior informed consent of all the indigenous peoples possessing the said knowledge. Obtaining the prior informed consent of one representative organization of indigenous peoples who possess such knowledge is sufficient to have legal access to the said knowledge. Nevertheless, this representative organization must inform as many indigenous peoples possessing collective knowledge as possible that it is beginning a negotiation and must take into account their interests and concerns.

LICENCE CONTRACTS

To have access to collective knowledge for the purposes of industrial or commercial application, asking and obtaining the prior informed consent of indigenous peoples who possess the knowledge is not enough. It is also necessary to negotiate and sign a licence contract for the use of collective knowledge. According to the law, terms that ensure an adequate payment for access to the collective knowledge and an equitable distribution of the benefits derived from its use must be included in that contract. These licences must be granted only by written contract and be recorded in a register maintained by the competent national authority, which is the National Institute for the Defence of Competition and Protection of Intellectual Property (INDECOPI). The law specifies the clauses that a licence contract must include, stating that INDECOPI shall not register those contracts failing to comply with these provisions.

Two of the clauses are worth a special mention. The first is the establishment of payments that indigenous peoples will receive.[1] These are: (i) initial monetary payment or an equivalent for its sustainable development; and (ii) a percentage of no less than 5 per cent of the value, before taxes, of the gross sales resulting from the marketing of the products developed directly and indirectly from the said collective knowledge, as the case may be. The second clause stipulates that sufficient information on the purposes, risks and implications of the said activity must be supplied.

Indigenous peoples shall receive the first payment mentioned above, and the second payment provided that the collective knowledge that has been licensed contributes to the development of a commercial product. This system of 'milestone payments' is justified on the basis that when a licence contract is negotiated, no one knows the real value of the knowledge that is being licensed.

The information shall be supplied to the representative organizations of indigenous peoples with whom the licence contract is being negotiated before the signature of the contract. However, this provision is useful as a tangible proof that the representative organizations that are granting a licence are acting with full knowledge of the facts, that is to say, they have given their prior informed consent.

The text of the legislation implies that only one representative organization of indigenous peoples who possess the collective knowledge that is being licensed may sign the contract, and that the signature of the contract by all the representative organizations of indigenous peoples is not needed.

COLLECTIVE KNOWLEDGE IN THE PUBLIC DOMAIN

The law gives a different status to collective knowledge in the public domain. Collective knowledge is in the public domain when it has been accessible to persons other than indigenous peoples through the media, such as publications, or when it is related to properties, uses and characteristics of a biological resource that are widely known outside the range of indigenous peoples. In such a case, it is not necessary to ask for the prior informed consent of indigenous peoples or to sign a licence contract. The law only provides that if the collective knowledge has passed into the public domain in the last 20 years, a percentage of the value, before taxes, of the gross sales resulting from the marketing of products developed from this knowledge shall be set aside for the Fund for the Development of Indigenous Peoples.

It seems reasonable to make an exception in such a case and not to require the prior informed consent or the signature of a licence contract, first, since it is very easy to have access to this kind of knowledge, and second, because it would be extremely difficult to determine which indigenous people or peoples possessed the knowledge before it passed into the public domain.

Nevertheless, it must be taken into account that, in many cases, collective knowledge has passed into the public domain without the consent of indigenous peoples. In some cases, indigenous peoples have given their consent for the use of their collective knowledge but not for its dissemination. In other cases, they have agreed to share their knowledge without being aware of the consequences that might follow. Considering this and recognizing the contribution of indigenous peoples to the development and preservation of this knowledge – which deserves some kind of compensation – it seems reasonable to set aside a percentage of the benefits derived from the use of this knowledge for the Fund for the Development of Indigenous Peoples.

REGISTERS

The law establishes three kinds of register. These are (i) the National Public Register of Collective Knowledge of Indigenous Peoples; (ii) the National

Confidential Register of Collective Knowledge of Indigenous Peoples; and (iii) Local Registers of Collective Knowledge of Indigenous Peoples. The objectives of these registers are, as the case may be, to preserve and safeguard the collective knowledge of indigenous peoples and their rights therein,[2] and to provide INDECOPI with information that enables it to defend the interests of indigenous peoples concerning their collective knowledge.[3]

None of these registers create legal rights in themselves. Indigenous peoples have rights over the collective knowledge they possess whether it is registered or not. Indigenous peoples may apply for the registration of the collective knowledge they possess in the National Public Register or in the National Confidential Register through their representative organizations. Indigenous peoples may also create their own local registers.

INDECOPI is in charge of the National Public Register. Given that this register is public, it is oriented to collective knowledge that is in the public domain. Indigenous peoples may apply for registration of public domain collective knowledge in this Register. Moreover, Article 17 states that INDECOPI shall record the public domain collective knowledge in this register.

This register has been created mainly for defensive reasons. According to Article 23, INDECOPI shall send the information contained in this register to the main patent offices of the world in order that they may use it better to screen patent applications in relevant technical fields for novelty and inventive step. The effectiveness of doing this will depend on the amount of information contained in the National Public Register, the way it is sent by INDECOPI, and the attitude of the different patent offices that receive it.

INDECOPI is in charge of the National Confidential Register. Third parties do not have access to this register. It is oriented to collective knowledge that is not in the public domain. Indigenous peoples may apply for registration of non-public domain collective knowledge they possess in this register.

Article 24 specifies that indigenous peoples may set up local registers according to their practices and customs. In my view, there is no need to mention this, because indigenous peoples have always been free to establish such registers.

THE FUND FOR THE DEVELOPMENT OF INDIGENOUS PEOPLES

This fund is created as a means of indirect compensation for all the indigenous peoples of Peru in recognition that they deserve a reward for contributing to the development and preservation of collective knowledge in the country. A percentage of the benefits obtained from the marketing of products developed from the collective knowledge shall be set aside for this fund. Article 8 specifies that a percentage of no less than 10 per cent of the value, before taxes, of the gross sales resulting from the marketing of products developed from collective knowledge shall be set aside for the fund. Article 13 states that if the collective knowledge has passed into the public domain in the last 20 years, a percentage of the value, before taxes, of the gross sales resulting from the marketing of products developed from this knowledge shall be set aside for the fund. In this case, it is not a fixed percentage.

The purpose of the fund is to contribute to the development of indigenous peoples through the financing of projects and other activities. The fund shall be administered by a committee comprising five representatives of indigenous peoples' organizations, and two representatives of the National Commission for the Andean, Amazonian and Afro-Peruvian Peoples. The members of this committee shall decide how to allocate the resources of the fund after having evaluated the development projects submitted by the concerned indigenous peoples.

THE NATURE OF THE PROTECTION CONFERRED

Indigenous people possessing collective knowledge shall be protected against the disclosure, acquisition and use of that collective knowledge without its consent and in a disloyal way, provided that the collective knowledge is not in the public domain. It shall also be protected against unauthorized disclosure in case a third party has legitimately had access to the collective knowledge. In this case, the third party will be forbidden to disclose it to others.

This law does not grant protection against any unauthorized disclosure, acquisition or use of collective knowledge. Protection is granted only if the unauthorized disclosure, acquisition or use has taken place in a disloyal way. The implementation of the law by the competent national authorities will probably give a better idea of what 'disloyal' means when speaking of disclosure, acquisition or use of the collective knowledge of indigenous peoples.

Indigenous peoples who possess collective knowledge may bring infringement actions against whoever violates the rights specified in the law and described above. An infringement action may also be brought when imminent danger exists that these rights may be violated. Infringement actions may also be brought ex officio by decision of INDECOPI.

Indigenous peoples may also bring actions claiming ownership and indemnification against a third party that uses, directly or indirectly, their collective knowledge, in a manner contrary to the provisions of this regime, as provided by the current legislation.

It is worth mentioning, finally, that the burden of proof falls on the defendant, whenever infringement of the rights of an indigenous people possessing collective knowledge is alleged.

INDECOPI AND THE INDIGENOUS KNOWLEDGE PROTECTION COUNCIL

The Office of Inventions and New Technologies of INDECOPI is competent to hear and decide in the first instance all matters concerning the protection of the collective knowledge of indigenous peoples. The Intellectual Property Chamber of the Tribunal for the Defence of Competition and Intellectual

Property of INDECOPI is competent to hear and decide all appeals in the second and last administrative instance.

The law creates an Indigenous Knowledge Protection Council, which shall be composed of five experts, three of them designated by the representative organizations of indigenous peoples, and two designated by the National Commission for the Andean, Amazonian and Afro-Peruvian Peoples. The functions of this council shall be to: (i) monitor and oversee the implementation of this protection regime; (ii) support the Administrative Committee of the Fund for the Development of Indigenous Peoples and the Office of Inventions and New Technologies of INDECOPI in the performance of their functions; (iii) give its opinion regarding the validity of licence contracts on collective knowledge of indigenous peoples; (iv) advise representatives of indigenous peoples, at their request, on matters related to this regime and, in particular, on the formulation and execution of projects within the framework of this regime; and (v) supervise the Administrative Committee of the Fund for the Development of Indigenous Peoples in the performance of its functions

This council will play a key role. Indeed, the success or failure of this protection regime relies, to a great extent, on its effective performance.

TRADITIONAL PRACTICES AND CUSTOMS OF INDIGENOUS PEOPLES

The following provisions of the law make specific references to the traditional practices of indigenous peoples:

- The protection regime shall not affect the traditional exchange between indigenous peoples of the collective knowledge protected under this regime.
- Indigenous peoples shall be represented by their representative organizations, respecting the traditional forms of organization of indigenous peoples.
- Indigenous peoples may organize local registers, according to their practices and customs.
- The Administrative Committee of the fund shall use, as far as possible, the mechanisms traditionally used by indigenous peoples for sharing and distributing collectively generated benefits.
- To settle disputes that may arise between indigenous peoples in the implementation of this regime, indigenous peoples may use their customary law and traditional forms of dispute settlement.

PROTECTION OF THE COLLECTIVE KNOWLEDGE OF INDIGENOUS PEOPLES AND INTELLECTUAL PROPERTY

Even though the new regime is independent of the protection provided by the current regional intellectual property agreements which are in force in Peru, such as Andean Community Decisions 345 and 486, these instruments are nonetheless linked by specific language contained in the latter two (see Chapter 25).

For example, the second complementary provision of the regime states that, if a patent application is filed for an invention related to products of processes obtained or developed from a collective knowledge, the applicant shall submit a copy of the licence contract as a prior requirement for the grant of the patent, unless this collective knowledge is in the public domain. It specifies that if this obligation is not complied with, the patent shall be denied or, as the case may be, invalidated.

To sum up, the new legislation deals with very complex issues. It uses interesting mechanisms. However, it is clear that different mechanisms may be used for the same purposes. Choices between different options have been taken when designing this law. Experience from the implementation of this law will show whether the choices taken were right or wrong.

NOTES

1 Regardless of these payments, indigenous peoples will also receive indirect compensation through the Fund for the Development of Indigenous Peoples (see below).
2 To be fulfilled by the National Confidential Register and by the local registers.
3 To be fulfilled by the National Public Register.

Annex 1

Agreement on Trade-related Aspects of Intellectual Property Rights (Extracts)

Members,

Desiring to reduce distortions and impediments to international trade, and taking into account the need to promote effective and adequate protection of intellectual property rights, and to ensure that measures and procedures to enforce intellectual property rights do not themselves become barriers to legitimate trade;

Recognizing, to this end, the need for new rules and disciplines concerning:

(a) the applicability of the basic principles of GATT 1994 and of relevant international intellectual property agreements or conventions;

(b) the provision of adequate standards and principles concerning the availability, scope and use of trade-related intellectual property rights;

(c) the provision of effective and appropriate means for the enforcement of trade-related intellectual property rights, taking into account differences in national legal systems;

(d) the provision of effective and expeditious procedures for the multilateral prevention and settlement of disputes between governments; and

(e) transitional arrangements aiming at the fullest participation in the results of the negotiations;

Recognizing the need for a multilateral framework of principles, rules and disciplines dealing with international trade in counterfeit goods;

Recognizing that intellectual property rights are private rights;

Recognizing the underlying public policy objectives of national systems for the protection of intellectual property, including developmental and technological objectives;

Recognizing also the special needs of the least developed country Members in respect of maximum flexibility in the domestic implementation of laws and regulations in order to enable them to create a sound and viable technological base;

Emphasizing the importance of reducing tensions by reaching strengthened commitments to resolve disputes on trade-related intellectual property issues through multilateral procedures;

Desiring to establish a mutually supportive relationship between the WTO and the World Intellectual Property Organization (referred to in this Agreement as 'WIPO') as well as other relevant international organizations;

Hereby agree as follows:

PART I
GENERAL PROVISIONS AND BASIC PRINCIPLES

Article 1
Nature and Scope of Obligations

1 Members shall give effect to the provisions of this Agreement. Members may, but shall not be obliged to, implement in their law more extensive protection than is required by this Agreement, provided that such protection does not contravene the provisions of this Agreement. Members shall be free to determine the appropriate method of implementing the provisions of this Agreement within their own legal system and practice.

2 For the purposes of this Agreement, the term 'intellectual property' refers to all categories of intellectual property that are the subject of Sections 1 through 7 of Part II.

3 Members shall accord the treatment provided for in this Agreement to the nationals of other Members.[1] In respect of the relevant intellectual property right, the nationals of other Members shall be understood as those natural or legal persons that would meet the criteria for eligibility for protection provided for in the Paris Convention (1967), the Berne Convention (1971), the Rome Convention and the Treaty on Intellectual Property in Respect of Integrated Circuits, were all Members of the WTO members of those conventions.[2] Any Member availing itself of the possibilities provided in paragraph 3 of Article 5 or paragraph 2 of Article 6 of the Rome Convention shall make a notification as foreseen in those provisions to the Council for Trade-Related Aspects of Intellectual Property Rights (the 'Council for TRIPS').

Article 2
Intellectual Property Conventions

1 In respect of Parts II, III and IV of this Agreement, Members shall comply with Articles 1 through 12, and Article 19, of the Paris Convention (1967).

2 Nothing in Parts I to IV of this Agreement shall derogate from existing obligations that Members may have to each other under the Paris Convention, the Berne Convention, the Rome Convention and the Treaty on Intellectual Property in Respect of Integrated Circuits.

Article 3
National Treatment

1 Each Member shall accord to the nationals of other Members treatment no less favourable than that it accords to its own nationals with regard to the protection[3] of intellectual property, subject to the exceptions already provided in, respectively, the Paris Convention (1967), the Berne Convention (1971), the Rome Convention or the Treaty on Intellectual Property in Respect of Integrated Circuits. In respect of performers, producers of phonograms and broadcasting organizations, this obligation only applies in respect of the rights provided under this Agreement. Any Member availing itself of the possibilities provided in Article 6 of the Berne Convention (1971) or paragraph 1(b) of Article 16 of the Rome Convention shall make a notification as foreseen in those provisions to the Council for TRIPS.

2 Members may avail themselves of the exceptions permitted under paragraph 1 in relation to judicial and administrative procedures, including the designation of an address for service or the appointment of an agent within the jurisdiction of a Member, only where such exceptions are necessary to secure compliance with laws and regulations which are not inconsistent with the provisions of this Agreement and where such practices are not applied in a manner which would constitute a disguised restriction on trade.

Article 4
Most Favoured Nation Treatment

With regard to the protection of intellectual property, any advantage, favour, privilege or immunity granted by a Member to the nationals of any other country shall be accorded immediately and unconditionally to the nationals of all other Members. Exempted from this obligation are any advantage, favour, privilege or immunity accorded by a Member:

(a) deriving from international agreements on judicial assistance or law enforcement of a general nature and not particularly confined to the protection of intellectual property;

(b) granted in accordance with the provisions of the Berne Convention (1971) or the Rome Convention authorizing that the treatment accorded be a function not of national treatment but of the treatment accorded in another country;

(c) in respect of the rights of performers, producers of phonograms and broadcasting organizations not provided under this Agreement;

(d) deriving from international agreements related to the protection of intellectual property which entered into force prior to the entry into force of the WTO Agreement, provided that such agreements are notified to the Council for TRIPS and do not constitute an arbitrary or unjustifiable discrimination against nationals of other Members.

Article 5
Multilateral Agreements on Acquisition or Maintenance of Protection

The obligations under Articles 3 and 4 do not apply to procedures provided in multilateral agreements concluded under the auspices of WIPO relating to the acquisition or maintenance of intellectual property rights.

Article 6
Exhaustion

For the purposes of dispute settlement under this Agreement, subject to the provisions of Articles 3 and 4 nothing in this Agreement shall be used to address the issue of the exhaustion of intellectual property rights.

Article 7
Objectives

The protection and enforcement of intellectual property rights should contribute to the promotion of technological innovation and to the transfer and dissemination of technology, to the mutual advantage of producers and users of technological knowledge and in a manner conducive to social and economic welfare, and to a balance of rights and obligations.

Article 8
Principles

1 Members may, in formulating or amending their laws and regulations, adopt measures necessary to protect public health and nutrition, and to promote the public interest in sectors of vital importance to their socio-economic and technological development, provided that such measures are consistent with the provisions of this Agreement.

2 Appropriate measures, provided that they are consistent with the provisions of this Agreement, may be needed to prevent the abuse of intellectual property rights by right holders or the resort to practices which unreasonably restrain trade or adversely affect the international transfer of technology.

PART II
STANDARDS CONCERNING THE AVAILABILITY, SCOPE AND USE OF INTELLECTUAL PROPERTY RIGHTS

Section 3: Geographical Indications

Article 22
Protection of Geographical Indications

1 Geographical indications are, for the purposes of this Agreement,

indications which identify a good as originating in the territory of a Member, or a region or locality in that territory, where a given quality, reputation or other characteristic of the good is essentially attributable to its geographical origin.

2 In respect of geographical indications, Members shall provide the legal means for interested parties to prevent:

(a) the use of any means in the designation or presentation of a good that indicates or suggests that the good in question originates in a geographical area other than the true place of origin in a manner which misleads the public as to the geographical origin of the good;

(b) any use which constitutes an act of unfair competition within the meaning of Article 10bis of the Paris Convention (1967).

3 A Member shall, ex officio if its legislation so permits or at the request of an interested party, refuse or invalidate the registration of a trade mark which contains or consists of a geographical indication with respect to goods not originating in the territory indicated, if use of the indication in the trade mark for such goods in that Member is of such a nature as to mislead the public as to the true place of origin.

4 The protection under paragraphs 1, 2 and 3 shall be applicable against a geographical indication which, although literally true as to the territory, region or locality in which the goods originate, falsely represents to the public that the goods originate in another territory.

Article 23

Additional Protection for Geographical Indications for Wines and Spirits

1 Each Member shall provide the legal means for interested parties to prevent use of a geographical indication identifying wines for wines not originating in the place indicated by the geographical indication in question or identifying spirits for spirits not originating in the place indicated by the geographical indication in question, even where the true origin of the goods is indicated or the geographical indication is used in translation or accompanied by expressions such as 'kind', 'type', 'style', 'imitation' or the like.[4]

2 The registration of a trade mark for wines which contains or consists of a geographical indication identifying wines or for spirits which contains or consists of a geographical indication identifying spirits shall be refused or invalidated, ex officio if a Member's legislation so permits or at the request of an interested party, with respect to such wines or spirits not having this origin.

3 In the case of homonymous geographical indications for wines, protection shall be accorded to each indication, subject to the provisions of paragraph 4 of Article 22. Each Member shall determine the practical conditions under which the homonymous indications in question will be differentiated from each other, taking into account the need to ensure equitable treatment of the producers concerned and that consumers are not misled.

4 In order to facilitate the protection of geographical indications for wines, negotiations shall be undertaken in the Council for TRIPS concerning the establishment of a multilateral system of notification and registration of geographical indications for wines eligible for protection in those Members participating in the system.

Article 24
International Negotiations; Exceptions

1 Members agree to enter into negotiations aimed at increasing the protection of individual geographical indications under Article 23. The provisions of paragraphs 4 through 8 below shall not be used by a Member to refuse to conduct negotiations or to conclude bilateral or multilateral agreements. In the context of such negotiations, Members shall be willing to consider the continued applicability of these provisions to individual geographical indications whose use was the subject of such negotiations.

2 The Council for TRIPS shall keep under review the application of the provisions of this Section; the first such review shall take place within two years of the entry into force of the WTO Agreement. Any matter affecting the compliance with the obligations under these provisions may be drawn to the attention of the Council, which, at the request of a Member, shall consult with any Member or Members in respect of such matter in respect of which it has not been possible to find a satisfactory solution through bilateral or plurilateral consultations between the Members concerned. The Council shall take such action as may be agreed to facilitate the operation and further the objectives of this Section.

3 In implementing this Section, a Member shall not diminish the protection of geographical indications that existed in that Member immediately prior to the date of entry into force of the WTO Agreement.

4 Nothing in this Section shall require a Member to prevent continued and similar use of a particular geographical indication of another Member identifying wines or spirits in connection with goods or services by any of its nationals or domiciliaries who have used that geographical indication in a continuous manner with regard to the same or related goods or services in the territory of that Member either (a) for at least 10 years preceding 15 April 1994 or (b) in good faith preceding that date.

5 Where a trade mark has been applied for or registered in good faith, or where rights to a trade mark have been acquired through use in good faith either:

(a) before the date of application of these provisions in that Member as defined in Part VI; or

(b) before the geographical indication is protected in its country of origin;

measures adopted to implement this Section shall not prejudice eligibility for or the validity of the registration of a trade mark, or the right to use a trade mark, on the basis that such a trade mark is identical with, or similar to, a geographical indication.

6 Nothing in this Section shall require a Member to apply its provisions in respect of a geographical indication of any other Member with respect to goods or services for which the relevant indication is identical with the term customary in common language as the common name for such goods or services in the territory of that Member. Nothing in this Section shall require a Member to apply its provisions in respect of a geographical indication of any other Member with respect to products of the vine for which the relevant indication is identical with the customary name of a grape variety existing in the territory of that Member as of the date of entry into force of the WTO Agreement.

7 A Member may provide that any request made under this Section in connection with the use or registration of a trade mark must be presented within five years after the adverse use of the protected indication has become generally known in that Member or after the date of registration of the trade mark in that Member provided that the trade mark has been published by that date, if such date is earlier than the date on which the adverse use became generally known in that Member, provided that the geographical indication is not used or registered in bad faith.

8 The provisions of this Section shall in no way prejudice the right of any person to use, in the course of trade, that person's name or the name of that person's predecessor in business, except where such name is used in such a manner as to mislead the public.

9 There shall be no obligation under this Agreement to protect geographical indications which are not or cease to be protected in their country of origin, or which have fallen into disuse in that country.

Section 5: Patents

Article 27
Patentable Subject Matter

1 Subject to the provisions of paragraphs 2 and 3, patents shall be available for any inventions, whether products or processes, in all fields of technology, provided that they are new, involve an inventive step and are capable of industrial application.[5] Subject to paragraph 4 of Article 65, paragraph 8 of Article 70 and paragraph 3 of this Article, patents shall be available and patent rights enjoyable without discrimination as to the place of invention, the field of technology and whether products are imported or locally produced.

2 Members may exclude from patentability inventions, the prevention within their territory of the commercial exploitation of which is necessary to protect ordre public or morality, including to protect human, animal or plant life or health or to avoid serious prejudice to the environment, provided that such exclusion is not made merely because the exploitation is prohibited by their law.

3 Members may also exclude from patentability:

(a) diagnostic, therapeutic and surgical methods for the treatment of humans or animals;

(b) plants and animals other than micro-organisms, and essentially biological processes for the production of plants or animals other than non-biological and microbiological processes. However, Members shall provide for the protection of plant varieties either by patents or by an effective sui generis system or by any combination thereof. The provisions of this subparagraph shall be reviewed four years after the date of entry into force of the WTO Agreement.

Article 28
Rights Conferred

1 A patent shall confer on its owner the following exclusive rights:

(a) where the subject matter of a patent is a product, to prevent third parties not having the owner's consent from the acts of: making, using, offering for sale, selling, or importing[6] for these purposes that product;

(b) where the subject matter of a patent is a process, to prevent third parties not having the owner's consent from the act of using the process, and from the acts of: using, offering for sale, selling, or importing for these purposes at least the product obtained directly by that process.

2 Patent owners shall also have the right to assign, or transfer by succession, the patent and to conclude licensing contracts.

Article 29
Conditions on Patent Applicants

1 Members shall require that an applicant for a patent shall disclose the invention in a manner sufficiently clear and complete for the invention to be carried out by a person skilled in the art and may require the applicant to indicate the best mode for carrying out the invention known to the inventor at the filing date or, where priority is claimed, at the priority date of the application.

2 Members may require an applicant for a patent to provide information concerning the applicant's corresponding foreign applications and grants.

Article 30
Exceptions to Rights Conferred

Members may provide limited exceptions to the exclusive rights conferred by a patent, provided that such exceptions do not unreasonably conflict with a normal exploitation of the patent and do not unreasonably prejudice the legitimate interests of the patent owner, taking account of the legitimate interests of third parties.

Article 31

Other Use Without Authorization of the Right Holder

Where the law of a Member allows for other use[7] of the subject matter of a patent without the authorization of the right holder, including use by the government or third parties authorized by the government, the following provisions shall be respected:

(a) authorization of such use shall be considered on its individual merits;

(b) such use may only be permitted if, prior to such use, the proposed user has made efforts to obtain authorization from the right holder on reasonable commercial terms and conditions and that such efforts have not been successful within a reasonable period of time. This requirement may be waived by a Member in the case of a national emergency or other circumstances of extreme urgency or in cases of public non-commercial use. In situations of national emergency or other circumstances of extreme urgency, the right holder shall, nevertheless, be notified as soon as reasonably practicable. In the case of public non-commercial use, where the government or contractor, without making a patent search, knows or has demonstrable grounds to know that a valid patent is or will be used by or for the government, the right holder shall be informed promptly;

(c) the scope and duration of such use shall be limited to the purpose for which it was authorized, and in the case of semi-conductor technology shall only be for public non-commercial use or to remedy a practice determined after judicial or administrative process to be anti-competitive;

(d) such use shall be non-exclusive;

(e) such use shall be non-assignable, except with that part of the enterprise or goodwill which enjoys such use;

(f) any such use shall be authorized predominantly for the supply of the domestic market of the Member authorizing such use;

(g) authorization for such use shall be liable, subject to adequate protection of the legitimate interests of the persons so authorized, to be terminated if and when the circumstances which led to it cease to exist and are unlikely to recur. The competent authority shall have the authority to review, upon motivated request, the continued existence of these circumstances;

(h) the right holder shall be paid adequate remuneration in the circumstances of each case, taking into account the economic value of the authorization;

(i) the legal validity of any decision relating to the authorization of such use shall be subject to judicial review or other independent review by a distinct higher authority in that Member;

(j) any decision relating to the remuneration provided in respect of such use shall be subject to judicial review or other independent review by a distinct higher authority in that Member;

(k) Members are not obliged to apply the conditions set forth in subparagraphs (b) and (f) where such use is permitted to remedy a practice determined after judicial or administrative process to be anti-competitive. The need to correct anti-competitive practices may be taken into account in determining the amount of remuneration in such cases. Competent authorities shall have the authority to refuse termination of authorization if and when the conditions which led to such authorization are likely to recur;

(l) where such use is authorized to permit the exploitation of a patent ('the second patent') which cannot be exploited without infringing another patent ('the first patent'), the following additional conditions shall apply:

(i) the invention claimed in the second patent shall involve an important technical advance of considerable economic significance in relation to the invention claimed in the first patent;

(ii) the owner of the first patent shall be entitled to a cross-licence on reasonable terms to use the invention claimed in the second patent; and

(iii) the use authorized in respect of the first patent shall be non-assignable except with the assignment of the second patent.

Article 32
Revocation/Forfeiture

An opportunity for judicial review of any decision to revoke or forfeit a patent shall be available.

Article 33
Term of Protection

The term of protection available shall not end before the expiration of a period of twenty years counted from the filing date.[8]

Article 34
Process Patents: Burden of Proof

1 For the purposes of civil proceedings in respect of the infringement of the rights of the owner referred to in paragraph 1(b) of Article 28, if the subject matter of a patent is a process for obtaining a product, the judicial authorities shall have the authority to order the defendant to prove that the process to obtain an identical product is different from the patented process. Therefore, Members shall provide, in at least one of the following circumstances, that any identical product when produced without the consent of the patent owner shall, in the absence of proof to the contrary, be deemed to have been obtained by the patented process:

(a) if the product obtained by the patented process is new;

(b) if there is a substantial likelihood that the identical product was made by the process and the owner of the patent has been unable through reasonable efforts to determine the process actually used.

2 Any Member shall be free to provide that the burden of proof indicated in paragraph 1 shall be on the alleged infringer only if the condition referred to in subparagraph (a) is fulfilled or only if the condition referred to in subparagraph (b) is fulfilled.

3 In the adduction of proof to the contrary, the legitimate interests of defendants in protecting their manufacturing and business secrets shall be taken into account.

Section 7: Protection of Undisclosed Information

Article 39

1 In the course of ensuring effective protection against unfair competition as provided in Article 10bis of the Paris Convention (1967), Members shall protect undisclosed information in accordance with paragraph 2 and data submitted to governments or governmental agencies in accordance with paragraph 3.

2 Natural and legal persons shall have the possibility of preventing information lawfully within their control from being disclosed to, acquired by, or used by others without their consent in a manner contrary to honest commercial practices[9] so long as such information:

(a) is secret in the sense that it is not, as a body or in the precise configuration and assembly of its components, generally known among or readily accessible to persons within the circles that normally deal with the kind of information in question;

(b) has commercial value because it is secret; and

(c) has been subject to reasonable steps under the circumstances, by the person lawfully in control of the information, to keep it secret.

3 Members, when requiring, as a condition of approving the marketing of pharmaceutical or of agricultural chemical products which utilize new chemical entities, the submission of undisclosed test or other data, the origination of which involves a considerable effort, shall protect such data against unfair commercial use. In addition, Members shall protect such data against disclosure, except where necessary to protect the public, or unless steps are taken to ensure that the data are protected against unfair commercial use.

PART VI
TRANSITIONAL ARRANGEMENTS

Article 65
Transitional Arrangements

1 Subject to the provisions of paragraphs 2, 3 and 4, no Member shall be obliged to apply the provisions of this Agreement before the expiry of a general period of one year following the date of entry into force of the WTO Agreement.

2 A developing country Member is entitled to delay for a further period of four years the date of application, as defined in paragraph 1, of the provisions of this Agreement other than Articles 3, 4 and 5.

3 Any other Member which is in the process of transformation from a centrally planned into a market, free-enterprise economy and which is undertaking structural reform of its intellectual property system and facing special problems in the preparation and implementation of intellectual property laws and regulations, may also benefit from a period of delay as foreseen in paragraph 2.

4 To the extent that a developing country Member is obliged by this Agreement to extend product patent protection to areas of technology not so protectable in its territory on the general date of application of this Agreement for that Member, as defined in paragraph 2, it may delay the application of the provisions on product patents of Section 5 of Part II to such areas of technology for an additional period of five years.

5 A Member availing itself of a transitional period under paragraphs 1, 2, 3 or 4 shall ensure that any changes in its laws, regulations and practice made during that period do not result in a lesser degree of consistency with the provisions of this Agreement.

Article 66
Least Developed Country Members

1 In view of the special needs and requirements of least developed country Members, their economic, financial and administrative constraints, and their need for flexibility to create a viable technological base, such Members shall not be required to apply the provisions of this Agreement, other than Articles 3, 4 and 5, for a period of 10 years from the date of application as defined under paragraph 1 of Article 65. The Council for TRIPS shall, upon duly motivated request by a least developed country Member, accord extensions of this period.

2 Developed country Members shall provide incentives to enterprises and institutions in their territories for the purpose of promoting and encouraging technology transfer to least developed country Members in order to enable them to create a sound and viable technological base.

Article 67
Technical Cooperation

In order to facilitate the implementation of this Agreement, developed country Members shall provide, on request and on mutually agreed terms and conditions, technical and financial cooperation in favour of developing and least developed country Members. Such cooperation shall include assistance in the preparation of laws and regulations on the protection and enforcement of intellectual property rights as well as on the prevention of their abuse, and shall include support regarding the establishment or reinforcement of domestic offices and agencies relevant to these matters, including the training of personnel.

PART VII
INSITITUTIONAL ARRANGEMENTS; FINAL PROVISIONS

Article 68
Council for Trade-Related Aspects of Intellectual Property Rights

The Council for TRIPS shall monitor the operation of this Agreement and, in particular, Members' compliance with their obligations hereunder, and shall afford Members the opportunity of consulting on matters relating to the trade-related aspects of intellectual property rights. It shall carry out such other responsibilities as assigned to it by the Members, and it shall, in particular, provide any assistance requested by them in the context of dispute settlement procedures. In carrying out its functions, the Council for TRIPS may consult with and seek information from any source it deems appropriate. In consultation with WIPO, the Council shall seek to establish, within one year of its first meeting, appropriate arrangements for cooperation with bodies of that Organization.

Article 70
Protection of Existing Subject Matter

1 This Agreement does not give rise to obligations in respect of acts which occurred before the date of application of the Agreement for the Member in question.

2 Except as otherwise provided for in this Agreement, this Agreement gives rise to obligations in respect of all subject matter existing at the date of application of this Agreement for the Member in question, and which is protected in that Member on the said date, or which meets or comes subsequently to meet the criteria for protection under the terms of this Agreement. In respect of this paragraph and paragraphs 3 and 4, copyright obligations with respect to existing works shall be solely determined under Article 18 of the Berne Convention (1971), and obligations with respect to the rights of producers of phonograms and performers in existing phonograms

shall be determined solely under Article 18 of the Berne Convention (1971) as made applicable under paragraph 6 of Article 14 of this Agreement.

3 There shall be no obligation to restore protection to subject matter which on the date of application of this Agreement for the Member in question has fallen into the public domain.

4 In respect of any acts in respect of specific objects embodying protected subject matter which become infringing under the terms of legislation in conformity with this Agreement, and which were commenced, or in respect of which a significant investment was made, before the date of acceptance of the WTO Agreement by that Member, any Member may provide for a limitation of the remedies available to the right holder as to the continued performance of such acts after the date of application of this Agreement for that Member. In such cases the Member shall, however, at least provide for the payment of equitable remuneration.

5 A Member is not obliged to apply the provisions of Article 11 and of paragraph 4 of Article 14 with respect to originals or copies purchased prior to the date of application of this Agreement for that Member.

6 Members shall not be required to apply Article 31, or the requirement in paragraph 1 of Article 27 that patent rights shall be enjoyable without discrimination as to the field of technology, to use without the authorization of the right holder where authorization for such use was granted by the government before the date this Agreement became known.

7 In the case of intellectual property rights for which protection is conditional upon registration, applications for protection which are pending on the date of application of this Agreement for the Member in question shall be permitted to be amended to claim any enhanced protection provided under the provisions of this Agreement. Such amendments shall not include new matter.

8 Where a Member does not make available as of the date of entry into force of the WTO Agreement patent protection for pharmaceutical and agricultural chemical products commensurate with its obligations under Article 27, that Member shall:

(a) notwithstanding the provisions of Part VI, provide as from the date of entry into force of the WTO Agreement a means by which applications for patents for such inventions can be filed;

(b) apply to these applications, as of the date of application of this Agreement, the criteria for patentability as laid down in this Agreement as if those criteria were being applied on the date of filing in that Member or, where priority is available and claimed, the priority date of the application; and

(c) provide patent protection in accordance with this Agreement as from the grant of the patent and for the remainder of the patent term, counted from the filing date in accordance with Article 33 of this Agreement, for those of these applications that meet the criteria for protection referred to in subparagraph (b).

9 Where a product is the subject of a patent application in a Member in accordance with paragraph 8(a), exclusive marketing rights shall be granted, notwithstanding the provisions of Part VI, for a period of five years after obtaining marketing approval in that Member or until a product patent is granted or rejected in that Member, whichever period is shorter, provided that, subsequent to the entry into force of the WTO Agreement, a patent application has been filed and a patent granted for that product in another Member and marketing approval obtained in such other Member.

Article 71
Review and Amendment

1 The Council for TRIPS shall review the implementation of this Agreement after the expiration of the transitional period referred to in paragraph 2 of Article 65. The Council shall, having regard to the experience gained in its implementation, review it two years after that date, and at identical intervals thereafter. The Council may also undertake reviews in the light of any relevant new developments which might warrant modification or amendment of this Agreement.

2 Amendments merely serving the purpose of adjusting to higher levels of protection of intellectual property rights achieved, and in force, in other multilateral agreements and accepted under those agreements by all Members of the WTO may be referred to the Ministerial Conference for action in accordance with paragraph 6 of Article X of the WTO Agreement on the basis of a consensus proposal from the Council for TRIPS.

NOTES

1 When 'nationals' are referred to in this Agreement, they shall be deemed, in the case of a separate customs territory Member of the WTO, to mean persons, natural or legal, who are domiciled or who have a real and effective industrial or commercial establishment in that customs territory.

2 In this Agreement, 'Paris Convention' refers to the Paris Convention for the Protection of Industrial Property; 'Paris Convention (1967)' refers to the Stockholm Act of this Convention of 14 July 1967. 'Berne Convention' refers to the Berne Convention for the Protection of Literary and Artistic Works; 'Berne Convention (1971)' refers to the Paris Act of this Convention of 24 July 1971. 'Rome Convention' refers to the International Convention for the Protection of Performers, Producers of Phonograms and Broadcasting Organizations, adopted at Rome on 26 October 1961. 'Treaty on Intellectual Property in Respect of Integrated Circuits' (IPIC Treaty) refers to the Treaty on Intellectual Property in Respect of Integrated Circuits, adopted at Washington on 26 May 1989. 'WTO Agreement' refers to the Agreement Establishing the WTO.

3 For the purposes of Articles 3 and 4, 'protection' shall include matters affecting the availability, acquisition, scope, maintenance and enforcement of intellectual property rights as well as those matters affecting the use of intellectual property rights specifically addressed in this Agreement.

4 Notwithstanding the first sentence of Article 42, Members may, with respect to these obligations, instead provide for enforcement by administrative action.
5 For the purposes of this Article, the terms 'inventive step' and 'capable of industrial application' may be deemed by a Member to be synonymous with the terms 'non-obvious' and 'useful' respectively.
6 This right, like all other rights conferred under this Agreement in respect of the use, sale, importation or other distribution of goods, is subject to the provisions of Article 6.
7 'Other use' refers to use other than that allowed under Article 30.
8 It is understood that those Members which do not have a system of original grant may provide that the term of protection shall be computed from the filing date in the system of original grant.
9 For the purpose of this provision, 'a manner contrary to honest commercial practices' shall mean at least practices such as breach of contract, breach of confidence and inducement to breach, and includes the acquisition of undisclosed information by third parties who knew, or were grossly negligent in failing to know, that such practices were involved in the acquisition.

Annex 2

The Convention on Biological Diversity (Extracts)

PREAMBLE

The Contracting Parties,

Conscious of the intrinsic value of biological diversity and of the ecological, genetic, social, economic, scientific, educational, cultural, recreational and aesthetic values of biological diversity and its components,

Conscious also of the importance of biological diversity for evolution and for maintaining life sustaining systems of the biosphere,

Affirming that the conservation of biological diversity is a common concern of humankind,

Reaffirming that States have sovereign rights over their own biological resources,

Reaffirming also that States are responsible for conserving their biological diversity and for using their biological resources in a sustainable manner,

Concerned that biological diversity is being significantly reduced by certain human activities,

Aware of the general lack of information and knowledge regarding biological diversity and of the urgent need to develop scientific, technical and institutional capacities to provide the basic understanding upon which to plan and implement appropriate measures,

Noting that it is vital to anticipate, prevent and attack the causes of significant reduction or loss of biological diversity at source,

Noting also that where there is a threat of significant reduction or loss of biological diversity, lack of full scientific certainty should not be used as a reason for postponing measures to avoid or minimize such a threat,

Noting further that the fundamental requirement for the conservation of biological diversity is the in-situ conservation of ecosystems and natural habitats and the maintenance and recovery of viable populations of species in their natural surroundings,

Noting further that ex-situ measures, preferably in the country of origin, also have an important role to play,

Recognizing the close and traditional dependence of many indigenous and local communities embodying traditional lifestyles on biological resources, and the desirability of sharing equitably benefits arising from the use of traditional knowledge, innovations and practices relevant to the conservation of biological diversity and the sustainable use of its components,

Recognizing also the vital role that women play in the conservation and sustainable use of biological diversity and affirming the need for the full participation of women at all levels of policy-making and implementation for biological diversity conservation,

Stressing the importance of, and the need to promote, international, regional and global cooperation among States and intergovernmental organizations and the non-governmental sector for the conservation of biological diversity and the sustainable use of its components,

Acknowledging that the provision of new and additional financial resources and appropriate access to relevant technologies can be expected to make a substantial difference in the world's ability to address the loss of biological diversity,

Acknowledging further that special provision is required to meet the needs of developing countries, including the provision of new and additional financial resources and appropriate access to relevant technologies,

Noting in this regard the special conditions of the least developed countries and small island States,

Acknowledging that substantial investments are required to conserve biological diversity and that there is the expectation of a broad range of environmental, economic and social benefits from those investments,

Recognizing that economic and social development and poverty eradication are the first and over-riding priorities of developing countries,

Aware that conservation and sustainable use of biological diversity is of critical importance for meeting the food, health and other needs of the growing world population, for which purpose access to and sharing of both genetic resources and technologies are essential,

Noting that, ultimately, the conservation and sustainable use of biological diversity will strengthen friendly relations among States and contribute to peace for humankind,

Desiring to enhance and complement existing international arrangements for the conservation of biological diversity and sustainable use of its components, and

Determined to conserve and sustainably use biological diversity for the benefit of present and future generations,

Have agreed as follows:

Article 1. Objectives

The objectives of this Convention, to be pursued in accordance with its relevant provisions, are the conservation of biological diversity, the sustainable use of its components and the fair and equitable sharing of the benefits arising out of the utilization of genetic resources, including by appropriate access to genetic resources and by appropriate transfer of relevant technologies, taking into account all rights over those resources and to technologies, and by appropriate funding.

Article 2. Use of Terms

For the purposes of this Convention:

'Biological diversity' means the variability among living organisms from all sources including, inter alia, terrestrial, marine and other aquatic ecosystems and the ecological complexes of which they are part; this includes diversity within species, between species and of ecosystems.

'Biological resources' includes genetic resources, organisms or parts thereof, populations, or any other biotic component of ecosystems with actual or potential use or value for humanity.

'Biotechnology' means any technological application that uses biological systems, living organisms, or derivatives thereof, to make or modify products or processes for specific use.

'Country of origin of genetic resources' means the country which possesses those genetic resources in in-situ conditions.

'Country providing genetic resources' means the country supplying genetic resources collected from in-situ sources, including populations of both wild and domesticated species, or taken from ex-situ sources, which may or may not have originated in that country.

'Domesticated or cultivated species' means species in which the evolutionary process has been influenced by humans to meet their needs.

'Ecosystem' means a dynamic complex of plant, animal and micro-organism communities and their non-living environment interacting as a functional unit.

'Ex-situ conservation' means the conservation of components of biological diversity outside their natural habitats.

'Genetic material' means any material of plant, animal, microbial or other origin containing functional units of heredity.

'Genetic resources' means genetic material of actual or potential value.

'Habitat' means the place or type of site where an organism or population naturally occurs.

'In-situ conditions' means conditions where genetic resources exist within ecosystems and natural habitats, and, in the case of domesticated or cultivated species, in the surroundings where they have developed their distinctive properties.

'In-situ conservation' means the conservation of ecosystems and natural habitats and the maintenance and recovery of viable populations of species in their natural surroundings and, in the case of domesticated or cultivated species, in the surroundings where they have developed their distinctive properties.

'Protected area' means a geographically defined area which is designated or regulated and managed to achieve specific conservation objectives.

'Regional economic integration organization' means an organization constituted by sovereign States of a given region, to which its member States have transferred competence in respect of matters governed by this Convention and which has been duly authorized, in accordance with its internal procedures, to sign, ratify, accept, approve or accede to it.

'Sustainable use' means the use of components of biological diversity in a way and at a rate that does not lead to the long-term decline of biological diversity, thereby maintaining its potential to meet the needs and aspirations of present and future generations.

'Technology' includes biotechnology.

Article 3. Principle

States have, in accordance with the Charter of the United Nations and the principles of international law, the sovereign right to exploit their own resources pursuant to their own environmental policies, and the responsibility to ensure that activities within their jurisdiction or control do not cause damage to the environment of other States or of areas beyond the limits of national jurisdiction.

Article 4. Jurisdictional Scope

Subject to the rights of other States, and except as otherwise expressly provided in this Convention, the provisions of this Convention apply, in relation to each Contracting Party:

(a) In the case of components of biological diversity, in areas within the limits of its national jurisdiction; and

(b) In the case of processes and activities, regardless of where their effects occur, carried out under its jurisdiction or control, within the area of its national jurisdiction or beyond the limits of national jurisdiction.

Article 6. General Measures for Conservation and Sustainable Use

Each Contracting Party shall, in accordance with its particular conditions and capabilities:

(a) Develop national strategies, plans or programmes for the conservation and sustainable use of biological diversity or adapt for this purpose existing strategies, plans or programmes which shall reflect, inter alia, the measures set out in this Convention relevant to the Contracting Party concerned; and

(b) Integrate, as far as possible and as appropriate, the conservation and sustainable use of biological diversity into relevant sectoral or cross-sectoral plans, programmes and policies.

Article 8. In-situ Conservation

Each Contracting Party shall, as far as possible and as appropriate:

(a) Establish a system of protected areas or areas where special measures need to be taken to conserve biological diversity;

(b) Develop, where necessary, guidelines for the selection, establishment and management of protected areas or areas where special measures need to be taken to conserve biological diversity;

(c) Regulate or manage biological resources important for the conservation of biological diversity whether within or outside protected areas, with a view to ensuring their conservation and sustainable use;

(d) Promote the protection of ecosystems, natural habitats and the maintenance of viable populations of species in natural surroundings;

(e) Promote environmentally sound and sustainable development in areas adjacent to protected areas with a view to furthering protection of these areas;

(f) Rehabilitate and restore degraded ecosystems and promote the recovery of threatened species, inter alia, through the development and implementation of plans or other management strategies;

(g) Establish or maintain means to regulate, manage or control the risks associated with the use and release of living modified organisms resulting from biotechnology which are likely to have adverse environmental impacts that could affect the conservation and sustainable use of biological diversity, taking also into account the risks to human health;

(h) Prevent the introduction of, control or eradicate those alien species which threaten ecosystems, habitats or species;

(i) Endeavour to provide the conditions needed for compatibility between present uses and the conservation of biological diversity and the sustainable use of its components;

(j) Subject to its national legislation, respect, preserve and maintain knowledge, innovations and practices of indigenous and local communities embodying traditional lifestyles relevant for the conservation and sustainable use of biological diversity and promote their wider application with the approval and involvement of the holders of such knowledge, innovations and practices and encourage the equitable sharing of the benefits arising from the utilization of such knowledge, innovations and practices;

(k) Develop or maintain necessary legislation and/or other regulatory provisions for the protection of threatened species and populations;

(l) Where a significant adverse effect on biological diversity has been determined pursuant to Article 7, regulate or manage the relevant processes and categories of activities; and

(m) Cooperate in providing financial and other support for in-situ conservation outlined in subparagraphs (a) to (l) above, particularly to developing countries.

Article 9. Ex-situ Conservation

Each Contracting Party shall, as far as possible and as appropriate, and predominantly for the purpose of complementing in-situ measures:

(a) Adopt measures for the ex-situ conservation of components of biological diversity, preferably in the country of origin of such components;

(b) Establish and maintain facilities for ex-situ conservation of and research on plants, animals and micro-organisms, preferably in the country of origin of genetic resources;

(c) Adopt measures for the recovery and rehabilitation of threatened species and for their reintroduction into their natural habitats under appropriate conditions;

(d) Regulate and manage collection of biological resources from natural habitats for ex-situ conservation purposes so as not to threaten ecosystems and in-situ populations of species, except where special temporary ex-situ measures are required under subparagraph (c) above; and

(e) Cooperate in providing financial and other support for ex-situ conservation outlined in subparagraphs (a) to (d) above and in the establishment and maintenance of ex-situ conservation facilities in developing countries.

Article 10. Sustainable Use of Components of Biological Diversity

Each Contracting Party shall, as far as possible and as appropriate:

(a) Integrate consideration of the conservation and sustainable use of biological resources into national decision-making;

(b) Adopt measures relating to the use of biological resources to avoid or minimize adverse impacts on biological diversity;

(c) Protect and encourage customary use of biological resources in accordance with traditional cultural practices that are compatible with conservation or sustainable use requirements;

(d) Support local populations to develop and implement remedial action in degraded areas where biological diversity has been reduced; and

(e) Encourage cooperation between its governmental authorities and its private sector in developing methods for sustainable use of biological resources.

Article 11. Incentive Measures

Each Contracting Party shall, as far as possible and as appropriate, adopt economically and socially sound measures that act as incentives for the conservation and sustainable use of components of biological diversity.

Article 12. Research and Training

The Contracting Parties, taking into account the special needs of developing countries, shall:

(a) Establish and maintain programmes for scientific and technical education and training in measures for the identification, conservation and sustainable use of biological diversity and its components and provide support for such education and training for the specific needs of developing countries;

(b) Promote and encourage research which contributes to the conservation and sustainable use of biological diversity, particularly in developing countries, inter alia, in accordance with decisions of the Conference of the Parties taken in consequence of recommendations of the Subsidiary Body on Scientific, Technical and Technological Advice; and

(c) In keeping with the provisions of Articles 16, 18 and 20, promote and cooperate in the use of scientific advances in biological diversity research in developing methods for conservation and sustainable use of biological resources.

Article 15. Access to Genetic Resources

1 Recognizing the sovereign rights of States over their natural resources, the authority to determine access to genetic resources rests with the national governments and is subject to national legislation.

2 Each Contracting Party shall endeavour to create conditions to facilitate access to genetic resources for environmentally sound uses by other Contracting Parties and not to impose restrictions that run counter to the objectives of this Convention.

3 For the purpose of this Convention, the genetic resources being provided by a Contracting Party, as referred to in this Article and Articles 16 and 19, are only those that are provided by Contracting Parties that are countries of origin of such resources or by the Parties that have acquired the genetic resources in accordance with this Convention.

4 Access, where granted, shall be on mutually agreed terms and subject to the provisions of this Article.

5 Access to genetic resources shall be subject to prior informed consent of the Contracting Party providing such resources, unless otherwise determined by that Party.

6 Each Contracting Party shall endeavour to develop and carry out scientific research based on genetic resources provided by other Contracting Parties with the full participation of, and where possible in, such Contracting Parties.

7 Each Contracting Party shall take legislative, administrative or policy measures, as appropriate, and in accordance with Articles 16 and 19 and, where necessary, through the financial mechanism established by Articles 20 and 21 with the aim of sharing in a fair and equitable way the results of research and development and the benefits arising from the commercial and other utilization of genetic resources with the Contracting Party providing such resources. Such sharing shall be upon mutually agreed terms.

Article 16. Access to and Transfer of Technology

1 Each Contracting Party, recognizing that technology includes biotechnology, and that both access to and transfer of technology among Contracting Parties are essential elements for the attainment of the objectives of this Convention, undertakes subject to the provisions of this Article to provide and/or facilitate access for and transfer to other Contracting Parties of technologies that are relevant to the conservation and sustainable use of biological diversity or make use of genetic resources and do not cause significant damage to the environment.

2 Access to and transfer of technology referred to in paragraph 1 above to developing countries shall be provided and/or facilitated under fair and most favourable terms, including on concessional and preferential terms where mutually agreed, and, where necessary, in accordance with the financial mechanism established by Articles 20 and 21. In the case of technology subject to patents and other intellectual property rights, such access and transfer shall be provided on terms which recognize and are consistent with the adequate and effective protection of intellectual property rights. The application of this paragraph shall be consistent with paragraphs 3, 4 and 5 below.

3 Each Contracting Party shall take legislative, administrative or policy measures, as appropriate, with the aim that Contracting Parties, in particular those that are developing countries, which provide genetic resources are provided access to and transfer of technology which makes use of those

resources, on mutually agreed terms, including technology protected by patents and other intellectual property rights, where necessary, through the provisions of Articles 20 and 21 and in accordance with international law and consistent with paragraphs 4 and 5 below.

4 Each Contracting Party shall take legislative, administrative or policy measures, as appropriate, with the aim that the private sector facilitates access to, joint development and transfer of technology referred to in paragraph 1 above for the benefit of both governmental institutions and the private sector of developing countries and in this regard shall abide by the obligations included in paragraphs 1, 2 and 3 above.

5 The Contracting Parties, recognizing that patents and other intellectual property rights may have an influence on the implementation of this Convention, shall cooperate in this regard subject to national legislation and international law in order to ensure that such rights are supportive of and do not run counter to its objectives.

Article 17. Exchange of Information

1 The Contracting Parties shall facilitate the exchange of information, from all publicly available sources, relevant to the conservation and sustainable use of biological diversity, taking into account the special needs of developing countries.

2 Such exchange of information shall include exchange of results of technical, scientific and socio-economic research, as well as information on training and surveying programmes, specialized knowledge, indigenous and traditional knowledge as such and in combination with the technologies referred to in Article 16, paragraph 1. It shall also, where feasible, include repatriation of information.

Article 18. Technical and Scientific Cooperation

1 The Contracting Parties shall promote international technical and scientific cooperation in the field of conservation and sustainable use of biological diversity, where necessary, through the appropriate international and national institutions.

2 Each Contracting Party shall promote technical and scientific cooperation with other Contracting Parties, in particular developing countries, in implementing this Convention, inter alia, through the development and implementation of national policies. In promoting such cooperation, special attention should be given to the development and strengthening of national capabilities, by means of human resources development and institution building.

3 The Conference of the Parties, at its first meeting, shall determine how to establish a clearing-house mechanism to promote and facilitate technical and scientific cooperation.

4 The Contracting Parties shall, in accordance with national legislation and policies, encourage and develop methods of cooperation for the development and use of technologies, including indigenous and traditional technologies, in pursuance of the objectives of this Convention. For this purpose, the Contracting Parties shall also promote cooperation in the training of personnel and exchange of experts.

5 The Contracting Parties shall, subject to mutual agreement, promote the establishment of joint research programmes and joint ventures for the development of technologies relevant to the objectives of this Convention.

Article 19. Handling of Biotechnology and Distribution of its Benefits

1 Each Contracting Party shall take legislative, administrative or policy measures, as appropriate, to provide for the effective participation in biotechnological research activities by those Contracting Parties, especially developing countries, which provide the genetic resources for such research, and where feasible in such Contracting Parties.

2 Each Contracting Party shall take all practicable measures to promote and advance priority access on a fair and equitable basis by Contracting Parties, especially developing countries, to the results and benefits arising from biotechnologies based upon genetic resources provided by those Contracting Parties. Such access shall be on mutually agreed terms.

3 The Parties shall consider the need for and modalities of a protocol setting out appropriate procedures, including, in particular, advance informed agreement, in the field of the safe transfer, handling and use of any living modified organism resulting from biotechnology that may have adverse effect on the conservation and sustainable use of biological diversity.

4 Each Contracting Party shall, directly or by requiring any natural or legal person under its jurisdiction providing the organisms referred to in paragraph 3 above, provide any available information about the use and safety regulations required by that Contracting Party in handling such organisms, as well as any available information on the potential adverse impact of the specific organisms concerned to the Contracting Party into which those organisms are to be introduced.

Article 22. Relationship with Other International Conventions

1 The provisions of this Convention shall not affect the rights and obligations of any Contracting Party deriving from any existing international agreement, except where the exercise of those rights and obligations would cause a serious damage or threat to biological diversity.

2 Contracting Parties shall implement this Convention with respect to the marine environment consistently with the rights and obligations of States under the law of the sea.

Article 23. Conference of the Parties

1 Conference of the Parties is hereby established. The first meeting of the Conference of the Parties shall be convened by the Executive Director of the United Nations Environment Programme not later than one year after the entry into force of this Convention. Thereafter, ordinary meetings of the Conference of the Parties shall be held at regular intervals to be determined by the Conference at its first meeting.

2 Extraordinary meetings of the Conference of the Parties shall be held at such other times as may be deemed necessary by the Conference, or at the written request of any Party, provided that, within six months of the request being communicated to them by the Secretariat, it is supported by at least one third of the Parties.

3 The Conference of the Parties shall by consensus agree upon and adopt rules of procedure for itself and for any subsidiary body it may establish, as well as financial rules governing the funding of the Secretariat. At each ordinary meeting, it shall adopt a budget for the financial period until the next ordinary meeting.

4 The Conference of the Parties shall keep under review the implementation of this Convention, and, for this purpose, shall:

(a) Establish the form and the intervals for transmitting the information to be submitted in accordance with Article 26 and consider such information as well as reports submitted by any subsidiary body;

(b) Review scientific, technical and technological advice on biological diversity provided in accordance with Article 25;

(c) Consider and adopt, as required, protocols in accordance with Article 28;

(d) Consider and adopt, as required, in accordance with Articles 29 and 30, amendments to this Convention and its annexes;

(e) Consider amendments to any protocol, as well as to any annexes thereto, and, if so decided, recommend their adoption to the parties to the protocol concerned;

(f) Consider and adopt, as required, in accordance with Article 30, additional annexes to this Convention;

(g) Establish such subsidiary bodies, particularly to provide scientific and technical advice, as are deemed necessary for the implementation of this Convention;

(h) Contact, through the Secretariat, the executive bodies of conventions dealing with matters covered by this Convention with a view to establishing appropriate forms of cooperation with them; and

(i) Consider and undertake any additional action that may be required for the achievement of the purposes of this Convention in the light of experience gained in its operation.

5 The United Nations, its specialized agencies and the International Atomic Energy Agency, as well as any State not Party to this Convention, may be represented as observers at meetings of the Conference of the Parties. Any other body or agency, whether governmental or non-governmental, qualified in fields relating to conservation and sustainable use of biological diversity, which has informed the Secretariat of its wish to be represented as an observer at a meeting of the Conference of the Parties, may be admitted unless at least one third of the Parties present object. The admission and participation of observers shall be subject to the rules of procedure adopted by the Conference of the Parties.

Annex 3

International Treaty on Plant Genetic Resources for Food and Agriculture (Extracts)

PREAMBLE

The Contracting Parties,

Convinced of the special nature of plant genetic resources for food and agriculture, their distinctive features and problems needing distinctive solutions;

Alarmed by the continuing erosion of these resources;

Cognizant that plant genetic resources for food and agriculture are a common concern of all countries, in that all countries depend very largely on plant genetic resources for food and agriculture that originated elsewhere;

Acknowledging that the conservation, exploration, collection, characterization, evaluation and documentation of plant genetic resources for food and agriculture are essential in meeting the goals of the Rome Declaration on World Food Security and the World Food Summit Plan of Action and for sustainable agricultural development for this and future generations, and that the capacity of developing countries and countries with economies in transition to undertake such tasks needs urgently to be reinforced;

Noting that the Global Plan of Action for the Conservation and Sustainable Use of Plant Genetic Resources for Food and Agriculture is an internationally agreed framework for such activities;

Acknowledging further that plant genetic resources for food and agriculture are the raw material indispensable for crop genetic improvement, whether by means of farmers' selection, classical plant breeding or modern biotechnologies, and are essential in adapting to unpredictable environmental changes and future human needs;

Affirming that the past, present and future contributions of farmers in all regions of the world, particularly those in centres of origin and diversity, in conserving, improving and making available these resources, is the basis of Farmers' Rights;

Affirming also that the rights recognized in this Treaty to save, use, exchange and sell farm-saved seed and other propagating material, and to participate in decision-making regarding, and in the fair and equitable sharing of the benefits arising from, the use of plant genetic resources for food and agriculture, are fundamental to the realization of Farmers' Rights, as well as the promotion of Farmers' Rights at national and international levels;

Recognizing that this Treaty and other international agreements relevant to this Treaty should be mutually supportive with a view to sustainable agriculture and food security;

Affirming that nothing in this Treaty shall be interpreted as implying in any way a change in the rights and obligations of the Contracting Parties under other international agreements;

Understanding that the above recital is not intended to create a hierarchy between this Treaty and other international agreements;

Aware that questions regarding the management of plant genetic resources for food and agriculture are at the meeting point between agriculture, the environment and commerce, and convinced that there should be synergy among these sectors;

Aware of their responsibility to past and future generations to conserve the World's diversity of plant genetic resources for food and agriculture;

Recognizing that, in the exercise of their sovereign rights over their plant genetic resources for food and agriculture, states may mutually benefit from the creation of an effective multilateral system for facilitated access to a negotiated selection of these resources and for the fair and equitable sharing of the benefits arising from their use; and

Desiring to conclude an international agreement within the framework of the Food and Agriculture Organization of the United Nations, hereinafter referred to as FAO, under Article XIV of the FAO Constitution;

Have agreed as follows:

PART I – INTRODUCTION

Article 1 – Objectives

1.1 The objectives of this Treaty are the conservation and sustainable use of plant genetic resources for food and agriculture and the fair and equitable sharing of the benefits arising out of their use, in harmony with the Convention on Biological Diversity, for sustainable agriculture and food security.

1.2 These objectives will be attained by closely linking this Treaty to the Food and Agriculture Organization of the United Nations and to the Convention on Biological Diversity.

Article 2 – Use of Terms

For the purpose of this Treaty, the following terms shall have the meanings hereunder assigned to them. These definitions are not intended to cover trade in commodities:

'In situ conservation' means the conservation of ecosystems and natural habitats and the maintenance and recovery of viable populations of species in their natural surroundings and, in the case of domesticated or cultivated plant species, in the surroundings where they have developed their distinctive properties.

'Ex situ conservation' means the conservation of plant genetic resources for food and agriculture outside their natural habitat.

'Plant genetic resources for food and agriculture' means any genetic material of plant origin of actual or potential value for food and agriculture.

'Genetic material' means any material of plant origin, including reproductive and vegetative propagating material, containing functional units of heredity.

'Variety' means a plant grouping, within a single botanical taxon of the lowest known rank, defined by the reproducible expression of its distinguishing and other genetic characteristics.

'Ex situ collection' means a collection of plant genetic resources for food and agriculture maintained outside their natural habitat.

'Centre of origin' means a geographical area where a plant species, either domesticated or wild, first developed its distinctive properties.

'Centre of crop diversity' means a geographic area containing a high level of genetic diversity for crop species in in situ conditions.

Article 3 – Scope

This Treaty relates to plant genetic resources for food and agriculture.

PART II – GENERAL PROVISIONS

Article 4 – General Obligations

Each Contracting Party shall ensure the conformity of its laws, regulations and procedures with its obligations as provided in this Treaty.

Article 5 – Conservation, Exploration, Collection, Characterization, Evaluation and Documentation of Plant Genetic Resources for Food and Agriculture

5.1 Each Contracting Party shall, subject to national legislation, and in cooperation with other Contracting Parties where appropriate, promote an integrated approach to the exploration, conservation and sustainable use of plant genetic resources for food and agriculture and shall in particular, as appropriate:

(a) Survey and inventory plant genetic resources for food and agriculture, taking into account the status and degree of variation in existing populations, including those that are of potential use and, as feasible, assess any threats to them;

(b) Promote the collection of plant genetic resources for food and agriculture and relevant associated information on those plant genetic resources that are under threat or are of potential use;

(c) Promote or support, as appropriate, farmers and local communities' efforts to manage and conserve on-farm their plant genetic resources for food and agriculture;

(d) Promote in situ conservation of wild crop relatives and wild plants for food production, including in protected areas, by supporting, inter alia, the efforts of indigenous and local communities;

(e) Cooperate to promote the development of an efficient and sustainable system of ex situ conservation, giving due attention to the need for adequate documentation, characterization, regeneration and evaluation, and promote the development and transfer of appropriate technologies for this purpose with a view to improving the sustainable use of plant genetic resources for food and agriculture; and

(f) Monitor the maintenance of the viability, degree of variation, and the genetic integrity of collections of plant genetic resources for food and agriculture.

5.2 The Contracting Parties shall, as appropriate, take steps to minimize or, if possible, eliminate threats to plant genetic resources for food and agriculture.

Article 6 – Sustainable Use of Plant Genetic Resources

6.1 The Contracting Parties shall develop and maintain appropriate policy and legal measures that promote the sustainable use of plant genetic resources for food and agriculture.

6.2 The sustainable use of plant genetic resources for food and agriculture may include such measures as:

(a) pursuing fair agricultural policies that promote, as appropriate, the development and maintenance of diverse farming systems that enhance the sustainable use of agricultural biological diversity and other natural resources;

(b) strengthening research which enhances and conserves biological diversity by maximizing intra- and inter-specific variation for the benefit of farmers, especially those who generate and use their own varieties and apply ecological principles in maintaining soil fertility and in combating diseases, weeds and pests;

(c) promoting, as appropriate, plant breeding efforts which, with the participation of farmers, particularly in developing countries, strengthen the capacity to develop varieties particularly adapted to social, economic and ecological conditions, including in marginal areas;

(d) broadening the genetic base of crops and increasing the range of genetic diversity available to farmers;

(e) promoting, as appropriate, the expanded use of local and locally adapted crops, varieties and underutilized species;

(f) supporting, as appropriate, the wider use of diversity of varieties and species in on-farm management, conservation and sustainable use of crops and creating strong links to plant breeding and agricultural development in order to reduce crop vulnerability and genetic erosion, and promote increased world food production compatible with sustainable development; and

(g) reviewing, and, as appropriate, adjusting breeding strategies and regulations concerning variety release and seed distribution.

Article 7 – National Commitments and International Cooperation

7.1 Each Contracting Party shall, as appropriate, integrate into its agriculture and rural development policies and programmes, activities referred to in Articles 5 and 6, and cooperate with other Contracting Parties, directly or through FAO and other relevant international organizations, in the conservation and sustainable use of plant genetic resources for food and agriculture.

7.2 International cooperation shall, in particular, be directed to:

(a) establishing or strengthening the capabilities of developing countries and countries with economies in transition with respect to conservation and sustainable use of plant genetic resources for food and agriculture;

(b) enhancing international activities to promote conservation, evaluation, documentation, genetic enhancement, plant breeding, seed multiplication; and sharing, providing access to, and exchanging, in conformity with Part IV, plant genetic resources for food and agriculture and appropriate information and technology;

(c) maintaining and strengthening the institutional arrangements provided for in Part V; and

(d) implement the funding strategy of Article 18.

Article 8 – Technical Assistance

The Contracting Parties agree to promote the provision of technical assistance to Contracting Parties, especially those that are developing countries or countries with economies in transition, either bilaterally or through the appropriate international organizations, with the objective of facilitating the implementation of this Treaty.

PART III – FARMERS' RIGHTS

Article 9 – Farmers' Rights

9.1 The Contracting Parties recognize the enormous contribution that the local and indigenous communities and farmers of all regions of the world, particularly those in the centres of origin and crop diversity, have made and will continue to make for the conservation and development of plant genetic resources which constitute the basis of food and agriculture production throughout the world.

9.2 The Contracting Parties agree that the responsibility for realizing Farmers' Rights, as they relate to plant genetic resources for food and agriculture, rests with national governments. In accordance with their needs and priorities, each Contracting Party should, as appropriate, and subject to its national legislation, take measures to protect and promote Farmers' Rights, including:

(a) protection of traditional knowledge relevant to plant genetic resources for food and agriculture;

(b) the right to equitably participate in sharing benefits arising from the utilization of plant genetic resources for food and agriculture; and

(c) the right to participate in making decisions, at the national level, on matters related to the conservation and sustainable use of plant genetic resources for food and agriculture.

9.3 Nothing in this Article shall be interpreted to limit any rights that farmers have to save, use, exchange and sell farm-saved seed/propagating material, subject to national law and as appropriate.

PART IV – THE MULTILATERAL SYSTEM OF ACCESS AND BENEFIT-SHARING

Article 10 – Multilateral System of Access and Benefit-sharing

10.1 In their relationships with other States, the Contracting Parties recognize the sovereign rights of States over their own plant genetic resources for food and agriculture, including that the authority to determine access to those resources rests with national governments and is subject to national legislation.

10.2 In the exercise of their sovereign rights, the Contracting Parties agree to establish a multilateral system, which is efficient, effective, and transparent, both to facilitate access to plant genetic resources for food and agriculture, and to share, in a fair and equitable way, the benefits arising from the utilization of these resources, on a complementary and mutually reinforcing basis.

Article 11 – Coverage of the Multilateral System

11.1 In furtherance of the objectives of conservation and sustainable use of plant genetic resources for food and agriculture and the fair and equitable sharing of benefits arising out of their use, as stated in Article 1, the Multilateral System shall cover the plant genetic resources for food and agriculture listed in Annex I, established according to criteria of food security and interdependence.

11.2 The Multilateral System, as identified in Article 11.1, shall include all plant genetic resources for food and agriculture listed in Annex I that are under the management and control of the Contracting Parties and in the public domain. With a view to achieving the fullest possible coverage of the Multilateral System, the Contracting Parties invite all other holders of the plant genetic resources for food and agriculture listed in Annex I to include these plant genetic resources for food and agriculture in the Multilateral System.

11.3 Contracting Parties also agree to take appropriate measures to encourage natural and legal persons within their jurisdiction who hold plant genetic resources for food and agriculture listed in Annex I to include such plant genetic resources for food and agriculture in the Multilateral System.

11.4 Within two years of the entry into force of the Treaty, the Governing Body shall assess the progress in including the plant genetic resources for food and agriculture referred to in paragraph 11.3 in the Multilateral System. Following this assessment, the Governing Body shall decide whether access shall continue to be facilitated to those natural and legal persons referred to in paragraph 11.3 that have not included these plant genetic resources for food and agriculture in the Multilateral System, or take such other measures as it deems appropriate.

11.5 The Multilateral System shall also include the plant genetic resources for food and agriculture listed in Annex I and held in the ex situ collections of the International Agricultural Research Centres of the Consultative Group on International Agricultural Research (CGIAR), as provided in Article 15.1a, and in other international institutions, in accordance with Article 15.5.

Article 12 – Facilitated Access to Plant Genetic Resources for Food and Agriculture within the Multilateral System

12.1 The Contracting Parties agree that facilitated access to plant genetic resources for food and agriculture under the Multilateral System, as defined in Article 11, shall be in accordance with the provisions of this Treaty.

12.2 The Contracting Parties agree to take the necessary legal or other appropriate measures to provide such access to other Contracting Parties through the Multilateral System. To this effect, such access shall also be provided to legal and natural persons under the jurisdiction of any Contracting Party, subject to the provisions of Article 11.4.

12.3 Such access shall be provided in accordance with the conditions below:

(a) Access shall be provided solely for the purpose of utilization and conservation for research, breeding and training for food and agriculture, provided that such purpose does not include chemical, pharmaceutical and/or other non-food/feed industrial uses. In the case of multiple-use crops (food and non-food), their importance for food security should be the determinant for their inclusion in the Multilateral System and availability for facilitated access.

(b) Access shall be accorded expeditiously, without the need to track individual accessions and free of charge, or, when a fee is charged, it shall not exceed the minimal cost involved;

(c) All available passport data and, subject to applicable law, any other associated available non-confidential descriptive information, shall be made available with the plant genetic resources for food and agriculture provided;

(d) Recipients shall not claim any intellectual property or other rights that limit the facilitated access to the plant genetic resources for food and agriculture, or their genetic parts or components, in the form received from the Multilateral System;

(e) Access to plant genetic resources for food and agriculture under development, including material being developed by farmers, shall be at the discretion of its developer, during the period of its development;

(f) Access to plant genetic resources for food and agriculture protected by intellectual and other property rights shall be consistent with relevant international agreements, and with relevant national laws;

(g) Plant genetic resources for food and agriculture accessed under the Multilateral System and conserved shall continue to be made available to the Multilateral System by the recipients of those plant genetic resources for food and agriculture, under the terms of this Treaty; and

(h) Without prejudice to the other provisions under this Article, the Contracting Parties agree that access to plant genetic resources for food and agriculture found in in situ conditions will be provided according to national legislation or, in the absence of such legislation, in accordance with such standards as may be set by the Governing Body.

12.4 To this effect, facilitated access, in accordance with Articles 12.2 and 12.3 above, shall be provided pursuant to a standard material transfer agreement (MTA), which shall be adopted by the Governing Body and contain the provisions of Articles 12.3a, d and g, as well as the benefit-sharing provisions set forth in Article 13.2d(ii) and other relevant provisions of this Treaty, and the provision that the recipient of the plant genetic resources for food and agriculture shall require that the conditions of the MTA shall apply to the transfer of plant genetic resources for food and agriculture to another person or entity, as well as to any subsequent transfers of those plant genetic resources for food and agriculture.

12.5 Contracting Parties shall ensure that an opportunity to seek recourse is available, consistent with applicable jurisdictional requirements, under their legal systems, in case of contractual disputes arising under such MTAs, recognizing that obligations arising under such MTAs rest exclusively with the parties to those MTAs.

12.6 In emergency disaster situations, the Contracting Parties agree to provide facilitated access to appropriate plant genetic resources for food and agriculture in the Multilateral System for the purpose of contributing to the re-establishment of agricultural systems, in cooperation with disaster relief co-ordinators.

Article 13 – Benefit-sharing in the Multilateral System

13.1 The Contracting Parties recognize that facilitated access to plant genetic resources for food and agriculture which are included in the Multilateral System constitutes itself a major benefit of the Multilateral System and agree that benefits accruing therefrom shall be shared fairly and equitably in accordance with the provisions of this Article.

13.2 The Contracting Parties agree that benefits arising from the use, including commercial, of plant genetic resources for food and agriculture under the Multilateral System shall be shared fairly and equitably through the following mechanisms: the exchange of information, access to and transfer of technology, capacity-building, and the sharing of the benefits arising from commercialization, taking into account the priority activity areas in the rolling Global Plan of Action, under the guidance of the Governing Body:

(a) Exchange of information

The Contracting Parties agree to make available information which shall, inter alia, encompass catalogues and inventories, information on technologies, results of technical, scientific and socio-economic research, including characterization, evaluation and utilization, regarding those plant genetic resources for food and agriculture under the Multilateral System. Such information shall be made available, where non-confidential, subject to applicable law and in accordance with national capabilities. Such information shall be made available to all Contracting Parties to this Treaty through the information system, provided for in Article 17.

(b) Access to and transfer of technology

(i) The Contracting Parties undertake to provide and/or facilitate access to technologies for the conservation, characterization, evaluation and use of plant genetic resources for food and agriculture which are under the Multilateral System. Recognizing that some technologies can only be transferred through genetic material, the Contracting Parties shall provide and/or facilitate access to such technologies and genetic material which is under the Multilateral System and to improved varieties and genetic material developed through the use of plant genetic resources for food and agriculture under the Multilateral System, in conformity with the provisions of Article 12. Access to these technologies, improved varieties and genetic material shall be provided and/or facilitated, while respecting applicable property rights and access laws, and in accordance with national capabilities.

(ii) Access to and transfer of technology to countries, especially to developing countries and countries with economies in transition, shall be carried out through a set of measures, such as the establishment and maintenance of, and participation in, crop-based thematic groups on utilization of plant genetic resources for food and agriculture, all types of partnership in research and development and in commercial joint ventures relating to the material received, human resource development, and effective access to research facilities.

(iii) Access to and transfer of technology as referred to in (i) and (ii) above, including that protected by intellectual property rights, to developing countries that are Contracting Parties, in particular least developed countries, and countries with economies in transition, shall be provided and/or facilitated under fair and most favourable terms, in particular in the case of technologies for use in conservation as well as technologies for the benefit of farmers in developing countries, especially in least developed countries, and countries with economies in transition, including on concessional and preferential terms where mutually agreed, inter alia, through partnerships in research and development under the Multilateral System. Such access and transfer shall be provided on terms which recognize and are consistent with the adequate and effective protection of intellectual property rights.

(c) Capacity building

Taking into account the needs of developing countries and countries with economies in transition, as expressed through the priority they accord to building capacity in plant genetic resources for food and agriculture in their plans and programmes, when in place, in respect of those plant genetic resources for food and agriculture covered by the Multilateral System, the Contracting Parties agree to give priority to (i) establishing and/or strengthening programmes for scientific and technical education and training in conservation and sustainable use of plant genetic resources for food and agriculture, (ii) developing and strengthening facilities for conservation and sustainable use of plant genetic resources for food and agriculture, in particular in developing countries, and countries with economies in transition, and (iii) carrying out scientific research preferably, and where possible, in developing countries and countries with economies in transition, in cooperation with institutions of such countries, and developing capacity for such research in fields where they are needed.

(d) Sharing of monetary and other benefits of commercialization

(i) The Contracting Parties agree, under the Multilateral System, to take measures in order to achieve commercial benefit-sharing, through the involvement of the private and public sectors in activities identified under this Article, through partnerships and collaboration, including with the private sector in developing countries and countries with economies in transition, in research and technology development;

(ii) The Contracting Parties agree that the standard material transfer agreement referred to in Article 12.4 shall include a requirement that a recipient who commercializes a product that is a plant genetic resource for food and agriculture and that incorporates material accessed from the Multilateral System, shall pay to the mechanism referred to in Article 19.3f, an equitable share of the benefits arising from the commercialization of that product, except whenever such a product is available without restriction to others for further research and breeding, in which case the recipient who commercializes shall be encouraged to make such payment.

The Governing Body shall, at its first meeting, determine the level, form and manner of the payment, in line with commercial practice. The Governing Body may decide to establish different levels of payment for various categories of recipients who commercialize such products; it may also decide on the need to exempt from such payments small farmers in developing countries and in countries with economies in transition. The Governing Body may, from time to time, review the levels of payment with a view to achieving fair and equitable sharing of benefits, and it may also assess, within a period of five years from the entry into force of this Treaty, whether the mandatory payment requirement in the MTA shall apply also in cases where such commercialized products are available without restriction to others for further research and breeding.

13.3 The Contracting Parties agree that benefits arising from the use of plant genetic resources for food and agriculture that are shared under the Multilateral System should flow primarily, directly and indirectly, to farmers in all countries, especially in developing countries, and countries with economies in transition, who conserve and sustainably utilize plant genetic resources for food and agriculture.

13.4 The Governing Body shall, at its first meeting, consider relevant policy and criteria for specific assistance under the agreed funding strategy established under Article 18 for the conservation of plant genetic resources for food and agriculture in developing countries, and countries with economies in transition whose contribution to the diversity of plant genetic resources for food and agriculture in the Multilateral System is significant and/or which have special needs.

13.5 The Contracting Parties recognize that the ability to fully implement the Global Plan of Action, in particular of developing countries and countries with economies in transition, will depend largely upon the effective implementation of this Article and of the funding strategy as provided in Article 18.

13.6 The Contracting Parties shall consider modalities of a strategy of voluntary benefit-sharing contributions whereby Food Processing Industries that benefit from plant genetic resources for food and agriculture shall contribute to the Multilateral System.

PART V – SUPPORTING COMPONENTS

Article 14 – Global Plan of Action

Recognizing that the rolling Global Plan of Action for the Conservation and Sustainable Use of Plant Genetic Resources for Food and Agriculture is important to this Treaty, Contracting Parties should promote its effective implementation, including through national actions and, as appropriate, international cooperation to provide a coherent framework, inter alia, for capacity building, technology transfer and exchange of information, taking into account the provisions of Article 13.

Article 15 – Ex Situ Collections of Plant Genetic Resources for Food and Agriculture held by the International Agricultural Research Centres of the Consultative Group on International Agricultural Research and other International Institutions

15.1 The Contracting Parties recognize the importance to this Treaty of the ex situ collections of plant genetic resources for food and agriculture held in trust by the International Agricultural Research Centres (IARCs) of the Consultative Group on International Agricultural Research (CGIAR). The Contracting Parties call upon the IARCs to sign agreements with the Governing Body with regard to such ex situ collections, in accordance with the following terms and conditions:

(a) Plant genetic resources for food and agriculture listed in Annex I of this Treaty and held by the IARCs shall be made available in accordance with the provisions set out in Part IV of this Treaty.

(b) Plant genetic resources for food and agriculture other than those listed in Annex I of this Treaty and collected before its entry into force that are held by IARCs shall be made available in accordance with the provisions of the MTA currently in use pursuant to agreements between the IARCs and the FAO. This MTA shall be amended by the Governing Body no later than its second regular session, in consultation with the IARCs, in accordance with the relevant provisions of this Treaty, especially Articles 12 and 13, and under the following conditions:

(i) The IARCs shall periodically inform the Governing Body about the MTAs entered into, according to a schedule to be established by the Governing Body;

(ii) The Contracting Parties in whose territory the plant genetic resources for food and agriculture were collected from in situ conditions shall be provided with samples of such plant genetic resources for food and agriculture on demand, without any MTA;

(iii) Benefits arising under the above MTA that accrue to the mechanism mentioned in Article 19.3f shall be applied, in particular, to the conservation and sustainable use of the plant genetic resources for food and agriculture in question, particularly in national and regional programmes in developing countries and countries with economies in transition, especially in centres of diversity and the least developed countries; and

(iv) The IARCs shall take appropriate measures, in accordance with their capacity, to maintain effective compliance with the conditions of the MTAs, and shall promptly inform the Governing Body of cases of non-compliance.

(c) IARCs recognize the authority of the Governing Body to provide policy guidance relating to ex situ collections held by them and subject to the provisions of this Treaty.

(d) The scientific and technical facilities in which such ex situ collections are conserved shall remain under the authority of the IARCs, which undertake to manage and administer these ex situ collections in accordance with internationally accepted standards, in particular the Genebank Standards as endorsed by the FAO Commission on Genetic Resources for Food and Agriculture.

(e) Upon request by an IARC, the Secretary shall endeavour to provide appropriate technical support.

(f) The Secretary shall have, at any time, right of access to the facilities, as well as right to inspect all activities performed therein directly related to the conservation and exchange of the material covered by this Article.

(g) If the orderly maintenance of these ex situ collections held by IARCs is impeded or threatened by whatever event, including force majeure, the

Secretary, with the approval of the host country, shall assist in its evacuation or transfer, to the extent possible.

15.2 The Contracting Parties agree to provide facilitated access to plant genetic resources for food and agriculture in Annex I under the Multilateral System to IARCs of the CGIAR that have signed agreements with the Governing Body in accordance with this Treaty. Such Centres shall be included in a list held by the Secretary to be made available to the Contracting Parties on request.

15.3 The material other than that listed in Annex I, which is received and conserved by IARCs after the coming into force of this Treaty, shall be available for access on terms consistent with those mutually agreed between the IARCs that receive the material and the country of origin of such resources or the country that has acquired those resources in accordance with the Convention on Biological Diversity or other applicable law.

15.4 The Contracting Parties are encouraged to provide IARCs that have signed agreements with the Governing Body with access, on mutually agreed terms, to plant genetic resources for food and agriculture not listed in Annex I that are important to the programmes and activities of the IARCs.

15.5 The Governing Body will also seek to establish agreements for the purposes stated in this Article with other relevant international institutions.

Article 16 – International Plant Genetic Resources Networks

16.1 Existing cooperation in international plant genetic resources for food and agriculture networks will be encouraged or developed on the basis of existing arrangements and consistent with the terms of this Treaty, so as to achieve as complete coverage as possible of plant genetic resources for food and agriculture.

16.2 The Contracting Parties will encourage, as appropriate, all relevant institutions, including governmental, private, non-governmental, research, breeding and other institutions, to participate in the international networks.

Article 17 – The Global Information System on Plant Genetic Resources for Food and Agriculture

17.1 The Contracting Parties shall cooperate to develop and strengthen a global information system to facilitate the exchange of information, based on existing information systems, on scientific, technical and environmental matters related to plant genetic resources for food and agriculture, with the expectation that such exchange of information will contribute to the sharing of benefits by making information on plant genetic resources for food and agriculture available to all Contracting Parties. In developing the Global Information System, cooperation will be sought with the Clearing House Mechanism of the Convention on Biological Diversity.

17.2 Based on notification by the Contracting Parties, early warning should be provided about hazards that threaten the efficient maintenance of plant genetic resources for food and agriculture, with a view to safeguarding the material.

17.3 The Contracting Parties shall cooperate with the Commission on Genetic Resources for Food and Agriculture of the FAO in its periodic reassessment of the state of the world's plant genetic resources for food and agriculture in order to facilitate the updating of the rolling Global Plan of Action referred to in Article 14.

PART VI – FINANCIAL PROVISIONS

Article 18 – Financial Resources

18.1 The Contracting Parties undertake to implement a funding strategy for the implementation of this Treaty in accordance with the provisions of this Article.

18.2 The objectives of the funding strategy shall be to enhance the availability, transparency, efficiency and effectiveness of the provision of financial resources to implement activities under this Treaty.

18.3 In order to mobilize funding for priority activities, plans and programmes, in particular in developing countries and countries with economies in transition, and taking the Global Plan of Action into account, the Governing Body shall periodically establish a target for such funding.

18.4 Pursuant to this funding strategy:

(a) The Contracting Parties shall take the necessary and appropriate measures within the Governing Bodies of relevant international mechanisms, funds and bodies to ensure due priority and attention to the effective allocation of predictable and agreed resources for the implementation of plans and programmes under this Treaty.

(b) The extent to which Contracting Parties that are developing countries and Contracting Parties with economies in transition will effectively implement their commitments under this Treaty will depend on the effective allocation, particularly by the developed country Parties, of the resources referred to in this Article. Contracting Parties that are developing countries and Contracting Parties with economies in transition will accord due priority in their own plans and programmes to building capacity in plant genetic resources for food and agriculture.

(c) The Contracting Parties that are developed countries also provide, and Contracting Parties that are developing countries and Contracting Parties with economies in transition avail themselves of, financial resources for the implementation of this Treaty through bilateral and regional and multilateral channels. Such channels shall include the mechanism referred to in Article 19.3f.

(d) Each Contracting Party agrees to undertake, and provide financial resources for national activities for the conservation and sustainable use of plant genetic resources for food and agriculture in accordance with its national capabilities and financial resources. The financial resources provided shall not be used to ends inconsistent with this Treaty, in particular in areas related to international trade in commodities.

(e) The Contracting Parties agree that the financial benefits arising from Article 13.2d are part of the funding strategy.

(f) Voluntary contributions may also be provided by Contracting Parties, the private sector, taking into account the provisions of Article 13, non-governmental organisations and other sources. The Contracting Parties agree that the Governing Body shall consider modalities of a strategy to promote such contributions.

18.5 The Contracting Parties agree that priority will be given to the implementation of agreed plans and programmes for farmers in developing countries, especially in least developed countries, and in countries with economies in transition, who conserve and sustainably utilize plant genetic resources for food and agriculture.

PART VII – INSTITUTIONAL PROVISIONS

Article 19 – Governing Body

19.1 A Governing Body for this Treaty is hereby established, composed of all Contracting Parties.

19.2 All decisions of the Governing Body shall be taken by consensus unless by consensus another method of arriving at a decision on certain measures is reached, except that consensus shall always be required in relation to Articles 23 and 24.

19.3 The functions of the Governing Body shall be to promote the full implementation of this Treaty, keeping in view its objectives, and, in particular, to:

(a) provide policy direction and guidance to monitor, and adopt such recommendations as necessary for the implementation of this Treaty and, in particular, for the operation of the Multilateral System;

(b) adopt plans and programmes for the implementation of this Treaty;

(c) adopt, at its first session, and periodically review the funding strategy for the implementation of this Treaty, in accordance with the provisions of Article 18;

(d) adopt the budget of this Treaty;

(e) consider and establish subject to the availability of necessary funds such subsidiary bodies as may be necessary, and their respective mandates and composition;

(f) establish, as needed, an appropriate mechanism, such as a Trust Account, for receiving and utilizing financial resources that will accrue to it for purposes of implementing this Treaty;

(g) establish and maintain cooperation with other relevant international organizations and treaty bodies, including in particular the Conference of the Parties to the Convention on Biological Diversity, on matters covered by this Treaty, including their participation in the funding strategy;

(h) consider and adopt, as required, amendments to this Treaty, in accordance with the provisions of Article 23;

(i) consider and adopt, as required, amendments to annexes to this Treaty, in accordance with the provisions of Article 24;

(j) consider modalities of a strategy to encourage voluntary contributions, in particular, with reference to Articles 13 and 18;

(k) perform such other functions as may be necessary for the fulfilment of the objectives of this Treaty;

(l) take note of relevant decisions of the Conference of the Parties to the Convention on Biological Diversity and other relevant international organizations and treaty bodies;

(m) inform, as appropriate, the Conference of the Parties to the Convention on Biological Diversity and other relevant international organizations and treaty bodies of matters regarding the implementation of this Treaty; and

(n) approve the terms of agreements with the IARCs and other international institutions under Article 15, and review and amend the MTA in Article 15.

19.4 Subject to Article 19.6, each Contracting Party shall have one vote and may be represented at sessions of the Governing Body by a single delegate who may be accompanied by an alternate, and by experts and advisers. Alternates, experts and advisers may take part in the proceedings of the Governing Body but may not vote, except in the case of their being duly authorized to substitute for the delegate.

19.5 The United Nations, its specialized agencies and the International Atomic Energy Agency, as well as any State not a Contracting Party to this Treaty, may be represented as observers at sessions of the Governing Body. Any other body or agency, whether governmental or non-governmental, qualified in fields relating to conservation and sustainable use of plant genetic resources for food and agriculture, which has informed the Secretary of its wish to be represented as an observer at a session of the Governing Body, may be admitted unless at least one third of the Contracting Parties present object. The admission and participation of observers shall be subject to the Rules of Procedure adopted by the Governing Body.

19.6 A Member Organization of FAO that is a Contracting Party and the member states of that Member Organization that are Contracting Parties shall exercise their membership rights and fulfil their membership obligations in accordance, mutatis mutandis, with the Constitution and General Rules of FAO.

19.7 The Governing Body shall adopt and amend, as required, its own Rules of Procedure and financial rules which shall not be inconsistent with this Treaty.

19.8 The presence of delegates representing a majority of the Contracting Parties shall be necessary to constitute a quorum at any session of the Governing Body.

19.9 The Governing Body shall hold regular sessions at least once every two years. These sessions should, as far as possible, be held back-to-back with the regular sessions of the Commission on Genetic Resources for Food and Agriculture.

19.10 Special Sessions of the Governing Body shall be held at such other times as may be deemed necessary by the Governing Body, or at the written request of any Contracting Party, provided that this request is supported by at least one third of the Contracting Parties.

19.11 The Governing Body shall elect its Chairperson and Vice-Chairpersons (collectively referred to as 'the Bureau'), in conformity with its Rules of Procedure.

Article 20 – Secretary

20.1 The Secretary of the Governing Body shall be appointed by the Director-General of FAO, with the approval of the Governing Body. The Secretary shall be assisted by such staff as may be required.

20.2 The Secretary shall perform the following functions:

(a) arrange for and provide administrative support for sessions of the Governing Body and for any subsidiary bodies as may be established;

(b) assist the Governing Body in carrying out its functions, including the performance of specific tasks that the Governing Body may decide to assign to it;

(c) report on its activities to the Governing Body.

20.3 The Secretary shall communicate to all Contracting Parties and to the Director-General:

(a) decisions of the Governing Body within sixty days of adoption;

(b) information received from Contracting Parties in accordance with the provisions of this Treaty.

20.4 The Secretary shall provide documentation in the six languages of the United Nations for sessions of the Governing Body.

20.5 The Secretary shall cooperate with other organizations and treaty bodies, including in particular the Secretariat of the Convention on Biological Diversity, in achieving the objectives of this Treaty.

Annex 4

Participants at the Regional Multi-stakeholder Dialogues on IPRs and Sustainable Development

Dialogues took place at: Cusco, Peru, 22–24 February 2001; Nyeri, Kenya, 30–31 July 2001; Tikal, Guatemala, 20–22 September 2001; Rajendrapur, Bangladesh, 19–21 April 2002; Dakar, Senegal, 30–31 July 2002. The participants were as follows:

Argentina

Carlos M Correa
Director
Meastría en Política y Gestión de la Ciencia y la Technología
CEA/Universidad de Buenos Aires

Bangladesh

Nasiruddin Ahmed
Deputy Secretary
Ministry of Commerce
Government of Bangladesh

Md Shameem Ahsan
Senior Assistant Secretary (UN)
Ministry of Foreign Affairs
Government of Bangladesh

Mahbub Alam
Anthropologist
Bangladesh Resource Centre for Indigenous Knowledge (BARCIK)

A B M Mahbub Alam
Assistant Chief
Ministry of Agriculture

Tariq Ali
Executive Assistant
BRAC Centre

H E Toufiq Ali
Ambassador
Permanent Mission of Bangladesh
Geneva

Debapriya Bhattacharya
Executive Director
Centre for Policy Dialogue

Samson H Chowdhury
Chairman
Square Group of Companies

Zafrullah Chowdhury
Projects Co-ordinator
Gono Shasthaya Kendra (GSK)

Syeda Rizwana Hasan
Programmes Director
Bangladesh Environmental Lawyers Association (BELA)

Md Gul Hossain
Fellow
Bangladesh Academy of Agriculture

Md Daniul Islam
Assistance Secretary
Ministry of Foreign Affairs
Government of Bangladesh

Nihad Kabir
Barrister, Partner
Syed Ishtiaq Ahmed & Associates

Mona Laczo
Regional Media and Advocacy Coordinator, South Asia
OXFAM, Bangladesh

Shishir Moral
Research Officer
Society for Environment and Human Development (SEHD)

Ainun Nishat
Country Representative
IUCN–World Conservation Union

Atiq Rahman
Executive Director
Bangladesh Centre for Advanced Studies (BCAS)

Mustafizur Rahman
Research Director
Centre for Policy Dialogue (CPD)

Md Safiqur Rahman
Director (Standards)
Bangladesh Standard and Testing Institution

Muhammad Abu Yusuf
Senior Assistant Secretary
Ministry of Science and Information and Communication Technology

Anisatul Fatema Yousuf
Head (Dialogue and Communication)
Centre for Policy Dialogue (CPD)

S M Kuddus Zaman
Secretary-in-Charge
Bangladesh Law Commission

Benin

Antoine Sileté Agbadome
Directeur du Commerce Extérieur
Ministère du Commerce de l'Artisanat et du Tourisme
Aurélien C Atidelga
GRAPAD

Toussaint Hinvi
Président
Bénin Nature

Eloï Laourou
Permanent Mission of Benin
Geneva

Charles Nouatin
Fédération des Unions de Producteurs du Bénin (FUPRO Benin)

Godefroy Macaire Chabi
Radio Nationale du Bénin

Bolivia

Julio Alvarado
Minister Counsellor
Permanent Mission of Bolivia
Geneva

Mario J Baudoin Weeks
Director General
Dirección de Biodiversidad

Juan Carlos Chavez Corrales
PRISMA

Brazil

David Hathaway
Asesor
Asesoría y Servicios a Proyectos en Agricultura Alternativa (AS-PTA)

Manoel Artigas Schirmer
Gerente de Articulação e Pesquisa
Bioamazônia

Burkina Faso

Henry Compaore
Social Alert
Burkina Faso

Rosine Jourdain
Chef de Mission
Médecins Sans Frontières

Jean-Didier Zongo
Professeur Université de Ouagadougou
Faculté des Sciences et Techniques

Brahim Ouedraogo
Inter Press Service (IPS)

Cameroon

Elvire Beleoken
EDUC Actions

Madeleine Ngo Louga
Health and Environment Program

Fosi Mbantenkhu Mary
Head of Biodiversity Unit
Ministère de l'Environnement et des Forêts (MINET)

Raphaël Owona Etende
Permanent Mission of Cameroon
Geneva

Colombia

Diana Pombo
Ministerio de Medio Ambiente

Ana María Hernández
Instituto de Investigación de Recursos Biológicos – Alexander von Humboldt

Costa Rica

Grethel Aguilar
UICN
Comisión de Derecho Ambiental
Costa Rica

Gabriela Hernández
UICN Consultant

Nora Martín
INBio

Jorge Cabrera Medaglia
Universidad de Costa Rica

José A Navarro
Registro de la Propiedad Industrial

Silvia Salazar
Legal Adviser on Intellectual Property
Universidad de Costa Rica

José Pablo Sánchez
Universidad de Costa Rica

Susana Vásquez
Ministerio Comercio Exterior

Eugenia Wo Ching
Centro de Derecho Ambiental (CEDARENA)

Ecuador

Cristián Espinosa
Permanent Mission of Ecuador
Geneva

Joy Woolfson
Consultora del IICA
Coordinadora del Grupo Nacional de Trabajo sobre Biodiversidad

Manuela González
UICN – Oficina Regional, América del Sur

Antonio Jacanamijoy
Coordinador General
Coordinadora de la Organizaciones Indígenas de la Cuenca Amazónica (COICA)

El Salvador

Zulma Ricord de Mendoza
Ministero de Medio
Ambiente/PNUD
Coordinadora Nacional del Proyecto
Biodiversidad

Raúl Moreno
FUNDE /Centro para la Defensa
del Consumidor

Ana Cecilia Peña
Ministerio de Medio Ambiente

Jorge Quezada
Director de Recursos Biológicos
Ministerio del Ambiente

Ethiopia

Imeru Tamrat
Action Aid Ethiopia

France

Anne Chetaille
Solagral

Guatemala

Marco Antonio Ramos
Ministerio de Ambiente

Velvet Berg
Ministerio de Economía

Jorge Cabrera Hidalgo
Grupo Kukulkan

Javier García Esquivel
Consultor

Mario René Mancilla
Asociación Guatemalteca para la
Conservación Natural

Javier Hernández Munguia
Ministerio del Ambiente

Mario Rodríguez
Iniciativa 7

Guinea

Fofana Bakary
Directeur Exécutif
Centre du Commerce International
pour le Développement

Honduras

Mayra Falck
Zamorne
María del Rosario Martinez
Dirección General de la Propiedad
Intelectual

Sandra Villars
Permanent Mission of Honduras
Geneva

India

Dr Biswajit Dhar
Senior Fellow
Research and Information System for
the Non-Aligned and Other
Developing Countries

Dr N S Gopalakrishnan
Associate Professor
School of Legal Studies
Cochin University of Science and
Technology

Mr Atul Kaushik
Deputy Secretary
Cabinet Secretariat
Government of India

Riya Sinha
National Coordinator (Scouting and
Documentation)
National Innovation Foundation

G Utkarsh
Consultant
Foundation for the Revitalisation of
Local Health Traditions (FRLHT)

Narendra B Zaveri
Advocate
Indian Drug Manufacturers
Association (IDMA)

Indonesia

Edy Pramono
President Director
PT Indofarma – Jakarta

Riza V Tjahjadi
National Coordinator
PAN Indonesia

Rachmi Untoro
Director of Community Nutrition
Ministry of Health

Ivory Coast

Yao Abraham Gadji
Chef de la Cellule Juridique
Ministère de l'Environnement et du Cadre de Vie

Adrien Kouadio
Permanent Mission of Ivory Coast
Geneva

Soro Nagolo
Direction de l'Office Ivoirien de la Propriété Industrielle

Kenya

Adronico O Adede
L'Etwal International

Robert J L Lettington
Law and Policy Consultant
International Centre of Insect Physiology and Ecology

H E Amina Chawahir Mohamed
Ambassador
Permanent Mission of Kenya
Geneva

Gichinga Ndirangu
Action Aid

Nelson Ndirangu
Permanent Mission of Kenya
Geneva

James Otieno-Odek
Senior Lecturer
University of Nairobi

Chris Ouma
Action Aid

Mali

Sidi Coulibaly
Directeur des Informations et des Programmes de Radio KLEDU

Oumar Niangado
Délégué de la Fondation Syngenta pour une Agriculture Durable

Mamadou Traore
Division de la Propriété Industrielle

Mauritania

Abou Abass
CERIC

Mohamed Y O Boumediana
Directeur-Adjoint de l'Industrie

Aly Fall
Université de Nouakchott

Habib Oould Hemeth
Permanent Mission of Mauritania
Geneva

Mexico

Juan Ignacio Domínguez
COMPITCH

Ana Karina González
Centro Mexicano de Derecho Ambiental (CEMDA)

H E Eduardo Perez Motta
Ambassador
Permanent Mission of Mexico
Geneva

Namibia

Michaela Figueira
Project Coordinator
Ministry of Environment and Tourism – Environmental Legislation Project

Mesag Mulunga
Trade Promotion Officer
Ministry of Trade and Industry

Nicaragua

Thomas Loudon
Comité de Servicios de Amigos

Juan Manuel Sánchez
Ministerio de Fomento, Industria y Comercio
MIFIC/Encargado de Propiedad Intelectual

Santiago Urbina
Permanent Mission of Nicaragua
Geneva

Niger

Amadou Tankoano
Professeur
Université Abdou Moumouni
Faculté des Sciences Economiques et Juridiques

Nigeria

Mathew P O Dore
Federal Ministry of Environment

Johnson Ekpere
Private International Consultant
University of Ibadan

Kent Nnadozie
Consultant

Pakistan

Zulfiqar Ahmad Khan
Partner
Kursheed Khan & Associates (Khursheed Khan Centre for Advancement of Research in Intellectual Property Laws)

Patricia Flynn Moore
IUCN Regional Environmental Law Programme, Asia

Mujeeb A Khan
Commercial Secretary
Permanent Mission of the Islamic Republic of Pakistan
Geneva

Panama

Aurelio Chiari
Asociación Dobbo Yala

Peru

Carmen Arana
Presidente del Grupo de Trabajo de Propriedad Intelectual de la Comision ALCA/Perú

Alejandro Argumedo
ANDES

Betty Berendson
Minister Counsellor
Permanent Mission of Peru
Geneva

Jorge Caillaux
Sociedad Peruana de Derecho Ambiental (SPDA)

Manuel Ruiz
Sociedad Peruana de Derecho Ambiental (SPDA)

Jose E Salazar B
Economist

Gustavo Suarez de Freitas
Pro Naturaleza

Begoña Venero Aguirre
Vocal de la Sala de Propiedad Intelectual
Tribunal del INDECOPI

Philippines

Leo Palma
Senior Councel
Advisory Centre on WTO Law

Elpidio V Peria
South East Asia Regional Initiatives for Community Empowerment (SEARICE)

M Angelina Sta Catalina
First Secretary
Permanent Mission of the Philippines
Geneva

Senegal

Taoufik Ben Abdallah
ENDA Tiers-Monde

Ibrahima Camara
Faculté des Sciences Juridiques et Politiques
Université Cheikh Anta Diop

Bacary Dabo
Journaliste à Sud Quotidien

Alioune Diallo
ENDA Tiers-Monde

Awa Dione
ENDA Tiers-Monde

Abdoulaye Diop
Ministère de l'Intérieur
Direction Sécurité Publique

Prosper Houer
PROMETRA International

Mariama Dramé Léye
Ministère du Commerce

Marième Mbengue
Journaliste à l'INFO 7

Seynabou Mbodji
ENDA Tiers-Monde

Jean Pierre Mendy
Ministère des PME et du Commerce

Doudou Sagna
Chef du Service de la Propriété Industrielle et de la Technologie
Ministère de l'Artisanat et de l'Industrie

Falou Samb
Permanent Mission of Senegal
Geneva

Aïcha Tall
Ministère de la Justice Dakar

Cheikh Tidiane Dièye
ENDA Tiers-Monde

Mamadou Racine Ba
ENDA Tiers-Monde

South Africa

Ellen M Mahlase
IUCN-World Conservation Union
South Africa Country Office

Motlalepula Gilbert Matsabisa
South African Traditional Medicines Research Group
University of Cape Town

Rosemary Wolson
Intellectual Property Manager
University of Cape Town
Office of Industry Liaison, Research Support Services

Sri Lanka

K Balasubramaniam
Advisor and Coordinator
Health Action International Asia-Pacific (HAI-AP)

Gothami Indikadahena
Counsellor (Economic and Commercial)
Permanent Mission of Sri Lanka
Geneva

Tanzania

Wilson Y F Marandu
Acting Director General
Tropical Pesticides Research Institute

S G Ngaga
Assistant Director, Agriculture (Trade & Policy)
Ministry of Industry and Trade

Thailand

Pornachai Danvivathana
Minister Counsellor
Permanent Mission of Thailand
Geneva

Jade Donavanik
Legal Consultant
Thailand Biodiversity Center

Jakkrit Kuanpoth
Associate Professor
School of Law
Sukhothai Thammathirat Open University

Weerawit Weeraworawit
Minister (Commercial Affairs)
Ministry of Commerce
Thailand

Togo

Koffi Edinam Danstey
Ingénieur Agronome
Point Focal National
Biodiversité/Biosécurité
Ministère de l'Environnement et des Ressources Forestières

Agbényo Dzogbedo
Programme Biodiversité/OGM
Les Amis de la Terre

Uganda

Joyce Banya
Permanent Mission of Uganda
Geneva

Sophia Kerwegi Apio
Senior Research Officer
Natural Chemotherapeutics Research Laboratory (MOH)

Donna Kabatesi
Director
Traditional and Modern Health Practitioners Together Against AIDS (THETA)

Sirali S M Mauso
Principal Policy Analyst
Ministry of Tourism, Trade and Industry

Venezuela

María Adela Rodriguez
Abogada y Asesora
Consejo Nacional de Tecnología

Ana Campos Duarte
Abogada
Ministerio de Ciencia y Tecnología

Ramiro Royero
Fundación para el Desarrollo de las Ciencias Físicas, Matemáticas y Naturales FUDECI

Zambia

Edward Chisanga
Permanent Mission of Zambia
Geneva

Mwananyanda Mbikusita Lewanika
National Institute for Scientific and Industrial Research

Lovemore Simwanda
Zambia National Farmers Union (ZNFU)

Zimbabwe

H E Boniface Guwa Chidyausiku
Ambassador
Permanent Mission of Zimbabwe
Geneva

Sarah Kimakwa
The PELUM Association

Gus Le Breton
Director
Southern Alliance for Indigenous Resources (SAFIRE)

Bellah Mpofu
Registrar of Plant Breeders' Rights
Seed Services

Departement of Research and
Specialists Services
Ministry of Lands and Agriculture

Andrew Mushita
Director
Community Technology and
Development Trust

IGOs

Maurice Batanga
Organisation Africaine de la
Propriété Intellectuelle (OAPI)

Susan Bragdon
International Plant Genetic
Resources Institute (IPGRI)

Dimas López
Comisión Centroamericana de
Ambiente y Desarrollo (CCAD)

Francis Mangeni
African Union Office in Geneva (AU)

Godwin Y Mkamanga
Director
SADC Plant Genetic Resources
Centre (SPGRC)

John Mugabe
African Centre for Technology
Studies (ACTS)

Monica Rosel
Comunidad Andina (CAN)

Marianne Schaper
Economic Commission for Latin
America and the Caribbean (ECLAC)

Jean-Luc Senou
Directeur du Commerce et de la
Concurrence
Union Economique et Monétaire
Ouest Africaine (UEMOA)

ICTSD

Nadine Keim
Chair
International Centre for Trade and
Sustainable Development (ICTSD)

Ricardo Meléndez-Ortiz
Executive Director
International Centre for Trade and
Sustainable Development (ICTSD)

Christophe Bellmann
Programmes Director
International Centre for Trade and
Sustainable Development (ICTSD)

David Vivas Eugui
Project Manager
Intellectual Property, Services and
Technology
International Centre for Trade and
Sustainable Development (ICTSD)

Heike Baumüller
Editor and Project Coordinator
International Centre for Trade and
Sustainable Development (ICTSD)

El Hadji Abdourahmane Diouf
Programme Officer
African Issues
International Centre for Trade and
Sustainable Development (ICTSD)

Marie Chamay
Programme Associate
Intellectual Property
International Centre for Trade and
Sustainable Development (ICTSD)

Quakers

Brewster Grace
Quaker United Nations Office
(QUNO)

Millius Palayiwa
International Relations Secretary
Quaker Peace and Service

Geoff Tansey
Quaker United Nations Office
(QUNO)

Jonathan Hepburn
Quaker United Nations Office
(QUNO)

Index